Innamincka Talk
A grammar of the Innamincka dialect of Yandruwandha with notes on other dialects

Innamincka Talk
A grammar of the Innamincka dialect of Yandruwandha with notes on other dialects

Gavan Breen

Published by ANU eView
The Australian National University
Canberra ACT 0200, Australia
Email: enquiries.eview@anu.edu.au
This title is also available online at http://eview.anu.edu.au

---

National Library of Australia Cataloguing-in-Publication entry

Title: Innamincka talk: a grammar of the Innamincka dialect of Yandruwandha with notes on other dialects

ISBN: 9781921934193 (paperback) 9781921934209 (online)

Subjects: Innamincka language--Dialects.
Innamincka language--Grammar.
Yandruwandha (Australian people)
Aboriginal Australians--Languages.
Queensland--Languages.

Other Creators/Contributors:
Australian National University

Dewey Number: 499.15

All rights reserved. No part of this publication may be reproduced, stored in a retrieval system or transmitted in any form or by any means, electronic, mechanical, photocopying or otherwise, without the prior permission of the publisher.

Original cover concept by Ciril's Printers. Cover by Ivo Lovric and layout by ANU Press.

Previous edition © 2004 Pacific Linguistics, Research School of Pacific and Asian Studies, The Australian National University

This edition © 2015 ANU eView

This book can be purchased from http://eview.anu.edu.au

Table of contents

Acknowledgments	xi
Preface	xii
Abbreviations and conventions	xiii
Map: Yandruwandha and neighbouring languages	xvii

1 Introduction — 1
  1.1 The Yandruwandha and their country — 1
  1.2 The linguistic affinities of the Yandruwandha language — 3
  1.3 Previous work — 4
  1.4 The informants — 5
  1.5 A comparison of the sources — 7
  1.6 The project — 8

2 The sound system — 10
  2.1 Introduction — 10
  2.2 Consonant phonemes — 11
    2.2.1 Voiceless stops — 11
    2.2.2 Voiced stops — 12
    2.2.3 Trill-released stops — 13
    2.2.4 Nasals — 14
    2.2.5 Laterals — 15
    2.2.6 Pre-stopped laterals — 16
    2.2.7 Rhotics — 17
    2.2.8 Glides — 18
    2.2.9 The apical contrast between unstressed vowels — 18
  2.3 Vowel phonemes — 19

3 Pronunciation — 21
  3.1 Description of the consonants — 21
    3.1.1 Voiceless stops — 22
    3.1.2 Voiced stops — 23

		3.1.3	Trill-released stops	24

		3.1.3	Trill-released stops	24
		3.1.4	Nasals	24
		3.1.5	Laterals	24
		3.1.6	Prestopped laterals	25
		3.1.71	Trill	25
		3.1.8	Glides	25
	3.2	Description of the vowels		25
		3.2.1	Distortion of word-final vowels	27
	3.3	Features of rapid speech		28
	3.4	Interphonemic alternations		29
	3.5	Extraphonemic exclamations		30
	3.6	Stress		30
		3.6.1	Phrase stress	33
		3.6.2	Intonation	33
4	**Organisation of sounds**			36
	4.1	Distribution of phonemes		36
		4.1.1	Consonant clusters	37
	4.2	Phoneme frequencies		39
5	**The sentence**			44
	5.1	Definitions		44
	5.2	Sentence types and constituents		46
	5.3	Word and phrase order		47
	5.4	Incomplete sentences		50
6	**Word classes and paradigms**			52
	6.1	Words		52
	6.2	Word classes		53
	6.3	Nominal paradigms		55
7	**Simple declarative sentences**			60
	7.1	Verbless sentences		60
	7.2	Intransitive sentences		62
	7.3	Transitive sentences		63
	7.4	Reflexive and reciprocal sentences		64
8	**Non-declarative simple sentences**			66
	8.1	Command sentences		66
	8.2	Questions		66
	8.3	Uncertainty and indefiniteness		68
	8.4	Negation		70
		8.4.1	*walya*	70

			vii

        8.4.2 *pani*   73
        8.4.3 *pudlu*   74

9 Nominal inflection   75

  9.1 Common noun inflection   75
      9.1.1 Nominative   75
      9.1.2 Vocative   76
      9.1.3 Operative   77
          9.1.3.1 Operative as a co-ordinator in a noun phrase   78
      9.1.4 Dative   79
      9.1.5 Locative   81
      9.1.6 Ablative   83
      9.1.7 Aversive   84
  9.2 Kinship terms   85
  9.3 Personal names   86
  9.4 Dual and plural nouns   87
  9.5 The personal interrogative   87
  9.6 Location nouns   88
  9.7 Directional terminology   89
  9.8 Singular personal pronouns   90
  9.9 Non-singular personal pronouns   93
  9.10 Inflection of third person and demonstrative pronouns and *yarndu*   94
      9.10.1 Singular third person pronoun inflection   94
      9.10.2 Non-singular third person pronoun inflection   97
      9.10.3 Inflection of demonstrative pronouns   97
      9.10.4 *Yarndu*   99
  9.11 The interrogative *yila-*   100
  9.12 Inflection of noun phrases   101
  9.13 Double case-marking   103
  9.14 The suffix *-ngi*   103

10 Noun-stem formation   106

  10.1 Noun roots   106
  10.2 Reduplication   107
  10.3 Compounds   109
  10.4 Non-productive noun-stem formatives   111
  10.5 Productive noun-stem formatives   112
      10.5.1 Dual   113
      10.5.2 Plural   113
      10.5.3 Other   114
      10.5.4 Proprietive   116
      10.5.5 Privative   116
      10.5.6 Comitative   117
      10.5.7 First person kin proprietive   118

		10.5.8	Second and third person kin proprietive	118
		10.5.9	Habitual action	119
		10.5.10	Formatives denoting characteristics	120
		10.5.11	Noun stem formation by inflectional suffixes	120
	10.6	Derivation of nouns from verbs		121

11 Verb inflection 125

11.1	Past tenses		126
11.2	Present tense		130
11.3	Future tense		130
	11.3.1	Immediate future	132
11.4	Specification of time of day		133
11.5	Imperative mood		136
	11.5.1	Negative imperative	136
11.6	Optative mood		137
11.7	Potential mood		138
11.8	Unspecified tense		138
11.9	Contemporaneous action		139
11.10	Repeated action		140
11.11	Immediate sequence		140
11.12	Simultaneous action		141
11.13	Number markers		142
11.14	Motion away		143
11.15	The 'now' present		144
11.16	Possible suffix, with unknown function		145
11.17	Inflection of verb phrases containing two verbs		146

12 Bound verb aspect markers 148

12.1	Action while going along	150
12.2	Action on passing	150
12.3	Action directed away	151
12.4	Action directed back	152
12.5	Arrival	154
12.6	Widespread action	156
12.7	Action around a centre	157
12.8	Continued action	158
12.9	Habitual action	159
12.10	Action at night	159
12.11	Action in the morning	159
12.12	Action directed in or across	160
12.13	Action directed downwards	162
12.14	Action directed upwards	163
12.15	Action directed across	163
12.16	Going a different way	164

12.17	Action for oneself	164
12.18	Following and completion	165
12.19	*-thanggu*	166
12.20	Order of aspect markers	167

13 Verb-stem formation — 169

13.1	Verb roots	172
13.2	Reduplication	172
13.3	Compounding of verbs	173
13.4	Compounding of nouns and verbs	174
	13.4.1 Derivation of verb phrases from abstract nouns	175
13.5	Compounding of adverbs and verbs	176
13.6	Non-productive verb-stem formatives	176
13.7	Productive verb-stem formatives	176
	13.7.1 Inchoative/transitiviser/applicative	177
	13.7.2 Inchoative verb phrases	180
	13.7.3 Causative *-ka*	181
	13.7.3.1 *-kanmana*	183
	13.7.4 Causative *-ma*	184
	13.7.5 Causative *-lka*	184
	13.7.6 Intransitivisation of transitive verbs	185

14 Variations on transitivity — 186

14.1	Verbs with *-yindri*	186
14.2	Pseudotransitive sentences	194
14.3	Ditransitive sentences	195

15 Coordination and subordination — 197

15.1	Compound sentences	199
15.2	Coordinate sentences	200
15.3	Complex sentences	201
15.4	Subordinate sentences	205
15.5	Quotation	205

16 Adverbs — 207

16.1	Modal adverbs	208
16.2	Aspectual adverbs	208
	16.2.1 *kali*	208
	16.2.2 *ngada*	209
	16.2.3 *ngurra*	209
16.3	Reciprocal adverbs	210
16.4	Adverbs of time	211
16.5	Adverbs of place	212
16.6	Directional adverbs	213

16.7	Demonstrative adverbs		214
16.8	Adverbs of manner		216
16.9	Adjectives/adverbs derived with the operative suffix		217
16.10	Other adverbs		219

17 Conjunctions, interjections and emphatic particles — 222

17.1	Conjunctions		222
17.2	Interjections		225
	17.2.1	Sentence introducers	225
	17.2.2	Sentence substitutes	228
	17.2.3	Exclamations	228
17.3	Emphatic particles		228

18 Clitics and emphatic suffixes — 230

18.1	Dual and plural		230
18.2	Similarity		231
18.3	Bound conjunctions		233
	18.3.1	*-ngu*	233
	18.3.2	*-ldra*	236
	18.3.3	*-ldrangu*	237
18.4	Emphatic suffixes		238
18.5	*-yukala* (clitic with unknown meaning)		240

References — 242

Acknowledgments

Naturally, I owe most to Ben Kerwin for the many hours of his time that he gave me for little financial reward over the years. I am indebted also to my other teachers, Tim Guttie, Maudie Naylon and her husband Bob, Willy and Alfie Harris and Hector Harrison, for work that was congenial to some of them but not all.

I am grateful to those members of Ben Kerwin's family who helped me in one way or another, in particular to his daughter Barbara and her husband Kevin Allen, of Burra, South Australia (later Broken Hill, New South Wales), and his daughter Joan and her husband Ron Dennis, of Roma, Queensland, with whom he was living during the periods when the major part of the fieldwork was carried out. They were friendly, cooperative and interested at all times. Ben's great-grandson Aaron Paterson was interested in recent years and helped with some useful information.

I thank my wife Rosalie, who came with me (with small children after the first year) on some field trips and kept me fed and washed. Also the many linguists whose brains I have picked over the years (including Claire Bowern, who gave me a copy of her unpublished work on Nhirrpi). Perhaps the most helpful of these was the anonymous referee who read the manuscript for Pacific Linguistics in a most thorough and painstaking fashion and made many valuable suggestions.

I wish to thank also the Australian Institute of Aboriginal Studies (now Australian Institute of Aboriginal and Torres Strait Islander Studies) for financing all of the fieldwork and most of the analysis and helping in other ways, and Monash University for equipment, typing and office accommodation during that time. The Burran and later Muda Aboriginal Corporations paid me for a little over a year, during which time the Institute for Aboriginal Development, Alice Springs, provided me with office accommodation and other services. The Queensland Herbarium, the Royal Botanic Gardens and National Herbarium, Sydney and the Royal Botanic Gardens and National Herbarium, Melbourne helped with information on plants. Thanks also to Helen Tolcher for some information, and to Brenda Thornley for the map.

Preface

Innamincka Talk is one of a pair of companion volumes on Yandruwandha, a dialect of the language formerly spoken on the Cooper and Strzelecki Creeks and the country to the north of the Cooper, in the northeast corner of South Australia and a neighbouring strip of Queensland. The other volume is entitled *Innamincka Words: Yandruwandha dictionary and stories.*

Innamincka Talk is a more technical work and is intended for specialists and for interested readers who are willing to put some time and effort into studying the language. Innamincka Words is for readers, especially descendants of the original people of the area, who are interested but not ready to undertake serious study of the language. It is also a necessary resource for users of *Innamincka Talk*.

These volumes document all that could be learnt from the last speakers of the language in the last years of their lives by a linguist who was involved with other languages at the same time. These were people who did not have a full knowledge of the culture of their forebears, but were highly competent, indeed brilliant, in the way they could teach what they knew to the linguist student. Although the volumes document only a small part of a rich culture, they are a tribute to the ability and diligence of the teachers.

Abbreviations and conventions

(a) Abbreviations used in interlinear translations

Abbreviations in interlinear translations are in small capitals, except those for person, number, gender and inclusivity of pronouns. Many of the lower-case glosses in interlinear translations are translations of the morphemes concerned when they are in their free form. For example, *nhina* 'sit, stay, be' is glossed 'sit' whether it is functioning as a verb stem or as a modifier of a verb meaning 'continuing action' or 'action during the day'. These are not listed here.

ABL	ablative	LOC	locative
ACC	accusative	NOM	nominative
APP	applicative	NP	near past
AVER	aversive	OP	operative
CAUS	causative	OPT	optative
COM	comitative	PAST	past tense
CONT	contemporaneous action	pl, PL	plural
DAT	dative	PLIMP	plural imperative
DEM	demonstrative	POT	potential
DISTORT	distortion (of final vowel)	PRES	present tense
du, DU	dual	PRIV	privative
DUIMP	dual imperative	PROP	proprietive
EMPH	emphatic	REMP	remote past
ERG	ergative	RR	reflexive/reciprocal
ex	exclusive	SEQ	immediate sequence
FARP	far past	sg, SG	singular
fem	feminine	SIM	simultaneous action
FUT	future tense	TR	transitive
GEN	genitive	TVR	transitiviser
GER	gerund	UNSP	unspecified tense
HAB	habitual	VOC	vocative
in	inclusive	1	first person
INCH	inchoative	1KIN	first person kin-proprietive
INST	instrumental	2	second person
INTR	intransitive	2KIN, 3KIN	second/third person kin-proprietive
IP	immediate past		
		3	third person

Some other morphemes are glossed in capitals, but not as abbreviated words, e.g. BUT, THEN, HERE.

(b) Abbreviations of names of languages and speakers

IY	Innamincka dialect of Yandruwandha
SY	Strzelecki dialect of Yandruwandha
Yw	Yawarrawarrka
TG	Tim Guttie
BK	Bennie Kerwin
MN	Maudie Naylon
WH	Willy Harris

Some other abbreviations used only in the companion dictionary volume are explained in the introduction to it.

(c) Cross-references to example sentences

Example sentences are referred to by the bracketed number, without using the word 'example'. Where the sentence is in the same chapter as the reference the number is just that of the example, as (31). Where the sentence is in another chapter the number of the chapter also is given; thus (9-31) is example 31 in Chapter 9.

Where the sentence is in §5.1 of the dictionary volume, *Innamincka Words*, which is a long ethnographic account, the reference is to A plus the sentence number, thus (A-115). Where the sentence is in §5.2 of the dictionary volume, which comprises texts with separate line numbering (except that a couple of very short texts have no line numbering), the reference uses the abbreviation S followed by the number of the story and the line number; thus (S10-7) is line 7 of story 10 in this chapter. The chapter number is not repeated if there is a series of examples from a chapter referred to; thus (9-31, 43, 47, 10-11) refers to three examples from Chapter 9 and one from Chapter 10.

(d) Source details for example sentences

Example sentences are identified with a letter identifying the file name of the electronic orthographic transcripts followed by the page number in the file. (Note that all examples from Tim Guttie have prefix T except one from file C, Strzelecki Yandruwandha examples have M, for Maudie Naylon, and Yawarrawarrka examples have Y; all other letters refer to material from Bennie Kerwin.) Copies of these transcripts have been deposited with the Australian Institute of Aboriginal and Torres Strait Islander Studies. Also deposited there are copies of handwritten transcripts which contain more phonetic information.

The files, which are arbitrarily named according to who was recorded, or where, or what year, or what number tape, or what dialect, are as follows, with the abbreviation in the left column and an explanation in the right column.

T	Trans Tim	Recording of Tim Guttie, 1967–68
C	Trans Con	Recorded at Con's Bore, 1968, mainly Ben Kerwin
W	Trans Wacol	Recorded at Wacol, Brisbane, 1971, BK

P	Trans Princess	Recorded at Princess Royal Station, Burra, 1972, BK
D	Trans 258.2	Long text on tape 258 side 2, 1972, BK
E	Trans 265.1	Long text on tape 265 side 1, 1972, BK
B	Trans Burra	Recorded in Burra, 1973, BK
R	Trans Roma	Recorded in Roma, 1974, BK
X	Trans 76	Recorded in Roma, 1976, BK
M	Trans Maudie	Strzelecki dialect, Maudie Naylon, Birdsville
Y	Trans Yaw	Yawarrawarrka, mostly Maudie Naylon

Many example sentences are edited, for example to remove false starts or mistakes which have been corrected by the speaker, delete repetitions, or combine parts which might be separated in the original by some speech in English.

(e) Note on glossing of examples

I prefer to use a practical orthography and so not to use hyphens in the language line in example sentences in a grammar or text (as opposed to an article), but many readers feel the need of them and so I have compromised in the grammar. I have *not* used hyphens in the following cases:

- before a word-final monosyllabic suffix or series of monosyllabic suffixes (so if the last two syllables of a word are hyphenated off, they must comprise a disyllabic morpheme);
- between the two components of a stem which is a reduplicated disyllable or a disyllable with another disyllable (glossed in the interlinear line with a lower-case word);
- between the two components of a reduplicated trisyllabic stem of which only the first two syllables are reduplicated, e.g. *payipayirri* 'not very long', glossed 'long-long', from *payirri* 'long';
- where the segmentation would be clear given that the first morpheme in a word must be of at least two syllables and the last, if not hyphened off, must be monosyllabic (so, for example, if SSS-SS represents three morphemes they must be SS S SS);
- between a stem and a following suffix *-ini* 'gerund (GER)', for which the initial vowel of the suffix replaces the final vowel of the stem, but for which hyphenation is problematic because this suffix-initial vowel is treated as part of the stem for purposes of stress and reduplication (thus the reduplicated form of *wawini* 'see-GER', from *wawa* 'to see', is not **wawawawini* but *wawiwawini*).

Finally, I have not used hyphens in the somewhat suppletive third person pronoun forms *nhutjadu, nhatjadu, yintjadu* and *nhantjadu* (although *-tjadu* is hyphenated off in longer forms).

The number of morphemes in a word is, of course, one more than the number of hyphens in its interlinear gloss (except that two zero suffixes, nominative on a noun and imperative on a verb, are not glossed). Note that monosyllabic suffixes are never glossed in lower case.

(f) Note on translation of examples

It is recognised that translation of a sentence from an Aboriginal language into colloquial English often cannot result in a faithful rendering, because certain distinctions which must be made in English are not necessarily made in the Aboriginal language (e.g. definite vs indefinite, singular vs plural; cf. Dixon 1972:xxiii). No attempt has been made in this grammar to use Dixon's solution of writing translations in unnatural English. Instead I have used the informants' own translations where available and not misleading, even when they differ in content from the Yandruwandha sentence; for example, "That's Mrs Geiger looking at the horses" for a sentence which does not contain the name 'Mrs Geiger' but instead the noun *wadlumpada* 'white woman'. It is felt that this difference is not misleading (given an interlinear translation). In a few cases where it seemed advisable [*sic*] has been added. Informants' own translations are given in double inverted commas. Alternatively, I have given not a translation but the English sentence that was used in eliciting the example. Thirdly, where these alternatives are unavailable or potentially misleading, I have given a fairly free translation. In the two latter cases I have used single inverted commas. Where the translation given is partly my own and partly the informant's I have used both single and double inverted commas, as in 'I should have eaten it "while it was there"', where the translation of the subordinate clause is the informant's.

Note that where words such as 'person', 'man' etc. are used in translations (interlinear or other) the adjective 'Aboriginal' is to be understood if the adjective 'white' is not used. The word 'blackfellow' is used occasionally in translations; I do not regard this as derogatory and neither did my informants, and I am sorry if any readers are offended. 'Whitefellow' also is used.

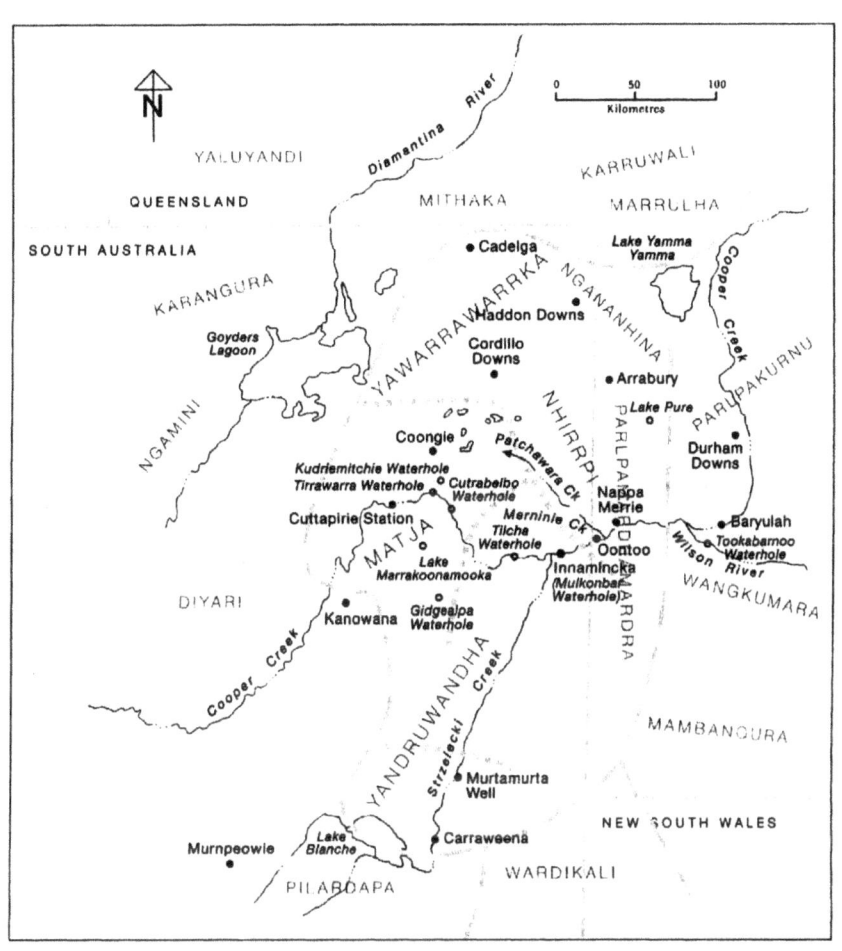

Yandruwandha and neighbouring languages

1 *Introduction*

1.1 The Yandruwandha and their country

The Yandruwandha were one of a group of tribes speaking dialects of the same language and living in the Lakes Country of northeastern South Australia. They first came to the notice of Europeans when they discovered the Burke and Wills Expedition in 1861. The exact dialect situation before white contact is unclear, but dialect or tribal names that have been heard include Innamincka or Thayipilthirringuda Yandruwandha, Strzelecki or Murnpeowie Yandruwandha, Biraliba, Nhirrpi or Nhirrpi Yandruwandha, Yawarrawarrka, Matja, Parlpamardramardra, Ngananhina, Ngapardandhirri and (using N.B. Tindale's spelling) Ngurawola. Tindale (1974) gave three names for the area: Yandruwandha (his Jandruwanta), Yawarrawarrka (his Jauraworka) and Ngurawola. The countries that he gave for them were as follows:

(p.213) Jandruwanta

South of Cooper Creek from Innamincka to Carraweena, on Strzelecki Creek.

(p.213) Jauraworka

North of Cooper Creek to Haddon Downs and Cadelga; at Cordillo Downs, west into sandhills east of Goyder Lagoon; east to about Arrabury; southeast nearly to Innamincka, but that area is also claimed by the Ngurawola and doubts exist.

(p.183) Ngurawola

At Arrabury and Durham Downs and the southwestern vicinity; west to Coongie Lakes; south to Lake Marrakoonamooka.

The name Biraliba is given by Capell (1963:Area L p.6) as the name of a dialect of Yandruwandha. However, it may be a mishearing of Pilardapa, the name of the language spoken to the south of Yandruwandha and used sometimes by Innamincka Yandruwandha speakers to refer to Strzelecki Yandruwandha.

The first mention of the name Ngurawola in writing seems (Hercus 2001) to be by Howitt (1904:449, 685 — referring to events in 1861). There are some other early references, including two improbable etymologies by Reuther (1981). My Strzelecki informant Maudie Naylon and her husband Bob, both first-language speakers of Wangkangurru, explained the meaning of this name as 'abandoned camp' (*nguda* 'camp', *warla* 'abandoned'), referring to the fact that nobody lived in that country any more, which meant that it was not a language or tribal name at all. A possible weakness of this etymology is that they gave *walpa* as the Wangkangurru equivalent of *warla*, and *walpa*

(Hercus, pers. comm.) actually means 'many'. However, it was clearly not an etymology made up at the time for my benefit, as I had heard the word used with, apparently, this meaning three years before. Other informants did not know the name, and regarded the western part of Tindale's Ngurawola area as being Yawarrawarrka country and the eastern part as Parlpakurnu (literally 'other language'; it refers to a dialect of the Wangkumara group (or the group as a whole), quite distinct from the Yandruwandha group of dialects).

Ngapardandhirri was given by Reuther (1981; information from Hercus 2001) as meaning 'the saltbush people', 'the marshland people'. It is made up of *ngapa* 'water' and *tantiri* (in Reuther's spelling) 'saltbush'. I am assuming that *tantiri* is the word that I have as *dandhirri*; the meaning I have for it is 'turkey bush' but Reuther may well be right. Reuther regarded them as a subgroup of Ngurawola.

Nhirrpi was a name used by Alice Miller for the variety of Yandruwandha she knew, recorded briefly by S.A. Wurm in 1957 (Bowern 2000). The name was given to me by Tim Guttie, who said that it was spoken at Arrabury. On another occasion Benny Kerwin placed it "somewhere round about Oontoo, between there and Nappa Merrie;[1] or between (Nappa Merrie and) Baryulah". (Oontoo is west of Nappa Merrie, where the Cooper crosses the Queensland–South Australia border; Baryulah is east of Nappa Merrie, and is a Wangkumara name.) According to Tolcher (2003:10) they were at Cullyamurra Waterhole (Callamurra on the 1:250,000 map) and Nappaoonie Waterhole, between Innamincka and Oontoo, and north along Merninie Creek. (This information ultimately from Benny Kerwin via his great-grandson Aaron Paterson — Tolcher, pers. comm.)

The name Parlpamardramardra, which means 'stony language', was given to me by Benny Kerwin as the language spoken between Innamincka and Nappa Merrie. However, on another occasion he seemed to say that there was a boundary between Parlpamardramardra and Parlpakurnu at Baryulah. On yet another occasion he said that Lake Pure and Tookabarnoo Waterhole were in Parlpamardramardra country; the former is north of Nappa Merrie and well inside Ngurawola country as delineated by Tindale, and the latter is on the Wilson River south of Baryulah and seems more likely to be in Wangkumara country. The name Yarramuddere recorded by Basedow in 1919 (Hercus, pers. comm.) may be a variant of this with *parlpa* replaced by *yawarri* (also 'language').

Ngananhina was also a name given by Tim Guttie for a language spoken at Arrabury. She said that it was different from Nhirrpi. On another occasion Benny Kerwin said that it was between Yawarrawarrka and Marrulha (i.e. east or northeast of Yawarrawarrka).

Matja was given by Benny Kerwin as the name of a variety of Yawarrawarrka spoken to the west of Innamincka, on the Cooper between his country and Diyari country. Specific placenames mentioned were Coongie, Tirrawarra and old Cuttapirie; he implied once that Cuttapirie was the upstream boundary. The Diyari boundary was said to be at or before Kanowana. (The map in Austin (1981a:3) puts the northeastern boundary of Diyari country to the west of Kanowana, suggesting that Kanowana was in Matja country.) Tolcher (2003:10) gave the western extent of Thayipilthirringuda country on the Cooper (and so presumably the eastern boundary of Matja) as Tilcha Waterhole.

It is interesting that both *matja* and *ngananhina* are time-related words in Yandruwandha. Matja means 'long ago', and *ngananhina*, literally 'do-sit', is the stem of the verbal form *ngananhinanhukada*, which means 'yesterday'. The name Thayipilthirringuda means literally 'grinding stone-chip-from' and refers to people from the area around Innamincka

---

[1] Also spelt Nappa Merry and Nappamerry on maps.

where there was a quarry where grinding stones were produced. Murnpeowie is the name of a station outside Yandruwandha country to the south; Maudie Naylon used it (pronouncing it more like 'Mumpy') to refer to the variety of Yandruwandha that she had learnt from a former husband — what I am calling Strzelecki Yandruwandha.

Benny Kerwin said that the Yawarrawarrka/Yandruwandha boundary ran between Cutrabelbo and Kudriemitchie. He specified a number of other placenames as being either Yandruwandha or Yawarrawarrka.

I am (arbitrarily) using Yandruwandha as a cover term for the whole language, which, like many Australian languages, does not have its own name. It seems clear that some of the names given above are alternatives to others. I have chosen to put Yandruwandha, Matja, Yawarrawarrka, Ngananhina, Nhirrpi and Parlpamardramardra — the names I have heard from my own informants — on the map. I have disregarded locations given for some of these groups in older sources (such as the 1907 letter from Alfred Walker to A.W. Howitt reproduced in Paterson, n.d.:90), having enough inconsistencies in the sources I have used without introducing more (although they are not gross).

Neighbouring languages were Diyari and Ngamini, and possibly also Karangura and Yaluyandi, on the west, Mithaka and perhaps Karruwali on the north, Marrulha on the northeast, Kungardutji(?), Wangkumara and Mambangura on the east, Wadikali on the southeast and Pilardapa to the south. (Kungardutji is a doubtful language name; see Breen 1990:22–23 and references given there. Other names recorded for this area include Yarumarra and Karendala. The Yandruwandha speakers called the language of this area Parlpakurnu, which simply means 'other language', and this is what I have called it on the map. Indications are that this refers to all dialects of the Wangkumara group, south as well as north of Wangkumara itself, although the name Wangkumara was used too. I have used it only for the area north of Wangkumara.) The Innamincka Yandruwandha speakers, as noted above, referred to Strzelecki Yandruwandha as Pilardapa. There were probably other similar identifications of dialects with more distantly related languages or other dialects further away in the same direction; another example noted was Maudie Naylon's referring to the Innamincka people as Parlpamardramardra, although she did also regard them as Yandruwandha ("different Yandruwandha").

The boundaries on the map are tentative and incomplete, reflecting my lack of knowledge of the details. The boundary line crossing the Strzelecki Creek north of Murtamurta Well divides Innamincka Yandruwandha from Strzelecki Yandruwandha, although I have not written these names on the map. I have not put in any boundaries between closely related languages surrounding this group; Wardikali is separated from the distantly related languages on either side, and the languages on the west and north, which I believe to have formed a dialect chain (see Breen 1971), are separated from those on the Cooper to the east.

Helen Tolcher has written (2003) 'Seed of the coolibah: a history of the Yandruwandha and Yawarrawarrka people'.

1.2 The linguistic affinities of the Yandruwandha language

Yandruwandha seems to be most closely related to a group of languages possibly forming a language chain, formerly spoken to the north, east and south. The best known of these are Diyari, described by Austin (1981a), and Ngamini. Its relationship to Wangkumara and related dialects to the east seems to be less close. However, the situation is not at all clear. In cognate counts of between 220 and 230 comparable items (based on the 250-word list used by Breen (1971), Yandruwandha shared 47% with Diyari, but only 40% of the 39 verbs that could be compared (and see Breen 1990, Chapter 7 on the significance of this). It shared 28% (and 22% of verbs) with Wangkumara. But its pronouns were much more similar to those of Wangkumara than Diyari, and these are a strong indicator of genetic relationship (see, for example, Blake 1988).

In the classification of all Australian languages by O'Grady, Voegelin and Voegelin (1966), based mainly on vocabulary lists, Yandruwandha[2] was classed as a dialect of the same language as Diyari, Ngamini, Karangura and Yaluyandi; other languages in this subgroup were Pilardapa, Yawarrawarrka and Karendala-Kungadutji-Pirriya-Marrulha-Karruwali (these five being classed as dialects of one language). These formed the Karna Subgroup of the Dieric Group. Other subgroups in this group were Ngura (languages to the east of Yandruwandha and Yawarrawarrka) and Yalyi (Karenggapa, Wadikali and Malyangapa to the southeast). To the north of the Dieric Group was the Pittapittic Group, which included Pitta-Pitta and Wangka-Yutjurru, to the west the Arabanic Group (Arabana and Wangkangurru) and to the northeast the Mitakudic Group, which (as Breen 1971:20 showed) was a case of mistaken identity, data for Mitakudi (Mayi-Thakurti, Cloncurry district) being attributed to Mitaka (Mithaka, east of Birdsville).

Breen (1971) reclassified all of the languages in these four groups which were in or close to Queensland, apart from Pirriya (Ngura Subgroup) as belonging to one group, which he called Karnic. He did not have data on the Arabanic Group or the Yalyi Subgroup, but assumed that the Arabanic languages, at least, were part of Karnic. He made substantial changes also to the internal relations within the group; for example, classing Yandruwandha and Yawarawarrka as dialects of one language, and Diyari, Ngamini, Yaluyandi, Mithaka and Karruwali as a chain of dialects forming one language. By 1990 (Breen 1990, Chapter 1) he was doubtful that Kalali and Badjidi (Ngura) were Karnic. Austin (1990) made the first attempt to reconstruct a proto-Karnic, but concluded that Arabana and Wangkangurru were not part of the group. Kalali and Badjidi were not mentioned, nor were the Yalyi languages. Bowern (1998) reinstated Arabana and Wangkangurru and also included Kalali, but excluded the Yalyi languages.

It is by no means clear at this stage that such a thing as a Karnic group of languages, exclusive reconstructable from a common ancestor, exists. Further work on the subgrouping in this area is currently in progress.

1.3 Previous work

The first published information on Yandruwandha is the 'Notes on the Aborigines of Cooper's Creek' by A.W. Howitt, published in Smyth's (1878) *The Aborigines of Victoria*. A wordlist from 'Cooper's Creek, in the neighbourhood where Burke and Wills died' was contributed by Howitt to Edward Micklethwaite Curr and published by him in Curr (1886–87). However, this is not Yandruwandha but Diyari. Words given for Yandruwandha and Yawarrawarrka in Howitt (1904) are more reliable, especially when they are contrasted with Diyari items (as on p.92–94) but are still not completely trustworthy — for example, at least some of the words given in the story on pages 802–803 are Diyari or Ngamini. This must cast some doubt on other aspects of Howitt's information

---

[2] This, and many of the other language names which follow, were spelt differently by O'Grady et al.

on the Yandruwandha. Howitt also describes a few hand-signs in Yandruwandha, interspersed with others in Diyari and other languages. There is an article by Howitt (1891) on the Diyari and related groups, and another by Howitt and Siebert (1904) on legends from the same area. Others to contribute wordlists from this area to Curr were H.G. Salmon from 'Koongi (Coongy) Lake Station' whose vocabulary was simply labelled 'Cooper's Creek' and W.H. Cornish, whose vocabulary was from 'Cooper's Creek, to the eastward of its northern branch'. Cornish labels the language of his list 'Yowerawoolka' although it is not clear that it is Yawarrawarrka and not Yandruwandha; for example, it has the word for 'woman', which in my data is clearly different, although related, in the two dialects, in its Yandruwandha form (*yiwa*, as compared to Yawarrawarrka *tjiwara*). Salmon's list seems also to be Yawarrawarrka; for example, it has the verb ending *-indri*, which is not found in Yandruwandha as I recorded it. Colin C. Wimberley published a short word list in 'Yarrawoorka' in the journal Science of Man in 1899, and there was a list by E. Sharpe in 'Yandra Wandra' in the same journal in 1901.

R.H. Mathews (1899, 1900) made references to the Yandruwandha and Yawarrawarrka without giving information on the language. Reuther (1981, a publication on microfiche of a translation of his 1891, 1899 and 1901 manuscripts) includes a fair number of Yandruwandha and Yawarrawarrka words and sentences in his monumental work on *The Diari*, including a grammatical sketch of 'Jandruwanta' which is discussed briefly in §1.5.

More recent work on these dialects includes a manuscript wordlist by N.B. Tindale and recordings by S.A. Wurm, B. Schebeck and D. Trefry. Bowern (2000) has studied some of Wurm's material, in the Nhirrpi dialect. A short wordlist in Yandruwandha is in Menning and Nash (1981). Two short articles on aspects of Yandruwandha, Breen (1976b, c), appear in Dixon, ed. (1976). There is some information on the languages in Hercus (1990). Austin (1988a, b, 1990) uses some data from Yandruwandha, as do Tchekoff (1985, 1987) and Breen (1974, 1993, 1997).

1.4 The informants

The data on the Innamincka dialect were obtained from the last two competent speakers: Nelly Parker, better known as Tim Guttie, and Benny Kerwin. Tim was first recorded in 1967, again in 1968, and passed away some time after that. Benny was first recorded in 1968, and then again in 1971–2–3–4 and finally in January 1976. The bulk of the information, therefore, came from him. He was an brilliant teacher and informant, although his knowledge was by no means complete, and our communication was hampered by the fact that he was hard of hearing, and also that he did not normally wear his false teeth.

Benny Kerwin, Man.gili,[3] was born about 1890 at Innamincka, South Australia, the only son of Jack Kirwan,[4] a white man who worked as cook and cowboy on various stations in the area, and an Aboriginal mother (who, however, was said to have had an Indian mother). He was brought up in the Birdsville area and his working life was spent mostly on

---

[3] Much of the following information on Benny Kerwin has already appeared in Hercus and Sutton, eds (1986) and in Breen, in Horton, ed. (1994). Some comes from Paterson (n.d.).

[4] Spelling of the name from Paterson (n.d.). I do not know how the spelling came to be changed. I have always written it Kerwin, but I don't remember where I got that spelling from. In any case, it is the spelling used now by the family.

properties in north-east South Australia and south-west Queensland as a ringer and drover. However, droving took him as far afield as Bedourie to the north and Adelaide to the south.

In 1906 he was employed as driver on the Cobb & Co. coach which carried the mail between Marree and Innamincka. On one occasion the horses bolted and the coach was smashed at Ackalana Crossing on Strzelecki Creek about 125 km from Innamincka. The coach was never replaced and for some time after that Benny carried the mail by packhorse.

While working at Nappa Merrie, Benny met his first wife, Nelly Parker, usually known (later, if not then) as Tim. Like Benny, she had a white father and Aboriginal mother, and she was employed as a housemaid. They were married about 1915. They had six children, of whom the first two died in childhood. The marriage broke up about 1932.

In 1927 Benny and his close friend Bill Gorringe represented Innamincka Station at a rodeo in Adelaide staged to celebrate the 75th birthday of Sir Sidney Kidman (Paterson n.d.; Tolcher pers. comm.). Performers were a couple of representatives from each of Kidman's stations.[5]

Benny's second wife was Mary Stafford (nee Moore), born at Cordillo of a white father and Aboriginal mother. They had seven children; Mary died at Broken Hill giving birth to the seventh, who also died. Most of this family were born at Tibooburra, New South Wales.

Benny lost an eye in an accident in 1953.

He was, needless to say, an expert horseman and was also noted for his nimble feet, and was in demand as a step-dancer at race balls even in his seventies.

Benny's last station job was at Arrabury in 1967. His last years were spent living with one or other of his children or, occasionally, grandchildren, and he was with his daughter Joan Dennis at Roma when he died on 8th January 1976.

Nelly Parker (Manngidrikani in Yandruwandha, Tim to many people[6]) was born at Nappa Merrie and brought up at Innamincka. She had a white father, who may have been John Conrick, the owner of Nappa Merrie (Paterson n.d.), and an Aboriginal mother. After leaving Benny she married Archie Guttie, but she and Benny were together again before she died in 1969.

Benny and Tim were the last two competent speakers of the Innamincka dialect of Yandruwandha and were generous in allowing their knowledge to be recorded for posterity. Benny's last session as a linguistic informant was less than a day before he died from a heart attack. He enjoyed this work and was cheerful, painstaking and competent to the end.

Maudie Naylon, whose life story appears in Horton, ed. (1994), was a native speaker of Wangkangurru but was a more or less good speaker of, and recorded in, a number of other languages, of which Yandruwandha and Yawarrawarrka were perhaps about numbers four and six. Her ability to keep her various languages apart was excellent when I first recorded her (when she was about 80) but deteriorated over the next ten years, and she did tend to mix these two quite a lot, although there is very little interference from Wangkangurru or other languages. However, one must have reservations about some of the vocabulary items she gave which differ from those given by others (where there are comparable items) and are the same as words from Ngamini (for instance; this was perhaps her second language),

---

[5] This corrects information given about this function in Kerwin (1986, in introductory notes by Breen) and Breen (1994).

[6] Manngidrikani is the name she told me. Tolcher (2003:139) gives her name as Timpicka, and this is the origin of the nickname Tim (Paterson, pers. comm.). Benny sometimes addressed her as Kila (or Killer?).

and words for which she gave the same form in Strzelecki Yandruwandha and Yawarrawarrka but for which different forms were given by others for the intervening Innamincka Yandruwandha. Study of Yandruwandha recorded by Schebeck and others should throw light on these.

Willy Harris, Alfie Harris and Hector Harrison were the sons of Walter Harrison, a Yandruwandha speaker, and grew up at Innamincka, but the language they spoke was Yawarrawarrka. Their knowledge was/is very incomplete. Willy and Hector are still alive at the time of writing.

Benny Kerwin, Tim Guttie and Maudie Naylon will generally be referred to by their initials throughout the grammar.

1.5 A comparison of the sources

Cognate counts were made of vocabulary from a long comparative list from seven sources, some of which, however, had only a small part of the total vocabulary. The sources were:

- Innamincka Yandruwandha: Benny Kerwin, Tim Guttie
- other Yandruwandha: Maudie Naylon, Reuther
- Yawarrawarrka: Maudie Naylon, Reuther, combined others (the three brothers Hector Harrison, Alfie Harris and Willy Harris, with also odd words from Benny Kerwin).

The counting was generous: if one list had words A and B for an item and another had A and C it was counted as a plus, even though study of the transcripts might have shown that one was the normal word and another perhaps an intrusion from another dialect. (This is particularly relevant to comparing the two Maudie Naylon lists.)

Comparable items for counts involving only the Kerwin, Guttie and Naylon lists ranged from 250 to nearly 400; counts involving the Harris list and one of the above involved 170–200 items, while counts involving the two Reuther lists had only from 50 to 100 comparable items. Items in the Harris list were sometimes untrustworthy — for example, the word given for 'eyebrow' was the word in a neighbouring language for 'eye'. Also there were some doubtful items in the Reuther list.

Cognate percentages ranged from a little over 71 to 92 for nominals and from 80 to 98 for verbs. Clearly only one language is involved; however, the figures for the two Naylon lists (89 and 95) are obviously inflated, due to her occasional confusion as to what belonged to which, and the same probably applies to the two Reuther percentages. Consequently, it is not possible to estimate how close the different dialects are to one another from these sources.

There are very few and only sporadic phonological differences between the dialects; the most salient involves a group of words beginning with /y/ in Yandruwandha and /tj/ in Yawarrawarrka (*yiwa/tjiwara* 'woman', *yada/tjada* 'boomerang', *yingka/tjingka* 'laugh', *yimpa/tjimpa* 'black').[7] This, and a couple of other differences involving single words, were absolutely consistent. One corresponding pair, *kilka* (Yn)/*kitka* (Yw) 'know', was not — Maudie Naylon used the former form in both dialects.

---

[7] The Nhirrpi corpus has *yiwa* 'woman' but *tjada* 'boomerang'.

Bowern (2000) compared 242 Nhirrpi words ('all the items in the Nhirrpi list that could be ascertained with reasonable confidence') with Innamincka Yandruwandha and found 78.5% common. The figure for Nhirrpi and Wangkumara (the Nhirrpi informant's first language) was only 18%.

The following table compares bound forms in the various sources. Only the minority that are not the same in all (as far as we know) are given. In the Reuther Yandruwandha list the items given to the right of another item are from example sentences in the Diari Dictionary or list of placenames, and tend to be more similar to Yandruwandha as described below than is his 'Jandruwanda' grammar, which is closer to Yawarrawarrka in modern sources. Bowern (2000) suggests that the grammar may be Matja.

Table 1-1: Comparison of bound forms

	Innamincka	Strzelecki	Reuther Jandruwanda	Nhirrpi	Yawarrawarrka
Nouns					
Operative	-li	-li, -lu/u-	-li	-li, (-ru?)	-li, -lu/u-
Dative	-ngadi	-ngadi	-ma	-adi	-ma
Locative	-yi	-yi	-nyi, -yi	-yi	-ni (H,R), -nyi (N,R)
Aversive	-puru	-yi (?)		-puru	-thudu
Pronouns					
1sg.GEN	ngakani	ngakani	kamanti, ngakani	ngandjani	kamanti
3sg:NOM:here	nhuniyi	nhunuyi	nhuniyi	—	nhunuyi
3sg:NOM:there	nhutjadu, nhunudu	nhunuku, nhunuwa, nhunurra	nhunuwa, nhunudu, nhutjadu[9]	nhunudu?[8]	nhunuku
Verbs					
immed. past	-na	-ni	-itha, -nhana	-na	-itha
far past	-lapurra	-lapurra	-iyapurra, -lapurra	—	-iyapurra
future	-nga	-nga nganarla	-inga	-iyala, -nga	-iya(la)
potential	-yi	-yi	-ipi	-yi	-ipi
diff. subj.	-rlayi	-rlayi	-irnanyi	—	-irnanyi
unspecified	-ri	-ri	-ri	—	-indri
Interrogatives					
when?	walpi		wintja	—	wintjama
how?	yilayarndu		yilari	—	yilaru

Some other differences in pronouns in Nhirrpi may result from errors; see §6.3.

1.6 The project

I first recorded Yandruwandha and Yawarrawarrka in 1967, as part of a linguistic survey of western Queensland, aimed at finding what languages were still remembered, who by

---

[8] Bowern gives deictic suffix -du as meaning 'near' and -kara/-yara as 'far'.
[9] Not in Reuther's grammar but in an example sentence in his dictionary.

and where. I visited many towns and properties and enquired for people who might remember an Aboriginal language, and when I found people who were willing and able to give me information I normally recorded them for half an hour or an hour, mainly to elicit vocabulary and sentences in the language. The elicitation used the lists of words and sentences given in Capell's (n.d.) booklet.

The following year I began work on a depth study of one of the languages I had recorded (Warluwarra), but while en route to work with or from working with speakers of this language in this and subsequent years I called on speakers of other languages that I had met in 1967, and some others who I met in later years, and did further work on these languages. (Wurm 1967 was a useful resource in these years; also I compiled my own resources, mainly lists of useful sentences to elicit particular grammatical forms, over the years.) After completing my Warluwarra project, I continued salvage work on numerous languages, funded by annual grants from the then Australian Institute of Aboriginal Studies.

The work continued to be based mostly on elicitation during these years, as most informants, being old people who had not spoken their own languages for years, were not able to tell coherent stories in the languages and had no-one with whom they could converse in the language. Benny Kerwin was one of the few who could tell a story of more than two or three sentences, and I began recording this sort of material from him in 1971. This produced some valuable ethnographic information as well as good stories and valuable data for grammatical analysis. However, my work on Yandruwandha was still very much part-time.

During 1975 I worked full-time on my Yandruwandha material for most of the year, and wrote a preliminary grammar (Breen 1975). This work uncovered many gaps in my knowledge of the language, and I compiled many pages of questions. At the end of the year I went to Roma, where Benny was living, and began work with him on New Year's Day 1976. This led to answers to most of my questions, but the work was cut short by Benny's sudden death on 8th January.

The work on the Strzelecki dialect of Yandruwandha and on Yawarrawarrka had never progressed beyond elicitation, and it too came to an end in 1976. Unfortunately, it had never been possible to do any of the work in Yandruwandha/Yawarrawarrka country.

In 1994–95, I was employed by the Burran Aboriginal Corporation, Bourke, New South Wales, to prepare a preliminary dictionary of Yandruwandha. The funding for this ran out after about nine weeks. In 2000–01 I was employed on a one-year contract by Muda Aboriginal Corporation, a successor to Burran, to produce usable tape transcripts, a grammar and a dictionary of Yandruwandha. The actual work took rather more than a year.

2 *The sound system*

2.1 Introduction

The sound system of Yandruwandha is characterised by a large number of consonant phonemes of which a fair proportion are very restricted in their occurrence, the status of a few being quite doubtful. There are a total of at least 28, perhaps 30, consonants including four compound phonemes; eight of these, including two of the compound phonemes, occur only following a primary stressed vowel or, occasionally, following a secondary stressed vowel in a compound stem. Even there some of the oppositions are sometimes lost. In addition, the opposition between apical-alveolar and apical-postalveolar points of articulation is neutralised in word-initial position and in unstressed environments.

In contrast to the complex consonant system is the typically simple Australian system of three vowel phonemes, and the simplicity of the phonotactics and morphophonology. All words end in a vowel, and there is only a limited range of consonant clusters, all diconsonantal. Virtually all bound morphemes have only a single form.

The phonemes are shown, using orthographic symbols, in Table 2-1.

Table 2-1: Yandruwandha phonemes

	Peripheral		Laminal		Apical		
	Bilabial	Velar	Dental	Alveopalatal	Alveolar	Postalveolar	Open
Voiceless stop	p	k	th	tj	t	rt	
Voiced stop	b	g	dh	dj	d	rd	
Trill-released stop					dr	rdr	
Nasal	m	ng	nh	ny	n	rn	
Lateral			lh	ly	l	rl	
Prestopped lateral					(dl)	(rdl)	
Trill				rr			
Glide	w			y		r	
Vowel	u			i			a

Note that in the spelling of Yandruwandha words the following simplifications are made:

- *n* and *l* are written instead of *nh* and *lh* respectively when *th* or *dh* follow, e.g. *nth* instead of *nhth*;
- *n* and *l* are written instead of *ny* and *ly* respectively when *tj* or *dj* follow, e.g. *ndj* instead of *nydj*;
- *t* and *d* are written instead of *rt* and *rd* respectively when they follow *rn*, e.g. *rnt* instead of *rnrt*;
- *d* and *dr* are written instead of *rd* and *rdr* at the beginning of a word, e.g. *dritji* instead of *rdritji* (but not within a word since /d/ can always contrast with /rd/ there; thus the reduplicated form of *drama* is *dramardrama*);
- the consonant cluster /n/ followed by /g/ is written *n.g* to distinguish it from the velar nasal, *ng*.

The consonant phonemes will now be illustrated and justified.

2.2 Consonant phonemes

2.2.1 Voiceless stops

The voiceless stops in IY and SY occur in all consonant positions except as first member of a cluster and, in the case of the apicals, word-initially. In Yw there are a couple of examples of /tk/ and in Matja the handful of words heard includes one with a /ttj/ cluster. Table 2-2 gives examples of each stop in each of the positions: word-initial, intervocalic and in a consonant cluster.

Table 2-2: Examples of voiceless stops

	Word-initial	Intervocalic	Consonant cluster
p	*pawa* 'seed'	*mapa* 'to gather'	*pampu* 'egg'
k	*karra* 'to tie'	*maka* 'fire'	*mingka* 'hole'
th	*tharra* 'to fly'	*matha* 'to bite'	*pintha* 'foreskin'
tj	*tjirri* 'acacia sp.'	*matja* 'long ago'	*pantja* 'knee'
t		*yita* 'away'	*kanta* 'over there'
rt		*warta* 'butt (of tree)'	*pirnta* 'waddy'

The voiceless apical-alveolar stop is one of the less frequent consonants, and the opposition between it and the apical-postalveolar stop is neutralised in some positions. /t/ is quite uncommon intervocalically and never occurs after an unstressed vowel except in loanwords. The apical-alveolar and laminal-dental consonants are often hard to distinguish in the speech of the three main informants — all old and the main one lacking in teeth. However, the oppositions between apical-alveolar and apical-postalveolar and between apical-alveolar and laminal-dental points of articulation are both well attested; the former by such pairs as *mini* 'to run' / *mirni* sentence introducer, *malka* 'mark' / *marlka* 'mulga', *pandi* 'dog' / *parndilka* 'maggot', *walkini* 'climb (gerund)' / *warlkini* 'fall (gerund)', and the latter by *yina* '2sg.ACC' / *yinha* '3sg.ACC', *thana* '3pl.NOM' / *thanha* '3pl.ACC', *pandi* 'dog' / *pandhi* 'down' and *paladi* 'particular' / *palha* 'bird'. A minimal pair for /th/ versus /t/ is *thitha* 'crotch' / *thita* 'bump, knob'. Compare also *kutawirri* 'rotten' with *nguthangutha* 'to stretch out' and *matha* 'to bite' with *thata* 'grease'. The best pairs we have for /t/ and /rt/

are *thata* 'grease' / *karta* 'crack' and, for Yw, *wita* 'hill' / *pirta* 'post'. Minimal pairs for /th/ and /tj/, in addition to that given in the table, are *thathi* 'step cut in tree trunk' / *thatji* 'clitoris' and *thalka* 'up' / *tjalka* '(eyes) to be open', and some subminimal pairs *withi* 'sore' / *pitji* 'coolamon', *ngathadi* 'younger sibling' / *ngatjada* 'camp', *kathi* 'meat' / *patji* 'good'.

2.2.2 Voiced stops

Australian languages have been generally thought of as lacking the voiced/voiceless distinction in stop phonemes, and although such a distinction has now been found in a significant number of languages the generalisation is still basically true. A majority of Australian languages do lack the distinction on the phonemic level, and in those languages which do have it it is restricted in some way; see Austin (1988a). In Yandruwandha the distinction is found only after stressed vowels (and almost always only after a primary stressed vowel) or in nasal–stop clusters. Note, however, that /rd/ occurs word-initially whereas /rt/ does not (e.g. *darla* 'skin'). For some of the voiced stop phonemes the evidence of an opposition with the corresponding voiceless stop is meagre; however, *in toto* the evidence for a full set of voiced stops is quite strong. Minimal and subminimal pairs are now given, with comments.

p/b There are four known minimal pairs and one of these will arouse cynical laughter; however, it is clearly genuine. This is *ngapa* 'water' / *ngaba* 'wet'. *Ngaba* occurs mainly in combined forms *ngabaka* 'to wet', *ngabangaba* 'wet', but once as a stem with locative inflection (and so *ngapayi* 'water-LOC' / *ngabayi* 'wet-LOC' is a minimal pair); the stop of *ngapa* remains unvoiced in such compounds as *ngapakurna* 'waterhole', *ngapatjili* 'soak (noun)', *ngapangarrka* 'river crossing' and others. Some other minimal pairs are *ngalba* 'light' (in weight) / *ngalpa* 'lap', also 'type of dance', *ngamburru* 'snot, nasal mucus' / *ngampurru* 'yellowbelly (fish)' and *palbarri* 'flat, smooth; level, not sloping much' / *palparri* 'boulder, bedded rock, big flat rock'. Other examples of the *p/b* opposition are found in the pairs *kapada* 'come on!' / *kabuta* 'hat', *ngapungapu* 'quiet' / *mabumabu* 'dark' and *tjumpurru, tjumpunyu*, both 'waxbill (zebra finch)' / *tjumbutjurrkuru* 'wild plum'.

k/g Minimal pairs include *kaka* 'near' / *kaga* 'to burp', *waka* 'tooth' / *waga* 'to move', *yika* 'to wash' / *yiga* 'wild orange', *yingkani* 'laugh (gerund)' / *yinggani* '2sg.GEN', *kalka* 'afternoon' / *kalga* 'dim'. Other pairs are *thangkananga* 'burn (INTR)-FUT' / *thanggurnanga* 'stand-CONT', *kurrkari* 'green' / *purrga* 'cramp', *pulka* 'to blow' / *pulgani* '3du.GEN', *thinkali* 'sideways' / *tjin.gini* 'beefwood'.

th/dh Minimal pairs are *kuthi* 'to come' / *kudhi* 'to hide', and *kathi* 'meat' / *kadhi* 'to be happy'. Further evidence is provided by the contrast between *manthi* 'bed' and *mandhirra* 'Acacia sp.' or *pandhi* 'down'.

tj/dj There are no minimal pairs. Some relevant pairs are *thatji* 'clitoris, stone knife' / *thadjingumini* 'mountain devil', also called 'thorny devil' (probably a compound derived from *thatji*), *ditjipa* 'to dry in the sun (TR)' / *didjipirri* 'to jump' (recorded only from TG), *muntji* 'to smother' / *mundja* 'sick' and *mundju* 'fly'. Intervocalic /dj/ is extremely rare.

t/d The very meagre evidence includes one minimal pair, *kanta* 'over there' / *kanda* 'shallow' and also *kutikutirri* 'winding' / *kuditharra* 'to forget'. There are very few examples of /t/ intervocalically; intervocalic /d/ is not a stop but a tap.

rt/rd Subminimal pairs include *martardaku* 'ankle' / *mardanpa* 'lizard sp.', *martimarti* 'peewee' / *pardi* 'dangerous creature', *yartu* 'full (of stomach)' / *mardu* 'social division', *kartiwirri* 'to dive' / *-ardi*, an emphatic suffix in which the first vowel may take a primary stress, *parntu* 'blunt' / *parndilka* 'maggot', *warnta* 'short' / *marnda* 'half way' and *ngarnda* 'forehead'.

Voiced stops occur only intervocalically and as the second member of a cluster, except for /rd/, which can also occur word-initially (being the only apical stop which can do so).

Table 2-3: Examples of voiced stops

	Word-initial	Intervocalic	Cluster
b		*yiba* 'to drink'	*yinba* 'to send'
g		*ngaga* 'throat'	*palgupalgu* 'meat'
dh		*thidharri* 'baby'	*mundha* 'greedy'
dj		*thadjingumini* 'mountain devil'	*mundju* 'fly'
d		*kadawa* 'edge'	*kanda* 'shallow'
rd	*darrpi* 'to turn'	*ngardu* 'nardoo'	*marnda* 'halfway'

Evidence of oppositions between voiced stops and laterals (simple or prestopped) is scarce, but there are a few pairs which suggest that they do exist. These include *kadhi* 'to be happy' / *kalhidi* 'mother-in-law', 'daughter-in-law', *puda* 'urine' / *pula* '3du.NOM', *pardi* 'dangerous creature' / *parli* 'father's sister' and *wardama* 'calm' / *wardla* 'nest'.

2.2.3 Trill-released stops

The trill-released stops, written /dr/ and /rdr/, are regarded as unit phonemes for the following reasons:

(a) at least one of them can occur word-initially, in which position a consonant cluster cannot (otherwise) occur;

(b) they form clusters with a preceding homorganic nasal or lateral; there are (otherwise) no triconsonantal clusters;

(c) trill-released stops in Yandruwandha correspond to voiced stops in the closely related languages to the west; see Table 2-4 for examples.

Table 2-4: Yandruwandha/Ngamini prestopped trill/stop correspondences

	Yandruwandha	Ngamini
'stone'	*mardra*	*marda*
'to get'	*mandri*	*manda* (gerund)
'willy wagtail'	*thindrithindri*	*thindithindi*
'to hold'	*pardra*	*parda*

Point (b) could easily be accounted for by writing the clusters as /nrr/, /lrr/, /rnrr/ and /rlrr/ instead of /ndr/, /ldr/, /rndr/ and /rldr/ respectively, since the stop could be interposed by a phonological rule of epenthesis. This is the solution adopted for Dieri (Diyari) by Trefry (1970) and it is probably also applicable to Wangkumara. As there is no word-initial opposition between [dr] and [ḍr̠] it would be possible to write /rr/ in this position, with a phonological rule to provide the initial stop. A point against this is the slow and careful pronunciation, occasionally heard when vocabulary is being elicited, of a compound word in which the second constituent begins in /rr/; thus, for example, mundjurrunga 'blowfly' (cf. *mundju* 'fly') was heard as two words, the second being [rúŋa], not [drúŋa] or [ḍrúŋa]. However, the main objection to this type of explanation is that no phonological rule could account for intervocalic [dr] or [ḍr̠]; note especially the opposition between *kadra* 'louse', *kardra* 'yam' and *karra* 'to tie'. The alternatives are to accept trill-released stops as phonemes or to regard them (intervocalically) as clusters of stop and trill. Only the former alternative enables us to represent the sounds in the same way whether they occur word-initially, intervocalically or in a cluster, without introducing word-initial clusters and triconsonantal clusters.

Note, however, that there is some alternation, at the phonetic level,[1] between trill-released stops in simple stems and stops in compound stems, e.g. *thadri* 'bank (of river)' / *thadripalapala* (heard as [ṭádipalapala]) 'both banks'.

Oppositions between trill-released stops and apical stops and rhotics are illustrated by the following sets: *kadra* / *kardra* / *karra* / *kara* 'maybe' / *kadawa* 'edge' / *kartakarta* 'saltbush', *mardri* 'heavy' / *martimarti* 'peewee', *kandra* 'top' / *kanta* 'over there' / *kanda* 'shallow', *mardra* 'stone' / *mara* 'hand' / *-mada* '2kin' / *marra* 'to redden (INTR)', *yita* 'that way' / *yirra* 'to wash' / *yidrayidra* 'flower', *marnardraku* 'tooth' / *mararrala* 'crab', *kardri* 'brother-in-law' / *kadi* 'to chase' / *karriwara* 'eaglehawk' (SY, Yw) / *karirri* 'creek', *kudri* 'swan' / *kurdikurdirri* ~ *kutikutirri* 'crooked' / *kuditharra* 'to forget' / *kurrikira* 'rainbow' / *kuriyirrika* 'to clean', *thadra* 'to push' / *thata* 'grease' / *tharra* 'to fly'.

Examples of word-initial trill-released stops include *dritji* 'sun', drama 'to cut', *drantha* 'fork (of tree)', *drukampada* 'frog sp.'.

Austin (1988b) is a comparative study of trill-released stops, their development and spread, in languages of this region.[2]

2.2.4 Nasals

The nasals can fill any consonant position in a word, except that the apical nasals do not occur word-initially (except for *nindri* 'net' and borrowed words like *nayipa* ~ *nalypa* 'knife'), and only the peripheral nasals may occur as the second member of a consonant cluster. Examples are given in Table 2-5. Phonemic oppositions are plentiful for all points of articulation.

---

[1] Because it involves a voiced alveolar stop, not a tap.

[2] As an anonymous referee notes, it may be that the trill-released stops arose from fortition, strengthening medial C in two-syllable words. This would link them with the 'heavy' prestopped laterals (see §2.2.6), and also suggest a historical source for the alternation in realisation of *thadri* as trill-released in the fortis context and voiced stop in the lenis context. The lack of prestopping (noted in §2.2.6) in *walarri* and *palapala* as opposed to *padla* would follow from the tendency to prestop in two-syllable words, not in longer words. It was noted also that most of the disyllabic words with 'light' laterals are function words; *darla* 'skin' is an exception.

Table 2-5: Examples of nasals

	Word-initial	Intervocalic	First member of cluster	Second member of cluster
m	*malka* 'mark'	*drama* 'to cut'	*yimpa* 'black'	*panma* 'to put out (fire)'
ng	*ngama* 'mother's brother'	*dranga* 'to sing'	*nhangka* 'to step on'	*marnngani* 'crayfish'
nh	*nhama* 'to touch'	*nganha* '1sg.ACC'	*drantha* 'limb (of tree)'	
ny	*nyalka* 'to miss'	*nganya* 'cloud'	*pantja* 'knee'	
n		*ngana* 'to tell'	*yinba* 'to send'	
rn	*nindri* 'net'	*marna* 'mouth'	*marnka* 'crack'	

There is some evidence of a possible opposition between a short and long apical-alveolar nasal. On a couple of occasions where *yina* '2sg.ACC' and *yina* 'emphatic marker' have both occurred in a sentence the former has had a noticeably longer nasal sound. For example:

[ŋáɻaḷàŋuínaŋáʈuín·a]

(1) *Ngararlangu   yina   ngathu   yina.*
    listen-PRES-yet EMPH   1sg:ERG   2sg:ACC
    'I'm still listening to you.'

However, the length in the final nasal here may well be conditioned by its position as the last consonant in the utterance. In the absence of a wider range and greater quantity of evidence there is no justification for postulating a second series of nasals.

2.2.5 Laterals

The lateral consonants occur only intervocalically and as first member of a consonant cluster. The laminal laterals cluster only with the homorganic stop and the apicals only with the peripheral stops and, in the case of /l/, with /dr/. Table 2-6 gives some examples.

Table 2-6: Examples of laterals

	Intervocalic	Cluster
lh	*pulhu* '3du.ACC' *palha* 'bird'	*malthi* 'cold' *palthu* 'road'
ly	*pulya* 'small' *walya* 'not'	*maltji* 'leg' *paltjapaltja* 'strong'
l	*pula* '3du.NOM' *paladi* 'individual'	*malka* 'mark' *paldri* 'to die'
rl	*purla* 'baby' *parli* 'father's sister'	*marlka* 'mulga' *parlpa* 'country'

16   *Chapter 2*

2.2.6 Prestopped laterals

Phonetically, three of the four laterals may be prestopped; this appears to be a development from a strong tendency in the language for consonants to be lengthened or geminated intervocalically after a stressed vowel. Phonemically there is some reason for regarding the apical-alveolar prestopped lateral as a phoneme, very little reason for making this distinction for the apical-postalveolars, and no reason in the case of the laminal-dentals. The laminal-alveopalatal lateral is never prestopped.

BK recognised the contrast between simple and prestopped laterals; to him the latter — or more correctly, perhaps, the words containing them — were, other things being equal, 'heavier' or 'deeper'.[3] He sometimes corrected my pronunciation, saying, for example, 'No, not light', or repeating a word with prestopped lateral when I pronounced it with a simple lateral. There is not, however, complete consistency in his statements as to whether a particular word was heavy or light; the root meaning 'help' was once said to be *wardli*, in contrast with *warli* 'house' and on another occasion to be *warli*, like 'house' but not like *wardla* 'bird's nest'. Nor was there complete consistency in his pronunciation, although some words, such as *padla* 'ground' were always prestopped and others, like *walarri* 'shade', never were.

There are several minimal or near-minimal pairs for the opposition between /l/ and /dl/; these include *ngali* '1du ex.NOM' / *ngadli* 'pigweed', *kalaka* 'yowers (a small plant with edible root nodules)' / *kadlaka* 'even' (accepted as a minimal pair during a discussion; however, *kalaka* also was used), *pula* '3du.NOM' / *pudla* 'to spill', *palapala* 'both' (e.g. in *thadripalapala* 'both banks of the river') / *padlapadla* 'dirty' (from padla 'dirt'), *Pulupulu*, a place name / *pudlupudlu* 'can't', *walarri* 'shade' / *wadlaka* 'to heap up' and *wadlangurru* 'sp. of pigweed'. The opposition is thus well established (although /l/ does often occur prestopped) This is not the case for the apical-postalveolars; it seems that this opposition did not occur in TG's speech but could be phonemic in BK's idiolect. In fact, there is little evidence in TG's speech that this lateral ever occurred prestopped. A pair illustrating the opposition in BK's speech is *darla* 'skin' / *wardla* 'nest'. Other examples did not stand up to checking; a few words, such as *parlaka* 'body' and *warli*, mentioned in the last paragraph, have been heard with prestopping but not often.

The interdental lateral in *palha* 'bird' is usually heard prestopped, especially in BK's speech. By contrast, it is never heard that way in *pulhu* '3du.ACC'. [dl] is also sometimes heard in *mulha* 'face' but never in mulhudu 'tucker'. Other morphemes in which intervocalic /lh/ occurs, never prestopped, include *walha* 'demonstrative adverb clitic', *walhini* 'boy, 16–17 years' (both only in TG's speech), *kalipilhipilhi* 'butterfly' and *kalhidi* 'husband's mother'.

I conclude that there is a phonemic opposition in the case of the apical-alveolar lateral, but there is not a clear division, rather some sort of continuum, between words with /l/ and words with /dl/. The dictionary has six morphemes with alternative spellings given with *l* and *dl*, but thirteen others given only with *dl* (although this does not mean that these never

---

[3]   This is not the only function of the contrast 'heavy/light' in his speaking about the language. Yandruwandha *ngardu* 'nardoo' was described as light in comparison to Yawarrawarrka *ngardru*. Likewise *palha* 'bird' was 'light', *padla* 'ground' 'deeper', referring to the distinction between interdental and alveolar. As another example of metalinguistic terminology, he said that *karra* was 'higher' than *kadra*.

occur with /l/, only that the number of occurrences of /dl/ is substantially greater). Also there is one given with both *rl* and *rdl*.

There is an idiolectal difference, or perhaps a dialectal difference, between the speech of MN and that of BK and TG; for example, the word for bad was heard as *madlandji* on four occasions from TG, eleven from BK and two from MN, and as *malandji* on six occasions from MN and never from the other two. Nevertheless, MN did use prestopped laterals often; she pronounced the word for 'ground, country, place' exclusively as *padla* (as did the younger Yawarrawarrka speakers) although on one occasion when she used the reduplicated form (meaning 'dirty') it was heard as *palapala*.

2.2.7 Rhotics

The existence of three phonemically separate 'r' sounds is conclusively shown by such sets of contrasted morphemes as *kara* 'maybe' / *kadawa* 'edge' / *karrawa* 'eaglehawk', *yada* 'boomerang' / *yarra* 'wide', some of the sets given in the next two paragraphs, and many others. However, the opposition is neutralised in consonant clusters, in which only /rr/ is written. Also some doubt was felt at one stage that the opposition between /d/ and /rr/ might have been confined to the consonant position following a stressed vowel, and the status of the opposition in the third syllable of words was investigated. Its validity was clear; there are words where both have been heard, but one minimal pair (for SY only) is *yulpudu* 'string' / *yulpurru* 'running (water)' and there are well-established pairs like *mulhudu* 'tucker' / *puthurru* 'dust', *kayidi* 'now' / *payirri* 'long', *ngathadi* 'younger sibling' / *maltharri* 'emu feathers' and *paladi* 'individual' / *walarri* 'shade'.

The separation of rhotics from laterals is illustrated by *warrkini* 'throw (GER)' / *warlkini* 'fall (GER)' / *walkini* 'climb (GER)', *thirri* 'angry' / *thili* 'side', *pirli* 'net' / *pidipidi* 'vigorously' / *pirripirri* 'white man', *padla* 'ground' / *paladi* 'individual' / *pada* 'inside' / *parrari* 'underneath',[4] *wardla ~ warla* 'nest' / *wara* 'who' / *wada* 'to wait' / *warra* 'arrive' (occurs only as a bound verb aspect marker), *madlandji* 'bad' / *mara* 'hand' / *-mada* 'your (as suffix to a kinship term)' / *marra* 'to redden (INTR)', *pula* '3du.NOM' / *kurla* 'burr' / *mura* 'thirst' / *muda* 'corroboree'.

Opposition between rhotics and stops is exemplified by the following sets: *warta* 'butt of tree' / *wara* / *wada* / *warra*, *karirri* 'creek' / *kartiwirri* 'to dive' / *kadi* 'to chase' / *karrini* 'tie (GER)', *yita* 'that way' / *yirra* 'to wash' / *tjida* 'to peel', *kuta* 'coat' (a loanword) / *kura* 'storm' / *kadawa* 'edge' / *kurra* 'to put down', *mara* 'hand' / *Mardanpa* 'place name', *pardaparda* 'to suck' / *pada* / *parrari*, *purda* 'unripe' / *puda* 'urine' / *purra* 'habitual action (stem formative)', *thata* 'grease' / *tharra* 'to fly'. /t/ and /d/ hardly contrast except in clusters with /n/, as the former rarely occurs intervocalically — eleven of the eighteen roots with intervocalic /t/ in the dictionary are loans.

/r/, like /d/, occurs only intervocalically. It occurs initially in the English loan *rabiti* 'rabbit' (but 'rope' is borrowed as *drupa*). /rr/ occurs intervocalically and also as the first member of clusters, e.g. in *purrtjina* 'to frighten', *warrkana* 'to spear', *darrpi* 'to turn'. Clusters of /rr/ with a nasal (/rrm/, /rrng/) are rare and do not contrast with the corresponding nasal–nasal clusters (/nm/, /nng/) (see also §4.1).

---

[4] As noted by a referee, *parrari* may be related to *padu* (which also has 'underneath' as one of its meanings). Note also Yawarrawarrka *parra* 'to lie down'.

2.2.8 Glides

As /r/ has been dealt with in §2.2.7, this section will deal with the glides /w/ and /y/. It was earlier proposed (Breen 1975) that it seemed more consistent with the phonetic facts of the language to assume that these glides do not occur before a stressed homorganic vowel, being rarely heard in this environment. Thus *iwa* not *yiwa* 'woman', *uldru* not *wuldru* 'narrow', *wawaindri* not *wawayindri* 'to look at one another' and so on. Reference was made to the contrast between what was then spelt *idraidra*, [ídraìdra] 'flower' and *parlayila*, [páḽêjla] 'Acacia sp.' and between *mitjiimpa*, [mít^jiìmpa] 'grass sp.' and *putiyita*, [pútì:ta] 'potato'.

This has been reconsidered because (a) further listening has shown that the glide is not as rarely heard as earlier thought, (b) *putiyita* is a recent loanword, and in any case there is contrast between the members of each of the two pairs of words quoted above in that the former in each case is a compound and has secondary stress on the third syllable while the latter is monomorphemic and shows diphthongisation of the vowel–glide–vowel sequence and consequent retraction of the secondary stress to the second vowel.

Some statistical evidence has suggested that there could be a contrast between suffixes -*i* (locative case of nominals, potential mood in verbs) and -*yi* (deixis 'here' on demonstrative pronouns). In a count made on the transcript of a long text by BK, stem-final /a/ before one of these suffixes was raised and fronted to [æ] or [e] as follows:

            before 'LOC'   9 of 39 instances
            before 'POT'   1 of 6 instances
            before 'here'   7 of 14 instances

and compare /a/ in the 'simultaneous action' suffix -*rlayi*   31 of 36 instances.

There was a little evidence of a glide other than [j] before the /i/ of the locative suffix: [ɹ] when the stem-final vowel was /a/ and [w] when it was /u/. This did not happen with the deictic (and evidence for the potential was lacking).

However, evidence from other recorded material, including the corpus obtained from TG as well as other material from BK, does not seem, on the surface, to support this analysis. No systematic study has been made, but there is, for example, a significant number of sequences of final /u/ and locative pronounced [uji]. Note, too, that the /yi/ of the 'simultaneous action' suffix is probably the locative suffix; see §11.12. Pending possible instrumental work on the tapes, locative and potential have therefore both been spelt -*yi*. This is, of course, consistent with the decision to write glides initially before homorganic vowels and in sequences which could have been analysed as diphthongs. It is consistent also with the fact that with the (few) established vowel-initial suffixes the initial vowel of the suffix replaces the final vowel of the stem (see, for example, §10.6).

2.2.9 The apical contrast between unstressed vowels

The apical contrast seems to be largely neutralised between unstressed vowels. All apical nasals and laterals occurring as onset to an odd-numbered syllable within a stem are regarded as neutral with regard to the apical distinction and are written as apical-alveolar. This would apply also to initial syllables, but the nasal hardly ever and the lateral never occurs there. It applies also to trill-released stops, but not to voiceless stops (because /t/ never appears in this position except in loan-words) or to voiced stops: /d/ does occur in this position, as does /rd/, but note that these two differ in manner as well as point of articulation, the former being realised as a tap, not a stop. This suggests that the reason for the absence of this opposition from these unstressed situations is the difficulty of hearing it, and when this difficulty is eased by a concomitant change in the manner of articulation the opposition is useful.

The position was complicated by a perception that in BK's speech there was a definite contrast between a retroflexed nasal in the very common word *ngakani* 'my, mine' and a non-retroflexed nasal in *yinggani* 'your (sg), yours' (and in all the other genitive pronouns). This may have been so for TG's speech too, although there is very little information on other than *ngakani* (mostly transcribed with retroflexion), but in MN's speech the final /ni/ on all the genitive pronouns was heard with retroflexion. Some of the non-singular genitive pronouns in the Innamincka dialect have optional *-ni*, presumably the same morpheme, added as a fourth syllable and this was never heard retroflexed.

In the case of the suffix *-rla* 'present tense' the point of articulation was frequently heard as alveolar in the overwhelmingly most common situation, in which it follows a disyllabic verb root or a disyllabic verb root modified by a disyllabic aspectual or other suffix. However, in the speech of the clearest speaker, MN, it was heard as retroflexed when it followed a trisyllabic or other odd-numbered stem (i.e. when it was following a vowel with some stress). It was concluded that the consonant in this suffix was underlyingly retroflexed and it is always written as such, although in the speech of BK and TG it was nearly always heard as alveolar after stems with an odd number of syllables.[5] Suffixes like *-na* 'immediate past tense', which could be heard as retroflexed in an unstressed situation, were alveolar after a stressed syllable and this is taken to be their underlying form. See also the notes on the pronunciation of apical consonants in some other suffixes in the last part of §3.1.

In the case of disyllabic suffixes like *-rlayi* 'simultaneous action' and *-rnanga* 'contemporaneous action', there would normally be some stress on the first syllable and so there would be a tendency for the first consonant to be retroflexed just as there is for a word-initial consonant. I have therefore written them with retroflexed consonants just as I have done for initial apical consonants of morphemes which are word-medial as a result of reduplication or compounding.

2.3 Vowel phonemes

The three vowel phonemes are /i/, /u/ and /a/. All may occur word-finally and in other syllables. A vowel sequence /aa/ occurs; sequences earlier phonemicised as /ai/ and /ii/ are now regarded as not distinct from vowel–glide–vowel sequences /ayi/ and /iyi/ respectively. Phonetically [i]-initial and (rare) [u]-initial words are phonemicised as beginning with /yi/ and /wu/ respectively.

---

[5] This could be a genuine dialectal difference (perhaps differentiating both Yw and SY from IY), or it could be due to the unclearness of their speech. I have written *-rla* for this suffix in their speech too, but perhaps wrongly. If I am wrong in this, it would seem that there is no distinction between the two apical series in bound morphemes in their dialect.

Table 2-7: Examples of vowels

	After initial homorganic glide	First syllable	Medial syllable	Final
i	*yirra* 'to wash'	*pirli* 'net'	*pakini* 'carrying'	*warli~wardli* 'house'
u	*wuldru* 'narrow'	*purla* 'baby'	*pakuna* 'dig-IP'	*warlu* 'who(ERG)'
a		*parli* 'father's sister'	*pakana* 'carry-IP'	*warla~wardla* 'nest'

Examples of /aa/ include *ngaandi* 'yes' and *mabaabi* 'dark'. The latter, as well as all other examples (except *ngaandi* and one other, *ngalaaku* 'I don't know'), is the result of reduplication and deletion of the initial consonant of the reduplicated form. Thus *mabaabi* represents an alternative pronunciation of *mabumabu*.[6] Other initial consonants deleted in this way are /k/ (only in MN's speech), as in *kalkaalkayi* 'yesterday' from *kalka* 'afternoon', and /y/, as in *yandhaandha-* from *yandha* 'to talk'.

---

[6] The reason for the change in the final vowel is not known.

3 *Pronunciation*

3.1 Description of the consonants

The consonants will be described in groups according to type of articulation — voiceless stops, then voiced stops and so on. However, a few features relevant to all consonants at a certain point of articulation will first be described. Section 3.3 will describe aspects of pronunciation noted only in relatively rapid speech.

Velar consonants are frequently labialised in the environment *u*-V or *u*C-V. Examples include:

[júkʷɪnɪŋàɾɪdʲi] *yukiningaditji* 'catch (fish) while swimming-GER-DAT-EMPH',

[d̪úkʷaŋa] *dukanga* 'take.out-FUT',

[t̪úɾat̪àwajùkʷaɾənəŋàldra] *thudathawayukarrarnangaldra* 'lie-go-at.night-CONT-BUT',

[ŋáluŋʷa] *ngalungga* '1du:ex:GEN'.

There is a general tendency for most consonants to be lengthened or geminated intervocalically following the primary stressed vowel (almost always the first vowel) of a word. It occurs most commonly in slow speech and in a two-syllable word. It has also been noted — at least for nasals — in a word-final syllable. It seems to involve two tendencies, both of which are applicable in disyllables: lengthening the consonant after a stressed vowel, and slowing down on the last consonant of an utterance. Examples include:

[máppɪnɪŋaɾi] *mapiningadi* 'gather-GER-purp'
[pák·ùɹɪdʲi] *pakuritji* 'dig-UNSP-EMPH'
[t̪át̪t̪i] *thathi* 'step cut in tree trunk'
[kútta] *kuta* 'coat' (English loan)
[n̪únnu] *nhunu* 'he'
[yíŋganni] *yinggani* '2sg:GEN'
[ŋám·a] *ngama* 'mother's brother'
[n̪án̪:a] *nganha* '1sg:ACC'
[mán̠ɖamàn̠ɖakùŋŋu] *marndamarndakurnu* 'here and there'
[n̪úllu] *nhulu* '3sg:ERG'
[káruwàl:i] *karruwali* 'boy'
[júḷḷu] *yurlu* 'straight'
[ká˞ɻa] *kara* 'maybe'
[ká·jjíɾi] *kayidi* 'now'

21

(1) [já̱tʊkaṯàŋgʊḏàlkalajàrra]
 yartuka-thanggu-thalkarla yada
 full-CAUS-stand-up-PRES hither
 'come up and feed [them]' (E4)

This tendency does not apply to the compound consonants, which are already long, nor to the laminal-alveopalatals (except /y/).

A lengthened /l/ has been noted before a consonant, [mʊ́lˑpɪnɪŋʊ̀ɾa] *mulpininguda* 'cut-GER-from'.

There is some tendency for alveolar phonemes to be retracted towards a postalveolar articulation in slow, careful speech (as for the benefit of a dull linguist). For example, *ngala* 'then', one of the commonest words in text, was repeated once as [ŋálạ] when I failed to hear it the first time; the pronoun *pula* '3du:NOM' repeated as [púlạ]. (An alternative in such cases is to lengthen a consonant after a stressed vowel, e.g. *pula* as [púlla].) The gerund formative *-ini*, a very common morpheme, is usually heard [ɪnɪ] but occasionally [ɪɳɪ]. Although numerically the former pronunciation preponderates, the latter has been heard in some slow repetitions; for example, BK repeated the word *pakathikiningadi* 'carry-return-GER-DAT' (composed of the four morphemes *paka, thika, -ini, -ngadi*) one morpheme at a time, as [páka/t̪hika/ŋáɾɪ/ íɳi] (with the morphemes in the wrong order). Similarly, TG said *thambanini* 'dancer' as [ṯámba/anínɪ]. This seems to contradict some facts given in §2.2.9, and it may be that the slowness of the speech gives the tongue time to move into a retroflexed configuration, thus counteracting the normal effect of the preceding stressed vowel.

3.1.1 Voiceless stops

The normal, or most common, pronunciation of the voiceless stops will be briefly described, followed by notes on the allophonic variations in various environments in which they occur.

- /p/ is typically a voiceless unaspirated bilabial stop.
- /k/ is a voiceless unaspirated velar stop.
- /th/ is a voiceless laminal-dental stop which may have slight fricative release. The closure is made by protruding the tongue tip a short distance between the upper and lower teeth.
- /tj/ is a voiceless stop with some friction in the release. The closure has not been observed visually but appears from the quality of the release fricative sound, to be alveopalatal. The tip of the tongue is in the vicinity of the lower teeth. The closure is occasionally retracted towards [c].
- /t/ is a voiceless unaspirated apical-alveolar stop.
- /rt/ is a voiceless unaspirated apical-postalveolar stop.

In word-initial position /p/ is occasionally realised with less tension and some voice, especially in English borrowings, e.g. [bági] *pagi* 'buggy', [búɹadlu] *puradlu* 'bridle', where the pronunciation is no doubt influenced by the English, and in the pronoun [búla] *pula* '3du.NOM', and adverb [báɾa] *pada* 'inside' in which the first vowel is often not stressed to the same degree as in most other words (this is a general tendency in pronouns and other "grammatical" words). Weakening and voicing are common in stops preceding secondary stressed vowels.

No variation has been noted for initial /k/.

/th/ is frequently retracted to apical-dental or even apicoalveolar position. This would not cause confusion in word-initial position; however, it happens also in other positions. It may be relevant that the informants were all old, TG was in very poor health, and BK did not usually wear his false teeth. A voiced allophone [d̪] or occasionally voiced fricative [ð] may be heard in *thana* '3pl.NOM'; this may be related to weakening of the stress (cf. the remark on *pula* above). It has also been noted rarely on other words, e.g. [ðítaðìta] *thitathita* 'rough'.

An occasional word-initial variant of /tj/ is an affricate, with much stronger friction than normal and possibly influenced by the English [tʃ], e.g. [tʃúga] *tjuga* 'sugar', [tʃíɟaɾi] *tjiradi* 'gum (from tree)' [tʃíŋɪnɪ] *tjin.gini* 'beefwood tree'.

The voiceless apicals do not occur word-initially.

Apart from labialisation of /k/ and lengthening, discussed above, there are no notable deviations from normal pronunciation after a primary stressed vowel.

Preceding a secondary stressed vowel and between unstressed vowels weakening and some voicing of stops is very common. It appears to depend to some extent on the degree of stress on the following vowel, being less likely with higher stress. This phenomenon sometimes gives a clue as to whether what we are dealing with should be analysed as a single word or a close-knit two-word compound. Thus we have [kínɪbàpa] *Kinipapa* 'Coopers Creek' but [kújapàɖi] *kuya pardi* 'fish sp.' (never [kínɪpàpa] or [kújabàɖi]). Note that the stress does not give a clue in this case. For *thangguthalka* 'to stand up', we have both [t̪áŋguʈàlka] and [t̪áŋguɖàlka]; this is clearly a compound but perhaps (as my intuitions, manifested in the way I wrote it in the field without any careful analysis, suggested) a more tightly bound compound than *kuya pardi* (which could perhaps be thought of as generic plus specific but probably better noun plus modifier, *kuya* 'fish', *pardi* 'dangerous (creature)').

In clusters the voiceless stops maintain their normal pronunciation, except that the laminals are occasionally produced with stronger friction.

3.1.2 Voiced stops

The voiced stops differ in their normal pronunciation from the corresponding voiceless stops in being articulated with less force and with voicing. Intervocalically, the voiced apical-alveolar stop is realised as a tap [ɾ]. Apart from that, little allophonic variation has been noted.

Occasionally a tap is repeated, to resemble a short trill, as in [játukaʈáŋguɖàlkalajàrra] *yartukathanggguthalkarla yada* 'full (in.stomach)-CAUS-stand-up-PRES hither', i.e 'come up and feed [them] for the time being'. In normal speech it may become a glide [ɹ] as in [pálaɹi] *paladi* 'individual'. Very rarely [d] has been heard: [kájidi] *kayidi* 'now'.

The only voiced stop to occur word-initially is /rd/ and in this position the opposition between the two apical voiced stops is neutralised, [d] being commonly heard. This also happens to some extent in initial position in the second or later morphemes of compound or reduplicated stems, where again /rd/ is the only apical stop to occur, e.g. in *thayirduda* 'to eat while walking along', *danthurdanthu* 'soft'.

Other variants noted for the voiced stop phonemes are a fricative [ð] as a variant of /dh/ intervocalically or in a cluster and following a stressed vowel, e.g. [páɳði] *pandhi* 'down', [t̪íðari] *thidharri* 'baby', a retraction of /dj/ parallel to that noted for /tj/ and lenition, sometimes to zero, of /dj/ in the cluster /nydj/ e.g. [mádlanʲi] *madlandji* 'bad', [wídɹwìdɹɪgànʲi] *wirdiwirdikandji* 'stir-SEQ'. The last may occur only in rapid speech and so will be more properly considered in §3.3. All of these variants occur only occasionally and are in free variation with the normal pronunciations. The environment for the retracted form of the laminal-alveopalatals is not known precisely but seems to involve a preceding /i/ and usually also a following /i/.

3.1.3 Trill-released stops

These are normally pronounced as voiced apical stops (alveolar or postalveolar) with trilled release. It is not clear whether the release from the apical-postalveolar stop closure is itself postalveolar or whether the tongue moves forward to the apical-alveolar position as for [r]. Variants include tap, fricative or glide release and, occasionally, absence of either the stop or the release. Thus *pardri* 'grub' may be [pád̠ri], [pád̠ɾi], [pád̠ɹ ̝i], [pád̠ɹi], or even [pád̠ɪ] and so homophonous with the normal pronunciation of *pardi* 'dangerous creature'. On rare occasions the stop phase has not been heard; note, from TG, [máŋaràku] *marnardraku* 'tooth' and [ᵈrámiràmini] and [ᵊrámiràmini] *dramirdramini* 'one who cuts'.) The stop has sometimes been not heard also in the cluster /ldr/, as in TG's [kálrukàlru] *kaldrukaldru* 'growl, bark'.

3.1.4 Nasals

All nasal phonemes are pronounced as voiced nasals with the point of articulation as for the corresponding voiceless stops. The most noticeable allophonic variation is the lengthening described in §3.2; in TG's speech, and mainly only for /n/, this lengthening may take the form of prestopping, e.g. [pádni] *pani* 'no!', [pádnma] *panma* 'put out (fire)'. Where a second nasal follows, the first may be entirely or partly replaced by the stop, e.g. [pádmini] *panmini* 'put out (fire)-GER'. A rare example involving another nasal is [púmmaɹi] *pumari* 'choke-UNSP'. An oddity, perhaps only in MN's speech, was the pronunciation of *kinyi* 'stealth, dishonesty' with a retracted tongue, [kíŋi].

3.1.5 Laterals

The laterals are voiced bilateral continuants; the points of articulation correspond to those of the voiceless stops. Like other consonants they may be lengthened or geminated (see §3.1); this process often results in prestopping. Examples of prestopping include [ṇúᵈlu] *nhulu* '3sg.NOM', [jʊ́ᵈl̠uw] *yurlu* 'straight', [pád̪la] and [páᵈla] *palha* 'bird'.

The apical-alveolar lateral is sometimes flapped, as in [ŋájɪmaɫa] *ngayimala* 'stomach', [kúɫuwa] *kuluwa* 'needlewood'. The same lateral is also sometimes dropped before a stop or trill-released stop; thus [kákajàba] *kakayalba* 'to split', [yǽɳɖudràŋu] *yarnduldrangu* 'how-BUT-YET' (= 'in the same way'), [pákanabàŋɖɪmòka] *pakanapandhimalka* 'carry-CAUS-down-OPT'.

3.1.6 Prestopped laterals

The prestopped laterals are composed of a voiced apical stop (alveolar or alveopalatal) with bilateral release. The stop may not be well defined — [ᵈl] or [ᵈȴ] — and rarely is not audible at all, e.g. [kúlɪni] *kudlini* 'cook-GER', [púlupʊlʊ] *pudlupudlu* 'can't'. Less rarely a variant consisting of a lengthened lateral with no noticeable prestopping is heard. Another rare allophone, noted on some occasions with the word *padla* 'ground, sand', is a well-defined stop followed by a syllabic lateral, [pádl̩a].

3.1.7 Trill

/rr/ is, in careful speech, a voiced apical-alveolar trill. In rapid speech it may be reduced to a single tap, especially when it is the first member of a cluster, as in [ʈʊ́rbanaɻi] *thurrbanari* 'spin-cause-UNSP', or further reduced to a fricative [ɹˆ] or glide [ɹ], as in [kágaɾɪ́la] *kagarrila* 'cockatoo', [báɪkʊlʊlɪ] *parrkululi* 'two-ERG'.

In the speech of MN a vowel was often heard between /rr/ and a following stop; thus *thirrtha* 'dog' as [ʈíriʈa], *pirrpari* 'pour-UNSP' as [píripaɻi].

3.1.8 Glides

Most commonly /w/ is a voiced bilabiovelar glide, /y/ a voiced palatal glide and /r/ a voiced apical-postalveolar glide. Little allophonic variation has been noted for /w/ and /r/; 0 is sometimes heard for the former, as in [káu] *kawu* 'yes' while a flapped version of the latter has been heard rarely. /y/ may also have a zero realisation in the environments *i-i* and *a-i*, as in [píjipiː]~[píːpiji] *piyipiyi* 'grey (of hair)', [ʈáwăɾaḷei] *thawawarrarlayi* 'go-arrive-SIM'. In the environment *u-i*, if the vowels are unstressed, /y/ may be realised (rarely) as zero or more commonly as a weak glide homorganic with the /u/, as in [kʊ́ɳʊwɪ] *kurnuyi* 'one-LOC'. In the second part of a reduplicated form the initial /y/ is sometimes realised as zero; this is fairly common in *yandhayandha* 'to talk' in which, however, the /y/ is signalled by the quality of the second vocoid, e.g. [jǽn̪d̪æ̀n̪d̪aḷa] (present tense). Note also [júndraʊ̀ndrə] *yundrayundra* 'far-far' (or "too far away"). Another rare allomorph in the unstressed environment *a-i* is a weak alveolar glide, e.g. [wáɾaɹ] *warrayi* 'all right'.

3.2 Description of the vowels

As in other three-vowel-phoneme Australian languages, the range of allophones of the vowels, and especially of the low vowel /a/, is wide.

/i/ is most commonly realised as [ɪ], as in [mín̪ɛja] *minhaya* 'what?', [múkʊpɪ̀ka] *mukupika* 'bony (bone-CHAR)', [íbɪnɪŋaɾi] *yibiningadi* 'drink-GER-purp', [tʲíri] *tjirri* 'acacia sp.'. Word-finally, before a stressed syllable or after /y/ it may be raised and fronted towards [i], e.g. [pájiri] *payirri* 'long', [wówɪnɪŋàɾi] *wawiningadi* 'see-GER-purp', [múḷaʈiˑ] *murlathi* 'lizard sp.'. As exemplified by the last example, final /i/ is occasionally lengthened. In word-initial /yi/ the vowel also is often lengthened and raised, e.g. [íːlʲiri] *yilyirri* 'hurry', [íˑwalədʲi] *yiwalitji* 'woman-ERG-EMPH'. The last example also shows reduction of /i/ to [ə] in an unstressed syllable; this is more common preceding an apical-postalveolar or velar consonant: [mínəɳɖɪja] *minirnanga* 'run-CONT', [n̪íŋgəwa] *nhinggiwa* 'there', [ʈáɾapàn̪ɖəɻi] *tharrapandhiri* 'fly-down-UNSP'. Word-finally following /y/ it may be omitted, e.g. [maj] *mayi* 'well', [káɾawɛj] *kadawayi* 'bank-loc'. Following /w/ a stressed /i/ may be rounded and sometimes retracted, thus [máɹawyt̪ʲu] or [máɹawùtyu] *marawitju* 'finger'. Other variants of /i/ are rare and unimportant.

/u/ in most environments is about [ʊ] — [kúpʊ] *kupu* 'arm', [n̪úlɾʊ] *nhuludu* '3sg:ERG-THERE'. When stressed it may be lengthened, raised and retracted, e.g. [mṳ:lpmin̪ʊra] *mulpininguda* 'cut-GER-from', [mú·kupìka] *mukupika* 'bony'. Before a laminal-alveopalatal or after /y/ it may be advanced to [ʉ], e.g. [jʉ́ndrʊ] *yundru* '2sg.OP', [n̪ʉ́t̪ʲaɾʊ] *nhutjadu* '3sg:NOM-THERE', [púlaɾʉt̪ʲi] *puladutji* '3du:NOM-THERE-EMPH'. Word-finally, in slow speech, it may be lengthened, e.g. [t̪úpʊ:] *thupu* 'smoke', or, at least in TG's speech, raised to a weak glide [uʷ].

Nhunu '3sg:NOM' with deictic suffix -*yi* 'here' is variously heard [n̪únəji], [n̪únʉji], [n̪úniji] and, as mentioned above (§2.2.8), it is spelt *nhunuyi* or *nhuniyi* according to speaker (or dialect?).

There are a couple of examples of a phenomenon somewhat similar to what I have called 'persistence of roundness' in describing Wakaya phonology; the rounded vowel /u/ resisting replacement by the initial vowel of a vowel-initial suffix. One is that the gerund suffix, -*ini* on most verbs, is -*ni* on the handful of /u/-final verb stems, such as *thanggu* 'to stand' and *paku* 'to dig' (and on one other verb; see §10.5.9, §10.6). Another is that the emphatic suffix -*ardi*, which often has a strong stress on the /a/, became -*wardi* in the one example in the corpus where it was added to a morpheme whose only vowel was /u/. (There are a couple of examples of -*ardi* replacing a final /u/ of a disyllabic morpheme. Given the paucity of examples this one example of retention of /u/ is no more than suggestive.)

(2)   *Nguni pirnangu wardi.*
      day   big-YET   EMPH
      'We've got plenty of daylight yet.' (X29)

/a/ is typically a low centralised vocoid about [ɐ], but written [a] above and in later sections, e.g. [t̪énɐ] *thana* '3pl.NOM', [t̪éwɐwɑɾɐn̪ɐ̀nɐ] *thawawarranhana* 'go-arrive-NP'. Following /y/ and often following the laminal-alveopalatal consonants, especially if stressed, it is fronted to [æ]. For example, [jǽɾɐ] *yada* 'boomerang', [jǽndu] *yarndu* 'how', [pít̪ʲænkɐ] *pitjanka* 'bony bream', [nʲǽlkɐɹi] *nyalkari* 'miss-UNSP'. Before /y/ unstressed /a/ may be raised as high as [ɛ] as in [mín̪kɛji]~[mín̪kaji] *mingkayi* 'hole-LOC', [mín̪ɛjɐ]~[mín̪ajɐ] *minhaya* 'what?', but stressed /a/ is much less affected, e.g. [maj] *mayi* 'well!', [t̪æjɪlɐ] *thayirla* 'eat-PRES'. Before a laminal-alveopalatal there may be a palatal off-glide as in [pédlɐʲd̪ʲɪ] *palhatji* 'bird-EMPH'. Following /w/ or a labialised velar /a/ may be retracted to [ɑ] or retracted and rounded to [ɒ], as in [wɒ́wɐŋɐ] *wawanga* 'see-FUT', [wárkɐn̪úkwaɾɐ] *warrkanhukada* 'throw-RECP'. It is not raised as high as [ɔ]; BK was on one occasion careful to point out the difference between English [wɔ́mɐ] and Yandruwandha [wɒ́mɐ] 'woma, species of snake'. Stressed /a/ is retroflexed before an apical-postalveolar consonant, e.g. [wɐ̣́tɐ] *warta* 'trunk (of tree)', [mɐ̣́n̪ɐ] *marna* 'mouth', [mɐ̣́dɾɐ] *mardra* 'stone'. /a/ is irregularly retracted and, rarely, rounded in some other environments, the details of which are not clear, e.g. [ŋɒ́kɐn̪ii] *ngakaniyi* '1sg:GEN-LOC', [t̪áwanʲd̪ʲi] *thawandji* 'go-SEQ', [kúnʲɐmàŋɐ] *kunyamanga* 'roll.up-FUT'. Unstressed or lightly stressed /a/ is often raised to [ə], especially before a retroflex, [kándranə̀ḷa] *kandranarla* 'up-INCH-PRES' (= 'going up'). In a sequence of two /a/s the unstressed one, always the first, is often dropped, resulting in a sequence of two stressed syllables, as in [mɐ́bɐ̀bi] *mabaabi* 'dark', [ŋɐ́lɐ̀ku] *ngalaaku* 'I don't know'. Note also [jǽn̪dæ̀n̪dɐlɐ] *yandhayandharla* 'talk-talk-PRES' and similar reduplicated forms in which deletion of the second [y] would leave two successive occurrences of /a/, and the first (unstressed) one of these is deleted.

There was some tendency for vowels to be nasalised between nasal consonants in TG's speech; this has not been noted for BK; e.g. [ŋɐ̃mɐ] *ngama* 'milk'.

Some details of allophonic variation for the vowel phonemes are still not clear; in particular there are some unexplained consistent differences in vowel quality in such pairs as [májɐ] *maya* 'name' and [méjɐtɐ] *mayatha* 'boss' (a loan word).

3.2.1 Distortion of word-final vowels

Distortion of word-final, and especially sentence-final, vowels is a feature of the speech of the Yandruwandha informants, especially TG. The function of such distortion appears to be emphasis — possibly to draw attention to the sentence as a whole rather than to the particular word involved. It seems to be most frequently used in imperative sentences and questions. The distortion is usually combined with stress and a rising pitch (symbolised ˜ in the examples).

Forms of distortion noted include raising of /a/ to a rising front diphthong and variants on this, e.g. [ãj], [ẽj] (moderately distorted), [ajẽj], [ɛjẽj] (strongly distorted), lowering of /i/ to a similar diphthong and variants of this, e.g. [ẽj], [ijẽj], and lowering of /u/ to a back rising diphthong, e.g. [ṍw], [uwṍw]. Other variants, (e.g. [ajã] for /a/, [wẽj] for /u/) seem to be isolated exceptions.

In the following examples the normal orthography will be used as far as possible, with stress marks and other symbols needed to transcribe the distorted sound superimposed. In interlinear transcriptions, henceforth as well as here, the gloss DISTORT will be used to signify that the final vowel is distorted, and to this extent the distortion will be given the status of a morpheme. The gloss will be preceded by a dot if no extra syllable is added to the word, and by a hyphen if the distortion involves the addition of a syllable. The morpheme or word affected by the distortion will be repeated in parentheses in its normal spelling at the end of each of the examples below.

(3) *Ay pátjikurnu nhutjaduwṍu!* (*nhutjadu*)
    eh good-one 3sg:NOM-THERE-DISTORT
    'He's a good fellow!' (T2)

(4) *Wáthi yada ngúnyẽy!* (*ngunyi*)
    stick hither give-DISTORT
    'Give me a stick!' (T2)

(5) *Yídlanggìniyẽy?* (= *yidlanggi yini*)
    where-2sg:NOM-DISTORT
    'Where are you?' (T5)

(6) *Káthi yíntjadu mándrithàrra-padẽy!* (*-pada*)
    meat 3sg:ACC:THERE get-fly-in.DISTORT
    'Get the meat out of the bag!' (T7)

(7) *Mínha-ngàdi ngànha yundru párndrineyẽy?* (*parndrina*)
    what-DAT 1sg:ACC 2sg:ERG hit-IP-DISTORT
    'Why did you hit me?' (T11)

3.3 Features of rapid speech

There are a number of phonetic phemonena which have been noted only in rapid (i.e. normal, as opposed to careful) speech. Further study may show that some pronunciations which were discussed in subsections of §3.1 should be included here.

Word-initially, and initially in the second part of a compound form, the velar nasal /ng/ is often realised as zero. Examples include [áru] *ngarru* 'only', [máɳaàrigànaɳadʲi] *marnangadikarnangatji* 'mouth-DAT-CAUS-CONT-EMPH' ('putting into your mouth'), [ṭánaàrpiṱa] *Thanangarrpira* 'Tenappera (place name)', [múdraæ̀nkuṱili] *Mudrangankuthili* (place name). There are also examples of dropping of initial /m/ from the second part of the reduplicated verb *mapamapa* 'to gather, to muster'. Note also *mabaabi*, sometimes [mábàbi] 'dark', as an alternative to *mabumabu*; in this case, however, the two forms are regarded as allomorphs. BK generally did not accept these pronunciations when they were repeated to him.

Elision of a word-final vowel has been noted on several occasions. For example:

(8) [múruwawájinìŋgani]
     Muduwa wayini   yinggani?
     child   how.many 2sg:GEN
     'How many kids have you got'? (in which also the initial /y/ of the
     final word is not pronounced) (T10)

(9) [ájkáliŋáṭpánmapàɳḍina]
     Ay kali   ngathu   panmapandhina.
     eh already 1sg:ERG   put.out-down-IP
     'I've already put it out'. (T5)

(10) [íˑbaɳɳáṭuɳàpa]
     Yibanga   ngathu   ngapa.
     drink-FUT   1sg:ERG   water
     'I want a drink of water'. (T2)

Also elided sometimes is the initial syllable of a word where it begins in a glide, as in two of the last three examples and the following where the glide is homorganic with the following vowel, and also in the following example in the second word where it is not.

(11) [míɳaːndruínʲtʲarupádɽəḻijéj]
     Minha yundru   yintjadu   pardrarliyey?
     what   2sg:ERG   3sg:ACC-THERE hold-PRES-DISTORT
     'What have you got there?' (T10)

(12) [ápaŋáŋaːraŋúnʲéj]
     Ngapa nganha   yada   ngunyey!
     water 1sg:ACC   hither give:DISTORT
     'Give me some water!' (T6)

It is difficult to judge which syllable has been elided in cases where the last syllable of one word is phonemically the same as or similar to the first syllable of the next.

(13) [kúdlaìndriṉànʲəmúḷuɾu]
 Kudla-yindringa nganyi   mulhudu.
 cook-RR-FUT   1sg:NOM tucker
 'I'm going to cook some tucker'. (T2)

One of the two contiguous /wa/ syllables is often elided from the verb *thawawarra* 'to go-arrive' (= 'to arrive, to come'). For example:

(14) [wálpiṉṯáwaraṉanɛjéja]
 Walpi yini   thawawarra-nhanɛyey?
 when 2sg:NOM go-arrive-NP-DISTORT
 'When did you get here?' (R4)

Occasional interchange of laminal phonemes may be related to the physical deficiencies of the informants. This usually affects the interdentals, mostly the stops, as in [wárkadʲìkaŋa] *warrkathikanga* 'throw-back-fut', [kárutʲìli] *karruthili* 'man-DU', [wánʲtʲiŋàɹi] *wanthingari* 'look.for-down', but does sometimes work the other way, as in occasional pronunciations of the emphatic suffix *-tji* as, for example, [ṯi] or [ðə].

3.4 Interphonemic alternations

There are a handful of examples of two allomorphs of a morpheme, or two closely related morphemes, differing only in that one has a voiceless stop while the other has a voiced stop. The cases of *ngapa* 'water' / *ngaba-* 'wet' and *thatji* 'clitoris, stone knife' / *thadjingumini* 'mountain devil' have already been mentioned (§2.2.2). One other probable case of this type of alternation is illustrated by the contrast marnardraku 'tooth' (cf. *marna* 'mouth') / *dragurdragu* 'spotted'.

Alternations between a trill-released stop in a simple form and a voiced stop in a compound form occur in the pairs *dritji* 'sun' / *ditjipa* 'to put in the sun to dry', and possibly in *windra* 'spear' / *windawinda* 'walking stick' (but BK did not accept any relationship between these two). *Thadri* 'bank (of river)' / *thadipalapala* 'on both banks' was formerly in this list, but this is now regarded as an example of a subphonemic alternation; see §2.2.7.

A possible isolated example of progressive vowel harmony is exhibited by the possible fossilised noun stem formative *-rri ~ -rru*, the former following stem-final /a/ and /i/ and the latter stem-final /u/. There are many examples, including *man.garri* 'girl', *malkirri* 'many', *thidharri* 'baby', *pilthirri* 'stone chips', *thakurru* 'later', *puthurru* 'dust'. Dictionary entries include 24 trisyllabic stems ending in /arri/, twelve in /irri/ and seventeen in /urru/, but none in /arru/, /irru/ or /urri/. An apparently anomalous form (heard in a text) which was changed on checking is *payipayirru* 'not very long' (cf. *payirri* 'long'). A slip of the tongue on the part of BK is of interest here; intending to say *kathi tjukurru* 'animal kangaroo' (= 'kangaroo') he said [káṯiritʲúk] before stopping and correcting himself.

An isolated example of regressive vowel harmony is seen in *nguthingi* 'my elder brother', formed by adding the suffix *-ngi* '1kin' to *nguthu* 'elder brother'. The same phenomenon occurs with some speakers with *nhunu* '3sg:NOM' and *pulhu* '3du:ACC' and the deictic suffix *-yi* 'here' (see above, §2.2.8 and §3.2).

Other isolated alternations are between the allomorphs *kulkupa* and *kulkuma* 'to jump' and between the two forms of the suffix meaning 'across' *-walpirri* and *-ngalpirri* (see §12.15).

There are a number of examples of fluctuation in the vowels in the Yawarrawarrka material: *nhangganima* and *nhangganama* '3sg:fem:DAT', *yingganany i* and *yingganinyi*

'2sg:LOC', *ngandjarra* and *ngandjarri* 'rain', *man.garri* and *man.garra* 'girl'. These were not isolated single instances, and there may be mixing of dialects involved. See also §11.16.

3.5 Extraphonemic exclamations

A sentence is frequently introduced by the interjection [aj] or [ɛj]. This is regarded as being outside the phonemic system and akin to the distorted final vowels (§3.2.1). There is probably no semantic significance in the phonetic difference between these two forms. Other, rarer, exclamations include [ɒː]. These exclamations are frequently pronounced with sharply rising pitch:

(15) [éj / mínajúndrupádɽalɛjéj]   [ɒː / pítʲanka]
 Ey, minha yundru pardrarleyey?   *Oh, pitjanka.*
 hey what 2sg:ERG hold-PRES-DISTORT
 "Hey, what are you catching?"   'Oh, bony.bream.' (T12)

(16) *Matja-nguda nhutjadu,   ay thipingu nhunudu.*
 long.ago-ABL 3sg:NOM-THERE eh alive-YET 3sg:NOM-THERE
 'He's very old but he's still alive'. (T11)

3.6 Stress

Basically, the primary stress in any word falls on the first syllable, with secondary stress on the third syllable of a four-syllable root or a trisyllabic word carrying a monosyllabic suffix and/or on the first syllable of any bound disyllabic morpheme, or on the first of a pair of bound monosyllabic morphemes if it does not tend to form a diphthong or long vowel with the preceding vowel (i.e. is not *-yi* after /a/ or /i/). A non-productive stem formative (like *-lu* in *parrkulu* 'two') is not treated as a bound morpheme but as part of the root. Secondary stresses are not always detectable. Examples (with morpheme boundaries shown by hyphens) include:

dárla	'skin'
dárla-li	'skin-ERG'
tjúkurru	'kangaroo'
tjúkurru-li or *tjúkurrù-li*	'kangaroo-ERG'
thálkapàrlu	'kangaroo rat'
yándha-yàndha-rnànga	'talk-talk-CONT'
máka-mùdu-li	'fire-ashes-ERG'
páku-pàdi-pàdi-ni	'dig-always-GER' ('always'='in-in')
kárrpa-ngà-la-tji	'sew-FUT-EMPH-EMPH'
páni-na-rlàyi-tji	'all-INCH-SIM-EMPH'
márni-pìka-na-rnànga	'fat-CHAR-INCH-CONT'

An alternative for words like the last example above, with a monosyllabic suffix preceding a disyllabic, is to have the secondary stress on the monosyllabic suffix; thus *-nà-rnanga* instead of *-na-rnànga*.

Note that the gerund formative *-ini* (with an allomorph *-ni*) does not behave as a disyllabic affix for the purpose of stress assignment; the initial /i/ replaces the final vowel of the preceding morpheme and functions as part of that morpheme, e.g. *kárrpi-ni-ngùda* 'sew-GER-ABL', from *karrpa* 'to sew'. On the other hand, the only other vowel-initial bound morpheme, the emphatic marker *-ardi*, is stressed on its first syllable and often even carries the primary stress, e.g. *nganyárdi* '1sg:NOM-EMPH' from *nganyi*. In a few other cases transfer of the main stress to a word-final distorted vowel has been observed, e.g. *mìni-pàndhi-ngêyéy* run-down-FUT-DISTORT. See §3.2.1 for examples of a second primary stress, also on a word-final distorted vowel (and there marked ˜ because the pitch is also noticeably rising). Stress may occasionally also be moved to the next syllable, to be on the syllable preceding an emphatic suffix, e.g. *ngána-rnangà-tji* 'tell-CONT-EMPH', *wáwa-la-purrà-tji* 'see-FARP-EMPH' (The far past inflection *-lapurra* functions, for purposes of stress, as *-la-purra*, although other evidence suggests that synchronically it is a single morpheme (see §11.1)).

Deletion of a syllable or a vowel may result in a secondary stress following on the next phonetic syllable after the primary stress. For example:

[yákàkaŋa] *yakayakanga* 'ask-ask-FUT'
[mábàbili] *mabaabili* 'dark-ERG'

Coalescence of two syllables into a long vocoid or diphthong has the same effect. For example:

[ŋálà:ku] *ngalaaku* 'I don't know'
[pá[àjⁱla] *parlayila* 'Acacia sp.'

A disyllabic bound morpheme is sometimes pronounced with a primary stress on its first syllable, and so realised as a separate word. The rules are not yet clear, but it may be obligatory for a noun phrase consisting of a generic term, such as *kathi* 'animal', *wathi* 'tree' or *ngapa* 'water', and a noun, optional for noun phrases consisting of a noun and an adjective or a numeral, and for long (including derived or modified) noun stems, and not permitted for noun phrases consisting (otherwise) only of a simple stem or simple stem with demonstrative, or for nominalised verbs in dependent clauses. Morphemes which may occur as separate words include the purposive and causal case inflections *-ngadi* and *-puru*, and the noun modifiers *-kurnu* 'other', *-mindji* 'proprietive' and *-ngurru* 'comitative'. The privative suffix *-pani*, which occurs also as a negative particle and so a separate word in its own right, may occur as a separate word even when associated with only a simple stem. This may also apply to the adverb formatives *-palapala* 'on both sides' and *-thanuthanu* 'in the middle'. It is clear that conditioning factors are only partly phonological. Examples include:

(17)   *ngápa páni*   (contrast   *nhíndapàni*
     water without   shame-without
     'got no water'   'got no shame') (both T11)

(18) *Márripàthi kàra ngányi tháwanga párndrithìkanga káthi kántu*
    tomorrow maybe 1sg:NOM go-FUT kill-return-FUT animal wallaby
    kúrnula.
    other-EMPH
    'Tomorrow I might go and get another wallaby [after having thrown a spear at one today and missed]'. (W3)

(19) *Ngúthu párrkulu míndji ngányi.*
    elder.brother two PROP 1sg:NOM
    'I've got two brothers' (in answer to 'How many ...?'). (R1)

(20) *Thawarla ngaldra, kundangali puru, wardamayi nhinanga,*
    go-PRES 1du:in:NOM wind AVER calm-LOC sit-FUT
    yandhiyandhini-ngadilatji.
    talk-talk-GER-DAT-EMPH-EMPH
    'Let's go and sit and talk [in the car], out of the wind'. (R7)

Alternation between one word (a primary and a secondary stress) and two words (two primary stresses) also occurs for many compound nouns, e.g. *ngapakaldri*, *ngapa kaldri*, lit. 'bitter water', often 'alcoholic drink'.

Grammatical words such as pronouns or auxiliary verbs may sometimes occur without a primary stress. For example:

(21) *wálya pànipànika mánggini-nguda*
    not all-all-CAUS burn-GER-ABL
    'before it had all burnt' (R7)

In some cases a primary stress on a grammatical word may be transferred to the last syllable of the preceding word, this word then having two primary stresses.

(22) [ŋánaḷámaj]
    nganarla may
    do-PRES well
    'does indeed' (D2)

(23) [íbaṭàwaŋájita]
    yibathawanga yita
    drink-go-FUT that.way
    'will drink while travelling there'. (D3, =A-108)

A word with an abnormal stress pattern is *ngaandi* 'yes', usually [ŋàándi].

Other deviations from the standard are not uncommon but may be random and unmotivated. One of the more common is a secondary stress on the second syllable of a three-syllable word, e.g. *yilànggi* 'where?', *yínggàni* '2sg:GEN'. Other non-standard patterns noted include *pálbárri* 'flat', *tháwathàwapádipadìni* 'walk-walk-always-GER' ('used to walk about'), *nhínathàrrathìkàrlangu* 'sit-fly-return-PRES-then' ('goes and visits then').

3.6.1 Phrase stress

The label 'phrase stress' is used in preference to 'sentence stress' for a strong stress which appears on at least one syllable in most sentences and more than once in many sentences, especially long ones. Up to seven stresses of this type have been noted in a sentence. The position of the phrase stress is unpredictable; it may even appear on a syllable that would not normally carry any word stress, as in the last two examples below. It may fall on any class of word. A few examples follow; the phrase stress is marked with an acute accent.

(24) *Nhinggiwa-ngadi pitjidi kúmani mandrithikanga.*
location-THERE-DAT pitchery bundle get-return-FUT
'[They] would go over there to get bundles of prepared pitchery.' (D3, =A-114)

(25) *Ngala thanayi kilkarla ngarru yárawarrangu thana*
then 3pl:NOM-HERE know-PRES only naked-THEN 3pl:NOM

thawathawa-padipadini.
walk-walk-HAB-GER
'These fellows think they used to walk about naked in those days.' (D4, =A-149)

(26) *Pirnapirna thanayi, thárrini-ngaditji ngana-rlayi, purndapárndringa,*
big-big 3pl:NOM-HERE fly-PURP-EMPH do-SIM nape hit-FUT

kudlanga yina, thayi-yindri-rnangatji.
cook-FUT EMPH eat-RR-CONT-EMPH
'The biggest ones, that were nearly ready to fly, they would kill and cook and eat.'
(D5, =A67)

(27) *Ngala pirlili ngámpurru-ngaditji páladi-ldrangu thana*
then net-INST yellowbelly-DAT-EMPH individual-BUT-YET 3pl:NOM

drakini-nguda, kurrarla yárndu-ldrangu, kinipapayi kurrapadari yita.
weave-GER-ABL put-PRES how-BUT-YET river-LOC put-in-UNSP that.way
'They weave a net of a different mesh, which they put into the water in the same way, for catching yellowbelly'. (D1, =A-24)

(28) *Kárnalitji thana pulka-padipadini kathi mardramítjiyi walya*
person-ERG-EMPH 3pl:NOM grill-HAB-GER meat stone-eye-LOC not

makamukuruyi.
fire-ashes-LOC
'The blackfellows used to grill their meat on [hot] stones, not in the hot ashes.'
(D3)

3.6.2 Intonation

Lacking any samples of real conversation, I have based this brief description of the main features of intonation in Yandruwandha mainly on the story given as Text 10 'Yandruwandha stories', in the second part of the text chapter of the dictionary volume. It includes some simulated conversation, including questions and exclamations. See also §3.2.1.

The basic intonation contour of a declarative sentence comprises a more or less level tone with a final drop. This may be varied by a rise in the tone at a particular point, mostly in association with higher stress. The sentence may be broken into smaller parts, each with its own sentence-type contour. These are illustrated in (29)–(31).

(29) *Thulathulakarlayi nganha.*
'They reckoned I was a stranger.' (R9, =S10-17)

(30) *Pula kilkanhukada walyanyadi ngathu ngararlayi.*
'Those two had thought I didn't understand.' (R9, =S10-31)

(31) *Ngapala, Diradili pula yandharnangatji, ngala ngathutji ngararlayi pulhu.*
'Well they were talking in Diyari, and I understood them.' (R9, =S10-16)

In the following example there is a high tone employed at the end of the sentence in correcting an error made earlier: *malkirri* should have been *ngalyi*.

(32) *Dritji kurnuyitji karna malkirri thawawarrandji — ngalyila.*
'One day another mob — another group — of blackfellows arrived.' (R9, =S10-20)

In a sentence of two short clauses that sets the scene for the story there is a slight rise in tone at the end of each clause.

(33) *Wilpadali nganyi thawalapurra; mandrithawari nganha walypalali.*
'Once I was travelling in a wagon — some white men picked me up.' (R9, =S10-1)

In a couple of sentences where additional material is added at the end there is no final fall, although the addition may be at a lower level.

(34) *Kilkarla ngathu yintjadu, ngarndri-ngapiri ngala nguthungama.*
'I know him, and his parents and relations.' (R9, =S10-24)

(35) *Walya nganyitji thawanga, puthangaditji.*
'I'm not going to the races.' (T11, =S1-3)

Questions have either a high tone initially, on the question word, or a rising or at least level tone at the end (or both).

(36) *Ngapala pula nganayindrirrnanga, "Yilangkinguda nhutjadu?"*
'Well they asked one another, "Where's he from?"' (R9, =S10-6)

(37) *Ngarrungu nhunu — Diradili nganha yakapadanga nga walypala yawarrili,*

"Yilangkinguda yiney?"
'Then he just asked me in Diyari, and then in whitefellow talk, "Where are you from?"' (The tone on the second line is higher from the start than that preceding it.) (R9, =S10–12)

(38) *Ey! Thawanga yini?*
'Hey, are you going [to the races]?' (T11, =S1-5)

The BK text includes an exchange of imperative sentences (S10-8 to 11), which are all on an evenly high tone (except that a declarative clause included in one utterance and a couple of extraphonemic ejaculations are on a lower tone) until the last which ends in a high rising tone.

(39) *'Yakapadaka yinha may!'*
'Well ask him!' (R9)

(40) *'A'ey, nhindalitji nganyi, yundru kay!'*
'Uhuh, I'm shy, you do it!' (R9)

(41) *'A'ay. Yundrungu yakapada may.'*
'Uhuh. You ask him!' (R9)

(42) *'A'ay yundru kay!'*
'Uhuh, you do it!' (R9)

4 *Organisation of sounds*

4.1 Distribution of phonemes

Syllable types in Yandruwandha (given the decision to write initial /yi/ and /wu/ instead of /i/ and /u/ and to write /y/ to break up vowel + /i/ sequences, and excluding the rare cases where a word has /aa/) are only CV and CVC. Words consist of at least two syllables, apart from the conjunctions *ya*, *ka* and *nga*. All words end in a CV syllable. The only VV sequence is /aa/, as in *ngaandi ~ ngaani* 'yes' in which the second /a/ is clearly syllabic and often carries primary stress, and *ngalaaku*, in which the /aa/ is realised as a long vowel or even as a short vowel carrying the primary stress. These are the two only words (apart from one or two loan words) containing an /aa/ which does not result from deletion of a consonant at a morpheme boundary (for example, in the second part of a reduplication).

Examples of words containing the various syllable types are now given:

CV: *mara* (CV–CV) 'hand', *tjukurru* (CV–CV–CV) 'kangaroo', *minirnanga* (CV–CV–CV–CV) 'run-CONT'.

CVC: *pandi* (CVC–CV) 'dog', *windrina* (CVC–CV–CV) 'enter-IP', *yurrkuyurrku* (CVC–CV–CVC–CV) 'dillybag', *Yinbarrka* (CVC–CVC–CV) 'Embarka (place name)'

Note, however, that there are some indications that the speakers may have regarded consonant clusters — even non-homorganic ones — as being not divided by syllable boundaries, so that there would be CCV syllables but not CVC syllables. Thus BK once divided *kurrumpala* 'spinifex' up as [kúru^m/^{m}bala], and TG, attempting to pronounce the half-forgotten word for 'porcupine (i.e. echidna)', (which is probably *karndilkatha*), gave [kándi/glaṭ], [kándiḷ/gaṭ] and [kándi/glgáṭ], in that order.

Owing to the extensive system of compounding of verbs and the fact that a word frequently has one, two or even three emphatic suffixes following its inflectional and other suffixes, words in Yandruwandha can be quite long. A text, chosen at random, had about 300 words of which there were 20 verbs of five syllables, 16 of 6, 8 of 7, 4 of 8 and 2 of 9, as well as nine other words (mostly nouns) of five syllables, 7 of 6, 7 of 7 and 2 of 8. See also §4.2.

The following phonemes may begin a word: non-apical voiceless stops, /ɖ/ (written *d*), non-apical nasals, /ɖr/ (written *dr*), non-apical glides. Note that the consonants classed as retroflex in this position do not contrast with any alveolar counterpart, are not as clearly retroflexed when utterance-initial as in postvocalic position, and are written without the initial *r*. Examples follow:

36

pirna 'big', *kanyi* 'sweat', *thupu* 'smoke', *tjilka* 'sinew', *durru* 'back', *milarri* 'hook', *ngarndri* 'mother', *nhadi* 'dead', *nyangi* 'moon', *dranga* 'to dance', *windra* 'spear', *yarndu* 'how'.

Apart from some English borrowings, the only word which does not fit this generalisation is *nindri* 'bag'.

The only phonemes which may end a word are the three vowels.

4.1.1 Consonant clusters

Consonant clusters are all binary and can be classified into several groups, with three clusters which do not fit into the classification. Also, two of the groups have gaps where there are no known examples of a cluster that would be expected to exist. The groups are: nasal followed by homorganic stop or trill-released stop, lateral followed by homorganic voiceless stop or trill-released stop, apical nasal or lateral followed by peripheral stop, trill followed by non-apical voiceless stop, and apical nasal followed by peripheral nasal. Table 6 shows the consonant cluster pattern; X shows a cluster that occurs and fits into the classification, 0 a cluster predicted by the classification, that does not occur, and + a cluster not predicted by the classification, that does occur. Note that most 0's involve /rl/ as first member.

Table 4-1: Consonant clusters

	p	k	th	tj	t	rt	b	g	dh	dj	d	rd	dr	rdr	m	ng
m	X						X									
ng		X						X								
nh			X						X							
ny				X						X						
n	X	X			X		X	X			X		X		X	X
rn	X	X				X	0	X				X		X	X	X
lh			X													
ly				X												
l	X	X			X		X	X				X				
rl	X	X				0	0	0					0			
rr	X	X	X	X			+								(+)	(+)

Yawarrawarrka also has a stop–stop cluster /tk/, e.g. in *kitka* 'to know' (cognate with Yandruwandha *kilka*; however, MN used the Yandruwandha pronunciation) and *mitka* 'lake'. In the almost totally unknown Matja dialect, of which BK remembered just a handful of words, the word 'to know' was given (several times) as *kittja*, with a /ttj/ cluster.

Examples of the various consonant clusters in Yandruwandha are now given; where possible one example of the cluster following a stressed vowel, one following an unstressed vowel in a trisyllable and one following an unstressed vowel and with a secondary stressed vowel following.[1] Note that the voiced/voiceless opposition is neutralised after an unstressed vowel and the voiceless stop symbol is used, although phonetically the stop may

---

[1] This type could be made by adding a suffix to the second type, but I have not done this.

be heard as voiced (especially in a homorganic nasal–stop cluster, as, for example, in *madlantji* 'bad').

Nasal + homorganic stop/trill-released stop

mp	*pampu* 'egg', *drukampada* 'frog sp.'
ngk	*mingka* 'hole', *thilingkurru* 'budgerigar'
nhth	*danthurdanthu* 'soft'
nytj	*muntji* 'to smother', *madlantji* 'bad', *tjuruntjuru* 'marrow (of bone)'
nt	*kanta* 'over there', *mithinti* 'carpet snake sp.'
rnrt	*warnta* 'short'
mb	*kamba* 'anthill'
ngg	*yinggani* '2sg.GEN'
nhdh	*pandhi* 'down'
nydj	*mundju* 'fly'
nd	*punda* 'mouse'
rnrd	*purnda* 'nape'
ndr	*kandra* 'top'
rnrdr	*marndra* 'to dip up (water)'

Lateral + homorganic voiceless stop or trill-released stop

lhth	*dultharri* 'bloodwood'
lytj	*kaltja* 'Acacia sp.', *thimbiltji* 'yam sp.'
lt	*kalta* 'blue-tongue lizard' (all examples are loan words)
rlrt	-----
ldr	*kaldri* 'bitter,' *pulyaldra* 'small-but' (morpheme boundary before /l/)
rlrdr	-----

Apical nasal + peripheral stop

np	*kanpa* 'visible, *Malkanpa* 'Innamincka (place name)'
nk	*thinka* 'side', *pitjanka* 'bony bream', *mukunkirri* 'ankle' (SY)
rnp	*pirnpi* 'to scatter (TR)' (only example)
rnk	*marnka* 'crack', *wilarnku* 'curlew'
nb	*thinba* 'to chisel'
ng	*ngan.gu* 'word'
rnb	-----
rng	*marngali* 'yellow goanna' (only example)

Apical lateral + peripheral stop

lp	*kalpurru* 'coolibah', *Kilyalpa* 'place name'
lk	*malkirri* 'many', *nhambalka* 'to cover', *karndilkatha* 'porcupine'
rlp	*parlpa* 'blade', *wirlpa* 'hole'
rlk	*marlka* 'red mulga', *warlka* 'to fall'
lb	*palbarri* 'boulder', *ngalba* 'light (weight)'
lg	*kalga* 'dim', *yulgani* 'your (dual)'
rlb	-----
rlg	-----

Trill + non-apical voiceless stop

 rrp *darrpi* 'to turn back'
 rrk *warrka* 'to throw', *kurrtjarrku* 'frog sp.'
 rrth *kurrthi thalpa* 'fallen leaves', *Kakurrthungayi* 'place name'[2]
    (also *thirrtha* 'dog' and two other examples in Strzelecki dialect)
 rrtj *purrtjina* 'to frighten'

Apical nasal + peripheral nasal

 nm *thanma* 'to swim'
 nng *Manngidrikani* 'personal name (Tim Guttie)'
 rnm *nyarnma* 'to block'
 rnng *marnngani* 'crayfish'

Miscellaneous

 rrg purrga 'cramp' (no other examples)
 (rrm) *dirrmi* 'sp. of bird' (no other examples, and this seems to be an alternative pronunciation of /nm/; see the dictionary)
 (rrng) *warrnganyi* 'on the left, left hand', also *wannganyi*

As the above list suggests, consonant clusters do not commonly follow an unstressed vowel.

4.2 Phoneme frequencies

Phoneme frequencies have been calculated for (a) the companion dictionary, counting all main headwords (i.e. excluding sub-heads) and (b) for the long ethnographic text given in that volume. The former involved a total of 1575 words, from 1375 dictionary entries but including some alternative forms (sometimes the second being a reduplication of the first) and some two-word entries. The words comprise mostly roots and longer words which cannot be analysed given my incomplete knowledge of the language. The text comprised 1380 words.

The dictionary list comprised 9310 phonemes, 4341 vowels (and so 4341 syllables) and 4969 consonants (and so about 47% vowels and 53% consonants). Words averaged 2.75 syllables and 5.9 phonemes. There was an average of about two clusters per five words, or one in every seven syllables. Ten per cent of the words with clusters have two; this is made up of 5.6% which are reduplications of roots with clusters and 4.4% which are not but which are mostly compounds, with one cluster in each part. There are nine trisyllabic words, which seem to be monomorphemic, with two clusters; for example, *thimbiltji* 'type of yam'. Most clusters follow a stressed vowel.

The text list comprised 9803 phonemes, 4712 vowels (48%) and 5091 consonants. Words averaged 3.4 syllables and 7.1 phonemes. There were 0.28 clusters per word, or two per seven words.

Table 4-2 gives percentage frequencies of the phonemes in the lexicon (upper figures) and the text (lower figures). For this table initial apicals were counted as retroflexed. Indeterminate apicals (following unstressed vowels) were counted as alveolar; this involved

---

[2] There is some doubt about the validity of this example; it is said to mean 'dead marpoo bush' and is presumably derived from *kakurru* 'marpoo bush (Acacia sp.)' (in Ngamini; the Yandruwandha word is *mandhirra*) and *thungga* 'rotten' plus *-yi*, the locative suffix.

53 third-syllable nasals in the dictionary and 21 in the text, 23 third-syllable laterals in the dictionary and 68 in the text (of which 54 were in the word *ngapala*). There would also be a small number in fifth and other syllables.

Table 4-2: Phoneme frequencies

p 6.1	k 7.1	th 3.1	tj 1.75	t 0.21	rt 0.41	total voiceless stops	18.7
4.9	5.1	3.3	2.5	0.11	0.15		16.1
b 0.72	g 0.80	dh 0.28	dj 0.34	d 1.62	rd 1.30	total voiced stops	5.1
0.20	0.27	0.16	0.09	2.07	0.68		3.5
				dr 1.22	rdr 0.35	total trill-released stops	1.58
				0.98	0.71		1.69
m 4.0	ng 3.0	nh 1.27	ny 1.12	n 3.4	rn 0.84	total nasals	13.5
2.20	5.7	1.11	0.42	4.4	1.70		15.6
		lh 0.35	ly 0.44	l 2.4	rl 0.82	total laterals	4.0
		0.44	0.37	3.9	1.07		5.8
				dl 0.38	rdl 0.021	total prestop lateral	0.40
				0.12	0		0.12
				rr 3.4			3.4
				2.5			2.5
w 2.9			y 2.3		r 1.46	total glide	6.7
1.79			3.4		1.44		6.6
13.7	10.9	5.0	6.0	12.6	5.2	totals for point of articulation	
9.1	11.1	5.0	6.8	14.5	5.4		
u 10.2			i 12.4		a 24.0		
6.8			14.1		27.1		

Differences between figures from the two sources can generally be attributed to the fact that words in the text are often inflected, and so phonemes which occur in common inflectional suffixes, emphatics and connectives (such as /tj/, /d/, /ng/, /n/, /l/, /y/, /i/ and /a/) have higher frequencies and phonemes which do not (notably the other voiced stops, /m/, /ny/ and /u/) have lower frequencies.

Features such as the infrequency of (voiceless) apical stops and laminal laterals, the dominance of /a/ over the other vowels, and the relatively high frequency of peripheral voiceless stops and nasals and of the trill, are shared with many Australian languages (although in languages which have only one stop series the frequency of the alveolar stop tends to be inflated by the high frequency of the /nt/ cluster).

The next two tables give frequencies of consonant–vowel sequences. Table 4-3, for the text only, gives overall figures and Table 4-4 gives word-initial frequencies (in the form percentage in lexicon/percentage in text). In the latter the single /ni/-initial word and the few loan words with initial /n/ or /r/ are disregarded.

Table 4-3: Consonant–vowel sequences in text

pa	7.2	ka	6.7	tha	4.5	tja	0.45	ta	0.15			rta	0.06
pi	1.74	ki	1.00	thi	1.70	tji	4.4	ti	0.08			rti	0.15
pu	1.32	ku	2.8	thu	0.76	tju	0.34	tu	0			rtu	0.11
ba	0.30	ga	0.25	dha	0.02	dja	0.06	da	1.72			rda	0.08
bi	0.13	gi	0.08	dhi	0.32	dji	0.15	di	2.5			rdi	0.21
bu	0	gu	0.23	dhu	0	dju	0	du	0.47			rdu	0.66
								dra	1.23			rdra	0.53
								dri	1.12			rdri	0.57
								dru	0.06			rdru	0
ma	2.6	nga	9.0	nha	1.00	nya	0.28	na	4.1			rna	1.63
mi	0.98	ngi	0.13	nhi	0.51	nyi	0.40	ni	2.8			rni	0.23
mu	0.74	ngu	2.3	nhu	0.40	nyu	0	nu	0.36			rnu	0.34
				lha	0.49	lya	0.40	la	4.6			rla	1.25
				lhi	0	lyi	0.11	li	1.74			rli	0.30
				lhu	0.13	lyu	0	lu	0.32			rlu	0.53
								dla	0.23			rdla	0
								dli	0.02			rdli	0
								dlu	0			rdlu	0
								rra	1.44				
								rri	0.98				
								rru	1.72				
wa	2.8					ya	2.4					ra	0.96
wi	0.89					yi	4.4					ri	1.80
wu	0.02					yu	0.38					ru	0.23

Of 89 possible CV sequences, three (/nga/, /pa/, /ka/) account for 23% of all sequences in the text and another four (/la/, /tji/, /yi/, /na/) account for another 17%. Another 13 account for another 29% so the remaining 69 account for less than a third of the total. A bias against velars (other than /w/) with following /i/ is common in inland Australian languages. Closer study of the data would show how much influence individual morphemes have on the figures; for example, /tji/ is quite common (208 occurrences in the text) but most of these (177) are word-final and probably all of these, certainly at least nearly all, are the emphatic suffix -*tji*. This could be regarded as biasing the figures, but it could perhaps be expected to do the same in almost any text or conversation. Another example is /rdu/, which is substantially more frequent than /rda/ and /rdi/, but this is almost entirely due to the frequency of the morpheme yarndu 'how, thus, that way' (orthographic *rnd* being, of course, /rn/+/rd/). This is a morpheme which would not be expected to be common in some other kinds of texts or conversations.

Table 4-4: Initial consonant–vowel sequences in lexicon and text

pa	7.6 / 8.8	ka	10.5 / 10.1	tha	3.9 / 12.2	tja	0.95 / 0.14
pi	4.6 / 4.1	ki	2.2 / 0.72	thi	2.8 / 1.45	tji	1.08 / 0
pu	5.7 / 2.4	ku	6.5 / 4.6	thu	2.7 / 1.45	tju	0.70 / 1.09
da	1.59 / 0.94	dra	0.63 / 1.09				
di	1.33 / 0.36	dri	0.32 / 0.22				
du	0.44 / 0.29	dru	0.25 / 0				
ma	7.3 / 6.5	nga	7.5 / 16.2	nha	1.46 / 0.29	nya	0.44 / 0.14
mi	2.3 / 2.2	ngi	0.19 / 0	nhi	0.70 / 1.38	nyi	0.25 / 0.29
mu	3.1 / 1.30	ngu	2.9 / 1.45	nhu	0.89 / 1.38	nyu	0.38 / 0
wa	7.9 / 4.9					ya	2.7 / 6.4
wi	3.0 / 2.3					yi	3.0 / 3.9
wu	0.13 / 0					yu	2.3 / 0.94

The most startling contrast between the two sources is for /tha/. This is due to the very high frequency of the third person plural pronoun *thana* and its inflected forms in the text; the nominative form alone accounts for ninety of 168 occurrences. The much higher figure for /nga/ in texts is due to the frequency of the connectives ngala and ngapala. The higher figure for /ya/ in texts is due partly to the frequency of *yarndu*, mentioned above.

The frequency of /a/ in initial syllables in the texts is 68%, much greater than that in the lexicon (52%) and than its overall frequency in all syllables, 56% in texts and 50% in the lexicon. This is undoubtedly due to the high usage of the connectives and the demonstrative mentioned in the previous paragraph. /u/ is substantially less common in text (14% overall, 15% in initial syllable) than in the lexicon (22% and 26% respectively). Part of this is attributable to a lower frequency of /u/ than of other vowels in bound morphemes. However, the ratio of /u/ to /i/ in initial syllables is higher in the lexicon than in the text, and I have no explanation for this at present.

Word-final vowel frequencies for the lexicon are: /a/ 53%, /i/ 30% and /u/ 18%. In texts /a/ is slightly lower and /u/ several per cent lower while /i/ is seven per cent higher, no doubt due to the frequency of emphatic -*tji* and the fact that several common suffixes have final /i/.

The most common consonant clusters in the lexicon are: /lk/ 60 occurrences, /ndr/ 58, /rrk/ 46, /lp/ 42, /nd/ 39, /ngg/ 36, /mb/ 32, /nhth/ 31, /nydj/ 28, /rnrd/ 27, /nk/ and /nytj/ 23, /mp/ 22 and /rrp/ 21. In the text the most common are: /ndr/ 56, /rrk/, /rnrd/ and /ldr/ 32, /lk/ 30, /rnrdr/ 25 and /lp/ 20. Figures for several others have dropped substantially; there are no examples of /nytj/ in the text. The rise in frequency of /ndr/ in the text can be attributed to its presence in some common words like *mandri* 'to get' and in the reflexive/ reciprocal suffix -*yindri*. The rise of /rnrdr/ is due mainly to the frequent use of *parndri* 'to hit, kill'. Other changes, like the paucity of clusters like /nd/, /nhth/ and /nytj/ in the text, can only be attributed to chance.

53% of words in the lexicon are disyllabic and 23% trisyllabic. The longest is of eight syllables, followed by seventeen of six syllables. In the text the percentage of disyllables is, as one would expect, substantially lower, at 37, but the percentage of trisyllables is almost the same as in the lexicon. Frequencies of longer words are, of course, higher in the text, and the two longest words are of eleven syllables, followed by one of ten and ten of nine syllables.

By far the most common pattern is for a word to have two syllables with /a/ as the vowel; these form more than 15% of the total in the lexicon and more than 20% in the text. Hercus (1994:54) noted that in Arabana/Wangkangurru morphemes there is a prohibition against /i/ and /u/ in successive syllables (in that order). This comes close to applying also in Yandruwandha. There is a single disyllable with this sequence: *witju* 'finger' or 'small stick' and this has been heard also as *wutju*. In trisyllables the only sequences that do not occur are five of the six possible sequences including /i/ followed by /u/; there are two 'iuu' words and one involves a morpheme boundary: *nhinggudu*, which comprises *nhinggi-*, which I translate as 'location' and the deictic suffix *-du* 'there' (and note the vowel harmony). The other, *wilpuru* 'rope' was heard only once in Strzelecki Yandruwandha. In fact, the strongest aspect of this near prohibition seems to be directed against this sequence in the last two syllables of a stem, although the suffix *-ngu* commonly follows a stem- or affix-final /i/.

Most final syllables of trisyllabic roots conform to a limited number of syllable shapes: of 122 trisyllabic common noun roots, 41 end in /rrV/ (and 23 of these in /rri/), 20 in /rV/, 11 in /dV/, 13 in /nV/ and 4 in /lV/ — a total of 89, or over 70%, with an apical-alveolar consonant or apical-postalveolar glide. Five have final /ka/. Eleven of the remaining 28 have CCV. Of these final syllables, there is evidence (other than the form of the reduplicated stem) that in some words (not included in the count) a final /rra/, /ni/, /li/, /lu/ or /ka/ is separable. For example, *parrkulu* combines with dual *thili* as *parrkuthili*, not **parrkuluthili*.

5 *The sentence*

5.1 Definitions

The definition of 'word' is discussed in §6.1 and will be taken for granted at this stage. See §6.2 for definition of the various classes of words.

A phrase is a unit made up of one or more words which communicates an image to the hearer (or reader, but written language did not exist in Yandruwandha when it was in use).

A sentence is a unit of speech made up of phrases and capable of standing alone to communicate some fact, probability, command or question (positive or negative in all cases) to the hearer. In fact, a sentence does not normally stand alone, but is supported by other sentences and by the shared knowledge of the speaker and hearer(s) so that the message conveyed is far more specific than it might otherwise be.

A phrase can be identified by the fact that it fulfils a function in building up a sentence which could also be fulfilled (with some alteration in the content but not the type of message) by a single word. Where the phrase comprises more than one word, at least one of the constituent stems must belong to the same major word class as the stem of a single word which could fulfil the same function. The words in a phrase need not be together, although if they are separated, and especially if one comes at the end of the sentence, the latter may be better analysed as a separate phrase in apposition with the former. This interpretation may be suggested by intonational or other cues.

A clause is a unit which could stand alone as a sentence (with perhaps some modification) but which is related to another clause (or other clauses) in such a way that together they form a single sentence. This definition is, of course, imprecise in that it depends on the interpretation of the phrase 'with perhaps some modification'; the differences between such modified clauses (subordinate clauses) and clauses which may stand alone as sentences will be described in Chapter 15.

Examples of sentences and clauses will be given in §5.3 and throughout the remainder of the grammar. Examples of typical phrases are given below:

(a) Noun phrases (must contain a nominal)

nganyi '1sg:NOM' 'I' (pronoun, as in (11, 12))

karna nhutjadu 'person 3sg:NOM:THERE' 'that (Aboriginal) person' (noun + pronoun; see (12-9))

minha karna 'what person?' 'which person?' (noun + noun; see (8-13))

ngamali 'mother's brother-ERG' 'uncle (as agent of transitive verb)' (noun in operative case; see (13-12)) *warlu* 'who-ERG' 'who? (as agent of transitive verb)' (interrogative pronoun in operative case; see (9-85))

thanha '3pl:ACC' 'them' (pronoun in accusative case; see (11-112))

ngathu muduwali '1sg:ERG child-ERG' 'I, (as) a child' (ergative pronoun, noun in operative case, see (9-21))

kathi thukathayini 'animal mussel eat-GER' 'water-rat' (noun + noun (noun + nominalised verb); see (A-27))

karna thula nhukuwanguda 'person stranger over.there-ABL' 'a stranger from over there' (noun + noun + adverbial phrase (= noun phrase = demonstrative pronoun in ablative case); see (9-150))

pandi ngakani 'dog 1sg:GEN' 'my dog' (noun + noun (genitive pronoun); see (9-110))

yiwa-nyadi 'woman-like' '(a person) resembling an (Aboriginal) woman' (noun; see (7-18))

yabali kathikathipuru 'fear-INST snake-AVER' 'frightened of the snake' (noun + adverbial phrase (= noun phrase = noun in aversive case); as in (7-19), where *nganyi* 'I' is the topic and the remainder is a (verbless) comment)

(b) Adverbial phrases (includes a subclass of noun phrases. An adverbial phrase may form part of, and qualify, a noun phrase or a verb phrase. There is an inconsistency in that a noun in operative case is regarded as an adverbial phrase when it refers to an instrument but not when it refers to the agent of an action.)

yingganiyi '2sg:GEN-LOC' 'with you' (pronoun in locative case; see (S5-7))

nhinggiwa 'location-THERE' 'there' (demonstrative; see (12-61))

yadamanili 'horse-INST' 'on horseback' (noun in operative case; see (S9-8))

ngatjada ngakaningadi 'camp 1sg:GEN-DAT' 'to my camp' (noun + noun (genitive pronoun) in dative case; see (10-27))

yiwa karrungadi 'woman man-DAT' '[it's] for the women and men' (noun + noun in dative case). (The two nouns here are coordinated; in the previous example one qualified the other. This was an elicited sentence.)

kunawarrku 'crossways (= at right angles)' (adverb; see (16-40))

pandhi 'down' (adverb; see (A-74))

(c) Verb phrases (must contain a verb)

thawarla 'go-PRES' 'is going' (verb; many examples, e.g. (7-26))

nhinapandhi 'sit-down' 'sit down' (verb (imperative); see (12-51))

nganha yada wawari '1sg:ACC hither look-UNSP' 'looked at me' (pronoun in accusative case + adverb + verb; see (16-37))

man.garri yinbana mandrithikiningadi purtu ngakani 'girl send-PAST get-return-PURP things 1sg:GEN' 'to get my things and bring them back' (noun + verb + adverbial phrase (nominalised verb in dative case + noun + genitive pronoun); see (20))

thawawindrirla ngalunggapuru 'walk-enter-PRES 1du:in:GEN-AVER' 'is walking away from us' (verb + adverbial phrase (=noun phrase = pronoun in aversive case); see (9-118))

Note that it is not necessary for all constituents of a phrase to be inflected; this will be discussed further in §9.12 (noun phrases) and §11.17 (verb phrases).

5.2 Sentences types and constituents

Sentences may be classified in various ways: according to whether they are statements (of fact or probability), questions, commands or suggestions; according to the number of verb phrases — none, one or more than one; according to whether the verb phrase (if any) includes an obligatory noun phrase (transitive sentences), an optional noun phrase (reflexive and reciprocal sentences) or no noun phrase (intransitive sentences); according to whether the sentence is complete in itself or depends on a preceding sentence or the context to supply (as opposed to identify) one or more missing constituents. Sentences containing more than one clause are subdivided according to whether all clauses remain unmodified (i.e. in the form they would have if they were simple sentences) or only one does. In the former case all clauses are of the same status and the sentence is described as compound; the clauses may be linked by conjunctions. In the latter case the sentence is described as complex; the unmodified clause is the main clause and the others are subordinate. In certain types of sentences the main clause (usually the only clause) is modified so that the sentence is dependent on a preceding sentence; this is then called a subordinate sentence. Compound, complex and subordinate sentences will be described in detail in Chapter 15.

Simple positive statement sentences consist basically of a noun phrase and a statement about the referent of the noun phrase. The statement, or predicate, is usually a verb phrase, but may be a noun phrase or adverbial phrase. The noun phrase (first mentioned) is the subject of the sentence, and is in nominative case if the sentence is not transitive and in operative or nominative case, according to whether its constituents have an operative case form or not, if the sentence is transitive. (I use the term 'subject' when the verb is intransitive, 'agent' when the verb is transitive, and 'subject' as a general term covering both.) The predicate, if a noun phrase, may be in any case form. In an intransitive sentence the predicate consists essentially of a verb, while in a transitive sentence it also includes a noun phrase, the object. The constituents of an object noun phrase are in accusative or nominative case according to whether or not they have an accusative case form. In reflexive and reciprocal sentences, where the underlying object coincides with or includes or overlaps with the agent, an object noun phrase is optional. Sentences of these types will be described in detail in Chapter 7.

A statement sentence may be transformed, by one of a number of devices, into a question or command sentence, and a statement, question or command may be negated. These devices include alteration of the intonation pattern, omission of subject noun phrase, use of appropriate (including zero) verbal inflection, use of particles (such as *walya* 'not') and use of interrogative pronouns or adverbs. Sentences thus formed will be described in Chapter 8.

Optional constituents in sentences may provide additional content for any phrase. Such constituents are adverbial phrases and consist most commonly of inflected nouns or demonstratives, but may also comprise an adverb or a combination of two or more words with adverbial function. They specify such often non-essential facts as location (of an actor, object or action), time, purpose, beneficiary, cause etc. Such phrases may be referred to as peripheral constituents, in contrast to the obligatory portions of the sentence which form its nucleus.

5.3 Word and phrase order

Word order is free in that the words comprising a sentence may be ordered in a variety of ways, even sometimes to the extent that the constituents of a phrase are separated. For example:

(1) *Puka ngathu nhapipandhina mardri.*
tucker 1sg:ERG mix-down-IP thick
'I mixed a thick damper.' (T9)

(2) *Nhipali ngapa marndrarla ngakani.*
wife-ERG water dip.up-PRES 1sg:GEN
'My wife will get water.' (T7)[1]

However, there are a number of rules which are adhered to fairly closely (perhaps in 90% of cases, in the corpus obtained from TG.) These are, in order of precedence:

(1) A question word takes first place.
(2) A negative particle takes first place.
(3) The constituents of a phrase are not separated.
(4) A pronoun appears as close to the beginning as possible without ever being first; in other words it aims to take second place.
(5) A peripheral constituent either precedes or follows the sentence nucleus.
(6) Peripheral constituents are not grouped together.
(7) A noun takes first place in the core of the sentence (disregarding peripheral constituents).
(8) Subject and object precede the verb.
(9) A personal pronoun precedes a demonstrative. (The third person pronouns are demonstrative pronouns.)
(10) Agent precedes object and, in a verbless sentence, topic precedes comment.

In a noun phrase a noun precedes any constituent (except an interrogative) that describes or identifies or delimits it, such as, for example, a demonstrative in (9, 17, 18), a word translated as an adjective in (10), a quantifier in (12) or a genitive pronoun in (15, 20). An exception can be seen in (16), in which the demonstrative *yintjadu* precedes the noun and number. These phrases count as words for the purpose of the above rules, unless they are discontinuous.

The following examples illustrate the rules (and occasional exceptions). Results of a somewhat more extensive study, based on text material, follow. Relevant rule numbers follow the translations; for example, the relevant rules for (3) are 1 and 4, and these govern the order; the sentence also conforms to rule 8 but this is irrelevant because the higher-ranking rules have already determined the order. For (4) the relevant rules are 4 and 5; 4 fixes the position of the pronoun and 5 allows the peripheral constituent to 'choose' first or last position, and so leave no option for the verb. X preceding a number means an exception to that rule.

---

[1] It is not certain here, and in (15) of which this was a repetition, that the genitive pronoun refers to the wife and not to the water. The translation given is the sentence that was used in the elicitation.

48 *Chapter 5*

(3) *Yila-kadi   yini   thawarlay?*
    where-DAT 2sg:NOM go-PRES.DISTORT
    'Where are you going?' (T5) 1, 4

(4) *Thawarla ngani   Malkanpa-ngadi.*
    go-PRES   1pl:ex:NOM Innamincka-DAT
    'We're going to Innamincka.' (T5) 4, 5

(5) *Wathili   ngathu   dranyina.*
    stick-INST 1sg:ERG hit(throwing)-IP
    'I hit him with a stick.' (T5) 4, 5
    (Two noun phrases in this sentence each consist of a nominal in operative case. One has instrumental function and is a peripheral constituent and an adverbial phrase; the other is the subject of the sentence.)

(6) *Madlantji nhutjadu.*
    bad   3sg:NOM:THERE
    'He's no good.' (T8) 7

(7) *Kathi ngathu   pardra-nhana nhinggiyi.*
    meat   1sg:ERG hold-NP   location-HERE
    'I had some meat here.' (W4) 4, 5, 7

(8) *Walya yina   yirrtjinatji!*
    not   3sg:ACC wake-CAUS-EMPH
    'Don't wake him!' (W2) 2, 4

(9) *Wathi nhuniyi   karrtjiwagawagarla.*
    stick 3sg:NOM-HERE turn-around-around-PRES
    'This machine is going round and round.' (W6) 3, 7

(10) *Kathi thungga ngathu   thayina.*
     meat   rotten   1sg:ERG eat-IP
     'I ate stinking meat.' (W7) 3, 4, 7

(11) *Walarri nganyi   wawa-yindrirla ngapayi.*
     shadow   1sg:NOM see-RR-PRES   water-LOC
     'I can see myself in the water.' (W8) 4, 5, 7

(12) *Dritji parrkulu nganyi   nhinanga Ngarndaparlungi.*
     sun   two   1sg:NOM sit-FUT   Arrabury-DAT
     'I'm going to stay at Arrabury for two days.' (T9) 3, 4, 5, 6, 7

(13) *Parndrina ngathu   yintjadu.*
     hit-IP   1sg:ERG 3sg:ACC:THERE
     'I hit him.' (T3) 4, 9

(14) *Parndrina nganha   nhuludu.*
     hit-IP   1sg:ACC 3sg:ERG-THERE
     'He hit me.' (T3) 4, 9

(15) *Nhipali   ngakani   ngapa   marndrarla.*
     wife-ERG 1sg:GEN water   dip.up-PRES
     'My wife will get water.' (T7) (Compare (2)) 3, 7, 8, 10

(16) *Minha-ngadi yintjadu wani kurnu yundru parndri-padapadarla?*
what-DAT 3sg:ACC:THERE song one 2sg:ERG sing-always-PRES
'Why are you always singing that same song?' (P12) 1, X4, 5, 7, 8
(The object noun phrase counts as a noun here, despite its order. Perhaps it precedes the subject because of its length.)

(17) *Muduwali thanayi kilkarla nganyi puthapirnatji.*
child-ERG 3pl:NOM-HERE know-PRES 1sg:NOM fast-big-EMPH
'These kids think I can run fast.' (P12) 3, 7, X10
(The object here is a separate, verbless, clause and perhaps, as in (16), takes a peripheral position in the core because of its length.)

(18) *Maka nhutjadu walya thangkanarla patjikurnu;*
fire 3sg:NOM:THERE not burn-INCH-PRES good-one

panmapanma-yindri-rnanga ngurra.
put.out-put.out-RR-CONT always
'That fire's not burning properly; it's going out all the time.' (P14) X2, 3, 5, 7; 5
(There are two clauses. The length of the subject phrase may be relevant again.)

(19) *Thawawarranatji nganyi, ngala ngandjarri warlka-rlayi.*
go-arrive-IP-EMPH 1sg:NOM then rain fall-SIM
'When I came here it was raining.' (P10) 4; (*ngala*) 7

(20) *Ngathu man.garri yinbana mandrithikini-ngadi purtu ngakani.*
1sg:ERG girl send-IP get-return-GER-DAT belongings 1sg:GEN
'I sent a girl to get my things.' (W6) X4, 5, 8, 10
(The peripheral constituent here is a three-word nominalised clause; see (g) below for the tendency determining its internal order.)

The following remarks are based on counts made on a long text (the ethnographic text in the dictionary volume), divided into 185 numbered parts (four have since been added) which as a first approximation are regarded as sentences. Division of a text in an Aboriginal language into units delimited by punctuation marks is difficult, as linking particles or adverbs such as, in the case of Yandruwandha, *ngala* 'then' and *ngapala*, translated 'then' or 'well' according to whether it introduces a sentence continuing a theme or starts a new theme, often take the place of the intonational changes which correspond (more or less) to punctuation marks in English. Most of the observations made here relate to clauses, not 'sentences'. A large number of the clauses in texts (in general) are elliptical, because one or more participants remain the same from one sentence to the next.

Generalisations that can be made from this study include:

(a) About one third of all sentences (and an uncounted number of other clauses) began with *ngala* or *ngapala*.

(b) Subject of an intransitive clause almost invariably (33 cases out of 34) preceded the verb. However, a subject pronoun was never in first position; a particle or conjunction or adverb always preceded it and only when there was no other core constituent did the verb precede the subject pronoun.

(c) Agent of a transitive verb tends to precede the object, but this is opposed in many cases by a stronger tendency for a noun (often representing new information) to precede a pronoun (never representing new information when it is the only word in a phrase).

(This may be a large part of the reason why the pronoun tends to take second place.) Thus, where there was a pronoun agent and a noun object the agent preceded the object in fifteen clauses and followed it in 25. This was the most common situation in transitive sentences in this text; there were practically no pronoun objects and only a few clauses where both agent and object were represented by nouns.

(d) When a core constituent began a (complete) transitive clause it was always the object (except in a few cases where it was the verb) if the agent was a pronoun, but when the clause began with an adverb or an inflected noun with adverbial function the agent pronoun most often (thirteen out of sixteen times) followed it and preceded the noun object. A sentence beginning with a particle followed by a core constituent was ordered in the same way as if the particle was not there.

(e) Discontinuous noun phrases were not uncommon; usually it was the object that was discontinuous and the constituents were usually separated by the verb.

(f) A large number of clauses began with a verb; about sixty in all, of which fourteen consisted only of a verb and only a handful were complete (not elliptical). This is due to the nature of the text which consisted of a series of descriptions of procedures and so was often made up of a series of clauses in which the agent and the object were the same and only the verb was new. On fifteen occasions one verb immediately followed another (excluding a couple of occasions where one of the verbs was adverbial, modifying the other).

(g) Where clauses were closely connected in a sequence of events there was a tendency for a verb to follow immediately after another, and any participants that had to be mentioned to follow after that.

Study of some other text material emphasised the variability of word order and the importance of the pragmatics. The samples were (a) texts 4 and 6, and (b) sentences given as speech of participants in texts 7, 9 and 10. One rule that was not often 'broken' concerned the location of non-nuclear constituents (other than one or two common adverbs like *ngala* 'then') outside the sentence nucleus, either before or after. The pragmatic considerations are often clear ('It's you then that I saw ...' with pronoun object preceding pronoun subject) or can be guessed (reversal of order for contrast between 'when [did] you arrive?' and 'came early you where from?' — one of the rare examples of an interrogative not in initial position).

5.4 Incomplete sentences

Omission of one or even more of the nuclear constituents from a sentence or clause where these can be supplied by a preceding sentence or by the non-linguistic context is common.[2] This is not to be confused with the omission of constituents from subordinate clauses; in these cases the morphemes which mark the clause as being subordinate specify (as part of their normal function) that omitted constituents are to be found in the main clause. Omission from subordinate clauses (and also omission of explicit tense specification from verbs in subordinate clauses and subordinate sentences) therefore

---

[2] A referee suggested that if first and second person pronouns are never omitted this might imply that omission of a subject or object implies third person. Unfortunatley, the corpus is not adequate to allow this to be studied. There are hardly any cases of omission of first person pronoun (and perhaps none of second) but there are hardly any situations where it might have happened.

The sentence 51

involves a type of substitution, akin to pronominalisation. This applies also to the omission of second person subject from imperative sentences.

Examples of incomplete sentences include:

(21) *Walya ngathu panmana.*
 not 1sg:ERG put.out-IP
 'I didn't put [the fire] out.' (T10)

(22) *Ay, kurrupu kara nhaniyi.*
 eh old.woman maybe 3sg:fem:NOM-HERE
 'This old woman might [be going to the races].' (T11, =S1-4)

(23) *Karirriyi pandhi waka, karlukarlu parndrirla.*
 river-LOC down there fish kill-PRES
 '[He's] down at the river, fishing.' (T2)

(24) *Ay walya ngali, kurnu nganyi.*
 eh not 1du:in:NOM one 1sg:NOM
 'It wasn't the two of us, it was just me [making the noise].' (B16)

In the following sentence the main clause of a complex sentence has been omitted.

(25) *Warluparndri-rlayi.*
 bark-hit-SIM
 '[He hit the dog] because [it] was barking.' (T12)

6 *Word classes and paradigms*

6.1 Words

The word in Yandruwandha could be defined phonetically: a section of an utterance, the first syllable and no other of which carries a primary stress. Study of the stress system as described above (§3.6) shows that there would need to be some modification to this derivation, but this will not be considered now.

Alternatively, a word could be defined as a unit which cannot be rearranged internally but which can be combined with other similar units with some freedom in the order. This definition, too, would need some modification, but this would not be great.

One complication arises from the apparent fluctuation between certain compound words and two word compounds, the constituents and the meaning of the compound being the same irrespective of whether the compound is (phonetically) realised as one word or two. An example is *ngapakaldri* ~ *ngapa kaldri* 'bitter water' or 'alcoholic drink' (*ngapa* 'water', *kaldri* 'bitter'). A possible solution might be to regard the one with the less predictable meaning as a compound and so one word, while the one with the predictable meaning is thought of as noun plus modifier or generic plus specific (whichever the particular one seems to be). However, this certainly does not apply to this particular compound, as witness the phrase

(1) *ngapa yibarla   kaldritji*
     water drink-PRES bitter-EMPH
     'drinking alcoholic drink' (W7)

in which the constituents of the compound are separated.[1] A similar example from Yw is the phrase *makali paruli* 'with a firestick' in which the operative suffix *-li* is added to both elements of what has been heard at other times as a single word. (On repetition the speaker used *maka paruli*.)

A similar complication is the tendency for disyllabic nominal inflectional suffixes and modifiers to be occasionally (phonetically) realised as separate words. Formatives or compounding endings may be realised as separate words if there is further derivation for inflection: thus *thalpapuru* 'deaf' is derived from *thalpa* 'ear' with a morpheme *-puru*

---

[1] A referee suggests that since, in some areas, the word for 'water' is used as a euphemism for 'grog', and in some areas the word for 'bitter' is also the word for 'grog', in this case *kaldri* is being used as a clarification rather than part of a discontinous compound. This could be, although I have no examples (in my rather small corpus) of either *ngapa* or *kaldri* being used alone to mean 'grog'. Also, as noted above, *ngapakaldri* can be pronounced as a single word.

which is not attested elsewhere. When causativised, in the word or phrase heard as thalpa *purukarla* 'is deafening [me]' it is heard as two words with a noticeably stronger stress on the /pu/ than in the simpler form.

I have tended to prefer the phonetics when writing words, as illustrated by the examples in the preceding paragraph. However, wherever the construction is clearly generic + specific I have written separate words.

6.2 Word classes

Words can be classified on morphological grounds into nominals, which may combine with members of a set of bound morphemes known as nominal inflections, verbs, which combine with a set of bound morphemes known as verbal inflections, and non-inflecting words which combine with neither (but may combine with certain other bound morphemes, as may nominals and verbs).

Nominals are divided on morphological grounds into nouns, the personal interrogative pronoun ('who?'), demonstrative pronouns and the interrogative 'where?'. Nouns are further subdivided into common nouns, kinship terms, personal names, nouns marked for plurality, location nouns (including place names, which may however be a separate subdivision) and compass points. Singular pronouns can be subdivided into personal (i.e. first and second person) and third person (which is also a demonstrative pronoun/adjective), and non-singular pronouns can be subdivided in the same way. Only singular pronouns have an ergative (or operative) form; nominative non-singular pronouns function as subjects of either transitive or intransitive verbs. Demonstratives form two subdivisions, one comprising yarndu 'how' and the other comprising the remainder.

Crossing over this classification, third person pronouns and other demonstrative pronouns form a group which is distinguished by the fact that its members combine with deictic suffixes. Also crossing over this classification is a grouping of location nouns, compass points and certain demonstrative pronouns which combine with only a limited number of inflectional suffixes.

A simple classification of nominals into nouns and pronouns is justified on syntactic grounds.

Further subdivision of common nouns on syntactic grounds is perhaps into: abstract nouns, which in their operative case form can form the predicate of a verbless sentence; auxiliary nouns, which combine with certain verbs in pseudotransitive sentences (in which they seem to form an object of an intransitive verb, whose subject is in the nominative case); and the remainder (and vast majority). *Minha ~ minhaya* 'what?' is an interrogative noun. Possibly another class is those nouns (= adjectives?) which can function as adverbs, e.g. *patji* 'good', *kurnu* 'one'.

A subdivision of the third person singular pronoun is into feminine and non-feminine forms, and there is consequently a syntactic classification of nouns into the same two genders according to which of the forms of the pronoun may substitute for or qualify the noun. This division exists only for singular nouns (number normally not being marked on nouns, however) and pronouns. The division is a clear one of female living creatures versus everything else (male living creatures, living creatures with sex not specified, plants and non-living things). Many nouns may be either feminine or non-feminine; thus:

(2) pandi   nhatjadu
    dog   3sg:fem:NOM:THERE
    'that bitch' (P1)

(3) pandi   nhutjadu
    dog   3sg:NOM:THERE
    'that dog' (male or unspecified).

Similarly, a kinship term which is unspecified for gender can be specified by combining it with a term with the appropriate gender, such as *ngathadi man.garri* 'younger sibling girl' = 'younger sister'.

A few possible exceptions to the rule have been noted: *ngan.gu* 'word, language', *yarru* 'yard (i.e. enclosure)' and *wathi parndriparndrini* 'axe' have been noted referred to by a feminine pronoun. In discussion on another occasion it was said that either feminine or non-feminine pronoun could be used with the last two of these (*ngan.gu* was not mentioned), and also with a couple of others (*wathi* 'tree' and wathi *mutuka* 'car', with *wathi* used as a generic, 'thing') but only the non-feminine was accepted with some others. In Strzelecki Yandruwandha there is an example of *kalpurru nhaniyi* 'coolibah 3sg.fem.NOM-HERE' while in Yawarrawarrka *ditji* 'sun' and *kurli* 'day' were used with the feminine pronoun (both on the same occasion, and there are no other examples). There seems to have been a change in this respect during the twentieth century; Reuther's (1981) Diari (Diyari) dictionary, which includes a substantial number of words from neighbouring languages including Yandruwandha and Yawarrawarrka, shows that something like a half of noun roots when his work was done around the turn of the century were feminine. Austin's (1981a) grammar shows that Diyari at the time of his research divided nouns into genders on the same basis as stated above for Yandruwandha. He made no mention of any exceptions, and the exceptions noted above for Yandruwandha and Yawarrawarrka are perhaps the last vanishing traces of an earlier comprehensive gender division. Bowern (2000) notes that in Nhirrpi some nouns occurred with feminine pronouns and some others with masculine, and it is not impossible that this dialect had retained the old system in its entirety. (Note that in interlinear translations feminine only is specified, with the gloss 'fem'; in all other cases the pronoun is non-feminine.)

Yet a further partial classification of some nouns is on the basis of their occurrence in two (or more) word units, the first member of which is one of a small set of generic terms such as *kathi* 'animal', *wathi* 'tree', *palha* 'bird' and some others. *Kathi*, for example, may be used with any animal that is used for food (*kathi* also means 'meat'), e.g. *kathi tjukurru* 'kangaroo', *kathi puluka* 'bullock', *kathi kantu* 'wallaby', *kathi thuka thayini* 'water rat', *kathi kurla* 'carney (lizard sp.)', *kathi warruwitji* 'emu', *kathi thuka* 'mussel'. These terms are not obligatory and are used with only a minority of nouns.

It was tentatively suggested on the previous page that those nominals that can function as adverbs could perhaps be separated into a class of adjectives. Another — larger — adjective class could contain those words which describe or specify another nominal and which follow that noun in a phrase (excluding those that already belong to a subclass of nominals, such as demonstratives, and excluding generic-specific phrases as discussed in the last paragraph). This would contain words which are translated into English as adjectives.

Verbs cannot be further subdivided on morphological grounds; classification into transitive, intransitive, reflexive etc. are made on syntactic grounds. (Note that a verb with the suffix *-yindri* can be reflexive, reciprocal, intransitive or transitive.)

Non-inflecting words can be divided into those that can form part of a compound or derived form, those that can combine only with emphatic suffixes and those that cannot combine with any bound morpheme. More useful is a syntactic/semantic classification into adverbs, conjunctions and sentence introducers, and sentence substitutes. Adverbs comprise adverbs of time, place, direction, manner and mood and demonstrative adverbs; the first two sets overlap a little.

It is most uncommon in Yandruwandha for words to belong to more than one of the major classes. A very few examples have been noted: *puda* 'urine' (noun) and 'to urinate' (verb), *kuna* 'faeces' and 'to defecate', *thirri* 'fight, aggression' and 'to fight' and possibly *yingka* 'laugh' and 'to laugh', *purrtji* 'nervous' and 'to frighten' and *mirrtja* 'noise' and 'to be noisy'. However, there is a lack of strong evidence for this duality. No pairs are proven by pairs of sentences in which they are inflected as nouns and as verbs. The first two pairs are fairly well attested, and these are both nouns and verbs in some other languages of the 'Karnic' area, such as Diyari and Pitta-Pitta. It is interesting to note, though, that in the handful of sentences where *thirri* seems to be a noun it has never had the nominal inflections that seemed to be appropriate in the particular case. The last four pairs mentioned are all well attested as verbs, but occur also as nouns derived by processes which are attested only with noun roots. See the various dictionary entries.

6.3 Nominal paradigms

For nouns only the common noun paradigm is given; nouns of other subclasses differ only in not having certain cases or in very minor ways. The vocative is omitted.

Table 6-1: Common noun paradigm

absolutive	*karna*	'person'
operative	*karnali*	
dative	*karnangadi*	
locative	*karnayi*	
ablative	*karnanguda*	
aversive	*karnapuru*	

In Yawarrawarrka, the operative is *-li* after final *a* or *i*, *-li* or, inconsistently from MN, *-lu* after final *u*; dative is *-ma*, locative *-nyi* (Reuther and MN) or *-ni* (Reuther and WH), and aversive *-thudu*. In Nhirrpi there is a doubtful occurrence of *-du* operative, but elsewhere *-li*; dative is *-adi* and no ablative is attested.

A number of the forms in the pronoun paradigms have never been elicited or heard in texts, but some have been accepted by BK when suggested to him. The gaps are all in the genitive-based forms (but not genitive itself), and in particular none of those involving the deictic suffix *-yi* 'here' are attested (so perhaps the gap left for locative + 'here' forms applies to all the genitive-based 'here' forms). Forms attested in these categories include all 1sg, locative for all except 1du:in and 2sg, dative for 1pl:in, 2sg, 2pl, 3sg, 3sg:THERE and 3sg:fem:THERE, ablative for 1du:ex, 2sg and 3sg:THERE, and aversive for 1du:in, 2sg:fem and 3du.

Table 6-2: Personal pronoun paradigm

	1sg	1du.in	1du.ex	1pl.in	1pl.ex
Nominative	*nganyi*	*ngaldra*	*ngali*	*ngandra*	*ngani*
Ergative	*ngathu*				
Accusative	*nganha*	*ngalunha*	*ngalinha*	*nganunha*	*nganinha*
Genitive	*ngakani*	*ngalungga*	*ngalingga*	*nganungga*	*nganingga*

(These non-singular genitives may have an additional suffix *-ni*, whether there is further affixation or not)

Dative	Genitive + *-ngadi*
Locative	Genitive + *-yi*
Ablative	Genitive + *-nguda*
Aversive	Genitive + *-puru*

	2sg	2du	2pl
Nominative	*yini*	*yula*	*yuda*
Ergative	*yundru*		
Accusative	*yina*	*yulhu*	*yunhu*
Genitive	*yinggani*	*yulgani*	*yunngani*
Dative	Genitive + *-ngadi*		
Locative	Genitive + *-yi*		
Ablative	Genitive + *-nguda*		
Aversive	Genitive + *-puru*		

Yawarrawarrka differs in that it has a suppletive first person singular genitive form: *kamanti*. Some of the genitive forms given by MN were different, for example *ngalini* for *ngalingga(ni)*, but forms heard from the younger speakers, and the fact that she was not consistent, suggest that she may have been using forms from another language. All of these forms are given in the dictionary.

The Nhirrpi data show several differences, but they do not seem to be very reliable. For first person singular genitive it has *ngandja(ni)*, *ngantja(ni)* and *ngandjini* (which seem to correspond to Wangkumara, the speaker's first language) instead of *ngakani*. For first person dual, there is no inclusive/exclusive distinction in the data; the forms attested are nominative *ngalu*, accusative *ngalhu* and *ngalunha*, genitive *ngalungga*, which show similarities to Innamincka inclusive forms. The only first person plural form is the genitive, which matches the Innamincka inclusive form. Second person forms are the same as in the Innamincka dialect.

Analysis of the forms in the above table suggests that *nga-* denotes first person, *yi-/yu-* second person, *-l-* dual, *-n-* plural. Accusative is *-nha* and genitive *-(ng)kani*. Any attempt at further analysis would be highly speculative, although the *-dra* of inclusive first person forms could perhaps be related to the *-dru* of *yundru* (and note also the *-dra* of *nhandra* '3sg.fem.ERG').

The third person pronouns are based on the four roots (or proto-roots) *nhu-* (but accusative is suppletive), *nha-*, *pula* and *thana* (respectively 'he/it', 'she', 'they two', 'they (plural)'). The dual and plural roots are so different from the singular roots and so widespread that it is rash to suggest that here again *-l-* denotes duality and *-n-* plurality.

The table does not include forms with the uncommon deictic *-wa*. This was once said to refer to something further away than *-(tja)du*, and this is supported by elicited material, although without natural speech it is impossible to be sure.

Where there is a choice in the table between final /uyi/ and /iyi/, the former was mostly heard from MN and the latter from BK and TG. The difference may be idiolectal rather than dialectal.

Table 6-3: Third person pronoun paradigm

Singular non-feminine			
	no deictic	here	there
Nominative	*nhunu*	*nhunuyi ~ nhuniyi*	*nhutjadu ~ nhunudu*
Operative	*nhulu*	*nhuluyi ~ nhuliyi*	*nhuludu*
Accusative	*yinha*	*yinhayi*	*yintjadu*
Genitive	*nhunggani*	*nhungganiyi*	*nhunggatjadu*
Dative	Genitive + *-ngadi*		
Locative	*nhungganiyi*		*nhunggatjaduyi*
Ablative	Genitive + *-nguda*		
Aversive	Genitive + *-puru*		

Feminine			
	no deictic	here	there
Nominative	*nhani*	*nhaniyi*	*nhatjadu ~ nhanudu*
Operative	*nhandra*	*nhandrayi*	*nhandradu*
Accusative	*nhanha*	*nhanhayi*	*nhantjadu*
Genitive	*nhanggani*	*nhangganiyi*	*nhanggatjadu*
Dative	Genitive + *-ngadi*		
Locative	*nhangganiyi*		*nhanggatjaduyi*
Ablative	Genitive + *-nguda*		
Aversive	Genitive + *-puru*		

A third alternative for the nominative 'there' form is *nhanidu*.

Dual			
	no deictic	here	there
Nominative	*pula*	*pulayi*	*puladu*
Accusative	*pulhu*	*pulhiyi*	*pulhudu ~ pultjadu*
Genitive	*pulgani*	*pulganiyi*	*pulgatjadu*
Dative	Genitive + *-ngadi*		
Locative	*pulganiyi*		*pulgatjaduyi*
Ablative	Genitive + *-nguda*		
Aversive	Genitive + *-puru*		

	Plural		
	no deictic	here	there
Nominative	*thana*	*thanayi*	*thanadu*
Accusative	*thanha*	*thanhayi*	*thanhadu*
Genitive	*thanngani*	*thannganiyi*	*thanngatjadu*
Dative	Genitive + *-ngadi*		
Locative	*thannganiyi*		*thanngatjaduyi*
Ablative	Genitive + *-nguda*		
Aversive	Genitive + *-puru*		

Note that there are no locative 'here' forms recorded; the locative and 'here' suffixes are both *-yi*. (In Yw the final /iyi/ of genitive 'here' forms is alternatively /ayi/.) The singular nominative forms *nhunudu, nhanidu, nhanudu* and *yinhadu* are rare and when used usually fluctuate with the more common form. For example:

(4) *Matja-nguda   nhutjadu,   ay thipingu nhunudu.*
     long.time-ABL 3sg:NOM:THERE eh alive-YET 3sg:NOM-THERE
     'He's very old but he's still alive'. (T11)

Nhirrpi forms mostly match the above, insofar as they are attested. *Nhia* and *nhiwa* are given as alternatives to *nhunu*, but the former is Wangkumara and the latter means 'female (animal)' in Innamincka dialect. *Nhunha* and *nhina* are given as well as *yinha*; the Wangkumara form is *nhinha*. Non-singular forms given all match the Innamincka forms.

The roots of the demonstrative pronouns are *nhinggu-* ~ *nhinggi-* and *nhuku-* ~ *nhuki-*. Only *nhinggu-* ~ *nhinggi-* is common. A stem *nhunggu-* also has been heard, but was not accepted later. Without natural speech in a real context it is difficult to determine the meanings of the demonstratives/deictics. According to BK, "*Nhinggiyi* means here, and *nhinggiwa* is over there, and *nhukiyi* is here somewhere". It seems that the stems with no deictic mean no particular where, and I gloss the stems as 'location'. It seems that it refers to location in time as well as in space: *nguni nhinggiyi* 'day location-HERE' = 'today'. BK's translation of *nhukiyi* (and, by implication, *nhukuwa*) is supported by some elicited examples, like (4), but not by all (see the dictionary entry). The paradigm of *nhinggi-* ~ *nhinggu-* is given; *nhuku-* ~ *nhuki-* always occurs with one or other of the deictic suffixes; the only example of it with an inflectional suffix is ablative *nhukuwanguda* (SY). The *-kala* deictic seems to refer to location in the vicinity of some known or named place[2] (compare *nhuku-* ~ *nhuki-*), while *-wa* could refer to some distant unnamed place. *-kala* is not used with this function on third person pronouns, but seems to be useable as an emphatic ending, as in *nhunukala* 'that's him!' As noted above, *-wa* seems to refer to something further away than *-du*. In the SY and Yw corpora *-yi* is by far the most common deictic. *-ku* is common in Yw and seems to be equivalent to *-(tja)du* in IY. *-wa* is not uncommon in both. Both *-du* and *-ku* are uncommon in the SY corpus. There are occasional occurrences of *-rra* in both, sometimes referring to something out of sight or far off, but not always. It may be an intrusion from another language.

(5) *Kinipapayi   nhukiyi   nhunu,   yilanggi kara.*
     Cooper's.Creek-LOC location-HERE 3sg:NOM where   maybe
     'He lives somewhere along the Cooper, I don't know where.' (X17)

---

2   BK translated *nhinggikala* as "there, like, he's round about there".

Table 6-4: Demonstrative pronoun paradigm

	here	there	there	about there
Nominative (= Locative)	nhinggiyi	nhinggudu	nhinggiwa, nhingguwa	nhinggikala
Dative	nhinggiyingadi	nhinggudungadi	nhinggiwangadi	nhinggikalangadi
Ablative	nhinggiyinguda	nhinggudunguda	nhinggiwanguda	nhinggikalanguda

The dative in Yw has -*ma* instead of -*ngadi*.

Nhinggi has rarely been heard without a deictic suffix:

(6) *Padla nhinggi-ngadingu nganyi thawarla.*
 place location-DAT-YET 1sg:NOM go-PRES
 'I'm going to the same place.' (X16)

The demonstrative/interrogative *yarndu* 'how' exists with no deictic suffix or with suffixes -*yi* 'here', -*du* 'there, -*kala* 'round about there', but takes no inflectional suffix.

Of the interrogatives, *wara* 'who' is inflected as an irregular proper noun and *minha* 'what' as a regular common noun, while *yi(d)la-* 'where' takes only locational suffixes.

Table 6-5: Interrogative pronoun paradigm

	who?	where?
Absolutive	wara ~ warnu ~ waranu	
Operative	waralu ~ warlu	
Genitive	warangi	
Dative	warangingadi	yilakadi ~ yidlakadi
Locative	warangiyi	yidlayi ~ yilanggi ~ yidlanggi ~ yilanggiyi ~ yidlanggiyi
Causal	warangipuru	
Ablative	waranginguda	yidlanguda ~ yilangginguda ~ yidlangginguda

Waranu is not well established, having been heard rarely and not clearly distinguished from *warnu*. *Wara* was the only absolutive form heard in SY. Operative *warali* was heard once on an SY tape. *Walpi* 'when' may take inflectional suffixes; an example of the Yw equivalent, *wintja*, with dative is given in (8-12).

7 *Simple declarative sentences*

7.1 Verbless sentences

Verbless sentences may be of the following types:

(a) equational; two noun phrases are equated to one another, the referent of one thus being identified or specified as a member of a class. For example:

(1) *Muduwa pulya nhuniyi,   karruwali, papa   ngakani.*
    child   small 3sg:NOM-HERE boy   daughter's.child 1sg:GEN
    'This little boy is my grandson.' (W3)

(2) *Pakitjampa yina nhutjadu.*
    buckjumper EMPH 3sg:NOM:THERE
    'He's a buckjumper.' (R3)

(b) kin-relational; the kinship between the members of the referents (obligatorily non-singular) of a noun phrase is specified by means of another noun phrase.

(3) *Puladutji   ngapiri-ngurru.*
    3.du:NOM-THERE-EMPH father-COM
    'Those two are father and son.' (R1)

(c) descriptive; some feature or aspect of the referent of one noun phrase is identified by means of another noun phrase. The statement (or identifying) noun phrase is frequently a term translated by an English adjective, and may be a derived stem (e.g. noun plus *-pika* 'characterised by'). Certain (abstract) nouns in operative case may also occupy this position (19).

(4) *Maltji withi.*
    leg   sore
    'My leg's sore.' (T6)

(5) *Ay ngawada nhutjadu.*
    oh thin   3sg:NOM:THERE
    'He's thin.' (T9)

(6) *Ngandjarri purra nhuniyi   padla.*
    rain   HABIT 3sg:NOM-HERE country
    'This is a rainy place.' (P30)

(d) Locative; the statement noun phrase specifies the location of the topic.

(7) *Nguda ngakani karirriyi.*
camp   1sg:GEN creek-LOC
'I'm camped at the creek.' (T2)

(8) *Nhutjadu thalkandra.*
3sg:NOM:THERE up-BUT
'[On the other hand] he's on top.' (T7)

(e) Dative; the statement noun phrase specifies the purpose or owner of the topic.

(9) *Yada nhutjadu karrukarru-ngadi.*
boomerang 3sg:NOM:THERE old.man-DAT
'That boomerang's for the old man.' (P12)

(10) *Nhutjadutji pandi-ngadildra.*
3sg:NOM:THERE-EMPH dog-DAT-BUT
'That [rug], [on the other hand] belongs to the dog.' (P15)

See also (10-51).

(f) Ablative; the statement noun phrase refers to the place or time of origin of the topic.

(11) *Ngarru nhipa mulha, parli-nguda.*
only spouse face father's.sister-ABL
"I can only marry one from my mother-in-law." (P11)

(The phrase *nhipa mulha* means 'eligible marriage partner'.)

(12) *Windra matja-nguda.*
spear long.time-ABL
'It's an old spear.' (T8)

(g) Possessive; the statement noun phrase identifies something possessed by the topic.

(13) *Muduwa-mindji ngala yini!*
child-PROP then 2sg:NOM
'You've got a baby now!' (P8)

(14) *Pandi patjikurnu ngurru nganyi.*
dog good-one COM 1sg:NOM
'I've got a good dog.' (T10)

(h) Privative; the statement noun phrase identifies something which is not (but could be) possessed by the topic.

(15) *Muduwa pani nganyi.*
child PRIV 1sg:NOM
'I've got no kids.' (T10)

(16) *Warluwarlu-pani nhutjadu.*
bark-PRIV 3sg:NOM:THERE
'That [dog] never barks.' (T12)

(i) comparison; the statement noun phrase identifies something which resembles the topic.

(17)　*Ay, pandi nhutjadutji   ngakani-nyadildra.*
　　　 eh dog   3sg:NOM:THERE-EMPH 1sg:GEN-like-BUT
　　　 'Eh, that dog's like mine!' (T11)

(18)　*Kuka karli payirri nhutjadutji   yiwa-nyadi.*
　　　 head hair long   3sg:NOM:THERE-EMPH woman-like
　　　 'He's got long hair like a woman.' (T11)

(For comparison of unequals see §9.1.5 and §18.2.)

Verbless sentences follow the normal rules for word order, insofar as they are applicable; the topic is equivalent to the subject of a sentence with a verb and (in a positive verbless statement) this takes first place unless it is a pronoun.

The following sentences illustrate verbless sentences with peripheral constituents.

(19)　*Yabali   nganyi   kathikathi-puru.*
　　　 fear-INST 1sg:NOM   snake-AVER
　　　 'I'm frightened of the snake.' (T2)

(20)　*Kali   nhutjadu   ngan.gutji yinggani patjikurnu.*
　　　 already 3sg:NOM:THERE   word-EMPH   2sg:GEN   good-one
　　　 'That's right.' (or 'Your words are correct.') (T2)

A phrase may function as a verbless clause in a longer sentence; for example, *manyu kurnu* 'it's a good job (that)' in (21).

(21)　*Manyu kurnu yundru   nganha nganana pandi-purutji   nhunggani,*
　　　 good one   2sg:ERG 1sg:ACC tell-IP dog-AVER-EMPH   3sg:GEN

　　　wathila   ngathu   mandrina, yaba ngunyingalatji   yinha.
　　　 stick-EMPH 1sg:ERG get-IP   fear give-FUT-EMPH-EMPH   3sg:ACC
　　　 'It's a good job you warned me about that dog; I got a stick and frightened it.' (X21)

(Perhaps *nhunggani* was actually *nhungganiyi*, with locative suffix.)

It will be noted that these example sentences are all translated into English with present tense verbs. If it is necessary to specify another tense or mood a dummy verb, normally *nhina* 'to sit, stay, live, be', in the appropriate tense or mood form is needed. See also §14.2.

7.2 Intransitive sentences

These consist basically of a subject noun phrase and a verb. Optional additional constituents include modifiers such as interrogative or negative particles (see Chapter 8) and adverbial phrases marking location, goal or origin of motion, cause, manner and so on. Examples of simple positive intransitive statements, with and without peripheral constituents, now follow.

(22)　*Wathara nhutjadu   darrkarla.*
　　　 wind   3sg:NOM:THERE   blow-PRES
　　　 'The wind's blowing.' (T9)

(23) *Warlkana nhutjadu wathi-nguda.*
 fall-IP 3sg:NOM:THERE tree-ABL
 'He fell out of the tree.' (T3)

(24) *Thinkali nganyi thudanhinarla.*
 side-INST 1sg:NOM lie-sit-PRES
 'I'm lying on my side.' (T7)

(25) *Tjukurru nhunu yita kulkupa-nhinarla.*
 kangaroo 3sg:NOM away jump-sit-PRES
 'The kangaroo's hopping away.' (T7)

Note that a clause like the first of (26) is not regarded as pseudotransitive (see §14.2) but simply as intransitive. The subject is *martardaku nganyi* 'my ankle', the genitive form of the pronoun not being used with body parts.

(26) *Martardaku nganyi dulyi-nhana, nganyi ngurrangu thawarla.*
 ankle 1sg.NOM twist-NP 1sg.NOM always-YET go-PRES
 'I hurt my ankle but I'm still going.' (R9)

In a sentence like

(27) *Kintha yunggudu ngaka-rnanga.*
 nose blood run-CONT
 '[His] nose is bleeding.' (T14, in S3)

the subject is probably best analysed as a phrase consisting of a single noun phrase with *yunggudu* inalienably possessed by *kintha* (like *kuka karli* 'head hair'). A further expansion of the subject phrase is possible as in the sentence (from the corpus for the Strzelecki dialect):

(28) *Mulha yunggudu nganyi ngakarla.*
 nose blood 1sg:NOM run-PRES
 'My nose is bleeding.' (M3)

7.3 Transitive sentences

Transitive sentences consist basically of subject noun phrase, object noun phrase and verb. Optional additional constituents are as for intransitive sentences; however, instrumental noun phrases are much more common and most other peripheral constituents, such as datives, locatives and ablatives, much less common.

(29) *Wani ngathu dranginga.*
 corroboree 1sg:ERG sing-FUT
 'I'm going to sing a song.' (T6)

(30) *Tjukurru ngathu windrali warrkana-nhana.*
 kangaroo 1sg:ERG spear-INST throw-APP-NP
 'I speared a kangaroo.' (T8)

(31) *Muduwa thidharri nhandra dan.ga-nhana.*
 child baby 3sg:fem:ERG find-NP
 'She had a baby yesterday.' (T6)

64 Chapter 7

(32) *Pandi nhuludu   ngurra parndrirla.*
      dog   3sg:ERG-THERE   always hit-PRES
      'He hits his dog often.' (T12)

(33) *Ngathinha   kurrana   nhinggiyi.*
      1sg:ERG-3sg:ACC   put-IP   location-HERE
      'I put it here.' (T12)

7.4 Reflexive and reciprocal sentences

A transitive verb may be converted to an intransitive verb by means of the suffix *-yindri*, to form one of a number of sentence types according to the relationship between the subject of the transitive verb, the object of the transitive verb and the subject of the intransitive verb. Two of these are types are common to many languages; these are:

(a) Reflexive sentences, which describe the sum of a set of actions, at least one in number, each of which has a single agent and a single patient which is identical with or an inalienably possessed part of the agent;

(b) Reciprocal sentences, which describe the sum of a set of actions, at least two in number, each of which has a single agent and a patient which does not coincide with or include the agent, but in which the sum of the agents and the sum of the patients form groups with at least one individual common to both.

Other functions of this suffix will be discussed in §14.1; only these two will be illustrated here.

Reflexive examples include:

(34) *Ngapayi   nganyi   nguya   wawa-yindrina.*
      water-LOC 1sg:NOM reflection   see-RR-NP
      'I saw myself in the water.' (T14)
      (One's reflection, like one's shadow, is inalienably possessed, as a body part.)

(35) *Purudu-ka-yindrina nganyi.*
      dry-CAUS-RR-IP   1sg:NOM
      'I dried myself.'[1] (T7)

(36) *Ngana-yindringa nganyi, walya yabalitji   ngana mayi.*
      tell-RR-FUT   1sg:NOM not   fear-INST-EMPH   do   EMPH
      "Telling myself not to be frightened." [lit. 'I tell myself, don't be frightened'] (R8)

(37) *Mirra-yindrina nganyi   marapukuli.*
      scratch-RR-IP 1sg:NOM hand-nail-INST
      'I scratched myself with my fingernail.' (B16)

Note that the following sentence is not reflexive:

(38) *Mitji ngathu   dukana   marawitju   pulyali.*
      eye   1sg:ERG   poke-IP hand-finger   small-INST
      'I poked my eye with my little finger.' (B16)

---

[1] MN used an ergative subject with no reflexive marking and no explicit object in a similar sentence.

Simple declarative sentences 65

Examples of reciprocal sentences include:

(39) *Yaka-yindriri kalkayi,   'Mayi, karlukarlutji wayinila   ngandra?'*
    ask-RR-UNSP afternoon-LOC EMPH fish-EMPH   how.many-EMPH 1pl:in:NOM
    'In the afternoon [they] ask one another "How many fish have we got?"'
    (D1, =A39)

(40) *Yiwa   pula   thawarla,   muduwa   ngala thuka-rnanga,*
    woman   3.du:NOM   go-PRES   child   then   carry-CONT

   warliwarli-ma-yindringa pula,   kurnulila   thukari,   ya
   help-help-CAUS-RR-FUT   3.du:NOM   one-ERG-EMPH   carry-UNSP and

   kurnulila   nhandra   thukandji.
   one-ERG-EMPH   3sg:fem:ERG   carry-SEQ
   'The two women are taking it in turns to carry the baby.' (P22)

(41) *Walya yina   thanayi   kilkarnanga, yila-yarndu ngandra*
    not   EMPH 3pl:NOM-HERE   know-CONT   where-how   1pl:in:NOM

   ngandja-yindri-lapurratji.
   call-RR-REMP-EMPH
   'These fellows now don't know how we used to be related to one another
   [i.e. the kinship system].' (D6)

Note that ambiguity between reflexive and reciprocal can be overcome by the use of additional specification; in the following example *paladi* 'separate, individual' and *warlima* 'to help' are used:

(42) *Puladutji   wani-ngadi   marndra-yindri-nhana   paladildra,*
    2.du:NOM-THERE-EMPH   corroboree-DAT   paint-RR-NP   individual-BUT

   ngala thanadutji   warlima-yindri-nhanaldra   marndra-yindri-rnanga.
   then   3pl:NOM-THERE-EMPH   help-CAUS-RR-NP-BUT   paint-RR-CONT
   'Those two fellows painted themselves for the corroboree, but the others painted
   one another.' (R8)

8 *Non-declarative simple sentences*

8.1 Command sentences

A command sentence is used to give an order (imperative) or make a suggestion or give permission (optative) and is characterised by the absence of an explicit subject (if the subject is in the second person). This absence is optional but normal. A minimal command sentence therefore consists of an intransitive verb, or an object noun phrase and a transitive or pseudotransitive verb, or two object noun phrases and a ditransitive verb. A negative command uses the negative particle *walya*, as in (5); there is no negative imperative affixation. See §8.4.1 for a construction in which *walya* is used for a negative permission (42, 43). A common additive is *may(i)*, which follows the verb and emphasises the command. See also §11.5, §11.6, §11.13 and §11.14.

(1) *Nhinathalka!*
     sit-up
     'Sit up!' (W4)

(2) *Makapani thambathambanakani   mayi yambarriyi.*
     fire-PRIV play-play-INCH-AWAY-PLIMP EMPH flat-LOC
     "Play away from the fire, out on the flat." (W3)

(3) *Ngapa nganha yada ngunyay!*
     water 1sg:ACC hither give:DISTORT
     'Give me a drink of water!' (T6)

(4) *Thuda-malka-yarndu nhunu.*
     lie-OPT-how(?)   3sg:NOM
     'Let him lie down.' (B16)

(5) *Walya wawa!*
     not   look
     "Don't look at him!" (X23)

8.2 Questions

Questions are of two types: choice questions, to which the answer is chosen from two or more alternatives (most commonly the alternatives are 'yes' and 'no'); and information questions, involving an interrogative, to which the answer expected is basically a word or phrase of the class for which the particular interrogative used normally substitutes. In addition, of course, an answer to either type of question could be *ngalaaku* 'I don't know' or some other confession of ignorance or doubt.

Questions of the choice type are differentiated from the corresponding statement sentences only by the intonation pattern, with a rising intonation at the end of the sentence nucleus.

(6) *Yabali   yini   kathikathi-puru?*
    fear-INST 2sg:NOM   snake-AVER
    'Are you frightened of the snake?' (T2)

(7) *Thawanga yini?*
    go-FUT   2sg:NOM
    'Are you going?' (T11, =S1-5)

There may be some distortion of the final syllable of a key word, as in (8), (10) or (9-11). Where an interrogative is used it normally takes first place in the sentence or clause; (9) is an exception.

(8) *Minha yundru   yintjadu   pardrarlayey?*
    what   2sg:ERG 3sg:ACC:THERE   hold-PRES-DISTORT
    'What have you got there?" (T10)

(9) *Muduwa wayini   yinggani?*
    child   how.many   2sg:GEN
    'How many kids have you got?' (T10)

(10) *Minha yundru   nganarley?*
     what   2sg:ERG tell-PRES.DISTORT
     'What did you say?' (T6) (Contrast (14-39). Note also (14-46).)

(11) '*Kathi   tjukurru   ngathu   parndrina.*' '*Wayi pirna ngala nhunu?*'
     animal kangaroo   1sg:ERG   kill-IP   how   big   then   3sg:NOM

    '*A, kathi   pirnatji.*'
     oh animal   big-EMPH
    'I killed a kangaroo.' 'How big was it?' 'Oh, a big one.' (P21)

Wari was sometimes used instead of *wayi* in sentences like this.

Example (12), in Yawarrawarrka, is the only instance of an inflectional suffix on a word for 'when'.

(12) '*Wintjama   yundru   wathiya   yinhaku   punga?*' '*Kayidima.*'
     when-DAT   2sg:ERG build-FUT 3sg:ACC-THERE humpy   soon-DAT
     'When are you going to put up that humpy?' 'Not long.' (Y10)

See §9.11, (9-3, 12, 101, 173) and the appropriate dictionary entries for additional examples of interrogatives, especially of those based on *yila-* ~ *yidla-* 'where'. Note that when the interrogative *minha* functions as an adjective (as in (17)) rather than a pronoun (as in (8) or (10)) it can qualify a human noun, for which *wara* 'who?' rather than *minha* would substitute as an interrogative pronoun. Alternative ways to ask 'Who are you?' are (from W5):

(13) Waranu   yini?   and   Minha karna   yini?
      who-NOM   2sg:NOM   what person   2sg:NOM

When a question sentence is subordinated as a quotation clause the interrogative need no longer denote interrogation. For example:

(14) Kali   ngathu   yinha   ngana-nhana, warnu   nganyitji.
      already   1sg:ERG   3sg:ACC   tell-NP   who-NOM 1sg:NOM-EMPH
      'I told him who I was.' (P12)

8.3 Uncertainty and indefiniteness

Uncertainty, indefiniteness, doubt and ignorance are most commonly expressed with the aid of the adverb *kara*. It is frequently used to modify what would otherwise be an information question, converting it into a statement of indefiniteness, doubt or ignorance, in which cases it can often be translated as 'I wonder' or 'I don't know'. In other cases (in which it can perhaps be regarded as modifying choice questions) it is translated by 'might' or 'maybe'. Where there are alternatives involved it may be translated 'or' (as could have been done in (17)). It follows the constituent of the clause to which it refers;[1] this may be nominal, verbal or adverbal.

The use of *kara* in association with an interrogative is illustrated in (15) to (18), and see also §9.11, (11-25) and (15-12).

(15) Manmarla   nhutjadu   ngakaniyi.'   'Minha-ngadi kara?'
      tell.a.lie-PRES 3sg:NOM:THERE   1sg:GEN-LOC   what-DAT   maybe
      'He's telling me a lie. 'Why does he tell me lies?" (C2) (More literally:
      '... I wonder why.')

(16) Waranu   kara   nhuniyi   thawarla ngatjada ngalunggani-ngadi.
      who-NOM   maybe   3sg:NOM-HERE   go-PRES   camp   1.du:in:GEN-DAT
      "There's somebody coming to our camp." (C5)

(17) Minha kathi   kara   nhutjadu   waka,   puluku kara,   nhandu
      what   animal   maybe 3sg:NOM:THERE   over.there bullock maybe   horse
      kara.
      maybe
      'There's some sort of animal over there; might be a bullock; might be a horse.' (T4)

(18) Thawawarrangatjila   walpi kara   nhani.
      go-arrive-FUT-EMPH-EMPH when   maybe 3sg:FEM.NOM
      "I don't know when she's coming home." (W2)

Other examples of *kara* are given below; see also (17), §17.1 and its dictionary entry.

(19) Marripathi   kara   nganyi   thawanga ...
      tomorrow   maybe   1sg:NOM   go-FUT
      "Tomorrow I might go ..." (W3)

(20) Dunka   yada   mayi; walpa-ngangalili   wawayila   yini,
      go.out   hither   EMPH   humpy-owner-ERG   see-POT-EMPH   2sg:NOM

---

[1] One exception to this ordering has been noted in a SY example.

winkama-rlayi   kara   yundru.
disappear-CAUS-SIM maybe   2sg:ERG
"You want to come out, boy, because the bloke that ... owns the humpy might see you shaking something, or think that you shook something." (W3)

(Note that *yini* should presumably be *yina*, 2sg:ACC.; 'shake' = 'steal'.)

(21) *Kilkarla   nhulu   walya   kara   ngathu   wawa-rlayi.*
     know-PRES   3sg:ERG   not   maybe   1sg:ERG   see-SIM
     'He thinks I can't see him.' (R6)

(See (18-18) for another way of saying this.)

(22) *Wathi   dranthayi   nhuniyi   ngarnma-yindrirlanga.   Mardramitjili   kara*
     tree   fork-LOC   3sg:NOM-HERE   stick-RR-PRES-EMPH   stone-eye-INST maybe

     ngathu   yinhadu   parndriparndringa,   kalgakarilatji.
     1sg:ERG 3sg:ACC-THERE   hit-hit-FUT   loose-CAUS-UNSP-EMPH-EMPH
     'It's jammed in the fork of the tree. Maybe I can hit it with a stone and loosen it.' (B15)

(23) *Nganyi   thawarla   yakathikanga   thawini-ngadi,   ngali   kara.*
     1sg:NOM   go-FUT   ask-return-FUT   go-GER-DAT   1du:ex:NOM   maybe
     'I'll go and ask if I can go with him.' (lit. 'I'm going and will ask about going, he and I maybe.') (X43)

The expression *pani kara* sometimes forms a very elliptical coordinate clause in a sentence, with the meaning 'or not'.

(24) *Ngathu   yinha   kapirla,   yakayakanga   yinha,   mardra   ngakani*
     1sg:ERG 3sg:ACC   follow-PRES   ask-ask-FUT   3sg:ACC   stone   1sg:GEN

     winkama-nhana,   ngunyithikanga   kara   nganha   nhulu,   pani   kara.
     disappear-CAUS-NP   give-return-FUT maybe   1sg:ACC 3sg:ERG   none   maybe
     'I'm going to follow him "and ask that bloke whether he shook my money and whether he'll give it to me back or not." (P7)

The rarely heard conjunction(?) *kayi* is probably another form of *kara*; however, it will be described in §17.1. The interjection *ngalaaku* (§17.2.2) also resembles *kara* in some ways.

If the potential mood form of the verb, described in §11.7, can function as the main verb of an independent sentence, this also could appropriately be included in this section. Indefiniteness may also be expressed by means of such nouns as *ngalyi* 'some', 'a few' and *kurnu* 'one'; both may also mean 'other' (cf. (15-19) for *ngalyi*, §10.5.3 for *kurnu*; cf. also *-ldra*, §18.3.2).

(25) *Pandi   nhuniyi   ngurra   marrtjirla,   karna   ngalyi   ngala   nhulu*
     dog   3sg:NOM-HERE   always   bark-PRES   person   some   then   3sg:ERG

     walya   matharla.
     not   bite-PRES
     "He's always barking but he never bites anybody." (W7)

(26) Ngarru ngathu   kurnu   kilkarlatji.
     only 1sg:ERG   one   know-PRES-EMPH
     'I only know one of you.' (W5)

8.4 Negation

8.4.1 *walya*

A clause is most commonly negated by the particle *walya* 'not', 'don't', which normally occurs as first word in the clause. It frequently occurs in a sentence of the form 'a, not b' where the clause 'b' is very elliptical (compare the use of *kara*, as in (15), (17) and (24)). Its Yawarrawarrka equivalent is *watja* or (heard from a younger speaker) *watka*.

(27) Ay, walya nganyi   yurarla,   mulhudu kudlini-ngadi.
     oh not 1sg:NOM   like-PRES   tucker   cook-GER-DAT
     'I don't like cooking.' (T14)

(28) Walya yinha   yirrtjinatji!
     not   3sg:ACC   wake-CAUS-EMPH
     'Don't wake him!' (W2)

(29) Ay, Yawarrawarrka nhutjadu,   walya Yandruwandha.
     oh Yawarrawarrka 3sg:NOM:THERE not   Yandruwandha
     'That fellow's a Yawarrawarrka, not a Yandruwandha.' (T14)

(30) Walya kilkini   maka pirna thangkakari   mardramitji warrkapandhinga,
     not   know-GER fire big   burn-CAUS-UNSP   stone-eye   throw-down-FUT

     mardramitjiyi kathitji   warrkapandhinga, walya maka-mukuruyi.
     stone-eye-LOC meat-EMPH   throw-down-FUT   not   fire-ash-LOC
     'They don't know about building a big fire and throwing stones on it and throwing the meat on the stones, not on the coals [to cook].' (D4)

Walya is often used with a gerund rather than with the appropriate imperative or indicative form of the verb; the first occurrence of *walya* in (30) is such a case and other examples are given below. The clause in which it occurs is therefore verbless, and the gerund functions as an agent noun; thus (31) could be translated 'Don't be a perpetual "lier"'. This type of construction is not confined to habitual, normal or long continued actions as might be expected; see (33) and (34). Omission of the topic from the verbless clause implies an imperative sentence (e.g. (31), (32)) unless the context — the other clause of the sentence as in (34) or (15-12) or the extralinguistic context as in (33) or a preceding sentence — shows that this is not the case and that the clause is merely elliptical.

(31) Walya ngurra   thudanhinini.
     not   always lie-sit-GER
     "Don't lie down all the time." (W4)

(32) Mirni kathi yintjadu   panthama, walya thayini.
     wait meat 3sg:ACC:THERE   smell   not   eat-GER
     'Smell that meat before you eat it.' (P8)

(33) Walyala   yada   ngatjada-ngaditji thawawarrini.
     not-EMPH hither camp-DAT-EMPH   go-arrive-GER
     'He's not coming to the camp.' (P4)

(34) *Nhutjadu   thawana   karnatji   ngarru nganha yada   wawari,*
      3sg:NOM:THERE go-IP   person-EMPH   only   1sg:ACC hither look-UNSP

  walya yandhini.
  not   talk-GER
  "He looked at me [as he walked past] and never said a word." (W1)

The meaning of *walya* may be extended to mean 'not, but should', i.e. it is used in conjunction with a past tense to mean 'should have' or with a present tense to mean 'should'. Note the two functions of *walya* in (36) and see also (35) and (16-22); (37) may be of this type too, given that *mirni* can mean 'how about'. Also, it can be used to refer to something that did not happen but if it had happened it would have had a certain result: 'if x had happened y would have happened'. The negative is in the main clause, which corresponds to the subordinate clause in the English translations; the other clause also may be negated. Thus the English construction is equivalent to either 'x did not happen for y to happen' or 'x did not happen and y did not happen'. See (38, 39, 10-27). Both of these usages are characterised by the negative marker not being in its usual initial position; there are few possible and no clear counter-examples to this. Of about forty examples of non-clause-initial negative, about one third are of one of these types. The retraction of the negative marker may function to reduce its scope to less than the whole clause and give it this irrealis function.

Other non-initial occurrences of walya include several instances of the expected situation where a question word precedes it and several others (such as (40)) where it may be that a subject or agent or object is given prominence (but also several, like (15-47), where both agent and object precede, indicating perhaps that the position of *walya* is free if it is not initial; see also (15-48)). There are also three examples of non-initial *walya* in different types of negative subordinate clause ('so that not', 'because not', 'when not'). An example is (41).[2]

(35) *Thayi-nhana walya ngathu,   kanpayi   ngada.*
      eat-NP   not   1sg:ERG   visible-LOC still
      'I should have eaten it while it was still there.' (R8)

(36) *Nhutjadu   walya yina   mardratji   ngunyithikarla,   walya*
      3sg:NOM:THERE not   2sg:ACC stone-EMPH   give-return-PRES   not

  pardranhinini.
  hold-sit-GER
  "He should pay you back the money; he shouldn't hang on to it." (W2)

(37) *Mirni walya thawa-malk-árdi!*
      wait not   go-OPT-EMPH
      'Will you go!' (B19)

(38) *Thawanhina-nhukadani walya nganyi,   wawanga kaku-madanitji.*
      go-sit-RECP   not   1sg:NOM   see-FUT elder.sister-2kin-EMPH
      'If I had come here yesterday I would have seen your sister.' (T12)

---

[2] The connection between the 'should' clause and the non-initial position of *walya* was observed, and its possible function suggested, by a referee (who also suggested the analysis of (37) as belonging to this type). This sparked my examination of non-initial *walya*, reported in these two paragraphs.

(39) *Ngathu   watja   yinhaku   kathi   thayini nganyi   watja mundjarla.*
    1sg:ERG   not   3sg:ACC:there   meat   eat-IP   1sg:NOM   not   be.sick-PRES
    'If I had eaten that meat I would have been sick.' (Y28)

(40) *Padri   kananggu   walya thayini muduwa karruwalitji.*
    grub   type.of.grub   not   eat-GER child   boy-ERG-EMPH
    'Boys [before being initiated] were not allowed to eat witchetty grubs.' (X14)

(41) *Purla,   thambathikayada!   Thanaku   watja wawinima,   walpa*
    little   play-return-hither   3pl:NOM-THERE   not   see-GER-DAT humpy

    thulanyi.
    strange-LOC
    'Little one, play back this way! So they won't see you, at the strange(r's) humpy.' (Y28)

The combination of *walya* with the dative form of the gerund denotes a prevention or forbidding: 'not letting'.

(42) *Nganggalhildra   thana   wani   thambana-padipadini. Walya*
    own-BUT   3pl:NOM   corroboree   dance-HAB-GER   not

    yiwali   wawini-ngadi,   yirrbandji   yina.
    woman-ERG   see-GER-DAT   forbidden   EMPH
    'They [the men] dance their own corroboree and the women don't watch, it's forbidden.' (P11)

This is the only example of *yirrbandji*, and it is not clear whether the clause preceding it is to be regarded as subordinate to the preceding sentence or governed by *yirrbandji*, which could be a verbal form.

(43) *Mirni   ngaldra   yandhayandharla, walya ngarini-ngadi   ngalunha*
    wait   1.du:in:NOM   talk-talk-PRES   not   hear-GER-DAT   1.du:in-ACC

    ngalyitji   (or   ngalyilitji ?).
    others-EMPH   (others-ERG-EMPH)
    'We'll have a talk, but "we don't want other people to hear us".' (R8)

The combination of *kali* 'already' with *walya* forms a qualified negative, with the meaning 'nearly'. See also the dictionary entry for *kali walya*.

(44) *Kali   walya ngathu   yinha   muthukana.*
    already   not   1sg:ERG   3sg:ACC   very-CAUS-IP
    'I nearly got it.' (i.e. speared a kangaroo) (T12)

(45) *Kali   walya nhuniyi   parntu; parntunarlatji.*
    already   not   3sg:NOM-HERE   blunt   blunt-INCH-PRES-EMPH
    'The axe is nearly blunt; it's getting blunt.' (P8)

It seems that the change to *parntunarla* here may have been a correction; on a later occasion BK said that the use of *kali walya* here was not correct, and *parntunarla* should be used. This suggests that *kali walya* is useable only with verbs, to describe an action or situation that nearly happens, and not to describe a state or quality.

8.4.2 *pani*

The particle *pani* may occur alone, as a sentence substitute, to mean 'no' (or 'none' or 'nothing').[3] Its combination with *kara* 'maybe' to form the elliptical coordinate clause 'or not' has been described above (§8.3 and (24)). It is not common as a free morpheme; the following sentences give some examples. See also (9-150).

(46) *Thawa-nhana nganyi,   ngatjadayi   thangguthikanga; pani   yinha*
     go-NP   1sg:NOM camp-LOC stand-return-FUT none   3sg:ACC

   wawaritji.
   see-UNSP-EMPH
   "I went there and visited the camp. I stopped there, like, but I couldn't see him."
   (P4)

(47) *Wadarla   ngali   yinha.   Thangguthalkana nganyi   palthu wawanga,*
     wait-PRES 1.du:ex:NOM 3sg:ACC stand-up-IP   1sg:NOM   road   see-FUT

   paningu   nhunu.
   none-YET 3sg:NOM
   'We're waiting for him. I stood up to look at the road but he's not coming yet.'
   (R7)

It is not clear whether *walya* could be substituted for pani in the above two sentences, and what the effect would be.

The proprietive suffix may combine with *pani*.

(48) *Pani-mindji nganyi ...*
     none-PROP   1sg:NOM
     "(I) went for nothing ..." (or 'I've got nothing') (M2)

Pani occurs most often in a bound(?) form as the privative suffix, as in:

(49) *Mawalila   nganyi, kathi-pani ngala ngandra.*
     hunger-INST-EMPH 1sg:NOM meat-PRIV   then   1pl:in:NOM
     "I'm hungry and we got no meat." (P5)

See §10.5.5 for more examples. With a gerund this construction rarely functions as a negative imperative, as in (10-48), and in:

(50) *Thawaka, nga(?)   purnunu-kini-pani.*
     go-AWAY   then(?) itchy-CAUS-GER-PRIV
     "Go away, don't tease me." (P29)

For notes on the use of *-pani* with a verb stem, see §10.6.

---

[3] As a referee points out, this is attested with a negative function in a number of languages of the region; these include Arabana, Diyari, Pitta-Pitta and Wangka-Yutjurru. See Austin (1990).

8.4.3 *pudlu*

Pudlu 'can't' — or better, perhaps, 'in vain' — can negate only sentences with indicative verbs. It occurs most commonly in the reduplicated form, *pudlupudlu*. There are few examples in the corpus; some more will be found in the dictionary entry.

(51) *Nhutjadu walki-nhana mardrayi, pudlupudlu.*
3sg:NOM:THERE climb-NP stone-LOC can't-can't
'He tried to climb the mountain but he couldn't.' (P12)

(52) *Pudlu ngunyingunyina, walya nhunu yurana. Ngathu ngurrangu*
can't give-give-IP not 3sg:NOM want-IP 1sg:ERG always-YET

thanhayi pardrana.
3pl:ACC-HERE hold-IP
'I tried to give him some (fruit) but he wouldn't have it. "I've still got it."' (P7)

9 *Nominal inflection*

Yandruwandha has an absolutive–ergative system for nouns (with marginal exceptions for some sub-classes of nouns), a nominative–accusative system for non-singular pronouns and a three-way system, with nominative, ergative and accusative all distinguished, for singular pronouns. The interrogative root *yila-* has a rather divergent system.

As ergative coincides in marking with instrumental the term 'operative' is used for the morpheme, although ERG for ergative or INST for instrumental, as appropriate, are used for interlinear glosses.

9.1 Common noun inflection

Examples are sometimes given using other classes of nouns if they behave in the same way with regard to the point under discussion.

9.1.1 *Nominative*

The nominative (or absolutive) case form of a noun is unmarked, i.e. has zero inflection, and has a range of functions. These include marking:

subject in an intransitive sentence:

(1) *Wathara nhutjadu darrkarla.*
    wind   3sg:NOM:THERE blow-PRES
    'The wind's blowing.' (T9)

(2) *Mulha yunggudu nganyi ngakarla.*   (Strzelecki dialect)
    nose blood   1sg:NOM run-PRES
    'My nose is bleeding'. (M3)

topic in a verbless sentence:

(3) *Minha maya nhutjadu?*
    what name 3sg:NOM:THERE
    'What's the name of that thing?' (T6)

comment in a verbless sentence (as well as topic in this example):

(4) *Wathi kuka pampaampu.*
    stick head round
    'The stick's got a rounded end.' (X49)

75

76   *Chapter 9*

subject in a reflexive or reciprocal sentence:

(5) *Pururrukayindrina   nganyi.*
    dry-CAUS-RR-IP   1sg:NOM
    'I dried myself.' (T7)

object in a reflexive or reciprocal sentence:

(6) *Maltji   nganyi   kudra-yindrina.*
    leg   1sg:NOM break-RR-IP
    'I broke my leg.' (T8)

object in a transitive sentence:

(7) *Thinamitji   nganha   nhuludu   nhangkana.*
    foot-toe   1sg:ACC 3sg:ERG-THERE   step.on-IP
    'He stepped on my toe.' (T8)

(8) *Ay   kilkarla   ngathu,   pukatji   kudlini-ngadi.*
    eh   know-PRES   1sg:ERG   tucker-EMPH   cook-GER-DAT
    'I know all about cooking.' (T8)

duration and location in time (see also §9.6):

(9) *Malthi   parrkulu   nganyi   nhinan.ga   Mardrapirnangiyi.*
    cold   two   1sg:NOM   sit-FARP   stone-big-GEN-LOC
    'I stayed at Planet Downs for two years.' (T9)

(10) *Ngara-nhana   ngathu,   dritji   parrkulu-parrkulu.*
     hear-NP   1sg:ERG   day   two-two
     'I heard it four days ago.' (P9)

In cases where a noun phrase consists of two or more words, only one word is normally inflected. The other word(s) in the phrase are then uninflected, but are regarded as being not in the nominative case but in the case of the inflected word. In other words the inflectional affix refers to the whole phrase. See §9.12 for further detail and examples.

9.1.2 Vocative

A few examples of a possible vocative case, with suffix *-a* which replaces the final vowel of the stem, have been noted. It is optional and the final vowel is distorted in a high proportion of cases; it may in fact be more correct to regard all the examples as cases of distortion (see §3.2.1), although distortion of /i/ and /u/ to [a] has rarely been noted elsewhere. Examples include:

(11) *Ngarndra!   Ngarndrey!   Nganyi   thawarley   karirri-ngadi?*
     mother-VOC mother-VOC:DISTORT   1sg:NOM   go-PRES:DISTORT river-DAT
     'Mum, can I go down to the river?' (T13)

(12) *Yini   ngala   karrukarra?*
     2sg:NOM   then   old.man-VOC
     "Oh, is that you, [old man]?" (W5) (Compare (11-100))

There are two specialised terms of address in Yandruwandha, *kan.ga* for men and *purdupa* for women. The former could be a vocative form of a word cognate with Wangkumara *kan.gu* 'boy'.

9.1.3 Operative

The form of the operative case suffix is *-li*; the few examples noted of *-lu* on a noun with stem-final /u/ are attributed to interference from neighbouring languages and have at times been corrected to *-li*. The modern Strzelecki Yandruwandha and Yawarrawarrka material has *-lu* after final /u/ and *-li* elsewhere (but is not entirely consistent in the use of *-lu*), but Reuther has *-li* only. The main functions are to mark the subject of a transitive verb (ergative function, as in (13)) and the instrument or material used in an action (instrumental function, as in (17, 20, 7-30)). These are glossed ERG and INST respectively. Two other functions will be discussed later in this section.

The subject of a transitive verb need not be animate nor the originator of any action (14, 15), although it normally is both. Instrumental nouns usually occur with transitive or reflexive/reciprocal verbs, but are also used with intransitive verbs (19, 20). An instrument need not be inanimate (18, 14-11). The 'use' of an instrument may be uncontrolled (16).

(13) *Pandili   nhuludu   nhambapandhina kathi.*
     dog-ERG 3sg:ERG-THERE bury-down-IP   meat
     'The dog buried the meat.' (T8)

(14) *Ngala wathi malkirrili   nganha   ngarndangarndamaritji.*
     then   tree   many-ERG 1sg:ACC block-block-CAUS-UNSP-EMPH
     "A lot of trees blocked me from getting through." (P5)

(15) *Ngandjarrili nganha   parndrina, ngabakana   nganha, ngabangabala*
     rain-ERG   1sg:ACC hit-IP   wet-CAUS-IP 1sg:ACC wet-wet-EMPH

     thikawarrana   nganyi.
     return-arrive-IP 1sg:NOM
     "I got wet in the rain and I came home wet." (C3-4)

(16) *Mardrali   nganyi   parndri-yindrina thina.*
     stone-INST 1sg:NOM hit-RR-IP   foot
     'I hit my foot on a rock.' (T12)

(17) *Marlkali   ngathu   thinba-nhana.*
     mulga-INST 1sg:ERG make-NP
     'I made [the boomerang] out of mulga wood.' (C5)

(18) *Kapada   ngaldra   thutjutjuli thawarla tjukurru pandringa.*
     come.on 1du:in:NOM dog-INST   go-PRES   kangaroo hit-FUT
     'Come on, we're going hunting kangaroos with dogs.' (C2)

(19) *Ngapala mabaabili   nhunu   kuthiwarra-rnanga ...*
     well   dark-INST 3sg:NOM come-arrive-CONT
     'Well he comes in the dark ...' (R3)

(20) *Kadlirla   nganyi   wirni kamurali.*
     wear-PRES 1sg:NOM hairstring-INST
     'I'm wearing a hair belt.' (P28)

-li locates an action in time in the following example (and perhaps (19)):

(21) *Kathi tjukurru ngathu parndri-lapurra muduwalitji.*
animal kangaroo 1sg:ERG kill-REMP child-ERG-EMPH
'I used to kill a lot of kangaroos when I was a young fellow.' (W2)

MN used operative to mark the part by which something is held or handled, as in:

(22) *Ngathu pardra-nhana yinhayi nhurali.*
1sg:ERG hold-NP 3sg:ACC tail-INST
'I caught it by the tail.' (M21)

However, BK used the unmarked noun for the part in a similar sentence (see the *kurni* entry in the dictionary).

The operative, in its instrumental function, is sometimes used where aversive or locative might be expected:

(23) *Pukuduli nhutjadu yandharla.*
dream-INST 3sg:NOM:THERE talk-PRES
'He's talking in his sleep.' (R5)

(24) *Paldri-nhana nhunu kundrukundruli.*
die-NP 3sg:NOM cough-INST
'He died of the flu.' (P5)

(25) *Durruli nganyi thikathikanarla.*
back-INST 1sg:NOM return-return-INCH?-PRES
'I'm walking backwards.' (P13)

(26) *Thinkali nganyi thudanhinarla.*
side-INST 1sg:NOM lie-sit-PRES
'I'm lying on my side.' (T7)

and perhaps

(27) *Pundrali nganyi yirrikarla.*
cold-INST 1sg:NOM shiver-PRES
'I'm shivering with the cold.' (T11)

Related to the usage exemplified in the previous paragraph, especially by the last example, is the use of an operative form as the complement of a noun in a verbless sentence, or to qualify a noun phrase or verb phrase. These forms are thus semantically adjectives or adverbs. They take no further affixation apart from emphatic markers. The stems involved are mostly abstract noun stems, some of which rarely (or never?) occur without the operative suffix. The identification of this suffix with the operative (as opposed to regarding it as homophonous with it) is supported by the presence in Ngamini, a dialect of a neighbouring language, of the same phenomenon; in this dialect the form of the relevant suffix (in all its functions) is *-nu*. This usage will be described in more detail in §16.9.

The operative suffix may be used in combination with, and following, the ablative suffix; see §9.1.6.

9.1.3.1 Operative as a co-ordinator in a noun phrase

Another use of the operative case form is in certain expansions of a noun phrase. Where the noun phrase is dual or plural and is expanded by a word or phrase which specifies one (or more if plural, but not all) of the members of the set denoted by the noun phrase, the item comprising the explanation can appear in the operative case form. Thus, *ngali nhulu* 'he and I' ('1du:ex:NOM 3sg:ERG') would be used as a transitive subject, but the same phrase would be used as an intransitive subject too, *ngani yiwathilili* 'the two women and I' (lit. 'we all not including you but including the two women', '1pl:ex:NOM woman-DU-INST'[1]).

(28) *Nhinanhina-nhana yula ngurra nhuludu walypalalitji,*
sit-sit-NP 2du:NOM always 3sg:ERG-THERE white.man-INST-EMPH

nhinggudungu.
location-THERE-YET
'You and that whitefellow have been sitting there all day.' (R10)

(29) *Yambarriyi ngali nhuludu yandhayandha-nhana, ngala*
open.place-LOC 1du:ex:NOM 3sg:ERG-THERE talk-talk-NP then

kurnulitji nhulu ngalinha ngara-rlayi, walpakuku-nguda.
one-ERG-EMPH 3sg:ERG 2du:ex:ACC hear-SIM humpy-inside-ABL
'He and I were having a talk outside and another fellow was listening to us from inside.' (R7)

See (68) and (142) for examples where the operative suffix was not used; the former is an example of a more general dropping of inflectional suffixes after a suffix *-ngi* (see §9.2). See (173) for an example of coordination of two nouns in a phrase, involving juxtaposition and inflection of both.

9.1.4 Dative

The dative suffix *-ngadi* denotes possession, beneficiary, purpose, reason, or destination (in time as well as in place, but not if the verb implies remaining at the destination or returning from it, when locative is used; see §9.1.5). *-ngadi* is frequently affixed to the gerund form of the verb; this will be discussed in §15.3. The corresponding Yawarrawarrka suffix is *-ma*, while Reuther's Jandruwanda distinguishes between dative *-ma* and genitive *-ngi*. This distinction is not made in the language as recorded from BK and others, but note the use of *-ngi* as genitive on proper names and non-singular nouns (see §9.3 and §9.4) and as first person kin proprietive (§9.2) and as a base to which other suffixes are added, and see especially §9.13.

possession

(30) *Nguthu karnakurnu-ngadi parndripada-nhana.*
elder.brother person-other-GEN hit-in-NP
'He hit the other fellow's brother.' (P3)

---

[1] I have glossed the operative suffix here as INST rather than ERG simply because 'with' could be used in an English translation; the function of the suffix is actually different from both.

possession or beneficiary

(31) Yada   nhutjadu   karrukarru-ngadi.
    boomerang   3sg:NOM:THERE   old.man-DAT
    'It's the old man's boomerang.' or 'That boomerang is for the old man.' (P12)

beneficiary

(32) Draka-rnanga yarnduldrangu wirnikamuratji yiwa-ngaditji   pirnaldra,
    weave-CONT   how-BUT-YET   hairstring-EMPH woman-DAT-EMPH   big-BUT

    karrini-ngadi panikaldra   nhambalka-yindrindji.
    tie-GER-DAT   nothing-CAUS-BUT   cover-RR-SEQ
    On the one hand they make a big one [hair-string apron] for women, to tie on to
    cover themselves completely.' (D4, =A-151)

purpose

(33) Karlukarlu-ngadi nganyi   thawarla.
    fish-DAT   1sg:NOM   go-PRES
    'I'm going fishing.' (T6)

(34) Nguthungama   ngakani   thawawarra-nhana wani-ngadi.
    elder.brother-mother's.brother 1sg:GEN   go-arrive-NP   corroboree-DAT
    'My relations came for the corroboree.' (B17)

destination, in time or space; see also (93, 94, 8-16, 13-5, 13-24). The term 'destination' is interpreted broadly here; destination in time refers to the time that has been arrived at when something happens, and (36) illustrates an unusual interpretation of spatial destination.

(35) Man.gili   nhunu   patjarla,   thawa-nhana nhunu   kirri-ngadi.
    Benny.Kerwin   3sg:NOM   sick-PRES   go-NP   3sg:NOM   clever-DAT
    "Benny's gone to see the doctor, he's sick." (T14, in S3)

(36) murnathitha-ngadi ngapa
    chest-DAT   water
    'chest-deep water' (X37)

reason

(37) Yiwa nhatjadu   yingkirla ngathani-ngadi.
    woman 3sg:fem:NOM:THERE   cry-PRES   child (of.woman)-DAT
    'That woman's crying for her baby.' (P4)

(Locative could be used instead of dative in this sentence.)

For discussion of the use of the dative as a stem formative see §10.5.11.

Note that inalienable possession, e.g. of a body part, does not require -ngadi for its expression. This applies also to one's name and seems to apply also to one's language, as in *walypala yawarri* 'white man's language'.

(38) Pandili   nganha   mara   mathani.
    dog-ERG   1sg:ACC   hand   bite-IP
    'The dog bit my hand.' (Y9)

In a sentence like this *nganha mara* could be thought of as object of *mathani*, or *nganha* could be thought of as object of a verb phrase *mara matha* 'to bite the hand of'.

9.1.5 Locative

The locative suffix *-yi* has the following functions:

- to mark location in space, including point of reference of a location word — e.g. behind X-LOC, see (39)–(42); the last two of these illustrate situations where a different case might have been used
- to mark motion to a location followed by rest in that location or return from it, (43)–(45)
- to mark accompaniment, (73), (132), (16-6)
- to mark location in time, (46, 47) and see (10-26)
- to mark the cause of or reason for an action or state (such as fear, anger, crying, laughing, running away), (48)–(50)
- to mark indirect objects, such as person looked for, person to whom speech is directed, also (at least in Yw) the target of something thrown (51, 116, 133) also (14-18, 19)
- to mark direct object of *minha ngana* 'do what' (attested only for SY; (52)),
- to mark the object of comparison 'than —' (attested only for Yw; (53)).

Reuther gave both *-yi* and *-nyi*, while for Yawarrawarrka he gave both *-ni* and *-nyi*, MN used *-nyi* (and *-yi* possibly only because of interference from Yandruwandha) and the younger speakers used *-ni*.

Unlike in some other languages of inland Australia, such as the Arandic group, where dative or allative is used for the location of the object of a transitive verb, Yandruwandha uses locative (40, 44, 45).

(39) *Minha-ngadi nhuniyi walpamarnayi thanggurla?*
what-DAT 3sg:NOM-HERE house-mouth-LOC stand-PRES
"What's he standing in front of the house for?" (W9)

(40) *Wawa parrariyi!*
look underneath-LOC
'Look underneath!' (W9)

(41) *Tjalparrika ngathu mardra thayiyi.*
sharp-CAUS 1sg:ERG stone grinding stone-LOC
'I'm going to sharpen it "on that grinding stone."' (P8)

(Probably the operative could be used instead of the locative in this case. The verb should be inflected.)

(42) *Ngapa yundra nhunu, ngatjadayi.*
water far 3sg:NOM camp-LOC
'The water's a long way from the camp.' (R5)

(Ablative could also be used; see (61).)

(43) *Mayi, nganyi yita windripada-rlayi, nguda yingganiyi?*
well 1sg:NOM that.way enter-in-SIM(?) camp 2sg:GEN-LOC
'Can I come in?' (T13)

82   *Chapter 9*

(or *windripadarlayi* may be enter-in-PRES-DISTORT.)

(44) *Mardramitji   warrkapandhina   ngathu   ngapayi,   ngapala   nhunu*
stone-eye   throw-down-IP   1sg:ERG   water-LOC   well   3sg:NOM

thawari   pulyurru-ngadi.
go-UNSP   mud-DAT
"I chucked a stone into the water, he went into the mud." (W9)
(Note the use of the dative — with allative function — in this example. The verb *warrka* 'to throw' carries the implication that the object will remain where it is thrown; the verb *thawa* 'to go' carries no such implication for its subject.)

(45) *Yinbana   ngathu   mandrithikini-ngadi   ngakani   storekeeper-yi,   ngathu*
send-IP   1sg:ERG   get-return-GER-DAT   1sg:GEN   storekeeper-LOC   1sg:ERG

man.garri   yinbana   mandrithikini-ngadi   purtu   ngakani.
girl   send-IP   get-return-GER-DAT   goods   1sg:GEN
"I sent a girl to go over there to the shop to get me what I wanted." (W6)

(46) *Matja   ngathu   yina   wawawawana-nhina-nhanatji;   padlakanpayi*
long.time 1sg:ERG 2sg:ACC look-look-APP-sit-NP-EMPH   ground-visible-LOC

nyadi yini   thawawarrini-ngadi.   (= 'at dawn')
like   2sg:NOM   go-arrive-GER-DAT
'I've been watching for you for a long time; I thought you would be getting here at dawn.' (P12)

(47) *Wawa-lapurra ngathu   nhanhadu,   muduwa   pulyayi.*
see-REMP   1sg:ERG   3sg:fem:ACC-THERE   child   small-LOC
'I saw her "when she was a little kid."' (W5)

See also §16.2.2 for the use of *-ngada* after the locative.

(48) *Minhayi   ngali   thirrinhanatji,   pitji   yina   nhulu   ngakani*
what-LOC   1du:ex:NOM fight-NP-EMPH coolamon EMPH 3sg:ERG 1sg:GEN

kudra-nhana.
break-NP
"We fought over that coolamon that he broke of mine." (P5) (lit. 'What did we fight over; the coolamon of mine that he broke.')

(49) *Kadhirla   nganyi   muduwayitji.*
be.happy-PRES 1sg:NOM child-LOC-EMPH
'I'm proud of my kid.' (P29)

(50) *Nganyi   ngilarli-ngana-rnanga   ngakani   muduwayi .*
1sg:NOM   sorry.for-INCH-CONT   1sg:GEN   child-LOC
'I'm sorry for my boy.' (M2)

(SY; dative could be used instead of locative, at least in IY.)

(51) *Thanhani   thaparla   nhutjadu,   ngakaniyi.*
tongue   poke.out-PRES 3sg:NOM:THERE 1sg:GEN-LOC
'He's poking his tongue out at me.' (P15)

(52) *Minha nganarla yini muduwayi?*
 what do-PRES 2sg:NOM child-LOC
 'What are you doing to the kid?' (M23)

(SY example. This could also have been expressed as a ditransitive sentence using *ngarrka* instead of *ngana* and with *muduwa* accusative — i.e. unmarked.)

(53) *Nganyi pirna muthu yinggananyi.*
 1sg:NOM big very 2sg:DAT-LOC
 'I'm older than you.' (Y11)

(Yw example. See (15-13, 14) and §18.2 for other ways of comparing.)

The following example seems to be of a different type from any of the preceding, and the locative suffix could possibly be substituted with the ablative. It is not clear if this would change the meaning. The aversive also could be used, but this adds an element of fear of what would have been done with the spear if I had not taken it, and also an implication that the old man had not actually got the spear yet.

(54) *Karrukarruyi yintjadu ngathu mamathikana, wathi windra.*
 old.man-LOC 3sg:ACC:THERE 1sg:ERG steal-return-IP tree spear
 "I took the spear off that fellow over there." (W8)

The use of the locative as a stem formative will be mentioned in §10.5.11.

9.1.6 Ablative

The ablative case, marked by the suffix *-nguda*, is used to denote origin, in a wide range of senses. These include the place from which a person or thing comes, whether the sentence involves motion or not (55, 56, 94, 95, 7-23), the mother from whom a person comes (7-11), the origin of some state (e.g. the object or instrument of action — simple or habitual — that gave rise to it, or the time of origin) (57, 58, 175, 7-12), the reference point of a statement about distance or direction (61), the point from which an action is directed (59, 62). In the last case if the action is transitive the operative suffix *-li* may be added after the ablative suffix ((62, 176), but compare (29)). In (174) a locative suffix *-yi* follows the ablative.

The ablative suffix is frequently affixed to the gerund form of the verb; this will be discussed in §15.3, especially the last page or so. (*-li* may also follow the ablative in such cases, where appropriate.)

See §10.5.11 for discussion of the use of *-nguda* as a stem formative.

(55) *Thayi-pilthirri-nguda ngali.*
 grinding.stone-chips-ABL 1du:ex:NOM
 'We're from the broken stone country.' (i.e. 'We're Innamincka people.') (C4)

It is not clear whether *-nguda* here is an inflectional affix or a stem formative, nor whether the distinction is relevant.

(56) *Thawawarra-nhana nhuniyi mulhapundra-nguda.*
 go-arrive-NP 3sg:NOM-HERE face-cold-ABL
 'This fellow came from the south.' (W8)

84 *Chapter 9*

(57) *Karrukarru nhuniyi   pada ngapakaldri-nguda yiba-nhana*
old.man 3sg:NOM-HERE inside water-bitter-ABL drink-NP

nhuliyi,   thudaarla   nhunu,   kurrayi ngana-rnanga.
3sg:ERG-HERE lie-NOW-PRES 3sg:NOM mad do-CONT
"Old Joe Smith, he's been on the rum, now he's choked down now, and he's asleep."
('choked down' = 'in a drunken sleep') (T14, =S2)

(58) *Ngapa-nguda nganyi.*
water-ABL 1sg:NOM
"I've been in the water before." (i.e. 'I can swim; I'm used to the water.') (B16)

(59) *Ngara-nhana ngathu   ngambungi-nguda.*
hear-NP 1sg:ERG mate-1KIN-ABL
'I heard about it from my mate.' (P11)

(Contrast the alternative construction with locative, as in:

(60) *Ngara-nhana ngathu   ngamangiyi.*
hear-NP 1sg:ERG mother's brother-1KIN-LOC
'I heard it from my uncle.' (B20))

(61) *Miri-nguda ngani   ngatjada kurrakurra-nhana, yundra.*
sandhill-ABL 1pl:ex:NOM camp put-put-NP far
'We camped a long way from the sandhills.' (R7)

(62) *Karrkapada-nhana nhulu   ngalinha, padawarra-ngudali.*
call.out-across-NP 3sg:ERG 1du:ex-ACC other side-ABL-ERG
'He sang out to us from across the river.' (R7)

-nguda in sentences like (62) may be best regarded as a nominal stem formative (see §9.13 and §10.5.11).

9.1.7 Aversive

The suffix *-puru* (*-thudu* in Yawarrawarrka; no equivalent could be elicited in Strzelecki Yandruwandha) marks the cause of some undesirable state or action, or something against which precautions (such as running away, or hiding) are taken. In one example (see the dictionary entry for *mama*) it seems to mark the origin of something taken; however, contrast the other two examples in that entry, in which locative and accusative are used. See the *mardri* entry in the dictionary for sentences in which the aversive and the dative seem to fulfil the same function (too heavy **for** X to lift); after using locative in a similar sentence (too hot for ...) BK agreed that locative could also have been used with 'heavy'. With a less superficial knowledge of the language we would probably be able to point to differences in meaning between these sentences with the different inflections.

Like other disyllabic nominal affixes, *-puru* can be pronounced as a separate word.

The aversive alternates with the locative (§9.1.5) in marking the cause of fear. For an example using the aversive for this purpose see (135). See also (7-21).

(63) *Thawa-rlayi yini, wawardudaw   pardi-puru.*
go-SIM 2sg:NOM see-along.DISTORT snake-AVER
'Watch out for snakes as you go along.' (P10)

(64) *Kathi wawawawanaw palha-puru.*
      meat see-see-APP:DISTORT bird-AVER
      'See that the hawks don't take this meat.' (P11)

(65) *Mulhudu ngandra kinikinikanga, ngapa yulpurru-puru.*
      tucker 1du:in:NOM store.up-CAUS-FUT water flood-AVER
      'We'd better get some extra tucker in in case the river floods.' (B15)

9.2 Kinship terms

In general, kinship terms behave exactly as common nouns in their morphology. One difference arises when the term is modified by the suffix *-ngi*, first person kin proprietive, which denotes that the term relates to the speaker (see §10.5.7). These terms are then generally used without further affixation, irrespective of their function in the sentence. Thus in the following examples one would expect nominative, ergative, ergative, dative, dative and locative or aversive marking. (In relation to (68), note the last part of §9.1.3, including (28).) In fact, in all of these cases the nominative form was used.

(66) *Mukuli kamingi nhulu draka-nhana.*
      bone-INST cousin-1KIN 3sg:ERG pierce-NP
      'He killed my cousin with the bone.' (P6)

(67) *Papangi nganha pirna-ka-lapurra.*
      mother's.father-1KIN 1sg:ACC big-CAUS-REMP
      "My granddad reared me." (C6)

(68) *Nguthingi ngali thawarla.*
      elder.brother-1KIN 1du:ex:NOM go-PRES
      'My brother and I are going.' (P21)

(69) *Yada nhutjadu ngapiringi.*
      boomerang 3sg:NOM:THERE father-1KIN
      'That boomerang belonged to my father.' (P12)

      (When I suggested *ngapiringingadi* here, BK said that would mean 'for my father'.)

(70) *Maka ngathu parndriparndrirla, ngapiringi.*
      firewood 1sg:ERG hit-hit-PRES father-1KIN
      'I'm cutting some wood for my father.' (P21)

      (When I suggested *ngapiringingadi* here, BK said that would mean 'to my father'.)

(71) *Windra ngathu winkamana ngapiringi.*
      spear 1sg:ERG disappear-CAUS-NP father-1KIN
      'I stole the spear from my father.' (W8)

However, there are a minority of examples in which an inflectional suffix is used after *-ngi* (after GB's suggestion, however, in the case of (72)).

(72) *Nguthingili nganha parndripada-nhana.*
      elder.brother-1KIN-ERG 1sg:ACC hit-in-NP
      'My brother hit me.' (P6)

86 *Chapter 9*

(73) *Thawarla   nganyi   nguthingiyi.*
      go-PRES   1sg:NOM   elder.brother-1KIN-LOC
      'I'm going with my brother.' (T11)

Contrast (73) with (68). See also (59) and (60).

There are also examples of *-ngi* affixed to a kinship term carrying forms of the second/third person kin proprietive suffix which is basically *-mala* (see §10.5.8); *-ngi* in this case, as in other cases to be discussed below, seems to have a genitive function. There is evidence also that it forms a base for further addition of inflectional suffixes: *nguthumalanginguda* 'from your elder brother', from BK; on the other hand we have *nguthumadali* 'his elder brother (ERG)', with no *-ngi*, from TG.

(74) *Kathi yundru   thayirla   ngapiri-malangi.*
      meat   2sg:ERG eat-PRES father-2KIN-GEN
      'You're eating your father's [part of the] meat.' (P21)

Note (for example, in (68) and (72)) that *nguthu* 'elder brother' + *-ngi* is *nguthingi*, not **nguthungi*. This vowel change does not apply with other terms with final /u/, such as *kaku* 'elder sister' (*kakungi* 'my sister') or *tharu* 'father-in-law' (*tharungi*).

There are indications that there is an accusative suffix *-nyi* usable with the second/third person kin proprietive. This was heard on several occasions and always on the object of a transitive verb, although there are occasions (see (10-38, 11-46)) when it did not appear.

(75) *Wawathikana yundru   muduwa, ngama-malanyi?*
      see-return-IP 2sg:ERG child   mother's brother-2KIN-ACC
      'Did you [child] go and see your uncle?' (X12)

(76) *Pula   thawanhana ngama-maladinyitji   wawathikanga?*
      3du:NOM go-NP   mother's.brother-3KIN-ACC-EMPH see-return-FUT
      'Did those two kids go and see their uncle?' (X12)

A suffix *-kaka* occurs in a phrase, not part of a coherent sentence, in text. I have no idea what it might mean.

(77) *Nguthungama-kaka,   nga   ngarndrikaku-kaka*
      elder.brother-mother's.brother-?   then   mother-elder.sister-?
      (probably) 'male relatives and female relatives' (E5)

9.3 Personal names

Only a handful of personal names are known and very little information is available on their morphology. It appears that they may not have been used often; people were addressed or referred to by means of kinship terms or by such terms as *karrukarru* 'old man' (not necessarily confined to old men, it appears, when used as a term of address). I was able to elicit sentences containing personal names and a vocative form of a personal name (with a distorted final vowel), but this should not be taken as indicating that personal names were used in these ways in practice; they are not commonly so used in still viable Central Australian languages. Reuther says that names of men ended in *-na* and names of women ended in *-ni* or *-nu*. This (a final *-ni* in the particular case) applied to only one of the five names I was able to collect. Compare *-nha* added to proper nouns in Arabana/ Wangkangurru (Hercus 1994:88).

Nominal inflection 87

One example is available of a suffix *-ngi*, homophonous with the first person kin proprietive but apparently a separate morpheme (see §9.13) and the same as that used in (74) and referred to also in §9.4, §9.5 and (the same morpheme?) in §9.6. It functions as a genitive.

(78)   *Ay Man.gilingi   nhutjadu.*
       eh Benny.Kerwin-GEN 3sg:NOM:THERE
       'That belongs to Benny.' (T14)

9.4 Dual and plural nouns

Dual is optionally marked on nouns by the suffix *-thili* (see §10.5.1) and plural by the suffix *-ndja* (see §10.5.2). *-ngi* may be added to such forms, and functions as a genitive, and (perhaps optionally) as a base for other bound forms. (Compare the use of the genitive as a base for other bound forms with pronouns (§9.8)). Examples are:

(79)   *Nganyi yandhayandhana pulganiyi,   yiwa-thilingiyi.*
       1sg:NOM talk-talk-IP   3du:GEN-LOC woman-DU-GEN-LOC
       'I talked to those two women.' (X6)

(80)   *karrundjangi*
       man-PL-GEN
       'belonging to those men' (B18)

(81)   *Muduwa yabali   nhutjadu   karrundjangiyitji.*
       child   fear-INST 3sg:NOM:THERE man-PL-GEN-LOC-EMPH
       'That kid's frightened of all those men.' (B18)

The construction in (81) can be contrasted with that (accepted and repeated) in:

(82)   *yadamanindjayi*
       horse-PL-LOC
       'with a mob of horses' (B24)

Reuther gives an accusative suffix *-na* (presumably *-nha*) for dual nouns but not for singular or plural. There is no information on this for the modern language.

9.5 The personal interrogative

The personal interrogative *wara* 'who?' (which also functions as a personal indefinite pronoun 'someone') differs in its morphology from common nouns in some respects:

(a)   it has a optional nominative (absolutive) case marker *-nu*, together with a suppletive nominative form *warnu*, but the unmarked form *wara* also may be used (83, 84);

(b)   the operative suffix is *-lu* (although there is one example of *warali*) and there is a suppletive operative form *warlu* (85);

(c)   the suffix *-ngi* functions as a genitive and also forms a base form to which other inflectional affixes can be added ((86); compare §9.4).

Examples will be found in the dictionary entries for *wara* (and subentries), *warlu* and *warnu*. Additional examples are:

88 *Chapter 9*

(83) Yinha yiwayi   yini   yandhayandha-nhanatji; ngathu   yulhu
    ?   woman-LOC 2sg:NOM   talk-talk-NP-EMPH   1sg:ERG   2du:ACC

   wawanhana yandhayandha-rlayi. Warnu   ngala   nhani?
   see-NP   talk-talk-SIM   who-NOM   then   3sg:fem:NOM
   'You were talking to a woman; I saw the two of you talking. Well, who was she?'
   (P7)

(84) Wara ngala yinha   nhulu   parndri-nhanatji?
    who   then   3sg:ACC   3sg:ERG kill-NP-EMPH
   'Who did he kill?' (B19)

(85) Walya ngathu   yintjadu   muduwa parndrina; warlu   kara
    not   1sg:ERG   3sg:ACC:THERE   child   hit-IP   who:ERG   maybe

   yintjadu   parndrina.
   3sg:ACC:THERE   hit-IP
   'I didn't hit him, someone else did.' (P15)

(86) Warangi-nguda yundru   mandrina?
    who-GEN-ABL   2sg:ERG   get-IP
   'Who did you take it from?' (B19)

   (Note that MN did not accept *waranginguda*, but said *waranguda*.)

(87) Waranyadi   nhani?
    who-like   3sg:fem:NOM
   'Who's she like?' (B19) (*Waranyadi* accepted and used)

9.6 Location nouns

Location nouns are those which normally combine only with the dative (with allative function usually) and ablative inflections, and do not combine with the other semantically appropriate inflection — locative. (Occasionally I suggested locative inflections on place names and they were accepted, but they were not used by informants except after *-ngi*, as noted below.)

It may possibly be appropriate to regard place names as a separate subclass of nouns, on the basis of occurrences of *-ngi*. This was heard only from TG, on two occasions, with locative *-yi* following, as in (89). I discussed these examples on occasions with BK; his responses were inconsistent (partly due perhaps to his hearing problem) but it seemed that he did not understand them. It could be that *-ngi* is dative and locative *-yi* follows it.

Note that the locative suffix *-yi* has been used as a stem formative in some place names, e.g. *Mingkayi* 'Minkie', from *mingka* 'hole' (see also §10.5.11). See also §10.3 for some discussion of the etymology of a few place names. A list of place names is given in the dictionary.

Nominative forms of location names refer to location in space or time, as appropriate.

(88) Ngarndrili   nganha   ngathani-ka-lapurra,   Malkanpatji.
    mother-ERG 1sg:ACC   child.(of.woman)-CAUS-REMP   Innamincka-EMPH
   'I was born at Innamincka.' (W7)

(89) *Dritji parrkulu nganyi nhinanga Ngarndaparlungiyi.*
    sun   two   1sg:NOM sit-FUT Arrabury-GEN-LOC
    'I'm going to stop at Arrabury for two days.' (T9)

(90) *Mirni nganyi nhinanga, matja thawini-ngadi.*
    wait 1sg:NOM sit-FUT long.time go-GER-DAT
    'I'm not going for a long time yet.' (P10)

(91) *Marripathi nganyi thawanga.*
    tomorrow 1sg:NOM go-FUT
    'I'm going away tomorrow.' (P9)

(92) *Thawarla ngani Malkanpa-ngadi.*
    go-PRES 1pl:ex:NOM Innamincka-DAT
    'We're going to Innamincka.' (T5)

(93) *Kathi marripathi-ngadi nhutjadu.*
    meat tomorrow-DAT 3sg:NOM:THERE
    'That meat's for tomorrow.' (R7)

(94) *Yundra nhuniyi Kinipapa-ngudatji.*
    far   3sg:NOM-HERE Cooper's Creek-ABL-EMPH
    'This place is a long way from Cooper's Creek.' (R7)

(but see (12-25))

(95) *Ngidlali nganyi, yundra-nguda, thawawarra-nhana.*
    sorry.for 1sg:NOM far-ABL go-arrive-NP
    'I'm sorry for [them] having to come so far.' (P31)

9.7 Directional terminology

The names of the four points of the compass are:

             North   *karawarra*

West *dritjiwindrini*   East *dritjirdunka,*
                                                witjukura

             South   *mulhapundra* (IY),
                     wakarramuku (SY, Yw)

The etymology of three of these is transparent: *dritjiwindrini* is 'sun-enter-GER', *dritjirdunka* is 'sun-go.out' and *mulhapundra* 'face (or nose)-cold'. Of the others, *warra*, as in *karrawarra*, means 'side', *witjukura* contains *witju* 'finger' and *kura* 'storm', and *wakarramuku* is close to a compound of *wakarri* 'nape' and *muku* 'bone'.

These differ from other nouns in that:

(a) they combine with only the locational inflectional suffixes, locative (no good examples, but accepted by BK), dative (with allative function), which is optional, and ablative;

(b) a form *-kadi*, in addition to *-ngadi*, has been noted for the dative. *(-kadi* is also the form that combines with *yila-* 'where?')

90   Chapter 9

The words *wannganyi* 'left' and *pinhani* 'right' seem to behave in the same way, except that BK did not accept the latter with a locative suffix (and was not asked about it with the former). 'Down' (*pandhi, ngari*) and 'up' (*thalka*) are adverbs and are discussed in §16.5.

The speakers had some difficulty remembering the directional names, and it may be that there was more morphology associated with them which has been lost. At times (as in (100)) *walpanggarra* 'north wind' was used because the speaker could not remember the word for 'north'.

(96) *Thawarla   nganyi   mulhapundra.*
      go-PRES   1sg:NOM   south
      'I'm going south.' (W8)

(97) *Ay, thawa-nhana nhunu   ay   mayi! Mulhapundra-ngadi.*
      eh   go-NP   3sg:NOM   eh   well   south-DAT
      'He's gone eh! South.' (W8)

(98) *Thawana   thana-waka   karawarra-kadi.*
      go-IP   3pl:NOM-over.there   north-DAT
      'They went north.' (T8)

(99) *Thawawarra-nhana   nhunuyi,   mulhapundra-nguda.*
      go-arrive-NP   3sg:NOM-HERE   south-ABL
      'He came from the south.' (W8)

(100) *walpanggarra   thadriyi*
      north (wind)   bank-LOC
      'on the north bank.' (X9)

Certain body-part words can be used as directionals and can then take the *-kadi* allomorph of the dative suffix. Data are scarce, but *durrukadi* '(shot him) from (or in?) the back' was given and *murnakadi* 'from the front' (*murna* 'chest') and *pangkithirrikadi* 'from the side' (*pangkithirri* 'ribs') were accepted. **Kandrakadi* 'from above' was not accepted; if you shot something from above *kandrangudali* would be used. (*Kandra* 'above' is, of course, not a body-part term.)

9.8 Singular personal pronouns

Inflectional affixes used with pronouns (both personal and demonstrative — §9.8 to §9.11) can be divided into two groups:

(i)   nominative, operative (if any), accusative, and genitive, which are either based on the nominative pronoun stem or are suppletive;

(ii) dative, locative, ablative and aversive, which use the same suffixes as nouns but add them to the genitive form of the pronoun.

Examples in this section are sometimes given using non-singular personal pronouns if they behave in the same way with regard to the point under discussion.

(a) Nominative

The nominative case form of singular personal pronouns is used as subject of an intransitive or reflexive sentence and the topic of a verbless sentence — a subset of the functions of nominative of nouns. Examples can be found in the dictionary entries for *nganyi* and *yini*; see also, among many, (7-13, 14, 15).

(b) Operative

The operative (or ergative) case form of singular personal pronouns is used as the subject of a transitive sentence.

(101) *Minha-ngadi nganha yundru parndrineyey?*
what-DAT 1sg:ACC 2sg:ERG hit-IP-DISTORT
'Why did you hit me?' (T11)

A combined first person singular operative–second person or demonstrative (non-feminine) singular accusative pronoun has been noted on several occasions. Forms noted are *ngathuna* '1sg:ERG-2sg:ACC' (see 11-9), *ngathunha* and *ngathinha* '1sg:ERG-3sg:ACC', and *ngathinhayi* '1sg:ERG-3sg:ACC-HERE'. Note that sometimes the final *u* of *ngathu* is retained and the initial *yi* of the second pronoun dropped, and sometimes the final *u* of *ngathu* and the initial *y* of the other pronoun are dropped.

(102) *Parndripada-nhana nganha nhulu, ngathunha*
hit-in-NP 1sg:ACC 3sg:ERG 1sg:ERG-3sg:ACC

parndrithika-nhana-ldrangu.
hit-return-NP-BUT-THEN
'He hit me, and I hit him back.' (B14-15)

(103) *Ngathinha ngana-nhana thangguthalkini-ngadi.*
1sg:ERG-3sg:ACC tell-NP stand-up-GER-DAT
'I told him to stand up.' (B15)

(104) *Pudlupudlu ngathinhayi thilpathilparla.*
can't-can't 1sg:ERG-3sg:ACC-HERE chase-chase-PRES
'I can't make him [a horse] go.' (T12)

(c) Accusative

The accusative pronoun is used to mark the object of a transitive verb. (101) illustrates it, as do:

(105) *Kuluwali nganha drakana.*
needlewood-ERG 1sg:ACC pierce-IP
'The needlewood pricked me.' (B3)

(106) *Wawa-yukarranga ngathu yulhu nguthu-ngurru.*
see-at.night-FUT 1sg:ERG 2du:ACC elder.brother-COM
'I'll see you and your brother tonight.' (B14)

See (b) in §9 for incorporation of the second person singular accusative pronoun as a suffix on the first person operative pronoun.

(d) Genitive

The genitive form of a pronoun is used to denote possession, and also forms a stem to which the dative, locative, ablative and aversive suffixes may be added. Since the genitive pronoun may also function as and be inflected as a noun (e.g. in (43)–(47)), confusion could arise between inflected forms of the pronoun, using the genitive as a base, and inflected forms of the genitive pronoun. For example, *ngakanipuru* could mean 'because of me' or 'because of mine'.

(107) *Nhunuyi   yulgani?*
      3sg:NOM-HERE 2du:GEN
      'Does this belong to you two?' (P26)

(108) *Nguthu   ngakani   yidlanggiyi?*
      elder.brother 1sg:GEN where-LOC
      'Where's my brother?' (T2)

The genitive is sometimes used where a dative would seem more appropriate:

(109) *Kubala ngathu   parrkulu mandrithikarla ngalungga.*
      bottle   1sg:ERG two   get-return-PRES   1du:in:GEN
      'I'll bring a couple of bottles home for you and me.' (C5)

Examples of the use of the genitive pronoun as a noun include:

(110) *Pandi yingganili   mathana ngakani   thirrirnanga pula.*
      dog   2sg:GEN-ERG bite-IP   1sg:GEN   fight-CONT   3du:NOM
      'Your dog bit mine in a fight.' (B15)

(111) *Warnu   kara   nhunuyi   thawarla, ngatjada ngalunggani-ngadi.*
      who-NOM maybe 3sg:NOM-HERE go-PRES   camp   1du:in:GEN-DAT
      'Someone's coming to our camp.' (C5)

(e) Dative

The dative case suffix is *-ngadi*, affixed to the genitive. It is rarely heard; directional adverbs or demonstratives are usually used if the function is allative.

(112) *Ngathu yina   yurarla   wawini-ngaditji, karna   yina kala,*
      1sg:ERG 2sg:ACC want-PRES see-GER-DAT-EMPH person EMPH there(?)

      ngakani-ngadi.
      1sg:GEN-DAT
      'I want you to see that man, for me.' (R3)

(113) *Walypala-ngadi mulhudu madlantji   nganungga-ngaditji.*
      white.man-DAT tucker   bad   1pl:in:GEN-DAT-EMPH
      'Whitefellows' tucker is no good for us.' (R5)

(f) Locative

The locative suffix is *-yi*, as for nouns, and is affixed to the genitive form. It functions as for nouns.

(114) *Muduwa yini   wanthi-yindrirla, nhunuyi   nhinarla ngalinggayi.*
      child   2sg:NOM look.for-RR-PRES 3sg:NOM-HERE sit-PRES   1du:ex:GEN-LOC
      "You're looking for the boy; he's sitting down here with me and him." (W5)

(115) *Muduwa   nhutjadu   winkawindrina   nganinggayi.*
      child   3sg:NOM:THERE   disappear-enter-IP 1pl:ex:GEN-LOC
      'That kid ran away from us.' (X10, accepted)

(116) *Manmarla   nhutjadu   ngakaniyi.*
      tell.a.lie-PRES 3sg:NOM:THERE   1sg:GEN-LOC
      'He's telling me a lie.' (C2)

(g) Ablative

The ablative suffix is *-nguda*, attached to the genitive. It is rarely heard; where it might be expected *-puru* (aversive) or *-yi* (locative) are used; see (115) and (118).

(117) *Ngalingga-nguda   nhunu   thawawindrina.*
      1du:ex:GEN-ABL   3sg:NOM   go-enter-IP
      'He went away from us two.' (P26)

(h) Aversive

The aversive suffix for pronouns, as for nouns, is *-puru*, but it is added to the genitive form of the pronoun. Its function is the same; no examples of the type of (119) have been noted for nouns but it is very likely that they would occur. Compare (118) with (115) and (119); the nature of the differences is not clear.

(118) *Thawawindrirla   nhunu   ngalungga-puru.*
      go-enter-PRES   3sg:NOM 1du:in:GEN-AVER
      'He's walking away from us.' (B24)

(119) *Walya ngala nhutjadu   mardri   ngakani-puru.*
      not   then 3sg:NOM:THERE   heavy   1sg:GEN-AVER
      'It's not too heavy for me.' (P2)

9.9 Non-singular personal pronouns

Non-singular personal pronouns differ in their morphology from singular personal pronouns in that they have no operative case form. The nominative form is therefore used for subject of a transitive verb as well as for the other functions it fulfils for the singular pronouns.

(120) *Wawana ngali   yintjadu.*
      see-IP 1du:ex:NOM 3sg:ACC:THERE
      'We saw him.' (T3)

(121) *Warnu yuda   thawawarrana?*
      who   2pl:NOM   go-arrive-IP
      'Who are you lot [who have] come here?' (W5)

(122) *Dan.ga-nhanangu yuda?*
      find-NP-YET   2pl:NOM
      "Did you fellows find him?" (P7)

A second distinction, not fully understood, is that the first person non-singular pronouns have two genitive forms, apparently the same in meaning. The longer form is distinguished by an affix *-ni*. This was discussed on two occasions with BK, who said that there was no difference. Only the longer form is recorded from TG (but this means only three words). BK usually used the shorter form. Note that the first and second person singular genitive pronouns have an invariable final *-ni*, and the demonstrative pronoun genitive forms often have it (see §9.10.1).

A word which seems to be *thanngamalala* appears in an incomprehensible sentence during a text. The first part can be compared to *thanngani* '3pl:GEN' while the *-mala* is like the second/third person kin proprietive (see §10.5.8). The speaker was thinking of the topic of kinship. I am not able to explain the word.

9.10 Inflection of third person and demonstrative pronouns and *yarndu*

The demonstrative/third person pronouns are characterised by deictic suffixes, which are optional with the third person pronouns and *yarndu* 'how, in this way' but seem to be obligatory with the demonstrative pronouns. Omission of these suffixes, where they are optional, occurs when the deixis has already been specified or when it cannot be specified (e.g. in some questions) as well as on some occasions when there seems to be no conditioning factor.

The deictic suffixes precede separable inflectional affixes (dative, locative, ablative, aversive) and follow other case forms (which cannot be segmented into stem and affix); see (133) for a word in which genitive marking precedes the deictic suffix and a locative suffix follows it.

The deictic suffixes are, basically, *-yi* 'here, this one', *-du (-ku* in Yw) 'there, that one' (the unmarked form), *-wa* 'there, that one' (or 'over there' in Yw) and *-kala* (not attested in Yw) which is rare but seems to be anaphoric on personal pronouns, as in *Nhunukala!* 'That's the one [whose name I was trying to remember]!', and 'round about' on demonstratives. Yw also has *-rra* 'distant'.

The unmarked form on IY pronouns does not occur often as 'stem + *-du*' but has idiosyncratic forms, comprising a shortened form of the stem suffixed with *-tjadu*, which, at least with some case forms, are far more common. IY-*wa*, not used much on pronouns and not attested with *yarndu*, was said once to be 'further away than *-du*', but no difference has been noted between their functions with other demonstratives, with which *-wa* is the more common; it is also much more common with pronouns in Yw than in IY.

Note also that *yarndu* may be suffixed to the interrogative root *yila-* 'where', to form the interrogative *yilayarndu* (~ [ilá.ɟəndu]) 'how'; see §9.11. *Yarndu* also occurs as a suffix following the optative verb mood marker *-malka*, with an unknown function, and in one example suffixed to a noun stem, also with unknown function. (See §9.10.4, footnote)

9.10.1 Singular third person pronoun inflection

Apart from the addition of the deictic suffixes these pronouns are inflected as are the singular personal pronouns, and the various inflected forms have similar functions. The following examples, which include also examples of non-singular third person pronouns where the form and function are as for the singular pronouns, illustrate the various cases.

Nominal inflection 95

(a) Nominative

(123) *Ngapa nhutjadu yibini-ngadi.*
water 3sg:NOM:THERE drink-GER-DAT
'That water's for drinking.' (W7)

(124) *Warrayi nhanudu nhinanhina-pada kanguyi.*
it's.all.right 3sg:fem:NOM-THERE sit-sit-in warm-LOC
"Let her stop in the warm." (T14)

(Repeated with *nhatjadu* instead of *nhanudu*.)

(b) Operative

(125) *Nhandu nhandra wawarla wadlumpadali.*
horse 3sg:fem:ERG look-PRES white.woman-ERG
"That's Mrs Geiger looking at the horses." (lit. 'That white woman is ...') (T9)

(c) Accusative

(126) *Ngathu yinha nganana nhinapandhini-ngadi.*
1sg:ERG 3sg:ACC tell-IP sit-down-GER-DAT
'I told him to sit down.' (W8)

(127) *Ngarru mulha malka ngathu thanhayi pardrarla nhanggani.*
only face mark 1sg:ERG 3pl:ACC-HERE hold-PRES 3sg:fem:GEN
'I've only got these photos of hers.' (W3)

For combined forms in which the accusative form of the singular non-feminine demonstrative/third person pronoun is suffixed to the operative form of the first person singular pronoun, see (b) in §9.8.

(d) Genitive

It appears that the suffix *-ni* is always present except when the deictic suffix *-tjadu* 'there' is used, when it is optional; compare (128) and (130).

(128) *Mardra mani nhangga-tjadu nhunuyi.*
stone money 3sg:fem:GEN-THERE 3sg:NOM-HERE
'This money belongs to her.' (B24)

(129) *Ngalingga nhunggani.*
1du:ex:GEN 3sg:GEN
'[It] belongs to me and him.' (P25)

Omission of a locative suffix from the pronoun constituent of a noun phrase has resulted in a genitive demonstrative/third person pronoun in:

(130) *Ngathu wakanirla thanngani-tjadu kathi tjipiyitji.*
1sg:ERG work-PRES 3pl:GEN-THERE animal sheep-LOC-EMPH
'I've been working with those sheep.' (W7)

The construction exemplified below, with the pronoun given twice, first with the genitive specified and then with the deictic specification, has been heard only once, and

96   *Chapter 9*

may be an alternative to the form with both specified together. As a translation of 'It belongs to that lot over there' BK gave

(131) *Thannga-tjadu,   or   thanngani thanadu,   nhutjadu.*
      3pl:GEN-THERE or 3pl:GEN   3pl:NOM-THERE 3sg:NOM:THERE (P25)

However, it is not completely clear that this is what it means; *thanngani thanadu* may mean 'those belong to them'.

(e) Dative

There are no suitable examples.

(f) Locative

As the locative suffix *-yi* is the same as the deictic suffix *-yi* 'here', a three-way ambiguity is possible. For example, *pulganiyi* may mean 'belonging to these two here' ('3du:GEN-HERE') 'with these two' ('3du:GEN-LOC') or 'with their (dual)' ('3du:GEN-LOC'), deixis being unspecified in the last two cases, which differ in that the former is functioning as a pronoun and the latter as a possessive adjective or noun. It appears that it is not possible to specify locative and 'here' in the one word. In (132) 'here' is specified in a separate word.

(132) *Nhinggiyi   nganyi   nhinanhinanga nhungganiyi.*
      location-HERE 1sg:NOM sit-sit-FUT   3sg:GEN-LOC
      'I'm going to sit down with this fellow here.' (P25)

(133) *Yandhayandharla nganyi   thannga-tjaduyi.*
      talk-talk-PRES   1sg:NOM 3pl:GEN-THERE-LOC
      'I'm talking to them.' (T3)

In the following example the locative suffix has been added to the nominative form, not to the genitive. There are no other such examples and this may be an error.

(134) *Ngali   nhinarla nhinggiyi   yandhayandhanga nhutjaduyi.*
      1du:ex:NOM sit-PRES location-HERE talk-talk-FUT   3sg:NOM:THERE-LOC
      'We're sitting here talking to that [tape recorder].' (W6, and see X11)

(g) Ablative

There are no suitable examples.

(h) Aversive

There are very few examples.

(135) *Ngapiri ngakani, yabali   nganyi   nhunggani-puru.*
      father   1sg:GEN fear-INST 1sg:NOM 3sg:GEN-AVER
      "I'm frightened of my dad." (W6)

9.10.2 Non-singular third person pronoun inflection

The non-singular pronouns differ from the singular only in that they do not have an operative case form, and so the nominative case form functions as subject of a transitive verb (as well as other functions it has for the singular pronouns).

(136) *Walypawalypala   yina   thanayitji.*
like.white.men   EMPH   3pl:NOM-HERE-EMPH
'They're just like white men.' (W3)

(137) *Walypalatji,   walyaldra   thanayi   yarndu-kalatji   nhina-lapurra.*
white.man-EMPH   not-BUT   3pl:NOM-HERE   how-ABOUT-EMPH   sit-REMP
'The white fellows (on the other hand) never lived like that.' (W10)

(138) *Ngaru ngakani   ngaranga   thanayi   muduwalitji.*
voice 1sg:GEN   hear-FUT   3pl:NOM-HERE   child-ERG-EMPH
'These kids will hear my voice [on the tape, "when I'm dead and gone"].' (W3)

9.10.3 Inflection of demonstrative pronouns

The demonstratives *nhinggi-* ~ *nhinggu-* and *nhuku-* are probably inflected only for dative and ablative and so correspond to the location nouns (§9.6). They are never attested as free forms; they occur with deictic suffixes (*-yi* in (139, 140), the latter with ablative, (144) with dative, and (146, 147); *-wa* in (141, 148); *-du* in (143) and, with dative, (144); *-kala* in (145, 149)). There is one doubtful example (11-1) of *nhinggi-* with no deictic suffixed with *-ngu* 'yet, still, then', which is also attested following the deictic *-kala* in (149, 151, 152). The other demonstratives are extremely rare and no inflected forms have been noted; however, it is assumed that (if these demonstratives are genuine) such forms would exist.

The following are examples of *nhinggi-* ~ *nhinggu-* (*nhinggi-* occurs with *-yi* and *-wa*, *nhinggu-* with *-du*). For some others see (165), (10-12), (11-1) and (18-28). Note the phrase *nhinggiwa thalka* 'up there' in (141); *nhinggiwa ngari* 'down there' also is attested.

(139) *Walya ngandra   yurarla   paldrini-ngadi nhinggiyi.*
not   1pl:in:NOM   want-PRES   die-GER-DAT   location-HERE
'We don't want [him] to die here.' (B25)

(140) *Nhinggiyi-ngudaldra   nhutjadutji.*
location-HERE-ABL-BUT   3sg:NOM:THERE-EMPH
'He's a local man.' (P30)

(141) *Minha ngana-lapurra yini,   nhinggiwa   thalka?*
what   do-REMP   2sg:NOM   location-THERE   up
"What were you doing up there?" (W7)

(asked of a person who had been away for a long time, and so, presumably, in a distant place)

(142) *Yiwa   thanadu   thirrirla   nhinggiwa   ngari.*
woman   3pl.NOM-THERE   fight-PRES   location-THERE   down
'Those women are fighting down there.' (W8)

98   Chapter 9

(143) Kurrapandhi nhinggudu   thanuthanu.
      put-down   location-THERE   in.the.middle
      'Put it down there, in the middle.' (P4)

(144) *Muduwa thana   mini-thikathikarla,   nhinggudu-ngadi   waka,*
      child   3pl:NOM run-everywhere-PRES   location-THERE-DAT   over.there

      minithikawarrandji   nhinggiyi-ngadila.
      run-return-arrive-SEQ   location-HERE-DAT-EMPH
      'Those kids are running about; they run over there and run back here.' (P13)

(145) *Ngarndaparlu nganyi   waka-na-nhukada,   nhinggi-kala.*
      Arrabury   1sg:NOM   work-INCH(?)-RECP   location-ABOUT
      'I worked on Arrabury before.' (W7)

Examples of *nhuku-*, which is uncommon, follow. Note the repetition of a phrase with nhukuwa replaced with *nhinggiwa* in (148).

(146) *Wadana   ngathu   thawawarrini-ngadi   kara   nhukuyi   thana,*
      wait-IP   1sg:ERG   go-arrive-GER-DAT   maybe   location-HERE   3pl:NOM

      ay paningu.
      eh   none-YET
      'I waited for them to come, but nobody came.' (P15)

(147) *Pulyala   kara   nhukuyi   nhunu   wathitji,*
      small-EMPH   maybe   location-HERE   3sg:NOM   machine-EMPH

      yandhayandha-rlayitji nganyi,   ngana-rnangatji   yunhu.
      talk-talk-SIM-EMPH   1sg:NOM   tell-CONT-EMPH   2pl:ACC
      'There must be only a little bit of tape left now, for me to talk to you fellows.' (D6)

(148) *Pulganiyi   nhunu   nhinanhinarla   nhukuwa,   nhinggiwa*
      3du:GEN-LOC   3sg:NOM   sit-sit-PRES   location-THERE   location-THERE

      nhunu.
      3sg:NOM
      'He's with them two, over there.' (W5)

(149) *Ngala   nhuku-kalangu,   nhunu   thawathawarla   kara.*
      then   location-ABOUT-YET   3sg:NOM   walk-walk-PRES   maybe
      "He must be walking around somewhere." (P4)

(150) *Walya thana   thirri-padipadinitji,   pani, ngarru pinyayi.   Karna   thula*
      not   3pl:NOM   fight-HAB-GER-EMPH   not   only   war-LOC   person   stranger

      nhukuwa-nguda   yada   thawa-rnanga   parndrithikangatji.   Minhayatji
      location-THERE-ABL   hither   go-CONT   kill-return-FUT-EMPH   what-EMPH

      pinyalitji.
      war-INST-EMPH
      'They never used to fight, except in a war. Strangers would come from over there [in their country] to kill and then go back. "That's what they used to call war."' (W10)

See also (12-25) and (S10-35).

The only examples of *nhunggu-* ~ *nhungku-*, both with deictic *-kala*, are the one in the dictionary entry and the following. This could be a variant of *nhinggi-* ~ *nhinggu-*.

(151) *Ngalaaku,   yidlanggi   kara   nhunu   nhinanga,   nhunggu-kalangu.*
      I.don't.know where   maybe   3sg:NOM   sit-FUT   location-ABOUT-YET
      "He's round about there sitting down somewhere." (P4) ['sitting down' = 'living']

The only example of *nhunuku-* is:

(152) *Mayi, wawathikana   yundru   pani?   Yidlayi   nhunuku--kalangu   thana?*
      well   see-return-IP 2sg:ERG   none   where-LOC   location-ABOUT-YET   3pl:NOM
      "Well, did you see anybody? Whereabouts are they?" (E7)

9.10.4 Yarndu

Yarndu is included in this section because it combines with the same deictic suffixes as the demonstratives; it has not been noted in combination with any inflectional affixes, although it is thought that it might combine with the ablative, thus being similar to those nouns denoting compass points.

The following examples illustrate the use of *yarndu*; it has no suffixation in (153); deictic *-yi* in (17-15); deictic *-du* in (154, 155) with *-ngu* 'yet, still, then' in the latter, and (17-15); and *-kala* in (137, 156). See also (12-25) and (18-46).

(153) *Walya nhulu   kilka-nhana, minha   ngana-rnanga kara   nhunu.   Walya*
      not   3sg:ERG   know-NP   what   do-CONT   maybe   3sg:NOM not

      yina   nganha   nhulu   dranyini-ngadi.   Yarndu   nganha
      EMPH   1sg:ACC   3sg:ERG   hit(throwing)-GER-DAT   how   1sg:ACC

      nhulu   dranyi-nhanatji.
      3sg:ERG   hit(throwing)-NP-EMPH
      'He didn't know what he was doing. He didn't intend to hit me. That's how he came to hit me.' (P5)

(154) *Walya yarndudutji   yandha!*
      not   how-THERE-EMPH   talk
      'Don't talk about that!' (P30)

(155) *Ngurra   nhutjadu   yandharla   yarndudungu.*
      always   3sg:NOM:THERE   talk-PRES   how-THERE-YET
      'He always talks that way.' (B22)

(156) *Wathi windra ngathu   warrka-nhana kandraldra, walya ngathu*
      tree   spear   1sg:ERG   throw-NP   top-BUT   not   1sg:ERG

      warrka-padipadini   yarndu-kalatji.
      throw-HAB-GER   how-ABOUT-EMPH
      'I threw the spear very high; I never used to throw it like that.' (P14)

100 *Chapter 9*

See the next section for *-yarndu* as a bound morpheme, and §11.6 for other uses of a morpheme with the same form.[2]

9.11 The interrogative *yila-*

The stem *yila-* ~ *yidla-* 'where?' has not been noted as a free form but occurs in at least the following inflected or combined forms:

yidlayi 'where at? (locative), noted only once;

yilanguda ~ *yidlanguda* 'where from?' (ablative) (see *yidlanguda* dictionary entry);

yilakadi ~ *yidlakadi* 'where?' (allative) (see both dictionary entries);

yilanggi ~ *yidlanggi* 'where?' (unmarked, locative) (157, 158);

yilanggiyi ~ *yidlanggiyi* 'where at?' (locative), uncommon, see *yidlanggiyi* dictionary entry;

yilangginguda ~ *yidlangginguda* 'where from?' (ablative) (159);

yilayarndu ~ *yidlayarndu* 'how?', 'which way?' (usually heard [ilá̪ɭəɳɖu] or [ilá̪ɭəndu] or even [ilá̪ɭənu]) (cf. *yarndu*, §9.10.4) (160, 161).

Note that all the above forms can function as indefinite pronouns as well as interrogative pronouns, e.g. 'somewhere', 'I don't know where.'

The frequency of the prestopped lateral varies with different forms; thus, for example, *yidlakadi* is quite uncommon and *yilakadi* very common, but *yidlanggi* is more common than *yilanggi*.

No meaning or function is known for *-ngki*. Note that the dative affix *-kadi* has also been noted with a compass point; see §9.7.

Examples include those in dictionary entries (see under both *yidla* and *yila*) and the following. See also (152) for the only known occurrence of *yidlayi*.

(157) *Yilanggi kara nhunu.*
 where maybe 3sg:NOM
 'I don't know where he is.' (W3)

(158) *Yilanggi ngathu pitjidi ngakani kurrana?*
 where 1sg:ERG pitchery 1sg:GEN put-IP
 'Where did I put my pitchery?' (W9)

(159) *Minha karna yini; yilanggi-nguda yini thawawarrana?*
 what person you where-ABL 1sg:NOM go-arrive-IP
 'Who are you and where do you come from?' (W5)

(160) *Yidla-yarndu kara nhunuyi yandharla.*
 where-how maybe 3sg:NOM-HERE talk-PRES

 Ngarnmangarnma-yindri-rnanga.
 grip-grip-RR-CONT
 'He's got a funny way of talking. "Hard to follow."' (B22)

---

2   One additional use of *-yarndu*, noted only once and possibly an error, was heard in:
 Minhayi ngarrkana muduwa-yarndu ...?
 what do-IP child-?
 'What did you do to the baby ...?'

Nominal inflection 101

(161) *Yidla-yarndu walpatji wathinanga?*
 where-how humpy-EMPH build-APP(?)-FUT
 'How do you build a humpy?' (P15)

Yila wayini (*wayini* 'how many') has been heard once:

(162) *Thawa-nhana nhunu, parndri-thikathikanga, yila wayini kara*
 go-NP 3sg:NOM kill-everywhere-FUT where how.many maybe

 nhulu parndri-nhana, yilayarndu kara nhulu parndri-nhana
 3sg:ERG hit-NP where-how maybe 3sg:ERG hit-NP

 kara pani kara.
 maybe nothing maybe
 'He went out hunting. I wonder how many he got, how he got on, whether he killed anything or not.' (B17)

9.12 Inflection of noun phrases

Up to this point this chapter has mainly described the inflection of single-word noun phrases (but see §9.1.3.1 for an exception). Inflection of noun phrases of more than one word (if they are headed — not involving coordination) is similar except that it is not necessary for all nominal constituents of the phrase to carry the appropriate inflectional suffix.[3] In general, especially if the phrase is not discontinuous, the inflectional suffix will occur on the last constituent (see (163) and also (14), (43), (47), (7-38), (8-16) and many others), or if it is a disyllabic affix it may follow the last constituent as a phonetically separate word ((65) and (7-14)). Where one constituent of the phrase is a generic such as *kathi* 'animal', *wathi* 'tree' with a specific term following, it seems never to carry an inflectional suffix (although the same word when not functioning as a classifier would do so) (see (41) and (164)). The inflectional suffix may also, but much less commonly, fall on the first word of a phrase ((165) and (5-2)), on another word than first or last (166) or on more than one word ((13) and (167)); the latter example is probably better treated as having two separate phrases, one added to clarify the other, as suggested by the pause between them.

Where a phrase consisting of a noun and a non-singular pronoun functions as subject of a transitive sentence the noun must carry an operative suffix ((165) and (168) — the latter perhaps involving two phrases); the non-singular pronoun has no operative case form. Where a phrase containing a pronoun is object of a transitive verb the pronoun must appear in its accusative case form ((169, 170); note that in both of these cases the noun phrase concerned consists of two constituents which are in a part–whole relationship). Where a phrase containing a pronoun fills any syntactic position other than subject, object or instrument, the pronoun may occur in the appropriate inflected form (43, 10-27, 8-16) or in the genitive form if another constituent is appropriately inflected ((10-27, last two words) and (171); the latter was repeated with the pronoun fully inflected). In (172) the genitive is the appropriate inflected form of the pronoun.

Co-ordinate noun phrases are separately inflected (173).

---

[3] For clarity, the relevant phrases in the examples in this section are underlined.

102   *Chapter 9*

(163) *Thudathawa-nhana nganyi* <u>*padla mudlu malkirriyi*</u>.
  lie-go-NP 1sg:NOM place bean.tree many-LOC
  'I camped yesterday in a place with a lot of bean trees.' (B15)

(164) <u>*Kathi thukali*</u>, *walya* <u>*kalpurru thalpali*</u>, *walya darlamurruli, ngarru*
  animal mussel-INST not coolibah leaf-INST not   bark-INST only

  <u>*kathi thukali*</u> *mandrirnanga.*
  animal mussel-INST get-CONT
  '[They] picked up [the nardoo paste and spooned it into their mouths] with a mussel [shell], not with a coolibah leaf and not with bark, only with a mussel [shell].' (D4, =A172)

(165) *Nganyi thawanga* <u>*yinggani-ngadi(?) padla*</u>, *nga* <u>*karnali*</u>   <u>*thana*</u>
  1sg:NOM go-FARP 2sg:GEN-DAT(?) country then person-ERG 3pl:NOM

  nganha nganananga, mardrangumuyi karnapalha nhina-rlayi. Walya
  1sg:ACC tell-FUT   stone-cave-LOC man-bird sit-SIM   not

  nganyi thawanga nhinggi-kala-ngaditji.
  1sg:NOM go-FUT   location-ABOUT-DAT-EMPH
  'I went to your (?) country, and the people told me there was a devil in a cave there. I'm not going near there.' (P11)

(166) <u>*Pandi parluli*</u>   <u>*yinggani*</u> *nganha matha-nhana.*
  dog white-ERG 2sg:GEN 1sg:ACC bite-NP
  'That white dog of yours bit me.' (R1)

(167) *Ngapala*<u>*maka*</u> <u>*pirna*</u> *thangkakari, ya mardramitji mandringa*
  well fire big burn-CAUS-UNSP and stone-eye get-FUT

  <u>*malkirrili, karnakurnu-karnakurnuli.*</u>
  many-ERG person-one-person-one-ERG
  'They would build up a big fire and everyone would collect stones.' (D3, =A-135)

(168) *Thayi-yindringa palhatji yarndu thana   parndri-padipadini,*
  eat-RR-FUT bird-EMPH how 3pl:NOM kill-HAB-GER

  <u>*karnalitji.*</u>
  person-ERG-EMPH
  'That's how the Aborigines used to catch birds to eat.' (D2, =A-58)

(169) *Kabow! Yulawarrali* <u>*yina*</u>   *muna parndrina!*
  bang-DISTORT owl-ERG 2sg:ACC chest hit-IP
  "Bang! The night-owl hit you in the chest!" (W9)

(170) <u>*Pangkithirri*</u> *nhulu* <u>*yinha*</u> *warrkana-nhana.*
  rib 3sg:ERG 3sg:ACC throw-APP-NP
  'He speared it in the ribs.' (B14)

(171) *Kapada,* <u>*thiliyi*</u> *ngakani nhinanga.*
  come.on side-LOC 1sg:GEN sit-FUT
  'Sit down alongside of me.' (W5) (Repeated with *ngakaniyi* '1sg:GEN-LOC'.)

Nominal inflection 103

(172) *Yilanggi kara thana pipatji, <u>nhanggani man.garri-ngaditji</u>.*
where maybe 3pl:NOM paper-EMPH 3sg:fem:GEN girl-GEN-EMPH
'I don't know where those letters are, belonging to that girl.' (W3)

(173) <u>*Walypalali karnali ngapa yibarla kaldritji*</u> *pirna, yabayi,*
white.man-ERG person-ERG water drink-PRES bitter-EMPH big fear-LOC

minha-ngadi kara, kurrari ngananga.
what-DAT maybe mad do-FUT
"Make you cranky when you drink too much."
(A closer translation, but omitting *yabayi* whose function in the sentence is not clear, would be:
'White men and black men drink a lot of grog, ...; I don't know why, it makes them cranky.'
Two phrases are underlined here; the first two words form one and the others the other.) (W7)

(174) *Yila-kadi ngandra pakanga, <u>minha kirri-ngadi</u>?*
where-DAT 1pl:in:NOM carry-FUT what clever-DAT
"Where are we gonna take her? What doctor will we take her to?" (W2)

9.13 Double case-marking

The use of two case suffixes on a word is partly covered by §10.5.11, which deals with the formative function of certain nominal inflectional suffixes. Affixation of case suffixes to genitive (which is, of course, not distinct from the dative in Yandruwandha) and ablative nouns is common cross-linguistically and examples can be seen in §10.5.11 and as (62, 175, 176). In the case of the ablative, at least, it is not always clear that it is best to regard the noun stem + ablative as a stem in its own right; in (175) it is easy enough to translate this 'stem' as 'a place where rain had fallen' but in (176) it is not so easy — 'the one through the hole' does not seem adequate. This applies also when the noun stem involved is a gerund (nominalised verb) as in (177) and (15-38).

(175) *Thuda-nhana ngali ngandjarri-ngudayi.*
lie-NP 1du:ex:NOM rain-ABL-LOC
'We camped at a place where rain had fallen.' (X43)

(176) *Wirlpa-ngudali nhuliyi nganha wawarla.*
hole-ABL-ERG 3sg:ERG-HERE 1sg:ACC look-PRES
'He's peeping at me through a hole.' (B11)

(177) *Yarnduldrangu ngana-kaldri ngandjarri warlkini-ngudayi.*
how-BUT-YET do-again rain fall-GER-ABL-LOC
'They would do it the same way again after it had rained.' (E9)

9.14 The suffix -*ngi*

A suffix -*ngi* appears in Reuther's Jandruwanda with the following functions:

1. as the dative suffix on common nouns (including kinship terms and adjectives), contrasting with genitive -*ma* (a contrast which is not made in the modern language, where -*ma* in Yawarrawarrka, -*ngadi* in Yandruwandha is used for both functions). (Reuther does not detail the actual functions of these morphemes; see §9.1.4 for some details for the modern language.)
2. as the dative suffix on nouns marked (with -*thili*) as dual. The genitive is basically -*ma*, but the combined dual + genitive suffix is not *-*thilima* but -*thilkanama* (-*dilkanama* in Reuther's spelling).
3. as the first part of a compound morpheme marking genitive on nouns marked (with -*ndja*) as plural; the dative of these nouns is given not as -*ngi* but as -*ni* (whatever that might represent), while the corresponding genitive is -*ngima*.
4. as the dative of proper nouns (personal names) which, according to Reuther, have a final syllable -*na* if masculine, -*ni* or -*nu* if feminine. He gives -*ma* as the genitive of masculine names, but -*ni* for feminine.
5. as the first element of a compound suffix marking ergative (his 'ablative') on feminine personal names. It replaces the final -*ni* (in this case) of the name. The suffix is -*ngili*.
6. as a suffix translated 'own' on masculine kinship terms (thus *ngapati* 'father', *ngapatingi* 'own father'), which is presumed to be a first person kin proprietive. It precedes inflectional suffixes. Since the dative of kinship terms also is -*ngi* (see 1) the dative of 'own' terms ends in -*ngingi*. The genitive of male 'own' kinship terms can be thought of as -*ma* added to the dative; i.e. they end in -*ngingima*.
7. as the first element of a compound suffix marking 'own' on feminine kinship terms; the second element is -*li* (thus *ngandri* 'mother', *ngandringili* 'own mother'). Inflectional suffixes (including -*ngi* dative and -*ma* genitive) follow.
8. as the dative of the second person plural pronoun. This is probably a mistake, as he has -*nji* (= -*nyi*) in this position for all other pronouns.
9. as a 'preposition' (i.e. a suffix) meaning 'in, on, after, to'. This may be a mistake too, as the present Yawarrawarrka locative suffix is -*nyi* or -*ni*.

In modern Yandruwandha -*ngi* has the following functions:

1. as the genitive (which includes dative function) of proper nouns, nouns marked for non-singular (dual or plural), and the personal interrogative *wara* 'who', and as the base for addition of other suffixes to these words. With *wara*, as with kinship terms, it is possible that the expected other inflectional suffix may be omitted, but there are no clear examples.
2. as a first person kin-proprietive suffix on kinship terms, which also may take the place of some other inflectional suffixes.
3. as a dative suffix (with at least genitive and benefactive functions) following the second and third person kin-proprietive suffix on kinship terms, and forming a base for further inflection (see §9.2, §10.5.8).

The data for modern Yandruwandha are quite incomplete and inconsistent and the above statement includes some assumptions; for example, that dative of dual is -*ngi*. This assumption is based on (79), in which the locative of a dual is -*ngi* plus the normal locative, -*yi*. Details, with examples, of modern (2) will be found in §9.2, while further details of (1) are found in §9.3, §9.4 and §9.6 and of (3) in §9.5.

These data are summarised in Table 9-1. There is little relevant information for Yawarrawarrka, so that column is mostly empty. The last two items in the Reuther Jandruwanda list, being probably mistakes, are omitted.

Table 9-1: Functions given for -*ngi*, and other affixes with these functions

Function	Jandruwanda	Yandruwandha	Yawarrawarrka
singular noun dative	-*ngi*	-*ngadi*	-*ma*
singular noun genitive	-*ma*	-*ngadi*	-*ma*
dual noun dative	-*thili-ngi*	-*thili-ngi*	
dual noun genitive	-*thilkanama*	-*thili-ngi*	
plural noun dative	-*ndja-ni*	-*ndja-ngi*	
plural noun genitive	-*ndja-ngi-ma*	-*ndja-ngi*	
proper noun dative	-*ngi*	-*ngi*	
proper noun genitive	-*ma* (masc.), -*ni* (fem.)	-*ngi*	
feminine proper noun ergative	*ni>ngi-li*		
'own' kin (masculine)	-*ngi*		
'my' kin		-*ngi*	
'own' kin (feminine)	-*ngi-li*		
'own' kin (masculine) dative	-*ngi-ngi*		
'own' kin (masculine) genitive	-*ngi-ngi-ma*		
'my' kin dative/genitive		-*ngi(?)*	
'own' kin (feminine) dative	-*ngi-li-ngi*		
'own' kin (feminine) genitive	-*ngi-li-ma*		
'who' dative	*wan(g)kananyi*	*wara-ngi*	*wara-ngi*
'who' genitive ('whose')	*wan(g)kana*	*wara-ngi*	*wara-ngi*
'your/his/her' kin dative/genitive		-*ngi*	

It is clear from Reuther's material that there are two morphemes involved here: -*ngi* as dative on certain classes of noun, and -*ngi* as marking first person possessor of kin. The kinship field, which probably earlier had quite complex morphology (to judge from comparisons with languages to the west and northwest), was not well remembered by the last speakers; this is a normal situation for last speakers in general.

Reuther's material gives no indication of -*ngi* on the personal interrogative, but the modern information in this case is clear and consistent (from MN as well as BK and TG) and is not doubted.

10 *Noun-stem formation*

Noun stems comprise:

(a) noun roots
(b) reduplicated noun roots
(c) combinations of two noun roots
(d) combinations of a noun root and a noun-stem formative
(e) combinations of a noun stem and an inflectional suffix
(f) combinations of a verb stem and a noun derivational suffix.

Group (e) words are rarely stems but there are a few examples.

10.1 Noun roots

The majority of noun roots are disyllabic; most of those of three syllables are believed or suspected to incorporate a no longer productive monosyllabic stem formative, while those of four syllables almost certainly are originally compounds (whether in Yandruwandha or in a language from which they were borrowed), although the components may not (now) exist in any other form in the language.

Trisyllabic roots include *parlaka* 'body', *tharralku* 'duck sp.' (a widespread word which may be a loan word in Yandruwandha), *tjiradi* 'gum (from tree)', *kadawa* 'bank', *karrawa* 'eaglehawk', *yunggudu* 'blood'. The more common final syllables of trisyllabic words, which may be former stem formatives, include /da/, in *maluda* 'shag' (or it may be *malurra*), *ngawada* 'light (in weight)', *ngatjada* 'camp', *nhukada* 'before', 'a day or two ago', *kapada* 'come here!'; /li/ in *Man.gili, Walkili, Warrguli* (all personal names), *marngali* 'sand goanna', *Mudlali* (placename), *nganggali* 'owner'; and /ni/ in *marnngani* 'crayfish', *kumani* 'pitchery bundle', *kanyini* 'mother's mother; daughter's child', *pinhani* 'right (hand)', *thapini* 'shoulder', *tjin.gini* 'beefwood (tree)', *walhini* 'adolescent boy'. The final syllable of the last group of words could possibly be related to the *-ni* ending on certain genitive pronouns (cf. §9.9), the occasional *-ni* occurring on *-mada* (§10.5.8) and/or the *-ni* of *ngathani* 'child of mother' (cf. *ngathalki* 'child of father').

Four-syllable stems which cannot, in the present state of knowledge, be further analysed, include *mangawarru* 'widow' (which may include an element *warru* 'white'), *karditjidi* 'cheek', *ngayimala* 'throat', *yuruwitja* 'horn', *mayikurru* 'rat', *karndilkatha* 'porcupine', *thilpirrutja* 'budgerigar', *drukambada* 'bullfrog', *Kinipapa* 'Coopers Creek', *kunuputha*

Noun stem formation 107

'dust' (perhaps including *putha* 'white'), *Yandruwandha*, the language name,[1] and others. Many of these (even the last) may be borrowed (as are such obvious examples as *putiyita* 'potato' and *thakumani* 'stockman'). Such words may be — as is the last — analysable in the language of origin.

There are a handful of unanalysable five-syllable roots, including *nyungumalinya* 'blind snake' and *Manngidrikani*, a personal name.

10.2 Reduplication

Reduplicated forms can be classified in two ways: on a semantic basis, according to the relationship between the meaning of the simple form (if any) and that of the reduplicated form; and on a structural basis between the simple and reduplicated forms. These classifications intersect in Yandruwandha. The former will be dealt with first.

The biggest class is that in which the simple form is not known to exist, either free or combined with any other (different) morpheme. Words in this class include *pirripirri* 'spirit, white man', *putjaputja* 'hawk sp.', *yaliyali* 'lizard sp.', *thanpathanpa* 'dotterel', *kalipilhipilhi* 'butterfly', *pirtipirti* 'red', *Pulupulu* (a placename), *palgupalgu* '(lean) meat', *kurtukurtu* 'rough'. Some of these names would be imitative of the sound of the creature named, such as *thindrithindri* 'willy wagtail'.

In another class the reduplicated form seems to be simply an alternative to the simple form. Examples are *pangga(pangga)* 'young man', *parru(parru)* 'yellow', *(pula)pulayarra* 'green' and *(kurra)kurrari* 'mad'.

In a third class the reduplicated form has the same meaning as the simple form, but the latter occurs only in compounds or derived forms. Thus *karlukarlu* 'fish', *karlukapi* 'fish sp.', *paltjapaltja* 'strong', *paltjaka* 'to strengthen', *kudhikudhi* 'hidden', *kudhithika* 'to go and hide'. Very likely also *pirripirri* 'spirit', *pirritjampa* 'to be tired'.

In a fourth class the reduplication modifies the meaning of the simple form; there are several subclasses according to the nature of the modification. In the major subclass the meaning is 'having a quality that is typical of the thing denoted by the simple form, but to a lesser degree'; thus the reduplicated form normally functions as an adjective, qualifying a noun. Examples are *padlapadla* 'dirty' from *padla* 'dirt, ground', *thurrpathurrpa* 'ashy, covered with ashes' from *thurrpa* 'ashes', *makamaka* 'hot' from *maka* 'fire', *malkamalka* 'piebald' from *malka* 'a mark', *paladi-paladi* 'different' from *paladi* 'individual', *ngabangaba* 'wet' from *ngapa* 'water', *thakuthakurru* 'slowly' from *thakurru* 'later', 'in a while', *walypawalypala* 'like a white man' from *walypala* 'white man', *dragurdragu* 'spotted' compare *marnardraku* 'tooth' (*marna* 'mouth'), *yilthayiltharri* 'frosty' from *yiltharri* 'frost', *karrukarru* 'old man' from *karru* 'man'. In *pukapuka* 'scrubby (country)', from *puka* '(vegetable) food' the connection is that the country is covered by plants which, while looking as if they might be food sources, are actually not, while *kathikathi* 'snake' (probably only venomous snakes) from *kathi* 'meat, edible animal' refers to the fact that venomous snakes were not regarded as edible.

The meaning of the reduplication seems to be 'result' in *kudhikudhi* 'hidden' from *kudhi-* 'to hide' (the only example of a noun derived from a verb root by simple

---

[1] When someone suggested that this name meant 'stony country' (probably on the basis of Wangkumara *yandra* 'stone') TG's reply was 'Not stony country. Just the name, what the God gave them'.

reduplication). Resemblances in meaning between simple and reduplicated forms are obscure and perhaps non-existent in *ngambungambu* 'ball', *ngambu* 'friend, mate'.[2]

There are a few cases of nouns denoting 'one who does such and such', derived by (partial) reduplication of a nominalised verb stem ('such and such' of course refers to the meaning of the verb stem). Thus *palyakini thapithapini* 'honeyeater' from *thapa* 'to suck' (gerund form *thapini*), *palyakini* 'sweetener' (itself derived from *palya* 'sweet', *-ka* causative), *kathi dramirdramini* 'butcher' from *drama* 'to cut', *kathi* 'meat' and *thinbithinbini* 'chisel' from *thinba* 'to chisel'. This process is productive; thus we have a phrase like *muduwa kadikadini* 'one who is always chasing the children' (*muduwa* 'child', *kadi* 'to chase').

Turning to the second method of classification, the vast majority of reduplicated forms simply involve repetition of the simple form, as *kanthakantha* 'grassy' from *kantha* 'grass', *mardramardra* 'stony' from *mardra* 'stone', *danthurdanthu* 'soft' from *danthu* 'soft' and many others listed above. There are a handful of examples of simple reduplication of a trisyllabic word; examples are *paladi-paladi* 'different' from *paladi* 'individual' and *parrkulu-parrkulu* 'four' from *parrkulu* 'two'.

A frequently used method of reduplication of trisyllabic stems involves reduplication only of the first two syllables; in all such cases the third syllable consists of a continuant and a vowel. Examples are *thakuthakurru* 'slowly' from *thakurru* 'later', *parrkuparrkulu* 'four' from *parrkulu* 'two', *tjalpatjalparri* 'sharp' from *tjalparri* 'sharp', *yilthayiltharri* 'frosty' from *yiltharri* 'frost', *walypawalypala* 'like a white man' from *walypala* 'white man' (illustrating the productivity of the rule, since it applies to a loan from English), *kurrakurrari* 'mad' from *kurrari* 'mad'; note also *yabayabali* "sort of half frightened" from *yabali* 'frightened' — see §9.1.3 for *-li*. The reduplicated nominalised verb stems, such as *thinbithinbini* 'chisel', also follow this pattern (but these involve a formative *-ini ~ -ni*). In all of these where the final syllable is not known to be a suffix it may be regarded as a fossilised formative, meaningless in the present-day language. The seemingly contradictory pair of meanings for reduplicated forms like *payipayirri* 'not very long', 'longer' from *payirri* 'long' and *pirnapirna* 'biggish, not very big, comparatively big, bigger, biggest' from *pirna* 'big' (and probably other similar forms) are comparable with *-ulkere* in Arrernte, which has the meanings (paraphrased) 'this type of', 'more or less (like this)', 'more' (see Henderson & Dobson 1994:582–583).

Partial reduplication, or more likely the compounding of a simple morpheme with a reduplicated morpheme, is exemplified by *marrikurukuru* 'early morning' (*marri-* occurs also in *marripathi* 'tomorrow' and other compounds), *kalipilhipilhi* 'butterfly', *Parlpamardramardra* (a language name; *mardramardra* 'stony', *parlpa* 'language' occurring also in *Parlpakurnu*, another language name), *pulapulayarra*, also *pulayarra* 'green', and *digirdigilyarra* 'dotterel'. Note also the two-word compound *pulyurru nyununyunu* 'swallow' ("because they always make a wrinkly nest with mud"; 'mud' is *pulyurru*).

Two possible reduplicated nouns which do not conform to the above patterns are known: *mabaabi* 'dark' (also *mabumabu*) and *tjuduntjudu* 'marrow (of bone)'. *Thutjutju* 'dog' could be a third.

A number of (collective) terms are composed of reduplicated compound forms containing the formative *-kurnu* 'other'; see §10.5.3. These are stressed as two word compounds.

---

[2] BK did not accept *ngambungambu* with the expected meaning 'friendly'.

10.3 Compounds

Compounds, which may consist of one or two words and may fluctuate between the two states, are of the form A + B, where A and B are morphemes (although in practice it may not be possible to attach a meaning to one or even both). The relationship between the meaning of A, B and the compound (C) takes one of several forms; it is difficult to arrive at an exact number because of the large number of cases where the meaning of A and/or B is not known. A tentative list, with examples, is as follows:

(a) C is that part or aspect of A which resembles or is a form of B (or perhaps C is one possible denotation of B, that associated with A). For example, *ngunuwirlpa* 'vagina' from *ngunu* 'women's genitals', *wirlpa* 'hole'; the vagina is that part of the women's genitals that is a hole, or alternatively 'vagina' is one of the meanings of *wirlpa*, and *ngunu* specifies that it is this meaning in this case, and not one of the others. Other examples are *maramitji* 'finger' and *thinamitji* 'toe' from *mara* 'hand' / *thina* 'foot', *mitji* 'eye', but also used of small discrete rounded objects, such as pebbles or seeds;[3] *thinathundru* 'sole' from *thundru* 'stomach'; *thinapirri* 'toenail' from *pirri* 'nail'; *thinawarta* 'heel' from *warta* 'trunk';[4] *marathangka* 'palm (of hand)' cf. *kuka thangka* 'brain' (*kuka* 'head'); *ngandjarri yindri* 'thunder' from *ngandjarri* 'rain' and *yindri* 'noise'; *ngandjarri kurni* 'lightning' from *kurni* 'penis, tail, lightning'; and perhaps *marnardraku* 'tooth' from *marna* 'mouth' and compare *dragurdragu* 'spotted'.

(b) C is characterised by a part or feature A which has the quality B, e.g. *mitjiparlu* 'duck sp.' from *mitji* 'eye', *parlu* 'white'; *thundruputha* 'cormorant' or 'diver (bird)' from *thundru* 'stomach' and *putha* 'white'; *pidriputha* 'sandfly' from *pidri* 'anus'; *mukukarta* 'skinny' from *muku* 'bone' and *karta* 'rattle'; *marapatji* 'expert' from *mara* 'hand', *patji* 'good'; *Mardrapirna* (a placename) from *mardra* 'stone' and *pirna* 'big';[5] *Ngarndaparlu* (a placename) from *ngarnda* 'forehead' and *parlu* 'white' (referring to a sacred rock there), *ngapakaldri* 'rum, whisky' from *ngapa* 'water', *kaldri* 'bitter'. Probably also *mulhapundra* 'south' from *mulha* 'face' and *pundra* 'cold'.

(c) C is composed of, or a type of, A and resembles B, e.g. *mardrakupu* 'grinding stone' from *mardra* 'stone', *kupu* 'arm'; *mardramitji* 'stone, pebble' from *mitji* 'eye' (and see (a) above); *kurla purralku* 'sp. of burr' from *kurla* 'burr, prickle' and *purralku* 'brolga'; *kurla kurrumpa* 'sp. of burr' from *kurrumpala* 'spinifex'; possibly *maramuku* 'fist' from *mara* 'hand', *muku* 'bone'.

(d) A is a type of generic; the meaning of C is the same as the meaning of B, but A, which is the material of which B is composed, or the source of B, or something else closely associated with B, is included as an optional first element. Examples are *ngapa yulpurru* 'flood' from *ngapa* 'water' and *yulpurru* 'running (water)'; *maka thurrpa* 'ashes' from *maka* 'fire', *thurrpa* 'ashes' (but possibly *maka thurrpa* may mean specifically 'hot ashes'); *maka thupu* 'smoke' from *thupu* 'smoke'; *maka matji* 'match'

---

[3] *Mitji* could be a stem formative, with the denotation 'something in small, discrete, rounded pieces'. Another possible formative of this type (referring to shape) is *yinka* 'something in long thin pieces', as in *wirniyinka*, given for 'a length of string'. Note, however, *pirlimitji* 'gill net' (where it could perhaps refer to the holes), *ngandjarri mitji* 'thunder cloud' and *pinyiyinka* 'shoulder'.

[4] *Warta* is 'trunk (of tree)' and possibly also human trunk, as in *wartamuku* 'hip' (*muku* 'bone').

[5] *Pirna* may be a stem formative: note *marnipirna* 'fat' (as adjective) from *marni* 'fat' and *puthapirna* 'fast' from *putha* 'fast'.

(*matji* 'match' is an English borrowing); *wathi windra* 'spear' from *wathi* 'tree', *windra* 'spear'; *mardra thayi* 'grinding stone' from *mardra* 'stone', *thayi* 'grinding stone'.

(e) A is a generic term and B (and C) the specific term; e.g. *kathi tjukurru* 'kangaroo' (*kathi* 'meat, animal'); *wathi kalpurru* 'coolibah' (*wathi* 'tree'); *karlu kapi* 'fish sp.' (*karlukarlu* 'fish', *kapi* 'fish sp.'). Change of meaning by change of generic term is illustrated by *palha purralku* 'brolga' (*palha* 'bird') and *kurla purralku* 'goathead burr' (*kurla* 'burr'). Note that some compounds using the same first components may be more appropriately classified in other groups; e.g. *kathi kurla* 'carney (lizard sp., also called bearded dragon)' from *kathi* 'animal' and *kurla* 'burr', presumably an animal that looks prickly like a burr, and so class (c). Note also *wathi windra* 'spear' in (d). *Puka paka* 'tobacco' may belong to this group — *puka* 'food', *paka* 'tobacco' (English borrowing).

(f) C denotes the agent of an action, specified by B, a nominalised verb, on A, e.g. (*kathi*) *thuka thayini* 'water rat'[6] from *thuka* 'mussel', *thayi* 'to eat'; *palyakini thapithapini* 'honeyeater' from *palyakini* 'sweetener' from *palyaka* 'to sweeten', from *palya* 'sweet' and *thapa* 'to suck' (this may be a description rather than a name); (*palha*) *purda thayini* 'plain turkey' from *purda* 'unripe (fruit)', *thayi* 'to eat' (and see §10.6 for more).

(g) C is a group comprising A and B and in some cases others, e.g. *ngarndri-ngapiri* 'parents' from *ngarndri* 'mother' and *ngapiri* 'father'; *nguthu-ngama* 'relations' (or possibly 'male relations') from *nguthu* 'elder brother', *ngama* 'mother's brother'; *ngarndri-kaku*, possibly 'female relations' from *ngarndri* and *kaku* 'elder sister'.

Other isolated compounds are formed in different ways, e.g. *dritjiwindrini* 'west' from *dritji* 'sun' and *windri* 'to enter', noun plus nominalised verb, where the noun is the agent of the action; *dritjirdunka* 'east' which is similar except that the verb is not nominalised (and in this it is unique); *dunka* is 'to enter'; *padlakanpa* 'dawn' from *padla* 'ground', *kanpa* 'visible'; *ngunamarnda* 'elbow' from *nguna* 'wing', *marnda* 'half way'.

More knowledge of the range of meanings of the components of compounds would result in a clarification of the methods by which they are formed and probably a reduction in the number of suggested methods.

A number of placenames were given translations by BK, although one or more of the components seem not to be Yandruwandha words. Examples are *kalumurlayi* "quiet heart" (but *kalu* is 'liver' in Yandruwandha and neighbouring languages), *murla* 'quiet' in Yawarrawarrka, "like if saying 'he's a quiet fellow'", *-yi* is the locative suffix); *kakurrthunggayi* "dead marpoo bush" (compare *kakurru* 'marpoo bush' in Ngamini — it is *mandhirra* in Yandruwandha), *thungga* 'rotten', *-yi* 'locative'; *kadripariwirlpa* "creek sky" (*kadri* 'creek' in Yawarrawarrka, *pariwirlpa* 'sky' which probably includes *wirlpa* 'hole'); *kalyamarru* "wide waterhole" (*marru* 'lake'); *kuyapidri* "fish's bum" (*kuya* 'fish', *pidri* 'anus').

The connection between a compound and possible components is often quite obscure, e.g. *mangawarru* 'widow', *manga* 'carpet snake', but may be quite straightforward within the (now largely forgotten) tribal culture and way of thinking. Thus one would not relate *kartakarta* 'saltbush' to *mukukarta* 'skinny' without the clue given by the literal translation

---

6   Once heard as *thukalithayini*, which may have been an error.

"crack crack" (presumably the noise of pods popping when one walks on the saltbush) and "rattly bones".

Among the more common first elements of compounds are the generics *kathi* 'animal', *palha* 'bird', *pardi* 'dangerous creature', *wathi* 'tree, thing', *kurla* 'burr', *maka* 'fire-related things', *ngapa* 'water-related things', *mardra* 'stone', *ngandjarri* 'rain', and also the body-part terms *kuka* 'head', *mitji* 'eye' (used for small rounded things), *marna* 'mouth', *mara* 'hand', *thina* 'foot' and *kuna* 'faeces'.

Second elements occuring two or more times include *parlu* 'white', *-putha* 'white' (the hyphen preceding indicates that it is not known as a free form or the first part of a compound), *-pirri* 'nail', *-ngunpurru* 'nail', *thangka* 'brain', *yimpa* 'black', *mitji* 'eye', *yindri* 'noise', *muku* 'bone', *-wali* (meaning unknown, in *karruwali* 'boy' from *karru* 'man' and *kirriwali* 'prentie' from (?) *kirri* 'lively'), *-puru* (meaning unknown, in *thalpapuru* 'deaf' from *thalpa* 'ear' and *mardrapuru* 'hailstone' from *mardra* 'stone') and *wita* 'hill'. *Warra* 'side', which could be related to the verb aspect marker *-warra* 'arrive' (§12.5) has not been heard as a free form but occurs in *padawarra* 'the other side', *yitapandhiwarra*, meaning not clear but used in reference to the sloping bank of a river, and *karawarra* 'north' (see Breen 1993) as well as in *warrakurnu* 'one side, other side'.

There does not seem to be any definite rule specifying whether a compound consists (phonetically) of one word or two. Compounds containing a classifier as first part normally consist of separate words and are always written that way. Usually where both components are disyllabic the compound is heard as one word, and where one is trisyllabic or longer it is two words.

Modification of either component is practically unknown; the only example (and heard only once) is *Kakurrthunggayi* (placename) where the final vowel of the first component has been dropped.

10.4 Non-productive noun-stem formatives

Many noun stems contain a final portion (one or, less commonly, two syllables) which appears, from its frequency of occurrence in the lexicon, to be some kind of affix and which is detachable, at least from some of the roots with which it occurs, but to which no meaning or function can be attached and which is not a productive stem formative. It is, of course, sometimes difficult to decide whether a suffix is or is not a productive stem formative or the second part of a compound (as witness (a) and (b) in the previous section, especially the first and third footnotes). Other similar cases are *-thitha* in *murnathitha* 'chest', *pidrithitha* 'crotch' and *nharrathitha* 'shield' (*thitha* also means 'crotch') and *-muku* in *maramuku* 'fist', *wartamuku* 'buttocks, hips' and *pulumuku* 'hip' (*muku* means 'bone').

Non-productive stem formatives include *-lu* on *parrkulu* 'two' (compare *parrkukurnu* 'three', *parrkuthili* 'two-dual') and perhaps on *thupulu* 'widower' (*thupu* is 'smoke'); *-ri* and *-di* on some kinship terms: *ngapiri* 'father' (Yawarrawarrka *ngapardi*), *ngalari* (meaning not clear), *patjiri* 'son-in-law', *kamiri*, 'social subdivision' ("meat") (cf. *kami* 'mother's father, cross-cousin'), *ngathadi* 'younger sibling', *yimadi* 'brother-in-law', *kalhidi* 'mother-in-law, daughter-in-law' (note also *tjinbiri* 'scar', *thupari* 'wild banana', *kurrari* ~ *kurrakurrari* 'mad'); and *-lki* and *-ni* on *ngathalki* 'son, daughter (father speaking)' and *ngathani* 'son, daughter (mother speaking)'. Another is *-ntji*, possibly an abbreviated form of the proprietive suffix *-mindji* although BK analysed Mardrantji (a placename) as *mardra* 'stone' plus *-windji*, the meaning of the latter being unknown to him.

Another example of this is in *kadrantji* 'snake sp.' (cf. *kadra* 'louse', but no connection has been established). Note also the final *-rra* and *-nyu* on *tjumpurra* ~ *tjumpunyu* 'waxbill (zebra finch)'; *-rra* occurs also on *malurra* 'shag' (also heard as *maluda*) and *matjurra* 'greenhead ant'.

A suffix of this type exhibiting vowel harmony is *-rri* ~ *-rru*, the latter after stem-final /u/ and the former after other stem-final vowels. Examples of words with these endings (with other examples of the same roots, where available, in brackets) are: *manharri* 'burr sp.', *man.garri* 'girl', *malkirri* 'many', *kudikudirri* 'crooked', *kayarri* 'tea tree', *karirri* 'creek' (cf. *kadri* in Yawarrawarrka, *karitjurru* in Mithaka and Pitta-Pitta), *dikarri* 'duck sp.' *kambarri* 'front', *kaparri* 'root', *ngandjarri* 'rain', *palbarri* 'boulder', *payirri* 'long' (reduplicated form *payipayirri*), *yiltharri* 'frost' (*yilthayiltharri* 'frosty'), *pilthirri* 'stone chips' (also *pilthipilthirri*), *thidharri* 'baby', *tjalparri* 'sharp' (also *tjalpatjalparri*), *walarri* 'shade', *wararri* 'bottom of net', *yambarri* 'flat', 'open (country)', *yawarri* 'word, language', *kalpurru* 'coolibah', *kapurru* 'armpit' (also *kapurrukutja*), *kamburru* 'Acacia sp.', *ngampurru* 'yellowbelly (fish sp.)', *pururru* 'dry', *thakurru* 'later' (*thakuthakurru* 'slow'), *ngunpurru* 'nail, claw', *thupurru* 'heart', *tjukurru* 'kangaroo', *yulpurru* 'flood,' *puthurru* 'dust, haze' (also *puthuputhurru*). Trisyllabic words ending in *-irru*, *-arru* or *-urri* are rare or non-existent.

10.5 Productive noun-stem formatives

Productive noun-stem formatives form noun stems with meanings completely predictable from the meaning of the stems to which they are affixed, and are discussed in the following subsections. A few stems so formed cannot, however, be regarded as simply modifications of the root, but form a new stem, more or less completely unpredictable (even if descriptive). These include *ngukumindji* 'black shag' (from *nguku* 'hook', *-mindji* 'proprietive'), *nharramindji* 'turtle' (*nharra* 'coolamon') and *kunapika* (see below); others may be *mundhapani* 'greedy' (*mundha* 'greedy', *-pani* 'privative') and *yuthapani* 'a poor hunter' (*yutha* 'hunting prowess'). Placenames containing formatives would also come into this category, e.g. *Mudrangangkuthili* (lit. 'yamstick-butt-dual').

In general the function of a productive noun-stem formative is not to produce a new lexical item but to modify a noun stem in a way comparable with the modification produced by an inflectional suffix or by a qualifier such as a numeral or adjective. The meaning of the resulting unit is completely predictable from its form (at least to a native speaker and perhaps with some help from the context). When the meaning is not predictable it must be included in even the most minimal lexicon. For example, *mawapika*, from *mawa* 'hunger' and *-pika* 'characterised by', clearly means '(someone/something) with a big appetite' or something similar. *Kunapika* (*kuna* 'faeces') would be understood as 'something that produces large quantities of faeces' and perhaps can be used in a sentence with this meaning. However, it has a specific meaning 'wood duck' which might possibly be guessable if one knows the characteristics of that duck well enough, but is hardly predictable. This makes it an item that must be included in the lexicon (and see §10.5.10 for this type of stem formation).

In the following subsections the effect of the productive noun-stem formatives as noun modifiers will be described and illustrated.

A few morphemes which may be productive noun-stem formatives have not been discussed below. These include *mitji*, *yinka* and *pirna* (see their dictionary entries) and also *nganggali* 'owner' as in *walpa nganggali* 'the owner of the humpy' or *nguthu nganggali* 'the one whose brother he is'. These all occur free, as nouns.

10.5.1 Dual

The optional dual formative is, as noted in §9.4, *-thili*. It is unusual in that it can also function as a clitic attached to pronouns or verbs, as described in §18.1. This usage seems to be quite rare; however, use of the number formatives on nouns also was rare, non-singularity usually being specified by pronouns or numerals or not at all.

Examples of *-thili* as a formative include

(1) *Pandi-thili   pula   thirrina.*
     dog-DU   2du:NOM   fight-IP
     "The two dogs fought just now." (P3)

(2) *Panggapangga-thili pula,   karruwali nhina-lapurratji, pintha-purru.*
     young.man-DU   2du:NOM boy   sit-REMP-EMPH   foreskin-PROP?
     'There were two young men, just boys, with foreskins.' (D1, =S6-1-2)

(3) *Muduwa-thilili pakawarranhana.*
     child-DU-ERG   carry-arrive-NP
     'The two children brought [them].' (B18)

-thili has also been noted suffixed to the numeral *parrkulu* 'two', from which the final syllable has been dropped: *parrkuthili*. In this case it seems to emphasise the duality — 'just the two (of us), no more'.

(4) *Mirni ngaldra   yandhayandharla, walya ngarini-ngadi   ngalunha*
     wait   1du:in:NOM   talk-talk-PRES   not   hear-GER-DAT   1du:in-ACC

     ngalyilitji.   Parrku-thili yina   ngaldra   yandhayandhalarla.
     some-ERG-EMPH two-DU   EMPH   1du:in:NOM   talk-talk-NOW-PRES
     'Come on, we'll have a talk. We don't want anyone else to hear us. Just the two
     of us are talking now.' (R8)

-thili is attested also on an adjective; an attempt to elicit a translation of the phrase 'tall men and women' was misunderstood and the word *payirrithili* 'two tall ones' was given.

There is a single example, in the Yawarrawarrka corpus, of *-pula* used as a dual formative, in *widapulayi* 'on both banks (of the river)'. This may be an intrusion from Wangkangurru, the first language of the speaker.

10.5.2 Plural

The plural formative is *-ndja* (the pronunciation *-nya* sometimes heard is believed to be a result of careless or rapid speech rather than an allomorph). There is doubt about whether *-ndja* (and *-thili*) is combinable with all nouns or only with human nouns and perhaps a few others. Thus:

(5) *yarru dakamirri-ngadi,*   but not   **yarru dakamirrindjangadi*
     yard   pelican-DAT

was accepted as 'yard for the pelicans' (B24), but

114   *Chapter 10*

(6)   yarru   yadamanindja-ngadi
      yard   horse-PL-DAT

was accepted as 'yard for a mob of horses'. (B24)

(7)   pirli   karlukarlu   malkirri-ngadi
      net   fish   many-DAT

is the accepted form for 'net for catching a mob of fish' (B24); *pirli karlukarlundjangadi* was not accepted. Uninflected words using these number formatives were accepted when suggested (and *mardrandja* 'a mob of hills' was actually given when I mistakenly translated it as *mardrathili*, which would be 'two hills') but they were never elicited, and when they were accepted they were sometimes followed by a more normal translation. Thus when I asked if 'a mob of dogs' could be called *pandindja*, the answer was 'Yes, *pandindja*, or *pandi malkirri* ['dog many'].' A similar answer was given immediately afterwards regarding *wathindja* 'a mob of trees'.

Plural words in *-ndja* are one of the groups of nouns which combine with the suffix *-ngi* (see 9-81).

(8)   Muduwa yabali   nhutjadu   karrundjangiyitji.
      child   fear-INST   3sg:NOM:THERE   man-PL-DAT-LOC-EMPH
      'The kid's frightened of all those men.' (B18)

Other examples of *-ndja* include:

(9)   Yiwa   walya wanitji   wawini-ngadi,   ngarru karru-ngadi yina,
      woman   not   corroboree-EMPH   see-GER-DAT   only   man-DAT   EMPH

      paladildra   thana   karrundjatji   thambana-padipadini.
      individual-BUT   3pl:NOM   man-PL-EMPH   dance-INCH-HAB-GER
      'The women weren't allowed to watch the corroboree; it was only for the men
      and they danced it on their own.' (P11)

(10) Yarndu   kurrakurrana-nhina-rnanga   karrukarrundjalitji.
      how   put-put-APP-sit-CONT   old.man-PL-ERG-EMPH
      'That's what the old people used to tell me.' (D5)

The formative is apparently intended to refer to both nouns in the following example:

(11) ... kurrupu   karrukarrundjatji   nhina-rlayi.
      old.woman   old.man-PL-EMPH   sit-SIM
      '... while the old people were still living.' (D6, in A-173)

10.5.3 Other

The suffix *-kurnu* means '(an)other'. The free morpheme *kurnu* means 'one'. *-kurnu* is frequently suffixed to *putha* 'time, occasion' and the resulting compound means 'next time', 'any more', 'again'.

(12) Minhanganarla   yini   nhinggudu   muduwa,   walpakurnuyitji?
      what-do-PRES   2sg:NOM   location-THERE   child   humpy-other-LOC-EMPH
      'What are you doing there kid, in someone else's humpy?' (W3)

(13) Mirni   nhulu   yakayaka-rlayi   puthakurnutji   nganhaya   nganandji
      wait   3sg:ERG   ask-ask-SIM   time-other-EMPH   1sg:ACC-?   tell-SEQ

ngathu   yinha.
1sg:ERG 3sg:ACC
'If he asks me next time I'll tell him then.' (D6)

(14) *Walyala   nganyi   mawali,   puthakurnu.*
not-EMPH 1sg:NOM hunger-INST time-other
'I'm not hungry any more.' (R5)

(15) *Dranyi-nhana   nganha   nhulu,   nyalkari,   karnakurnunyadi   kilka-rnanga.*
hit(throwing)-NP 1sg:ACC 3sg:ERG mistake-UNSP person-other-like know-CONT
"He hit me in a mistake; like if he meant to hit someone else and he hit me." (P5)

(16) *Thawarla ngani   ngapakurna-kurnu-ngadila.*
go-PRES 1pl:ex:NOM waterhole-other-DAT-EMPH
'We'll go to another waterhole.' (P31)

-*kurnu* seems to combine with a third person pronoun in the following example, although it occurs as a phonetically separate word:

(17) *Warnu   ngala   nhunu   kurnutji?*
who:NOM then   3sg:NOM other-EMPH
"Who's the other fellow?" (R10)

The root *patji* 'good' usually occurs with -*kurnu* suffixed; in this case the suffix has no discernable function.

Reduplication of stems in -*kurnu* is used to specify 'all', as in *karnakurnu-karnakurnu* 'everybody' (*karna* 'person'), *padlakurnu-padlakurnu* 'everywhere' (*padla* 'country'), *mulhakurnu-mulhakurnu* 'all kinds' (*mulha* 'face'), *mudakurnu-mudakurnu* 'all kinds of corroborees' (*muda* 'corroboree'), *ngunikurnu-ngunikurnu* 'every day' (*nguni* 'day'), and, with what may be a slightly different function, *marndakurnu-marndakurnu* 'here and there', 'now and then' (*marnda, marndakurnu* 'half way'). The last one may not be a noun. These reduplicated forms are occasionally pronounced as single words. Inflectional suffixes are known only at the end, as in (19). Examples of their use include:

(18) *Ngunikurnu-ngunikurnu   nganyi   thawa-nhana, walya   pipini.*
day-other-day-other   1sg:NOM go-NP   not   rest-GER
'I went every day, never had a spell.' (B14)

(19) *Ngapala   maka pirna   thangkakari,   ya   mardramitji mandringa malkirrili,*
well   fire   big   burn-CAUS-UNSP and stone-eye   get-FUT   many-ERG

karnakurnu-karnakurnuli.
person-other-person-other-ERG
'Well, they would build a big fire and everyone would collect stones.' (D3, =A135)

(20) *Ngan.gu ngathu   kilkarla   ngalyi, ngarru ngathu*
word   1sg:ERG know-PRES few   only   1sg:ERG

marndakurnu-marndakurnu   mandripadarlanga   ngan.gutji.
half.way-other-half.way-other   get-in-PRES-EMPH   word-EMPH
'I know a few words; I can just pick up a word now and then.' (P13)

See also (S6-17) and note the repetition of forms conveying the idea of 'everywhere' in this sentence.

10.5.4 Proprietive

The suffix -*mindji* means 'having', in the sense of 'inalienably possessed'. It is suffixed to the stem denoting the person (e.g. kinship term), thing or quality possessed. Thus *malkamindji* 'striped' from *malka* 'mark', *nguyamindji* 'well built', 'good looking' from *nguya* 'good appearance'. Other examples are illustrated in the following sentences:

(21) Ngan.ga-mindji ngathu wawanhana.
    beard-PROP 1sg:ERG see-NP
    'I saw [a man] with a beard.' (B15)

(22) Walya ngupa nhinggudutji, minha-mindji kara nhutjadu.
    not swim location-THERE-EMPH what-PROP maybe 3sg:NOM:THERE
    'Don't swim there, it's dangerous [lit ... there might be something there].' (P31)

(23) Pampu nhutjadu purla-mindji.
    egg 3sg:NOM:THERE young-PROP
    'That egg has a chicken in it.' (R10)
    (Here an animate object is 'possessed' by an inanimate object.)

(24) Nguthu parrkulu-mindji nganyi.
    elder.brother two-PROP 1sg:NOM
    'I've got two brothers.' (R1)
    (This is in answer to the question 'How many brothers have you got?' Another way to say this is *Nguthu parrkulu ngakani* 'elder.brother two 1sg:GEN' and it seemed, from the context, that there was some difference between these two ways but it is not at all clear what it might be.)

There is one example from the Strzelecki dialect of the suffix -*mindji* being used with the negative *pani* 'nothing'; this occurs also in some other closely related languages (e.g. Ngamini, Wangka-Yutjurru).

(25) Pani-mindji nganyi.
    nothing-PROP 1sg:NOM
    "[I] went for nothing ..." (M2)

The suffix -*purru* has been heard only with the noun *pintha* 'foreskin'; see (2). -*purru* is the normal proprietive suffix in Arabana and Wangkangurru (Hercus 1994:90).

10.5.5 Privative

The privative suffix, to some extent semantically the converse of the proprietive but also denoting lack of something which would have been alienably possessed, is -*pani*. This is clearly an allomorph of the same morpheme as the free form *pani* 'not', 'none', 'nothing', and in fact does occur sometimes phonetically as a separate word; see (26, 17-5). Note in particular the interposition of an emphatic suffix between the noun and *pani* in (26). See (7-15, 16) for other examples. Note also the use of a genitive pronoun where nominative might have been expected in (27).

(26) Ngapatji panila.
    water-EMPH nothing-EMPH
    'There's no water [here]'. (T13)

(27) *Thawawarra-nhanatji walya yini   ngatjada ngakani-ngadi, kathila*
      go-arrive-NP-EMPH   not   2sg:NOM camp   1sg:GEN-DAT   meat-EMPH

   walya ngathu   yina   ngunyini-ngadi, ngala yini   thawawarrana,
   not   1sg:ERG 2sg:ACC give-GER-DAT   then 2sg:NOM go-arrive-IP

   kathi-paniyila   ngakani.
   meat-PRIV-LOC-EMPH 1sg:GEN
   'If you had come to my camp yesterday I would have given you some meat, but you've come now when I've got none.' (W2)

(28) *Nguthu-pani   nhutjadu,   ngarru kaku.*
     elder.brother-PRIV 3sg:NOM:THERE   only   elder.sister
     'He's got no brothers, only sisters.' (R1)

(29) *Nyalkanyalkari, kathi-panila   thikawarranga.*
     miss-miss-UNSP meat-PRIV-EMPH   return-arrive-FUT
     "[I] missed [the kangaroo] and had to come home without [meat]." (P5)

The compound *mara pani* means 'empty-handed'; see the dictionary entry in the companion *Innamincka Words*. Suffixation of *-pani* to a gerund (nominalised verb) is illustrated in §10.6. The suffixation of *-pani* has no discernable function in *mundhapani* (~ *mundha*) 'greedy'.

10.5.6 Comitative

The name 'comitative' is used here for a suffix whose functions range from 'possession' of kin (30)–(33) through accompaniment (34) to alienable possession (37). Examples (35) and (36) have elements of accompaniment and also alienable (and uncontrolled in the latter) possession. This has been briefly discussed by Breen (1976a). As a kin-possessive suffix it is added to a kinship term to denote a group of people, one or more of whom is called by that term by the other(s). In all of the examples the group consists of two people, but since there is no such restriction in at least some other languages (e.g. Pitta-Pitta, the Arandic languages, Wakaya, the Mayi languages; see Breen 1976a), and there is no such restriction when the suffix has its 'accompaniment' function, it is assumed that the group can be larger. The form of the suffix is *-ngurru*. It was sometimes heard as a separate word (36, 7-14). In its possession (kin and otherwise) function it differs from *-mindji* in that it does not refer to inalienable possession and means 'having with one' rather than 'owning' or 'having as a feature'. Contrast *nhipamindji* 'married' (i.e. 'having a spouse') with *nhipangurru* 'married couple', also translatable as 'with (or accompanied by) one's spouse'.

(30) *Nguthu-ngurru   ngali   nhuludu.*
     elder.brother-COM   1du:ex:NOM 3sg:ERG-THERE
     'That fellow and I are brothers.' (R1)

(31) *Puladutji   ngathalki-ngurruldra.*
     3du:NOM-THERE-EMPH   child(of.man)-COM-BUT

   or

118   *Chapter 10*

(32)   *Puladutji   ngapiri-ngurru.*
       3du:NOM-THERE-EMPH father-COM
       'Those two are father and son.' (both R1)
       (Or the meaning could be 'father and daughter'. *-ldra* in (31) could be translated as 'on the other hand', and contrasts the sentence with the previous one elicited, which is (30).)

(33)   *Nguthu-ngurruli   pula   yadamani   ngalungga   paka-nhana.*
       elder.brother-COM-ERG 3du:NOM horse   1du:in:GEN take-NP
       'Those two brothers took our horses.' (X15)

(34)   *Pandi-ngurru nhunu   thawa-nhana.*
       dog-COM   3sg:NOM go-NP
       'He went with his dog.' (P3)

(35)   *Nharrathitha-ngurru thirri kara   nhunu   thawanhana.*
       shield-COM   fight   maybe   3sg:NOM go-NP
       'He took his shield; he might expect trouble.' (P7)

(36)   *Kulkupa-windringa nhunu,   wathi windra ngurru.*
       jump-enter-FUT   3sg:NOM stick spear   COM
       '[The kangaroo] hopped away with the spear still in it.' (R5)

(37)   *Mara ngathu   pardrarla padla-ngurru.*
       hand 1sg:ERG   hold-PRES sand-COM
       'I've got a handful of sand.' (P30)

10.5.7 First person kin proprietive

The suffix *-ngi*, homophonous with the genitive inflection (see §9.3, §9.14), is added to kinship terms to denote that the relationship is to the speaker; i.e. it can be translated 'my' (or 'our', if appropriate[7]). The omission of inflectional suffixes after *-ngi* has already been noted (§9.2). Note that with *nguthu* 'elder brother' (but not other kinship terms with final /u/) there is regressive vowel harmony — *nguthingi*, not **nguthungi*.

For examples of *-ngi* see (9-66)–(9-73).

10.5.8 Second and third person kin proprietive

A suffix, heard variously as *-mada, -madani, -mala* and *-malani*, is added to kinship terms to denote that the relationship is to the person or persons addressed; thus it can be translated 'your'. (The forms with /d/ are from TG, and those with /l/ from BK.) The *-ni* seems to be optional and meaningless; thus Yidlanggi *ngarndrimalani*? 'Where's your mother?' was given immediately after Yidlanggi *ngapirimala*? 'Where's your father?'. The suffix seems, however, in some examples to have a third person reference, being translated 'his' or 'her'. It has been difficult to elicit sentences with this morpheme; BK preferred to use genitive pronouns or let the context specify whose kin was referred to, and I was often reduced to asking questions like 'Could you say that with *ngarndrimala*?'

---

[7]   There are no examples of *-ngi* used for non-singular first person possessor (as in *nguthingi ngalunggani* 'our (dual inclusive) brother') but my suggestion that this would be so was accepted. The corresponding second/third person forms also can refer to non-singular possessors.

The same suffix, or more often variants of it, denotes that the relationship is to a third party: 'his', 'her', 'their'. The evidence from BK, which is quite substantial but, unlike the data in most other fields, quite inconsistent and confusing, tends to suggest that there is a form *-maladi* which has third person reference, while *-mala(ni)* has second person reference.

Note that the genitive suffix *-ngi* (see §9.14) occurs with nouns carrying this suffix (9-74), and can function as a base to which other inflections can be added (see §9.2). There are examples, however, of inflections simply being omitted, e.g. *nguthumala* 'your brother' where the ergative *nguthumalali* or *nguthumalangili* was expected.

(38) *Marripathi nganyi thawarla kaku-madani wawanga.*
tomorrow 1sg:NOM go-PRES elder.sister-2kin see-FUT
'I'm going tomorrow to see your sister.' (T12)

(39) *Parndrirla yinha nguthu-madali.*
hit-PRES 3sg:ACC elder.brother-2kin-ERG
'He's getting belted by his brother.' (T14)

See also the last paragraph of §9.9 for a possible other use of *-mala*.

10.5.9 Habitual action

The suffix *-purra* is added to a noun (which may be a nominalised verb) denoting a state or action, to denote 'one who is habitually in that state or performing that action'. For example *kinyipurra* 'thief' from *kinyi* 'dishonesty, stealth', *mukapurra* 'one who is usually asleep' from *muka* sleep', *warluwarlupurra* '[dog] that barks a lot' from *warlu(warlu)* 'bark', *yuthapurra* 'good hunter' from *yutha* 'hunting' (the converse is *yuthapani*, with the privative suffix) and *yandhinipurra* 'a good talker' from *yandhini*, gerund form of *yandha* 'to talk'. *Parndrinipurra* 'bully' (from *parndri* 'to hit') was given when I suggested *parndripurra*, and *pubinipurra* 'heavy smoker' (from *puba* 'to smoke') was accepted. *Wakapurra* 'hard worker' is derived from the loan word *waka* 'work'.

Ngandjarri purra 'rainy' was heard as two words, but this is probably just an example of the occasional pronunciation of a disyllabic bound morpheme as a separate word.

One form which appears to be based on a verb root is *yingkapurra* 'someone who is always laughing'. However, *yingka* also combines with the nominal inflectional suffix *-li* (see §16.9) and with *ngunyi(ngunyi)* (see §13.4.1), which otherwise combines only with (abstract) nouns, and this suggests that it can function as a noun stem as well as as a verb stem.[8] (Another peculiarity of *yingka*, probably quite unrelated, is that its gerund is *yingkani*, not the expected *yingkini*.)

A similar formative, *-pika*, is described in the next section; note that *mirrtjapurra*, *mirrtjapika* and *mirrtjapirna* (from MN) have all been heard for 'noisy' (from *mirrtja* 'noise'; *pirna* is 'big'). *Pirna* combines with two other stems that are attested with *-purra*: *yutha* and *thirri*. *Thirri*, like *yingka*, seems to function as both a verb stem and a noun stem; see (1, 35).

---

[8] After eliciting *yinkapurra* I suggested *yingkapurra* 'someone who is always crying' and BK accepted this. However, he may well have heard it as *yingkinipurra*, the form I would (now) expect.

10.5.10 Formatives denoting characteristics

The suffix *-pika*, glossed CHAR, is added to a noun stem denoting some object, quality or state, to form a stem denoting someone who or something which is characterised by possessing or being affected by that object, quality or state. Examples include *mirrtjapika* 'noisy' from *mirrtja* 'noise', *marnipika* 'fat (as an adjective)' from *marni* 'fat (noun)', *mawapika* 'big eater' from *mawa* 'hunger', *thidripika* 'jealous' from *thidri* 'jealousy', *puthapika* 'racehorse', 'very fast' from *putha* 'the races', also *putha* 'to gallop', 'to move fast' (and the normal verb 'to run' in Yawarrawarrka; *putha*, a different morpheme, also means 'occasion', as in *puthakurnu* 'once'), *ngunipika* 'daylight' from *nguni* 'day', *mukupika* 'bony' from *muku* 'bone' and *yabapika* "frightened fellow" from *yaba* 'fear'.

The word *pirna*, basically 'big', is usable as a formative with, it seems, the same function; *ngunipika* and *nguni pirna* were used in two very similar sentences one immediately after the other. Note also *marnipirna* = *marnipika*, and see the last paragraph of the previous section. *Puthapirna* also is attested and said to be faster than *puthapika*; see the dictionary entries.

Pirna also is interchangeable with *patji* 'good' in at least the phrase *kunparri pirna* ~ *kunparri patji* 'very lucky'.

Another formative with a similar meaning is *kanpa*. There are two entries for *kanpa* in the dictionary, one for *kanpa* 'visible' and one for *kanpa* glossed as 'very(?); susceptible to'; it is, in fact, not at all clear how it should be glossed. The latter is exemplified by the phrase *kanpa kudrini* 'brittle, easily broken', and combines with *muthu* 'very, really' to form *kanpamuthu*, glossed 'very', as in *wirlpa kanpamuthu* 'very fast'. This *kanpa* (if they really are different words) is assumed to be the formative involved in *mawakanpa* 'hungry person'[9] (contrast *mawapika* above), *murakanpa* 'thirsty person', *yabakanpa* 'frightened person' (see (S8-4)), *kinyikanpa* 'thief' (also *kinyipurra*) and, from MN and derived from a nominalised verb, *manmini kanpa* 'liar'. *Padlakanpa* 'daylight' (lit. 'ground-visible') would be derived from the other *kanpa*. (Note also *padla muthu* 'sand'; it appears that of the range of meanings of *padla*, 'sand' is 'real *padla*'. See also §16.8 on *muthu*.)

10.5.11 Noun stem formation by inflectional suffixes

Formation of a possessive noun by affixation of the dative inflection (with genitive function) to a noun stem is productive although not common. Possessive pronouns are formed in the same way ((d) in §9.8) and note also the use of genitive forms of certain nouns and pronouns as a base to which some inflectional suffixes may be added (see §9.4, §9.5, §9.8). Examples of possessive nouns are rare; there are two in the following sentence.

(40) *Walyangu muduwa-ngadilitji pandi matha-nhana, walypala-ngadili*
 not-YET child-DAT-ERG-EMPH dog bite-NP white.man-DAT-ERG

 pandi matha-nhanatji.
 dog bite-NP-EMPH
 'The kid's dog didn't bite me, the white fellow's did.' (B16)

---

[9] A referee points out, however, a word *ka(r)npa* 'empty, hungry' in Barngarla.

Note also that a verb stem formative may be added to a noun with dative inflection (in the examples in the corpus the inflection has allative function) as in *marnangadika* 'to put into the mouth' (*marna* 'mouth', *-ka* 'causative').

Formation of a noun stem by means of the ablative suffix *-nguda* is illustrated in (9-62) and (9-176). The process illustrated there produces stems which function as noun stems with necessarily predictable meaning, but they are nonce words and not lexical items in the sense of requiring inclusion in the dictionary. The words *Thayipilthirringuda* 'people of the Innamincka Yandruwandha' (*thayi* 'grinding stone', *pilthirri* 'chips'), (*palha*) (*ngapa*) *mingkanguda* 'mountain duck' (*palha* 'bird', *ngapa* 'water', *mingka* 'hole') and (*pardri*) *ngurraputhanguda* 'grub in whitewood tree' (*pardri* 'grub', *ngurraputha* 'whitewood tree') are examples of lexical items derived with *-nguda*. *Kayidinguda* 'new' (*kayidi* 'now'), *matjanguda* 'old' (*matja* 'long time') and *pandjanguda* 'old' (*pandja* 'long time') may be noun stems (and note also in SY *manyanguda*, which, however, is translated as 'long ago', not 'old', and *manya* is not otherwise attested). Another SY example is *kakanguda* 'close' (*kaka* 'close'). The ablative suffix in some of these cases seems to have a locative rather than an ablative function, although in examples like (9-62) and (9-176) it could be regarded as ablative in that it defines the point from which the action is directed (and note the use of 'from' or 'through' in the English versions).

There are also some placenames formed with the locative suffix *-yi*. Examples are *Mingkayi* 'Minkie' (*mingka* 'hole'), *Kukuyi* 'Cooquie' (*kuku* 'inside, deep'), *Kalumurlayi* (English name not known; from *kalu* 'liver' and *murla* 'quiet' but translated "quiet heart"), *Pukapurdayi* 'Bookabourdie' (*puka* 'fruit', *purda* 'unripe') and *Thurrpayi* 'Tooroopie' (*thurrpa* 'ashes'); note also *Dalan.garanyi* 'Dullingari', which must to be a Yandruwandha placename (assuming it is correctly located) but may contain the Yawarrawarrka locative suffix *-nyi*.

10.6 Derivation of nouns from verbs

A noun stem is formed from a verb by means of the gerund formative *-ini ~ -ni*. Nominalisation of a verb in this way and inflection of the nominalised stem for dative or ablative case is a very common method of expressing the verbal concept in a subordinate sentence; this is illustrated in (45) and (46) but will be discussed in greater detail in §15.3. The gerund often forms an agent or instrument noun, which is sometimes used to replace a verbal form in a negative clause (discussed above in §8.4.1, but see (49)). Another use of the gerund is to combine with the verbal aspect marker *-padapada* to give a past habitual meaning, 'used to ...'; see §12.9.

The form of the gerund formative is *-ini* for all verbs with stem-final /a/, with one exception (*yingka* 'to laugh', gerund *yingkani*).[10] The initial vowel of the suffix replaces the final vowel of the stem; thus *wawa* 'to see' becomes *wawini*. If the verb stem is reduplicated this replacement vowel behaves as a stem vowel so that it is present in both occurrences, as in *dramirdramini* from *drama* 'to cut'. Note also *-padipadini*, the past habitual marker, from *-padapada* 'habitual action'. It is hard to see what connection the aspect marker *-padapada* has to the aspect marker *-pada* 'in, across', see §12.9.

---

[10] This does not seem to be the case with its Yw counterpart, *tjingka*, however; purposive *tjingkinima* is attested. The gerund of the Yw word *putha* 'to run' was heard as *puthani* (in *puthaninguda* 'after running') but this requires confirmation in view of the occasional interchange of /i/ and /a/ in that dialect (or in MN's speech).

122   *Chapter 10*

With stem-final /u/ the gerund formative is *-ni*; thus *thanggu* 'to stand' becomes *thangguni*. With stem-final /i/ the distinction between *-ini* (with the first vowel of the suffix replacing the stem-final vowel) and *-ni* is not relevant.

Note that the verb 'to cry' is *yingki* with gerund *yingkini*; if the verb *yingka* 'to laugh' behaved regularly it would also have gerund *yingkini*.

Examples of agent nouns, many of which are compounded of a noun stem plus the nominalised verb, include (as well as those given at (f) in §10.3):

kathi dramirdramini	'butcher' ('meat-cutter')
kathi pirnngini	'butcher' ('meat-skinner')
kathi parndrini	'butcher' ('meat-killer')
makawarlawagini	'a good cook' (derivation not fully known; *maka* 'fire', *waga* 'to shift'; compare *warla* to *wadha* in *makawadhawarrka* 'to stack firewood')
wani thambanini	'dancer' (*wani* 'corroboree', *thambana* 'to dance' (intransitive))
karna parndrini	'murderer' (*karna* 'person', *parndri* 'to kill')
(nhutjadu) muduwa kadikadini	'(that) fellow who's always chasing the kids' (*muduwa* 'child', *kadi* 'to chase')

It is clear that some nouns of this type are nonce coinages, such as the last in the above list. Note also *kaniparndrini*, for a hawk whose correct name the informants could not remember (*kani* 'carney (lizard sp.)', *parndri* 'to kill').

Examples of instrument nouns include:

dramirdramini	'knife' (cf. the first name for 'butcher', above)
*wathi parndriparndri*ni	'axe' (*wathi* 'tree', 'wood', *parndri* 'to hit')
marapardrini	'handle', as in:

(41) *Mardrathakiyi ngathu marapardrini kurranga.*
stone-axe-LOC 1sg:ERG hand-hold-GER put-FUT
'I'm going to put the handle on the axe.' (P6)

The gerund suffix denotes ability or propensity to perform the action expressed by the verb in *karna thula parndrini* '[people who] kill strangers' and *mulha wawayindrini* 'reflection of face' ('ability to see your own face') and with negation:

(42) *Palha purla pudlu tharrini.*
bird small can't fly-GER
'That bird can't fly.' (X20)

(Or *tharrinipani*, with privative *-pani*, could be used instead of *pudlu tharrini*. *Tharrapani*, heard on one occasion, was later said to be incorrect.)

Other examples of the use of gerunds include: *dritjiwindrini* 'west' (*dritji* 'sun', *windri* 'to enter') and, in sentences:

(43) *Maltji kudra-yindrini nhutjadu.*
leg break-RR-GER 3sg:NOM:THERE
'That fellow's got a broken leg.' (T8)

(This example does not seem to be consistent with others; *kudrayindrininguda* 'break-RR-GER-ABL would seem to me to be more correct.)

(44) *Minha-ngadi yundru wathi nhuludutji yada thinbarla;*
what-DAT 2sg:ERG tree 3sg:ERG-THERE-EMPH boomerang chisel-PRES

ngarru kudra-yindrini yina nhutjadutji wathi.
only break-RR-GER EMPH 3sg:NOM:THERE-EMPH wood
'Why do you make a boomerang from that wood, it just breaks.' (P5)

(45) *Nganarla yinha nhandra walya thanmini-ngaditji.*
tell-PRES 3sg:ACC 3sg:fem:ERG not swim-GER-DAT-EMPH
"[She's] telling him not to swim." (P11)

(46) *Marnipirna-kini-ngudatji, ngapala thana parndriri, thayingalatji.*
fat-big-CAUS-GER-ABL-EMPH well 3pl:NOM kill-UNSP eat-FUT-EMPH-EMPH
'They made them big and fat, and then they killed them and ate them.' (P29)

The following two examples suggest that the agent with a gerund derived from a transitive verb stem does not require ergative marking. However, this is contradicted by examples like (15-25) and (15-27). In the case of (47) it is possible that there was haplology, *karruwalitji* being said instead of *karruwalilitji*. In the case of (48) it could be that the sentence is to be thought of as two (or even three) clauses and the final one has no overt agent (and compare (15-39)).

(47) *Padri kanangku walya thayini muduwa karruwalitji.*
edible.grub grub.sp. not eat-GER child boy-EMPH
'Boys [before circumcision] couldn't eat witchetty grubs.' (X14)

(in discussion about prohibitions on certain people eating certain things)

(48) *Kali, karrula nhutjadu, padri kanangkutji thayini-ngadi.*
all.right man-EMPH 3sg:NOM edible.grub grub.sp.-EMPH eat-GER-DAT
'He's a man and can eat witchetty grubs now.' (X14)

There is one example of compounding of a gerund with *-purra* (10.5.9):

(49) *Yandhini-purra nhutjadu karrukarru, walya marna dapini.*
talk-GER-always 3sg:NOM:THERE old.man not mouth shut-GER
'That old man's a good talker; he never shuts his mouth.' (W4)

Compounding of a gerund with the privative suffix *(-)pani* (§10.5.5) is a very uncommon way of forming a negative imperative (see also §8.4.2).

(50) *Palthu ngarndamini-pani!*
road block-CAUS-GER-PRIV
'Get out of the way!' (P29) (i.e. 'Don't block the road', or perhaps better 'Unblock the road'.)

Examples of a purposive (i.e. gerund + dative) form in a main clause are rare, and are interpretable as verbless clauses. An example (with two main clauses) is:

(51) *Ngapa nhutjadu yibini-ngadi walya mara yika-yindrini-ngadi.*
water 3sg:NOM:THERE drink-GER-DAT not hand wash-RR-GER-DAT
"That water's for drinking, not to wash your hands." (W7)

Adding the nominal privative suffix *-pani* to a gerund gives a form which expresses inability to perform the action denoted by the verb stem. Thus *tharrinipani* (said of a baby bird) means 'can't fly'. 'Can't' is more likely to be expressed with the adverb *pudlu* 'in vain' (see §8.4.3) and there is practically no information on this construction. *-pani* can also be suffixed to a verb stem to form a negative imperative; see §11.5.1.

11 *Verb inflection*

Verbs in Yandruwandha may be inflected for tense, mood, number and subordination. However, the system is not simple, as one tense form is marked by a nominalisation, one of the tense markers is alternatively a marker of subordination, and some time specification is by means of stem formatives, not inflectional suffixes.

Five past tenses are distinguished by inflectional suffixes; these are designated 'immediate past' (IP), 'near past' (NP) (a day or so), 'recent past' (RECP) (a few days), 'far past' (FARP) (weeks or months) and 'remote past' (REMP) (years). Nominalisation of a verb stem which has been marked for habitual action gives a form which denotes a habitual action in the past; see §12.9. Further specification of tense can be made by means of stem formatives which denote action in the early morning, during the day or at night; these may be used with present and future tenses as well as past, and also with subordinate and nominalised forms. The use of these formatives will be described after the sections on tenses, rather than in the chapter on Verb Aspect, which deals with other formatives which modify the verb.

There is one present tense form, denoting an unmarked present and also normal or habitual action (the combination of habitual formative with present tense inflection is rare). The present tense form may be modified by an affix which precedes the tense inflection and which denotes that the thing which is happening now was not happening before.

A suffix which denotes future action is also used to mark consequential action (and so subordination).

Mood and number marking are interrelated in that number (dual or plural of subject) is marked only in the imperative mood; the singular imperative form is the verb stem. The other modal marking is for potential action ('might' or, in a subordinate clause, 'lest'). A number of inflections could be said to mark subordination although the clause concerned need not be grammatically subordinated to another clause in the same sentence. These include a suffix denoting continuing action contemporaneous with some other action in the past, or, in a text, an action performed in the general period to which the text refers; a suffix denoting that the tense is the same as that of the verb in the preceding clause or sentence; a suffix denoting a repeated action ('again'), a suffix denoting immediate consequence and a suffix basically denoting simultaneous action, as well as the future tense marker referred to above. None of these verb forms (except the future when it is used to indicate future time) contains any direct indication of tense.

Table 11-1 summarises the verb inflections of Yandruwandha and (very incompletely) Yawarrawarrka, and gives the section where each is discussed. No differences between Innamincka and Strzelecki Yandruwandha are known.

Table 11-1: Verb inflection

	Yandruwandha	Yawarrawarrka	Section
Past tenses:			
Immediate past	*-na*	*-ni*	§11.1
Near past	*-nhana*	*-itha*	§11.1
Recent past	*-nhukada(ni)*	?	§11.1
Far past	*-n.ga*	?	§11.1
Remote past	*-lapurra*	*-iyapurra*	§11.1
Other tense and aspect inflections:			
Present tense	*-rla*	*-rla*	§11.2
The 'now' present	*-la-, -a-, -li-, -ya-*	*-la- + ?*	§11.15
Future tense	*-nga*	*-iya*	§11.3
Immediate future	*-nga nganarla*	*-iya nganarla*	§11.3.1
time of day specification	*-thalka, -warrka, -yukarra, -nhina*	?	§11.4
Unspecified tense	*-ri*	*-indri*	§11.8
Contemporaneous	*-rnanga*	?	§11.9
Repeated action	*-kaldri*	?	§11.10
Immediate sequence	*-ndji*	?	§11.11
Simultaneous	*-rlayi*	*-(i)rnanyi*	§11.12
Moods:			
Imperative	*-0*	*-0*	§11.5
Negative imperative	*-pani*		§11.5.1
Optative	*-malka, -yarndu, -malkayarndu*	?	§11.6
Potential	*-yi*	*-ipi*	§11.7
Other:			
Dual	*-li*	?	§11.13
Plural	*-ni*	?	§11.13
Motion away	*-ka*	*-rrka?*	§11.14

11.1 Past tenses

The five past punctiliar tenses are:

- immediate past, denoting action within the last hour or two, marked by *-na*;
- near past, denoting action within the last day or two, marked by *-nhana*;
- recent past, denoting action within the last few days, marked by *-nhukada* (BK) ~ *-nhukadani* (TG);

- far past, denoting action within the last few years, marked by *-n.ga*;
- remote past, denoting action many years before, marked by *-lapurra*.

Corresponding Yawarrawarrka forms, insofar as they are known, are, respectively, *-ni*, *-itha*, (not known), (not known), *-iyapurra*. The last was also used several times as a translation of 'used to' (compare Yandruwandha *-padipadini*, see §12.9). MN often used *-ni* for immediate past in SY.

Some of these affixes are worthy of further mention. *-nhana* could be a compound affix containing *-na* as its second element, but there is no evidence apart from its phonological form to suggest this. *-lapurra* could be a compound affix incorporating *-purra*, a noun-stem formative denoting habitual action. There is no suggestion of habitual action in the meaning of this tense form, but there is in the meaning of its Yawarrawarrka counterpart, *-iyapurra*. *-nhukada* was heard on two occasions as a separate word following a verb stem with suffix *-la* (*thawala nhukadatji* 'went some time ago' and *kuditharrala nhukada* 'forgot before'; see the *minha* entry in the dictionary); this led to the supposition that it was a bound form of an adverb meaning 'before', 'yesterday'. It is now thought that the *-la* is an emphatic suffix; compare the use of the same suffix on *pakala warranana*, discussed in §12.

The time scales given above for the various past tenses are not strictly adhered to; in particular there is overlap between *-nhana* and *-nhukada*, and their relative ordering seems to be suspended when the formative *-nhina* 'action during the day' is used. However, *-nhana* may be used for action earlier today while *-nhukada* is not. It can refer to actions up to a fortnight or more ago and so overlaps to some extent with *-n.ga*. Probably all of the past tenses are compatible with *matja* 'long ago; before', which can refer to quite a short time ago although its primary meaning is 'long ago' and certainly further back than *nhukada*.

Note that *ngaranhinanhukadani* (TG) ~ *ngananhinanhukada* (BK), derived from the verb stems *ngara* 'to hear' and *ngana* 'to do','to tell' respectively, and *-nhina* 'action during the day', functions as an adverb with the meaning 'yesterday'. Also TG used *ngarathalkana* (*-thalka* 'action in the morning') to mean 'this morning', and BK accepted *nganathalkana* as having that meaning. It is not clear whether *ngarayukarrana/nganayukarrana* could be used as an adverb meaning 'last night'; BK agreed that *nganayukarrana* could, but then said it as *nganayukarranhana*, i.e with a different tense suffix, and translated it as 'went last night', suggesting that it was functioning as a verb, not an adverb. On another occasion he gave *nganayukarranhukada* for 'last night (yesterday during the night)'.

BK stated definitely that *-nhukada* refers to events further back in time than *-nhana*, and this is supported by the following example, in which both are used:

(1) '*Karlukarlu ngathu parndri-nhana malkirri.*' '*Yidlanggiyi?*'
    fish   1sg:ERG kill-NP   many   where-LOC

    '*Nhinggiyingutji ngaldra parndrithika-nhukada.*'
    location-HERE-YET-EMPH 1du:in kill-return-RECP
    'I caught a lot of fish.' 'Where?' 'At the same place where you and I caught [some] last time.' (R2)

Similarly, the relative order of *-na* and *-nhana* is illustrated by the example

128 *Chapter 11*

(2) *Walya ngathu yinha kandri-nhana, ngala nhunu thawawarranangu.*
  not 1sg:ERG 3sg:ACC call-NP then 3sg:NOM go-arrive-IP-THEN
  'I didn't call him but he still came.' (P8)

There are a couple of examples where *-na* refers to a distant past time; both occur in a text. For example:

(3) *Walya yina thana wawatharrana, kali yina thana*
  not EMPH 3pl:NOM see-fly-IP already EMPH 3pl:NOM

  paldritharrana matja.
  die-fly-IP long.time
  'They haven't seen all that; they all died long ago.' (D5)

Deviations from the expected tense form may depend to some extent on the circumstances; for example, consider the sentence:

(4) *Kayidila thanadu thawawarra-nhana, yilanggi-nguda kara.*
  now-EMPH 3pl:NOM-THERE go-arrive-NP where-ABL maybe
  'They have only come lately, I don't know where from.' (D3, =A-120)

where the reference is to the coming of rabbits to the Cooper's Creek area. The time involved here is at least a number of years, probably decades, but, in comparison with the time the native animals have been in the area, is quite insignificant, and so the adverb *kayidi* 'now' and the near past tense are used.

Note also that the tense form used to express, say, 'action this morning' would depend on the time of day when the utterance was made; if one were speaking early in the morning it would probably be *-thalkana (-thalka* 'action in the morning'), but if one spoke in the afternoon *-thalkanhana* would be likely.

The following sentences exemplify the past tenses. No attempt is made to illustrate all possible combinations of formative and inflection; some have been heard only when I have specifically elicited them, others have been suggested by me and accepted while others, which may be possible, have neither been elicited nor suggested. It is not clear whether the informant's acceptance of a form meaning, say, 'died a long time ago at night' means that it would ever, in practice, be used.

-na:

(5) *Kali ngathu yibana.*
  already 1sg:ERG drink-IP
  'I just had a drink.' (T6)

(6) *Pandi-thili pula thirrina.*
  dog-DU 3du:NOM fight-IP
  "The two dogs fought just now." (P3)

-nhana:

(7) *Thawa-nhana yini thantjiyipa-ngadi, walyala nganha nganari,*
  go-NP 2sg:NOM town-DAT not-EMPH 1sg:ACC tell-UNSP

  purtu ngathu yura-nhana mandrini-ngadi nganha.
  goods 1sg:ERG want-NP get-GER-DAT 1sg:ACC
  'You should have told me you were going to town. I wanted you to get me some things.' (P8)

(8) *Thirri-nhana pula nganahinanhukada.*
fight-NP   3du:NOM yesterday
'They had a fight yesterday.' (P3)

(9) *Pukudu ngathuna pardra-nhana.*
dream 1sg:ERG-2sg:ACC hold-NP
'I dreamt about you last night.' (T5)

-nhukada(ni):

(10) *Dritji parrkulu nganyi nhina-nhukada.*
day two 1sg:NOM sit-RECP
'I stopped there two days ago.' (P24)

-n.ga:

(11) *Kilkarla yundru kathi tjukurru ngaldra yinha parndrin.ga,*
know-PRES 2sg:ERG meat kangaroo 1du:in:NOM 3sg:ACC kill-FARP

yini kuthithikan.ga.
2sg:NOM come-return-FARP
'Do you remember that kangaroo we killed last time you were here.' (P11)

(12) *Wiki kurnu nganyi dritji parrkulu nhinathawan.ga.*
week one 1sg:NOM day two sit-go-FARP
'I stopped there two days last week.' (P24)

(13) *Muduwala thawathawalarla nhutjadu, wawathikan.ga ngathu*
child-EMPH go-go-NOW-PRES 3sg:NOM see-return-FARP 1sg:ERG

marrkamarrka-rlayi.
crawl-crawl-SIM
'The baby can walk now; he was crawling when I was here before.' (X47)

-lapurra:

(14) *Ngarndritji ngakani paldri-lapurra matja, walya ngathu*
mother-EMPH 1sg:GEN die-REMP long.time not 1sg:ERG

nhanha kilkarlatji.
3sg:fem:ACC know-PRES-EMPH
"My mother died before I can remember her." (C5)

(15) *Muduwatji yini yingki-lapurra.*
child-EMPH 2sg:NOM cry-REMP
'You used to cry a lot when you were a baby.' (W2)

(16) *Ngarndrili nganha ngathani-ka-lapurra, Malkanpatji.*
mother-ERG 1sg:ACC child(of.woman)-CAUS-REMP Innamincka-EMPH
'I was born at Innamincka.' (W7)

Unexplained omission of past tense inflection has been noted on occasions; see §16.8 and §18.3.3.

11.2 Present tense

The suffix *-rla* is used to denote action in the present (17), intended action in the near future (18), a state (21), duty (when used with *walya* 'not', (20)) or probability (with *kara*, (19)) in present time, and a normal condition or habitual action (22), (23). The same suffix is used in Yawarrawarrka.

(17) *Muduwa nhutjadu yingkirla.*
child 3sg:THERE cry-PRES
'The baby's crying.' (T2)

(18) *Kayidi nganyi papana-ngarirla.*
now 1sg:NOM start-INCH-down-PRES
'I'll start directly.' (P12)

(19) *Thawawarrarla kara nhunu, pani kara.*
go-arrive-PRES maybe 3sg:NOM nothing maybe
"He might come, and he might not." (T13)

(20) *Nhutjadu walya yina mardratji ngunyithikarla.*
3sg:NOM:THERE not 2sg:ACC money-EMPH give-return-PRES
"He should pay you back the money." (W2)

(21) *Thudarla thanaduwaw.*
lie-PRES 3pl:NOM-THERE-DISTORT
'They're lying down.' (T3)

(22) *Pandi nhuliyi ngurra parndrirla.*
dog 3sg:ERG-HERE always hit-PRES
'That fellow's always hitting his dog.' (T12)

(23) *Muduwa wayini yundru pardrarla?*
child how.many 2sg:ERG hold-PRES
'How many kids have you got?' (T10)

11.3 Future tense

The term 'future tense' for this verb form may be a misnomer; 'desiderative mood' may be more appropriate for its use in independent clauses. Note that immediate future action is denoted by the present tense suffix. The future tense marker *-nga* marks:

- intention, desire, permission or future time in an independent clause (24, 25, 26);
- consequential action in a main clause, in a situation in which there is a connected series of sentences, as in a text or coordinate clauses; thus such a sentence or clause is subordinated to the first in the series (28);
- purpose in a subordinate clause.

In the latter two uses, the subject of the verb in *-nga* is the same as the subject of the preceding clause or the main clause. (28) is an exception to this; contrast it with (29) and (30). Other exceptions are (15-19) and (S6-4). Austin (1981b:319) says that *-nga* and *-iningadi* (see §15.3) form a same subject/different subject pair in implicated (i.e.

purposive) clauses and this is partly correct, but both have other uses and the statement needs substantial qualification.

The corresponding Yawarrawarrka suffix is *-iya*; this occurred in the only example using future tense from one of the younger informants, and in about one third of cases from MN, who knew Yandruwandha better and often mixed the two, using *-nga* most of the time. Thus the Yawarrawarrka equivalent of Yandruwandha *thawanga* 'will go' is *thawiya*. Some of MN's translations suggest that the function of the suffix is desiderative mood rather than future tense, but this is clearly not possible in all cases (for example, where the subject is 'rain').

Subordinate clauses and subordinate sentences will be discussed in more detail later (§15.3 and §15.4).

The following examples illustrate the uses of *-nga*:

(24) *Yibanga   ngathu   ngapa.*
   drink-FUT 1sg:ERG water
   'I want a drink of water.' (T2)

(25) *Minha ngarrkanga kara   ngandra.   Yila-kadi ngandra   pakanga?*
   what do-FUT   maybe 1pl:in:NOM where-DAT 1pl:in:NOM carry-FUT
   "Don't know what we going to do with her. Where are we gonna take her?" (W2)

(26) *Mulha malka, yundru   wawanga   malkirri thanhayi   ngakani,   mulha*
   face   mark 2sg:ERG see-FUT many   3pl:ACC-HERE 1sg:GEN face

   malka mandrini-nguda.
   mark   get-GER-ABL
   "I got a lot of photos here that have been taken, if you like to look at them." (W3)

(27) *Ngarru puka   ngandra   thayingatji,   kathi pani.*
   only   tucker 1pl:in:NOM eat-FUT-EMPH meat   nothing
   'We've only got bread to eat, no meat.' (R2; see also M21)

(28) *Wathi-nguda nganyi   warlka-nhana nga   ngambutji   ngakani   yingkanga*
   tree-ABL   1sg:NOM fall-NP   then mate-EMPH 1sg:GEN laugh-FUT

   nhunu.
   3sg:NOM
   'I fell out of a tree and my mate just laughed at me.' (R8)

(29) *Thawa yadów,   warlimanga   nganha!*
   go   hither:DISTORT help-CAUS-FUT 1sg:ACC
   'Come here and help me.' (P8)

(30) *Mulhudu-pani ngani   thawa-nhana. Kurnula   nhunu   thikarla*
   tucker-PRIV 1pl:ex:NOM go-NP   one-EMPH 3sg:NOM return-PRES

   mandrithikanga pukalatji.
   get-return-FUT tucker-EMPH-EMPH
   'We came without any tucker. One of us will have to go back and get some.' (R2)

Where *-nga* denotes intention, this may be an intention in past time. For example:

(31) *Ay karrukarra! Muka nganyi thudapandhinga. Yundru nganha*
eh old.man:VOC sleep 1sg:NOM lie-down-FUT 2sg:ERG 1sg:ACC

yirrtjinana.
wake-TVR-IP
'Hey, old man, I was going to have a sleep. You woke me up.' (W1)

-nga in a subordinate clause may have an irrealis meaning ('would have') if the main clause is negative and in a past tense. For example:

(32) *Ngananhinanhukada walya yini thawawarra-nhana, wawangatji*
yesterday not 2sg:NOM go-arrive-NP see-FUT-EMPH

ngakani kaku.
1sg:GEN elder sister
"You seen my sister if you'd come day before yesterday." [or 'You didn't come yesterday to see my sister.'] (W2)

The future is used in (33) where a nominalised purposive (i.e. gerund + dative) verb would be expected; compare (10-51).

(33) *Patjikurnu thayingatji thana.*
good-one eat-FUT-EMPH 3pl:NOM
'They're good eating' (i.e. good to eat). (D1, =A-29))

11.3.1 Immediate future

The verb *ngana* 'to do' (in present tense) in association with a verb in the future tense forms a construction that can be translated as 'was just about to', 'was on the point of', or equivalent:

(34) *Yini thawawarrana kayidi, ngala nganyitji thangguwindringala*
2sg:NOM go-arrive-IP now then 1sg:NOM-EMPH stand-enter-FUT-EMPH

nganarla.
do-PRES
"He came just in time, he was just going to go, see." (W1)
(Not a direct translation, but from the viewpoint of a third person.)
See also (18-14)

A similar construction, but with the other verb nominalised rather than in the future tense, is illustrated in the next two examples. In (35) *ngana* is in the simultaneous action form, and in (36) in the immediate past. The purpose of these variations is not clear.

(35) *Dan.ga-nhana ngathu, paldrini-ngadila ngana-rlayi.*
find-NP 1sg:ERG die-GER-DAT-EMPH do-SIM
'When I found him he had nearly died.' (B15)

(36) *Mulhudu nganyi thayi-yindrini-ngadi nganana, wawangarina*
tucker 1sg:NOM eat-RR-GER-DAT do-IP see-down-IP

thawawarra-rlayila.
go-arrive-SIM-EMPH
'I was just going to have a feed, but then I saw him coming.' (X14)

This former construction is much more common in the Strzelecki Yandruwandha and Yawarrawarrka corpora (and in Diyari, see Austin 1981a:88–92) and clearly is not confined to the immediate future use; thus, in Strzelecki Yandruwandha:

(37) *Marrikudukudu   nhunudu   thawanga   nganarla.*
     tomorrow.morning   3sg:NOM-THERE   go-FUT   do-PRES
     'I'm going tomorrow morning.' (M14)

In elicited sentences in Strzelecki Yandruwandha the *-nga ngana-* construction is used for future tense in about 60% of cases and occasionally in subordinate clauses, and the verb + *-nga* in about 40% as well as in many subordinate clauses. In Yawarrawarrka, where it was common for MN to use Yandruwandha forms, *-iya ngana-* was used only a few times for future and only once in a subordinate clause, *-nga ngana-* was used about one third of the time for future and in a few subordinate clauses, *-iya* was used about one third of the time for future but only once in a subordinate clause, and *-nga* was used about one third of the time for future and quite often in subordinate clauses.

All dialects used only the present tense suffix *-rla* or the simultaneous action suffix — *-rlayi* in Yandruwandha, *-irnanyi* in Yawarrawarrka — on *ngana-* in this type of construction. (36) is the only exception known.

In a couple of cases MN used *ngana-* with a purposive form, as in the Yawarrawarrka example (and compare the use of dative in subordinate clauses described in §15.3):

(38) *Yini   yada   thawani,   nganyi   thawinima   nganarla.*
     2sg:NOM hither   go-IP   1sg:NOM   go-GER-DAT   do-PRES
     'You came when I was just about to go.' (Y11)
     (MN's translation: "I wanted to walk, just as you come.")

The use of *ngana-* in the following example in IY is quite different, and refers to an example in sequence. It is not clear what its function is here; it would seem that it could have been omitted without changing the meaning.

(39) *Nga   ngarru   makathurrpala   thana   dringarnanga*   and   *drangkanga*
     then only   hot-ash-EMPH   3pl:NOM   scrape-CONT   sweep-FUT

     nganangatji.
     do-FUT-EMPH
     'When there are only hot ashes left they scrape and sweep them away.' (D3, =A138)

11.4 Specification of time of day

The use of formatives to give additional specification of time is not obligatory. The formatives which can be used are *-thalka*, which probably refers particularly to early morning, *-warrka* also 'action in the morning' (but only uncertainly attested), *-nhina* 'action during the day' and *-yukarra* 'action at night'. *-warrka* is rare but BK, when asked for the meaning of *Thawawarrkana nhunu*, after some thought, said 'That's just the same as saying "this morning". Same as *thawathalkana. Thawawarrkana nhunu* just the same.' However, see §12.11 for another interpretation.

Each of these occurs as a free morpheme and each, except *-yukarra*, has also some other function as a verb stem formative (which will be described at a later stage). *Thalka*, as a free morpheme, is the adverb 'up' and the formative *-thalka* can, and usually does, denote 'action directed upwards'[1] (§12.14). *Warrka* is the verb 'to throw' and occurs as a formative in the word *makawadhawarrka* 'to heap up firewood' (see also §12.11). *Nhina* is the verb 'to sit, to stay' and as a verb-stem formative *-nhina* denotes 'action continuing for some time' (§12.8). *Yukarra* is a verb meaning 'to lie', also 'to spend the night' but rarely occurs as a free morpheme.

The majority of time of day references in verbs occur with the past tenses, but this may simply be the result of the nature of the corpus. It seems likely that any of them can occur with any or almost any verb inflection. They are actually attested with three past tenses, present tense, future tense, gerund (plus ablative, to give the sense 'after doing') and simultaneous action. Examples include:

-thalkana:

(40) *Maka yundrutji wangathalkana ...*
fire   2sg:ERG-EMPH make-up-IP
'You made the fire this morning …' (X25)

(41) *Thawawindri-thalkana nhunu.*
go-enter-up-IP   3sg:NOM
'He went away this morning.' (P9)

-warrkana:

(42) *Thambana-thika-warrkana nganyi ngakamarra.*
dance-INCH-return-throw-IP 1sg:NOM a while ago
'I was dancing a while ago.' (T7)

-yukarrana:

(43) *Thawa-yukarrana nganyi waruwaruyi.*
go-at.night-IP 1sg:NOM dark-in
'I was walking in the dark.' (P13)

(BK made it clear, when asked, that *-yukarra* meant 'at night' and not just 'in the dark'.)

-nhinanhana:

(44) *Walya yina nganyi ngurra thudathudanhina-nhana.*
not EMPH 1sg:NOM always lie-lie-sit-NP
"I haven't been sleeping all day" (i.e. 'I was sleeping for a while, but not for the whole day'). (P15)

-yukarranhana:

(45) *Wani ngandra thambana-yukarra-nhana, mirni kilkanhinarlala*
corroboree 1pl:in:NOM dance-INCH-at.night-NP wait know-sit-PRES-EMPH

---

[1] Compare Wangkumara, in which the suffix *-pa* denotes both 'action in the morning' and 'action directed upwards'.

ngathu.
1sg:ERG
'I'm just thinking about that corroboree last night.' (B17)

-nhinanhukada(ni):

(46) *Thawanhina-nhukadani walya nganyi, wawanga kaku-madanitji.*
go-sit-RECP not 1sg:NOM see-FUT elder.sister-2kin-EMPH
'If I had come here yesterday I would have seen your sister.' (T12)

Another possible example (depending on how the *nhina* is to be interpreted) is at (12-39).

-thalkanhukada:

(47) *ngarathalka-nhukada.*
hear-up-RECP
'[I] heard yesterday morning.' (P9)

-yukarrarla:

(48) *Malthi yini mirrka-pani thangguthanggu-yukarrarla, walya*
cold 2sg:NOM clothes-PRIV stand-stand-at.night-PRES not

yini pundrali?
2sg:NOM cold-INST
'Aren't you cold walking about [in the cold] at night with no shirt on?' (B16)

-thalkarla:

(49) *Putha thana minithalkarla, marripathi.*
races 3pl:NOM run-up-PRES tomorrow
'The races are on tomorrow.' (T11, in S1-1)

-yukarranga:

(50) *Thawa-yukarranga nganyi, walyala kara wawanga ngathu yina.*
go-at.night-FUT 1sg:NOM not-EMPH maybe see-FUT 1sg:ERG 2sg:ACC
'I'm going tonight and I mightn't see you again.' (P15)

(51) *Kathi ngali parndri-nhana, ya kudla-yukarranga yinha,*
meat 1du:ex:NOM hit-NP and cook-at.night-FUT 3sg:ACC

parndrala ngali walthathikana.
cooked-EMPH 1du:ex:NOM carry-back-IP
'We killed [a kangaroo], cooked it overnight and carried it home already cooked.' (R6)

-thalkanga:

(52) *Ngandjarri kara marripathi warlkathalkanga.*
rain maybe tomorrow fall-up-FUT
'It might rain tomorrow.' (P31)

-yukarrini-nguda:

(53) *Pirritjampanarla nganyi, wani thamba-na-yukarrini-nguda ngurra.*
tired-INCH-PRES 1sg:NOM corroboree dance-INCH-at.night-GER-ABL always
'I'm tired from dancing all night.' (W7)

-yukarra-rlayi:

(54) Ngapala mini-yukarra-rlayi thana warrkanapada-rlayildrangu.
well run-at.night-SIM 3pl:NOM throw-APP-in-SIM-BUT-YET
'When they run at night they spear them then too.' (?) (E8, =A33)

See also (12-38) for an example of *-nhini-nguda* which may have a time reference.

11.5 Imperative mood

The imperative form of a verb is marked by a zero morpheme (which is not glossed in the interlinear line of an example sentence), and is used for commands (both positive and negative). Certain other morphemes occur only with imperatives and optatives (§11.6); these are the two subject number markers *-li* and *-ni* (§11.13) and the suffix *-ka* which denotes action directed away from the speaker and/or hearer or their vicinity (see §11.14). Where a number marker occurs with *-ka* it follows it. Distortion of the final vowel of an imperative verb is quite common (55).

The imperative is often followed by the particle *mayi* (often [*may*]), which adds emphasis to the command. It has been variously translated as 'well', 'what' and 'what now' (the first being more appropriate to its function with imperative and the others more appropriate to its other functions — see §17.3), but none of these is adequate. *Mayi* immediately follows an imperative verb unless the directional *yada* intervenes.

The subject of an imperative verb is normally in the second person and not expressed. Two examples of an imperative with a third person subject have been noted ((58) — note however that the second person has been used in the translation — and (9-124)) and one of an imperative with first person subject, probably mistaken as it was repeated with the verb in present tense; see (17-15).

(55) Kurrapandhaw!
put-down:DISTORT
'Put [that] down!' (T7)

(56) Walya wathiyi karithalkaw!
not tree-LOC climb-up:DISTORT
'Don't climb that tree!' (T7)

(57) Kantha mangga mayi! Pulkapada mayi!
grass burn EMPH blow-in EMPH
'Burn the grass!' (C3)

(58) Karna kurnu nhulu ngapa marndrathika.
person one 3sg:ERG water dip.up-return
'One of you go and get the water.' (R2)

For earlier discussion of command sentences see §8.1.

11.5.1 Negative imperative

The suffix *-pani*, homophonous with the particle described in §8.4.2 and the noun modifier described in §10.5.5 and assumed to be the same morpheme, may be added to a verb stem (and so to the positive imperative form). The information on this point is very limited as the informants never used the construction and its existence came to light only while I was seeking information on the different morpheme *-pani* in the verb *winkapani* 'to run away'. The suffix is used to tell or advise the addressee not to carry out the action denoted by the verb stem. Thus:

(59) *Ay, thawa-pani nganyi.*
      eh   go-PRIV   1sg:NOM
      Translated as "You don't want to go; don't go; or you can't go, anything like that". (B20)

As explained by BK the difference between *wawapani* (*wawa* 'to see') and *wawinipani* (adding *-pani* to the gerund form of the verb) is that the former 'means "Oh, you can't see him". Like if there's a man sick and they tell you you can't go and see him', whereas the latter expresses a physical inability to see something. As illustrated in §8.1 and §11.5, a negative imperative sentence normally uses the negative particle *walya* with the positive imperative suffix.

11.6 Optative mood

The optative, whose function is to convey a weak command or permission, is marked by *-malka*, *-yarndu* or both together, *-malkayarndu*. *-yarndu* alone is not common. This morpheme is homophonous with *(-)yarndu* 'how' but the relationship between the two is not known.

The optative *-malka*, like the imperative, combines with *-ka* and the number markers; these precede the optative suffix. There are no examples of these markers occurring in conjunction with *-yarndu*.

The subject of an optative verb may be second or third person; it is not clear whether a first person subject is permitted. Where the subject is omitted it is assumed to be second person.

(60) *Mirniwa   yandhayandha-malk-ardi,   ngararlangu   yina   ngathu   yina.*
      wait-EMPH talk-talk-OPT-EMPH   listen-PRES-YET   EMPH   1sg:ERG   2sg:ACC
      "You keep on talking, I'm still listening to you." (B15)

(61) *'Thutjutjuli kathi yinggani   thayina.' 'Kawu warrayi   thayi-malkayarndu*
      dog-ERG   meat   2sg:GEN   eat-IP   yes   all.right eat-OPT

      nhulu.'
      3sg:ERG
      'The dog's got your meat!' "Oh, he can eat it." (B16)

(62) *Pirritjampanarla   nhunu;   warrayi   nhunu   yukarra-pandhi-malkayarndu.*
      tired-INCH-PRES   3sg:NOM   all.right 3sg:NOM   lie-down-OPT
      'He's tired. "He can lay down, sleep."' (B16)

(63) *'Waranu   yiniyey?'   ['Gavan.'] 'Ngandra ngala, thawapada-malka.'*
      who-NOM   2sg:NOM-DISTORT   [Gavan]   oh   then   go-in-OPT
      "Who's there?" ["Gavan"] "Oh, well, come in then." (T5)

11.7 Potential mood

A potential event, something that might happen, is expressed in Yandruwandha in one of two ways. Where the event is regarded as good or neutral the particle *kara* 'maybe' (see §8.3) is used with a verb of the appropriate tense, or in a verbless sentence. Where the event is undesirable and is a possible result of some other event or planned event the potential mood form of the verb is used (cf. Dixon 1972:112–113). The nearest English equivalent is the word 'lest'. (However, note (16-63).)

The potential is marked by the suffix *-yi*. The Yawarrawarrka equivalent is *-ipi*; thus Yawarrawarrka *mathipi*[2] = Yandruwandha *mathayi* 'might bite'. Examples include:

(64) *Warrayi, paldripaldriyi yini ngapayi.*
leave.it die-die-POT 2sg:NOM water-LOC
"Don't go down to the river, you might get drowned." (T13)

(65) *Winkamana ngathu nhunggani wathitji, ngurra parndriyilatji*
disappear-CAUS-IP 1sg:ERG 3sg:GEN stick-EMPH always hit-POT-EMPH-EMPH

nganinha.
1pl:ex.-ACC
"I planted his stick so he won't belt us any more." (R6) (planted = hid)

(66) *Muduwa thika yadayayi, pandilila yina mathayi.*
child return hither-DISTORT dog-ERG-EMPH 2sg:ACC bite-POT
"Come away from there boy, the dog will bite you." (W3)

As in some other languages, there is some relationship in function between the verbal potential suffix and the nominal aversive suffix *-puru*. This is illustrated by the following two examples.

(67) *Walpa-ngadi yada paka purtutji yinggani ngandjarri-puru.*
humpy-DAT hither carry swag-EMPH 2sg:GEN rain-AVER
'Bring your swag inside in case it rains.' (R10)

(68) *Purtu yada windrimapada, pandili purumayi.*
swag hither enter-CAUS-in dog-ERG urinate-POT
'Bring the swag inside "so the dog won't piddle on it."' (R10)

The potential may be most correctly regarded as a marker of subordination rather than mood.

11.8 Unspecified tense

The suffix *-ri* on a verb denotes that the tense is not specified in that verb but is to be inferred from the context, either because it has already been stated in a preceding clause or sentence, because the extralinguistic context makes it clear or because it does not matter. If a sentence or part of a sentence is repeated, even with alterations as in (72), *-ri* often replaces the tense marker. When a Yandruwandha verb is referred to in an English

---

[2] *Mathapi* also has been heard.

sentence the *-ri* form is usually used.³ The Yawarrawarrka equivalent seems to be *-indri*, although *-ri* was often used, especially by MN.

The functions of the unspecified tense form, the future tense when functioning as a marker of consequence (§11.3) and the contemporaneous form *-rnanga* (§11.9) overlap to some extent and the differences between them are not completely clear. All three are very common in texts, *-nga* (future and consequence) being the most common of all verb forms and *-ri* next with *-rnanga* its only possible rival. The subject of the verb in *-ri* is nearly always the same as the subject of the preceding verb, but there are a number of exceptions; see (A-18, 25-26, 45-47, 70-71). (In (A-26 the subject is a subset of the subject of (A-25).)

The following examples illustrate the use of the unspecified tense:

(69) *Ngathu yina wawana yundratji, ngapala yina walya kilkari.*
1sg:ERG 2sg:ACC see-IP far-EMPH well 2sg:ACC not know-UNSP

repeated as:

Yundra ngathu yina wawana, walya yina kilkanga.
far 1sg:ERG 2sg:ACC see-IP not 2sg:ACC know-FUT
"I seen you a long way and I didn't recognise you." (W5)

(70) *Pirnanangatji nhunu karrungaditji, ngapala nhunu kathi*
big-INCH-FUT-EMPH 3sg:NOM man-DAT-EMPH well 3sg:NOM animal

parndrini nhinari.
kill-GER sit-UNSP
'He's going to be a butcher when he grows up.' (W4)

(71) *Nhinapandhinga nganyi, pipiri.*
sit-down-FUT 1sg:NOM rest-UNSP
'I'll sit down and have a spell.' (R8)

(72) *Nguthingi ngathu winkamana, or mama-yindriri, windra.*
elder.brother-1KIN 1sg:ERG disappear-CAUS-IP or steal-RR-UNSP spear
'I took the spear off my brother.' (W8)

See also (15-15).

11.9 Contemporaneous action

The suffix *-rnanga* denotes a continuing action or state, in the present unless it is subordinate to a main clause or in a text. If subordinate to a main clause it denotes action contemporaneous with, but extending over a longer time than, the action described by the main verb, and with the same actor as the main verb. Austin (1981b) contrasts *-rnanga* with *-rlayi* (see §11.12) as marking same-subject relative and different-subject relative clauses respectively (and defines his usage of relative, which is broader than its more common use). In text it denotes a time contemporaneous with the period of the story, and

---

³ MN often code-switched between Yandruwandha and Pidgin, and when she denoted the tense or mood by *bin* (past tense) or *mait* (potential) she used the *-ri* suffix on the verb. Thus:
Ngathu kathi bin nhinalkari, and *thirrtha bin ngakani thayiri.*
1sg.ERG meat sit-CAUS-UNSP dog 1sg.GEN eat-UNSP
'I had some meat but the dog ate it.' (M4)

140   *Chapter 11*

so replaces a past tense. Sentences where *-rnanga* is used when the subject is different from the subject of the preceding verb are rare but include (A-65) and (A-84) (and see (A-66); these do not involve relative clauses, however. The contemporaneous form was often given when a verb was elicited in isolation, as 'What is the word for breathing?'

(73)   *Kanyi ngaka-rnanga.*
       sweat run-CONT
       '[I'm] sweating.' (T6)

(74)   *Kathi   tjukurru   ngathu   wawana,   thawa-rnanga   nhinggiyi-ngadi.*
       animal kangaroo 1sg:ERG see-IP   go-CONT   location-HERE-DAT
       'I saw a kangaroo while I was coming here.' (W1)

(75)   *Karna   nhutjadu   thawarla   thayithayi-yindri-rnanga.*
       person 3sg:NOM:THERE   go-PRES   eat-eat-RR-CONT
       "He's having a feed as he's walking along." (W1)

See also (15-13). Note the use of *-ri* for a momentary action and *-rnanga* for a continuing action in:

(76)   *Drama-yindri-nhana   nganyi,   mara   yilkari,   kathi   pirnnga-rnanga.*
       cut-RR-NP   1sg:NOM hand   slip-UNSP animal skin-CONT
       'I accidentally cut myself while I was skinning the kangaroo.' (R1)

11.10 Repeated action

The suffix *-kaldri* denotes (a) a repeated action and (b) an action that restores the previous state of affairs. In both cases it can be translated 'again'. It is not used of repetitive or often repeated actions. See (A-69) for a sentence in which *-kaldri* seems to be combined (but perhaps by mistake) with *-nga*.

(77)   *Purrirla   nhunu,   nguluka-yindriwaganga,   ya   winkathikapada-kaldri.*
       hide-PRES 3sg:NOM end-CAUS-RR-around-FUT and disappear-return-in-AGAIN
       'He's hiding, and he peeped out and then ducked back in again.' (B11)

(78)   *Thingapada-kaldri   nhulu   karna   kurnulitji,   thadri-ngadilatji,*
       pull-in-AGAIN   3sg:ERG person one-ERG-EMPH bank-DAT-EMPH-EMPH

       dukanga   ya   parndringa   palhalatji.
       pull out-FUT and kill-FUT   bird-EMPH-EMPH
       'One of the men pulled [the net] back in to the bank, and [they?] pulled out the ducks and killed them.' (E3)

11.11 Immediate sequence

The suffix *-ndji* marks an action that immediately follows another action. It may occur in a main clause in which case the tense depends on that of the preceding sentence. The action involved need not be caused in any way by that of the preceding sentence or clause. There are a number of examples in texts: (S6-4 and 8, 8-10, 9-3, 10-3, 18, 20 and 36). See also (14-49).

(79) *Thawawindrina nhunu, mukala nganyi thudapandhindji.*
     go-enter-IP   3sg:NOM sleep-EMPH 1sg:NOM lie-down-SEQ
     'As soon as he went I had a sleep.' (P8)

(80) *Thawarlatji nhunu, mukala nganyi thudapandhindji.*
     go-PRES-EMPH 3sg:NOM sleep-EMPH 1sg:NOM lie-down-SEQ
     'As soon as he goes I'm going to have a sleep.' (P8)

(81) *Darngaritji ya karrandji yinha.*
     find-UNSP-EMPH and tie-SEQ 3sg:ACC
     'If [we] could find [some rope we] could tie him up.' (R8)

Where a clause with a verb in *-ndji* follows a clause with a verb in *-rlayi* (which does not normally occur in main clauses; see §11.12) the *-rlayi* clause functions as a conditional clause and the verb in *-ndji* seems to have an imperative function.

(82) *Yakayaka-rlayitji nhulu, nganandji yinha, 'Ay marrikudhi-nhana*
     ask-ask-SIM-EMPH 3sg:ERG tell-SEQ 3sg:ACC oh go.early-NP

     nhunu'.
     3sg:NOM
     "If he asks you tell him he went early." (X25)   (The two 'he's' are different)

In the following example the verb of the main clause has been omitted, but can be assumed to be similar in nature to that of the other clause. The sentence as it stands is ambiguous as to time and duration (as is the translation given for it).

(83) ... *Nhingguwa-ngadi waka, minithikawarrandji*
     location-THERE-DAT over.there run-return-arrive-SEQ

     nhinggiyi-ngadila.
     location-HERE-DAT-EMPH
     "He run over there and he run back here." (P13)

11.12 Simultaneous action

The suffix *-rlayi (-irnanyi* or *-rnanyi* in Yw) is added to a verb in a subordinate clause to indicate that the action referred to is simultaneous with or the cause of (and continuing up to the time of) the action referred to in the main clause. It thus includes as a special case a verb which is the complement of a verb of sensing or knowing. In texts a verb with *-rlayi* inflection may (occasionally) function as the main or only verb of a sentence;[4] in such cases the sentence sometimes begins with *ngala*, which could be translated 'meanwhile', and can always be thought of as subordinate to a previous sentence. Examples (several with *ngala*) are (S8-8, 9-8, 21 and 27, 10-4, 17, 31 and 32). (88) was given in response to an elicitation.

The subject of a verb in *-rlayi* is nearly always different from the subject of the main verb, as in (84, 85) and (18-11) (and see §11.9); there are a couple of examples where this seems not to be so ((86) and (87)) but the situation is not completely clear. A main verb can govern more than one *-rlayi* clause, as in (A-62, 173, 180), or a second subordinate

---

[4] It is often difficult to decide where sentence breaks appear in text, however. It has been essentially on the basis of intonation.

142   *Chapter 11*

clause may use a different verb, as in (89) (in which, however, the third clause could just as well be thought of as subordinate to the second as to the first). (A-81) has three successive verbs with *-rlayi* (and it seems that there ought to be a fourth) as subjects are switched back and forth.

-rlayi could possibly be a compound suffix comprising the present tense suffix *-rla* and the locative *-yi*. If this is so the word *wawawawariyi* in (85) may illustrate replacement of *-rla* by *-ri*. However, I was not able to elicit *-riyi* again. Locative is used for a different subject form over a wide area of south-central Australia (see Austin 1981b:331).

(84)   *Pandi nhuliyi   parndrina yinha,   ngurra   mirrtja-rlayi.*
       dog   3sg:ERG-HERE   hit-IP   3sg:ACC   always   be.noisy-SIM
       'He hit the dog because it was barking.' (W7)

(85)   *Ngararla ngathu thawathawa-rlayi, wawawawariyi,   minha karna kara*
       hear-PRES 1sg:ERG go-go-SIM   look-look-UNSP-?   what   person maybe

       thawathawa-yukarrarla.
       go-go-at.night-PRES
       'I can hear someone walking around, looking around (?). It might be someone walking about in the dark.' (R6)

(86)   *Ngurrangu   nhunu   yingkirla,   katjakatja-rlayi   kara.*
       always-YET   3sg:NOM   cry-PRES   sting-sting-SIM   maybe
       'He's still crying, 'must be still hurting him.'' (R8)

       (*Katjakatja* seems to be intransitive but its grammar is complex; see the dictionary entry.)

(87)   *Ngapala kaldrapantjiri,   thawawarra-rlayi thana.*
       well   call.out-UNSP   go-arrive-SIM   3pl:NOM
       'They're singing out as they come (to let us know they're coming).' (R6)

(88)   '*Thawarla nganyi,   kathi parndrithikanga.' 'Kawu, kala ngathu   maka*
       go-PRES   1sg:NOM meat hit-return-FUT   yes   back 1sg:ERG fire

       thangkaka-rlayi.'
       burn-CAUS-SIM
       'I'm going out to get some meat.' 'OK, for my part I'll light a fire.' (X14)

(89)   *Wawana ngathu   yinha   thawathalka-rlayi, wawa-thikathikanga.*
       see-IP   1sg:ERG 3sg:ACC go-up-SIM   see-everywhere-FUT
       'I saw him walk up and then have a look around.' (X14)

11.13 Number markers

The dual suffix *-li* and the plural suffix *-ni* mark number of the subject of imperative and optative verbs. They are glossed DUIMP and PLIMP. Compare the dual and plural exclusive first person pronouns *ngali* and *ngani*. The dual and plural markers *-thili* and *-ndja* (see §10.5.1 and §10.5.2) can also occur on verbs but are not regarded as inflectional suffixes (see §18.1 for notes on this phenomenon).

Verb inflection 143

(90) *Ngapa pakali   marndrathika-pandhili! ...... Putha-pika ngala yula!*
water quick-ERG dip.up-return-down-DUIMP speed-CHAR then 2du:NOM
'Get some water quickly! ...... You were quick!' (P6-7)
(The second sentence is supposed to have been spoken after the two came back.)

(91) *Walya murlathi yintjadu   parndrili, pardrali   yintjadu.*
not   lizard.sp. 3sg:ACC:THERE hit-DUIMP hold-DUIMP 3sg:ACC:THERE
'Don't kill the lizard [you two], keep it.' (P12)

(92) *Ngandjarri thawawarrarla, muduwa yada winkapadani,   ngandjarri*
rain   go-arrive-PRES child hither disappear-in-PLIMP rain

puru.
AVER
"Rain coming, come inside so you won't get wet" (to children). (W4)

(93) *Nhinapandhini-malka.*
sit-down-PLIMP-OPT
'Sit down, all of you.' (P3)

Since the imperative suffix is zero it is not possible to determine an order for it in relation to the number marker. However we should be able to determine an order for number marker and optative, and could assume that this applies also to imperative. This turns out to be not consistent, however; in (93) number marker precedes optative, but in (18-54) we have an order optative-directional-number marker. Number markers are rare in the corpus and there are no other relevant examples.

11.14 Motion away

Motion away or direction of action away from the speaker, addressee or some other reference point may be marked in the verb by a suffix *-ka* or by a stem formative *-windri*. The former will be dealt with here; the latter in §12.3. *-ka* has been noted only with imperatives and optatives and can have the meanings 'do in a direction away' as in (94) and (96) or 'go away and do' as in (95) and (17-27). It may be followed by number markers. This gives rise to a problem with ordering; as noted above, (93) seems to show that the number marker *-ni* precedes *-malka*; (95) seems to show that *-ka* precedes *-ni*; however, *-ka* follows *-malka* — BK would not accept **thawakamalka* but insisted on *thawamalkaka* '(you) can go away'.

(94) *Wagaka   yita!*
shift-AWAY away
'Move over!' (P2)

(95) *Maka-pani thambathambanakani   mayi yambarriyi.*
fire-PRIV   play-play-INCH-AWAY-PLIMP EMPH flat-LOC
"Play away from the fire, out on the flat." (W3)

(96) *Kathi yita pandi ngunyikaw!*
meat away dog give-AWAY:DISTORT
'Give the meat to the dog.' (T7)

Yawarrawarrka, and perhaps SY, has a suffix *-rrka* which may be related to *-ka*. It is known to combine only with the verbs *thawa* 'to go' and *putha* 'to run', and is always followed by *-windri* 'away' (which, however, seems to be permissible without it). Other suffixes may follow the *-windri* (which is glossed 'enter', from its meaning as a free form; see §12.3).

(97) *Ay nhunu thawarrka-windritha watjala ngakaninyi ngampawindriri.*
 oh 3sg:NOM go-rrka-enter-NP not-EMPH 1sg:GEN-LOC tell-enter-UNSP
 'Oh, he went away without telling me.' (Y17) (Last syllable unclear)

11.15 The 'now' present

An augmented form of the present tense, apparently comprising a separate suffix preceding the present tense suffix *-rla*, is used to state that something which was not happening before is happening at the time of speaking. The augmenting suffix can be rendered in translation by the word 'now', which should be read with some emphasis. The augmenting suffix has alternative forms: *-la* (or *-rla*) or *-a* following stem-final /a/ and *-li* (or *-rli*) or *-ya* following stem-final /i/. There are no examples in the corpus with stem-final /u/. The choice between the alternatives may be partly a matter of idiolect but the situation is not at all clear. The doubt regarding the nature of the lateral is due to difficulty in transcription; it often falls in a position in which the alveolar/retroflex distinction is neutralised. Furthermore, there is a possibility sometimes of uncertainty as to whether we have *-la* 'now' + *-rla* 'present' or *-rla* 'present' + *-la* 'emphatic'. There is one example of *-li* and two of *-ya* with stem-final /a/; one of the latter is in the word *kimanayarla* 'swelling up now', but *kimanaarla* has also been heard from the same speaker. The other is in *thudayarla* 'lying down now'; *thudalarla* has also been heard from the same speaker, BK, and *thudaarla* (and all the other forms with *-a*) from TG. On a later occasion BK did not accept a suggested *thudayarla* but replaced it with *thudalarla*. On another occasion he used *thirrilarla* 'fighting now', but accepted *thirriyarla* as an alternative. Only the *-la* form was attested in Yawarrawarrka.

There are also a couple of examples of *-la* preceding the simultaneous action marker *-rlayi*.

The possibility that the augmented present tense suffix might in fact be a reduplicated present tense suffix was considered. Note replacement of an initial consonant by zero or /y/ in cases like *mapaapa* and *mapayapa*, from *mapa* 'to gather', 'to muster' (and also by /l/ in *kilkalilka* from *kilka* 'to know'). However, there are obvious difficulties with this analogy, not the least of which is the fact that BK did not accept some of these reduplicated verb forms when they were repeated to him, and if the preferred interpretation of (102) is believed it can probably be dismissed altogether.

There is one example of *-la*, which could be 'now', following *-nga* FUT, but there is no corroboration, the order is not what would be expected, and it could just as well be an emphatic suffix. There is another example (S9-6) where such a suffix precedes the future, and this seems more plausible.

Examples of the 'now' present include the following (and see Text 2):

(98) *Ngarrtjiyarla   nhunuyi.*
burn-NOW-PRES 3sg:NOM-HERE
'The fire's burning now.' (having just been lit. The previous sentence elicited was 'Light the fire'.) (T5)

(99) *Mulhudu ngathu   pirna thayipandhina, thundrutji   nganyi*
tucker   1sg:ERG big   eat-down-IP   stomach-EMPH 1sg:NOM

kimanaarla.
swollen-INCH-NOW-PRES
"I ate too much and I'm full up now, and my stomach's swollen." (T9)

(100) *Karrukarru, yini   thawalarla!   Walpila   ngathu   yina*
old.man   2sg:NOM go-NOW-PRES when-EMPH 1sg:ERG 2sg:ACC

wawangatji?
see-FUT-EMPH
"Old man, you are going, now! When will I ever see you again?" (W1)

(101) *'Pilitjimani nhutjadu nhina-padipadini.' 'Minhanganalarla   nhunu?'*
policeman 3sg:NOM sit-HAB-GER   what-do-NOW-PRES 3sg
'He used to be a policeman.' 'What's he do now?' (X21)

The clearest example with -*rlayi* is:

(102) *Mulhudu nganyi   thayi-yindringa, ngala yinitji   thawawarrala-rlayi.*
tucker   1sg:NOM eat-RR-FUT   then 2sg:NOM-EMPH go-arrive-NOW-SIM
'I was just going to have a feed when I saw you coming.' (W1-2)

(Alternatively, the last word could be:

thawawarralarlay
go-arrive-NOW-PRES:DISTORT

but present tense seems less likely.)

11.16 Possible suffix, with unknown function

There are four examples in the corpus in which stem-final /a/ of a verb is changed to /i/ (in addition to the many cases where the initial vowel of the suffix -*ini* replaces stem-final /a/). Two of these were in successive sentences elicited from TG. These are:

(103) *Thawawarringa kara   nhunu.*
go-arrive-i-FUT maybe 3sg:NOM
'He might come.' (T13)

(104) *Ngandjarri warlkathalkanga.*   repeated as:
Ngandjarri warlkathalkinga
rain   fall-up(-i)-FUT
'It's going to rain.' (T13)

When these sentences were repeated to BK he found them acceptable, but was unable to suggest any difference between them and the corresponding sentences without the -*i*.

The other examples were elicited from BK:

146   *Chapter 11*

(105)   *Yandhiyandhinga   ngali,   nhunu   nhina-rlayitji.*
        talk-talk-i-FUT   1du:ex:NOM   3sg:NOM   sit-SIM-EMPH
        'We'll have a talk while he's here.' (R6)

        (*yandha* 'to talk'; note that the vowel change affects both realisations of the verb root, just as it does when *-ini* combines with a reduplicated verb (see §10.6).)

(106)   *Ngathu   wakanirla   thanngani-tjadu   kathi   tjipiyitji.*
        1sg:ERG   work-INCH-i-PRES   3pl:GEN-THERE   animal   sheep-LOC-EMPH
        'I work with those sheep.' (W7)

    There is one Yawarrawarrka example:

(107)   *Kara   ngathu   yinhaku   warrkinga   kara,   pani   kara.*
        maybe   1sg:ERG   3sg:ACC-HERE   throw-i-FUT   maybe   not   maybe
        'I might be able to shift it, or maybe not.' (Y11)

This could be a result of confusion between the Yandruwandha future suffix *-nga* and the Yawarrawarrka suffix *-iya* (used in the preceding elicited sentence; a couple of minutes earlier on the tape there is a change from *-iya* to *-nga* in two successive sentences). As for the Yandruwandha examples, there are no clues to the meaning or source of the *-i*. It is hard to believe that it could be simply a mistake.

11.17 Inflection of verb phrases containing two verbs

The only phrases containing two verbs, one being in apposition with the other, are those involving one of the verbs of completion. These are *panina ~ panipanina* and *panika ~ panipanika*, both meaning 'to do completely' or 'everyone to do'. *Pani(pani)na* is intransitive and *pani(pani)ka* transitive. They would appear to be derived from a morpheme **pani-* meaning 'all' or 'complete' but this is not known in any other context; in fact, the free morpheme *pani* has an apparently opposite meaning 'none', 'nothing'. Obviously the connection is that when something is completed there is nothing left to do.[5]

When occurring in a phrase with another verb these verbs of completion do not carry any inflectional suffix (even if the other verb is nominalised). When one of these verbs is the only verb in the phrase it is inflected as any other verb.

Examples include (A-130) and:

(108)   *Ngandra   thawarla   panina.*
        1pl:in:NOM   go-PRES   nothing-INCH
        "Everybody go." (W5)

(109)   *Karna   thana   panipanina   thawa-nhana,   ngala   yinitji,*
        person   3pl:NOM   nothing-nothing-INCH   go-NP   then   2sg:NOM-EMPH

        minhayildra   walya   thawa-nhana.
        what-LOC-BUT   not   go-NP
        'All the [other] people went away, why didn't you go?' (P15)

---

5   The Western Desert languages are another group where a verb meaning 'finish, complete' is derived from a noun meaning 'nothing'.

Verb inflection 147

(110) *Kali   ngathu   yawarri   panikala   kilkarla.*
  already 1sg:ERG language   nothing-CAUS-EMPH   know-PRES
  'I know the language completely now.' (P13)

(111) *Panmana ngani,   walya panipanika   manggini-nguda.*
  put.out-IP 1pl:ex:NOM not nothing-nothing-CAUS burn-GER-ABL
  'We put [the fire] out before it did much damage.' (R7)

In one example *panina* is followed by *-ngu*, presumably the bound conjunction described in §18.3.1; its function is not clear.

(112) *Wawa-thikathikana nhulu,   paninangu   thanha.*
  see-everywhere-IP 3sg:ERG nothing-INCH-THEN 3pl:ACC
  'He had a look at everyone.' (X19)

Another circumstance where a verb phrase might contain two verbs is where one is a verbal time word, such as *ngananhinanhukada* 'yesterday'. In this case, of course, the inflection on the time word is invariable. An example is (32).

12 *Bound verb aspect markers*

A number of formatives, most of which occur also as free forms or are related to free forms, are added to verb stems to specify verb aspect. The term 'aspect' here is used in a broad sense; aspect markers specify such things as 'action while the agent is travelling', 'action directed upwards', 'action on one's own behalf' and 'action over a wide area'. They also include those morphemes, discussed above (Chapter 11), which specify the time of day of an action. The functions of the various bound aspect markers, which are all disyllabic or longer, are illustrated in the following sections.

The affixes described in §12.1 to §12.5 are all associated with motion, those in §12.6 and §12.7 with location, §12.8 to §12.11 with time, §12.12 to §12.16 with direction, §12.17 can specify the beneficiary of an action and §12.18 refers to an action carried out thoroughly. This classification is not rigid, however; for example, one of the affixes associated with motion has a secondary function relating to the beneficiary, as does one of the affixes associated with location.

Of the fifteen bound verb aspect markers which also occur as free forms, ten are verbs and five are adverbs. Two others are reduplicated forms of verbs and one of an adverb. Three are not related to any known free morpheme. They are virtually always stressed as bound morphemes; one small piece of contrary evidence is the appearance on one occasion of what seems to be an emphatic suffix on the root: *pakala warranana* 'carry-EMPH arrive-APP-IP' 'brought [them] for [me]'. Note that *warra* is not known as a free morpheme, and it is clear from the context that it was not intended to function as one on that occasion. The separation of the root and the affixation of the emphatic suffix to it occurred in an unnatural context in which the difference between two very similar words was being explained to the linguist.

Occurrence of two bound aspect markers on a verb is not uncommon. The order of aspect markers is discussed in §12.20.

The following example, taken from a text (A-73 to 76), gives some idea of the frequency and usefulness of bound aspect markers (which are in bold type) in Yandruwandha.

(1) *Ngapala kudru pakuri   ngari, nga   yankala   kurrawagandji   nga*
    well   hole   dig-UNSP down   then   bough-EMPH   put-around-SEQ   then

   windripandhinga   palha   mukuli.   Ngapala pandhi wirlpinhina-rnanga,
   enter-down-FUT   bird   bone-INST well   down   whistle-sit-CONT

   ngala kathi   thana   ngarangaramini-rlayila,   warruwitjilitji.
   then   animal 3pl:NOM hear-hear-run-SIM-EMPH   emu-ERG-EMPH

148

Thawawarranga   thangguwagawaganga,   ngala   karna   nhunu
go-arrive-FUT   stand-around-around-FUT   then   person   3sg:NOM

purrinhina-rlayi ngari   mingkayi.   Ngarrungu   thangguthalkawarrandji
hide-sit-SIM   down   hole-LOC   only-still   stand-up-arrive-SEQ

dranyingalatji   yadali.
hit.(throwing)-FUT-EMPH-EMPH   boomerang-INST

'Well, they would dig a hole and put boughs around it. Then [a man] would get down into the hole and whistle with a bird bone, and the emus would hear it as they were passing. They would come and stand around, while that man hid down in the hole. Then he would just jump up and hit [one] with a boomerang.' (D2)

Table 12-1 summarises these aspect markers; they are given in alphabetical order and the section where each is discussed is given. The second column gives an indication of the function, the third gives the gloss for those markers which are not known as free forms, and the fourth gives the gloss for those markers which are known as free forms, which is also the normal gloss of the free form (and so not necessarily indicative of the function of the bound form). There is one exception, *yukarra*, which has different glosses as a free form and as a bound form.

Table 12-1: Bound aspect markers

Marker	Function	Non free-form gloss	Free-form gloss	Section
mini	do on passing, do and go, go and do		run	12.2
ngari	downwards		down	12.13
nhina	continued action		sit	12.8
pada	in, into, across		inside	12.12
padapada	habitual	HAB		12.9
pandhi	downwards		down	12.13
rdaka	a different way(?)	?		12.16
rduda	while going		along	12.1
thalka	upwards; in the morning		up	12.14
thanggu	for some time(?), every day(?)		stand	12.19
tharra	following; completion, thoroughness		fly	12.18
thawa	do on passing, do and go, go and do		go	12.2
thayi	do for oneself		eat	12.17
thika	action directed back, do and return; do on behalf of another		return	12.4
thikathika	widespread action, action affecting many objects	everywhere		12.6
waga (also *wagawaga*)	around a centre		around	12.7
walpirri	across		across	12.15
warra	arrival	arrive		12.5
warrka	in the morning(?)	(none)		12.11
windri	action directed away or followed by movement away		enter	12.3
yukarra	at night	at night	spend the night	12.10

12.1 Action while going along

The formative *-rduda* denotes a continued or frequently repeated action carried out while the actor is travelling. It is to be distinguished from the formatives *-thawa* and *-mini* (see §12.2). *-rduda* is not related to any free morpheme in present-day Yandruwandha.

(2) *Nhipangurru nganyi thawanhana, paltjapaltjana-rduda-rnanga.*
     spouse-COM 1sg:NOM go-NP strong-strong-INCH-along-CONT
     'My wife and I have been struggling along.' (i.e. finding the going hard) (B23)

(3) *Maka nhutjadu manggardudarla.*
     fire 3sg:NOM-THERE burn-along-PRES
     'The bushfire's burning along.' (B11)

Other verbs derived in this way include *thayirduda* "to eat along", i.e. 'eat while going along' (*thayi* 'to eat'), *nhinarduda* 'to travel in a vehicle' (*nhina* 'to sit') and *yibayibarduda* 'to drink (at intervals) while travelling' (*yiba* 'to drink '). See (9-63) for another example.

12.2 Action on passing

Two morphemes, *-thawa* and *-mini*, seem to have the same function: to denote that an action is performed in an interval between stages in a journey, or that the agent begins to go somewhere immediately after performing the action, or performs the action on completing his travelling, or performs an action, lasting a comparatively short time, while in motion. These functions are to be distinguished from those of *-rduda* (§12.1) which denotes a continuing action contemporaneous with the motion.

As free morphemes *thawa* is the verb 'to go', 'to walk' and *mini* the verb 'to run'. To some extent it appears that *-thawa* and *-mini* are affixed to different verb roots, but there are some roots which may combine with either. These include *ngarangara* (from *ngara* 'to hear', 'to listen'), *thuda* 'to lie' and *thanggu* 'to stand'. *Yawathawari* and *yawaminiri* (*yawa* 'to spread') were coined by me and both accepted by BK: he translated the former as "you went past and made your bed, and you went on somewhere" and the latter as "just the same". *mandri* 'to get', *panima* 'to finish (intr.)', *parndri* 'to hit', 'to kill', *wawa* 'to see', *paku* 'to dig', *yiba* ' to drink', *waltha* 'to carry', and *nhina* 'to sit' have all been heard with *-thawa*, while *karra* 'to tie', *thawa* 'to go', *thika* 'to return' and *winka* 'to die' have been noted with *-mini*. *Thawathawa* and *minimini* occur but their meanings show that they are reduplicated forms.

The English verb 'to pass (someone going)' is translated as *wawathawa* 'see-go' or *wawathawawarra* 'see-go-arrive', or as *ngardrawarrka(thawa)* 'behind-leave(-go)'.

There are a couple of examples of reduplication of combined forms in *-thawa*: *mandrithawa-mandrithawa* 'to pick up here and there' and *thudathawa-thudathawa* 'to have two or three days on the road (travelling by day and camping at night)'. Compare *mandrithawa* 'to stop and pick up' in (16-31), and *thudathawa* in (6) below.

Examples include (1) (above), (A-17), and the following:

(4) *Pipa yintjadu walthathawana kundangalili. Wayi kaka kara.*
     paper 3sg.ACC-THERE carry-go-IP wind-ERG question near maybe
     'The paper was blown away by the wind. "I don't know how far."' (P5)

(5) Nhinanhinathawana nhunu.
     sit-sit-go-IP   3sg:NOM
     'He came and sat down for a minute.' (P10)

(6) Karirriyi   nganyi   thudathawana.
     creek-LOC   1sg:NOM lie-go-IP
     'I camped at the creek while I was on the way here.' (P10)

(7) Yila-kadi   yini   thangguminiwindrinayay?
     where-DAT   2sg:NOM stand-run-enter-IP-DISTORT
     'Where did you get up and walk away to?' (W5)
     (See §12.3 for -windri)

(8) Ngathu   nhipa-ka-lapurra   nhantjadu,   nhani
     1sg:ERG   spouse-CAUS-REMP   3sg:fem:ACC-THERE   3sg:fem:NOM

     thawamini-warrarlatji.
     go-run-arrive-PRES-EMPH
     'That woman I used to be married to came here.' (R10)

(9) Karna   nhutjadu   thawamini-warrana   ngarrungu   karrtjipandhindji.
     person   3sg:NOM-THERE   go-run-arrive-IP   just-YET   turn-down-SEQ
     'That fellow came here for a minute and then he just turned around and went away.'
     (W8) (see §12.5 for -warra)

12.3 Action directed away

The formative *-windri* denotes action (a) directed away from or (b) followed by movement away from the speaker or some other point of reference. As a free morpheme *windri* is the verb 'to enter' and as such could imply movement towards the speaker as well as movement away from him. Compare Ngamini, in which the (presumably) cognate form *wirri* 'to enter' has a bound allomorph denoting 'arrival' (which is denoted by *-warra* in Yandruwandha).

The following verbs, as they appear in the corpus, seem to have meanings suggested by (a) above, rather than (b):

pakawindri	'to carry away'
thawawindri	'to go away'
tharrawindri, tharrawindritharra	'to fly away' (see §12.18 for *-tharra*)
tharratharrawindri	'to hurry away' (*tharratharra* 'to hurry' is a reduplicated form of *tharra* 'to fly')
wagawindri	'to move (residence) away'
yinbawindri	'to send away'
ngunyiwindri	'to give to someone going away'
kudhiwindri	'to sneak off' (*kudhi* 'to hide')

Verbs for which (b) seems more appropriate include:

kurrawindri	'to leave (TR)' (*kurra* 'to put down')
warrkawindri	'to leave (TR)' (*warrka* 'to throw (away)')

(*warrka* in compounds such as this seems to have a meaning somewhat different from its normal meaning. The object of *warrkawindri* is a person, that of *kurrawindri* a thing.)

thangguwindri	'to get up to go, to get up and go' (*thanggu* 'to stand')
thangguminiwindri	'to stand up and walk away' (see §12.2 for -*mini*)
winkaminiwindri	'to duck off' (*winka* 'to run away', 'to disappear').

However, there is some overlap; for example, *thawathalkana* was once given as an alternative to *thangguwindrithalkana* (*-thalka* here referring to action in the morning).

Examples of the use of *-windri* include (11-34) and:

(10) Nhunu   thawawindrina,   mardratji   pakawindriri,   walya
      3sg:NOM   go-enter-IP   stone-EMPH   carry-enter-UNSP   not

      ngunyini   yinhayi.
      give-GER   3sg:ACC-HERE
      "He ran away with the money and never gave it to you." (W2)

(11) Ngathu   yina   mardra   ngunyiwindringa.
      1sg:ERG   2sg:ACC   stone   give-enter-FUT
      'I'll give you some money.' (spoken to a person belonging to another community) (W4)

12.4 Action directed back

The formative -*thika* fulfils one of four functions: it denotes action (a) directed back to or (b) followed by a return to camp, or to some other point of recent origin of the actor, and in most cases also preceded by movement to the location of the action, or (c) action directed back to the point of origin of an action to which it is a response, or (d) action carried out on behalf of someone other than the actor. Function (a) is illustrated by (15, 16), function (b) by (12, 13, 14), function (c) by (14-49) and (16-21) and function (d) by (17) and (18). Function (b) is probably primary, to judge from BK's translations of forms I made up ('went and did X', with 'and came back' added sometimes). Function (d) is obviously related to function (b), since it would normally imply going to the other person's camp or some other place, performing the action and then returning home. However, (c) also involves the implication that the actions are the type which would normally be carried out in one's own camp. Functions (a) and (b) are far more common than (c). Function (b) involves actions which would not normally be thought of as implying any direction; thus *nhinathika* and *thangguthika* would both mean 'to go and stay somewhere for a short time and then return home', *thudathika* 'go and camp somewhere and then return home'. When the verb is transitive, both agent and object are normally directed towards the camp, although in at least one case ('send back') it is only the object.

-*thika* is one of the most frequently used verb stem formatives. Verbs containing this affix in the corpus are listed below according to the function of the suffix. The root will not be translated separately except where necessary. As a free form *thika* is the verb 'to return'.

Function (a)

darrpithika	'to turn back'
kadithikathalka	'to chase back up' (-*thalka* 'up')
minithika	'to run back'

minithikawarra	'to run back' (also function (b)) (*-warra* 'arrival')
nhinathikapandhi	'to sit back down' (*-pandhi* 'down')
pakathika, pakanathika	'to bring back', 'to carry home'
winkathikapada	'to duck back in' (*-pada* 'in')
yinbathika	'to send back home'
thukathika	'to carry back'
walthathika	'to carry back'
walthayindrithika	'to carry back for oneself'
winkathika, winkapanithika	'to run back home'

Function (b)

kunathika	'to defecate'
marndrathika	'to get (water)', 'to dip up'
mandritika	'to get'
mandrithikapada	'to get out'
mapathika	'to muster', 'to gather', 'to pick up'
minithikawarra	'to run there and back' (also function (a))
nhinatharrathika	'to go and visit' (*nhina* 'to sit')
pakuthika	'to dig up'
parndrithika	'to kill'
pudathika	'to urinate'
thangguthika	'to go and visit' (*thanggu* 'to stand')
thambanathika	'to dance'
wanthithika	'to look for'
warrkathika	'to leave [over there]' (*warrka* 'to throw')

Function (c)

nganathika	'to tell [someone] back'
ngunyithika	'to give back'

Function (d)

nhapithika	'to mix (damper)'
dringathika	'to scrape'
windrithika	'to rub'
thinbathika	'to chisel'
wawawawanathika	'to look after'

Three verbs in *-thika* cannot be fitted into the above categories, at least with the translations at present available. These are:

kudhithika	'to go and hide'
kuthithika	'to have been [in a place] before' (*kuthi* 'to come')
nhinathika	'to return'

The following examples illustrate the use of *-thika*.

(12) *Warana nhutjadu nhinggiyi nhinathikana?*
who-NOM 3sg:NOM-THERE location-HERE sit-return-IP
'Who's that fellow who was here a while ago.' (T12)

(13) *Thawa-nhana yini   thangguthikanga thannganiyi, karna*
     go-NP   2sg:NOM stand-return-FUT 3pl:GEN-LOC person
     thulayitji.
     stranger-LOC-EMPH
     'You went and visited those strangers at their camp.' (R1)

(14) *Kathi-ngadi ngaldra   thawarla parndrithikanga.*
     animal-DAT 2du:in:NOM go-PRES kill-return-FUT
     'We're going out kangaroo hunting today.' (C2)

(15) *Thikapandhi mayi, walkithikapandhi mayi, warlkayila   yini.*
     return-down EMPH climb-return-down EMPH fall-POT-EMPH 2sg:NOM
     "Climb down because you might fall off." (W3)

(16) *Yundrali wawathikana   nganha nhulu.*
     far-ERG look-return-IP 1sg:ACC 3sg:ERG
     'He looked back at me [when he was a long way away].' (W1)
     (but *wawathika* is more often used to mean 'go and see, go and visit')

(17) *Windrithikana ngathu yinha,   parlaka panipanika.*
     rub-return-IP 1sg:ERG 3sg:ACC body   nothing-nothing-CAUS
     'I rubbed him all over.' (B10)

(18) *Dringathikari.*
     scrape-return-UNSP
     "Well you went over there and *dringari* for somebody."
     (B10, word suggested by GB and translated by BK)

12.5 Arrival

The suffix *-warra* denotes 'arrival'; the action is directed towards the vicinity of the speaker or some other reference point and has actually reached that vicinity or appears to be soon to do so (19, 20, 22). Alternatively, it may sometimes denote that the action has been or is being carried out to completion (21, perhaps 22, perhaps 23). *Warra* is not known as a free form.

(19) *Pirripirri nhutjadu   thawawarrarla.*
     white.man 3sg:NOM-THERE go-arrive-PRES
     'The white man's coming.' (T7)

(20) *Ngathu pulhu   walthawarranala.*
     1sg:ERG 3du:ACC carry-arrive-IP-EMPH
     'I carried them in to the camp.' (W1)

(21) *Nga kurnutji   nhunu   thangguthalkawarranga, wawayindripandhiringu.*
     then one-EMPH 3sg:NOM stand-up-arrive-FUT   look-RR-down-UNSP-THEN
     'Then one of them stood right up and looked down at himself.' (E1, in S6-5)

(22) *Thikawarranatji   nhaniyi,   kudhikudhi, windriwarranga,*
     return-arrive-IP-EMPH 3sg:fem:NOM-HERE hidden   enter-arrive-FUT
     walya ngathu nhanha   wawa-rlayi, purrtjinawarrana
     not   1sg:ERG 3sg:fem:ACC see-SIM   frightened-CAUS-arrive-IP

nganha   nhandra.
1sg:ACC 3sg:fem:ERG
"She sneaks in, in the back way and give me a fright." (W5)

(The function of -*warra* in *purrtjinawarrana* is not clear; it may denote 'on arrival' or it may mean 'really, properly.')

(23)   *Warrkawarrana-nhanatji   ngathu   yinha,   ngala   nhulutji   maka*
       throw-arrive-APP-NP-EMPH 1sg:ERG 3sg:ACC then   3sg:ERG-EMPH fire

   wangangarini-ngadi   ngana-rlayi.
   light-down-GER-DAT   do-SIM
   'When I left him he was just about to light the fire.' (X15)

When I asked about the stem *warrkawarra* on another occasion, I was told that it could be used of someone carrying a load of (fire)wood back and dumping it. Clearly in that case it has the 'arrival' meaning, which it does not seem to have in (23) unless[1] it is the other person, the object, who has just arrived (as in (24)).

(24)   *Mayathali nhulu   nganawarrana nhipa   nhunggani patja-rlayi*
       boss-ERG   3sg:ERG tell-arrive-IP spouse   3sg:DAT   be.sick-SIM

   warliyi,   yinbathikana   nhulu   yinha.
   house-LOC   send-return-IP 3sg:ERG 3sg:ACC
   'The boss told [him] when he got there that his wife was sick in the house, and sent him [up there].' (X50)

See also (1).

The -*warra* of *ngukuwarra* 'to vomit' and *wilawarra* 'to sit on one's haunches' is probably not the same morpheme. This may also be true of -*warra* in *thilpawarra* 'to notify'. The function of -*warra* in *karrtjikarrtjimawarra* 'to stir up'(?) is not clear.

Other verbs in -*warra* include:

kanpanawarra	'to appear' (*kanpa* 'visible', -*na* inchoative)
kulkupathalkawarra	'to jump out'
kurrakurrawarra	'to camp (on arrival)'
kuthiwarra	'do come', 'to arrive'
minithalkawarra	'to run up'
miniwarra	'to come (of a car)'
minithikawarra	'to run back', 'to run there and back'
nganawarra	'to inform'
pakawarra	'to bring'
thikaminiwarra	'to go back for a while'
windrimawarra	'to put in'
warlkawarra	'to fall'

---

[1] As a referee suggests.

156   *Chapter 12*

12.6 Widespread action

The formative *-thikathika*, occasionally heard as *-thigathiga*, denotes action over a wide area or affecting many objects; in particular it probably means action over the whole of the available area or affecting all the available objects. It is a reduplicated form of the formative *-thika*.

(25)   *Nhuludu   ngana-thikathikarla   madlandji   nhukiyi   nganyi,*
       3sg:ERG-THERE   tell-everywhere-PRES   bad   location-HERE   1sg:NOM

       ngala   nhunutji   yarnduldrangu.
       then   3sg:NOM-EMPH   how-BUT-YET
       "He's telling everyone I'm no good, but he's just the same." (P10)

(26)   *Yuda   thawa-padapadarla walya padlakurnu-padlakurnu*
       2pl:NOM   go-HAB-PRES   not   place-one-place-one

       wawa-thikathikanga.
       look-everywhere-FUT
       "You fellows ought to go and have a look all round the place." (D3)

(27)   *Walya mini-thikathika   ngurratji,   pirritjampanayila   yini.*
       not   run-everywhere   always-EMPH   tired-INCH-POT-EMPH   2sg:NOM
       'Don't run around all the time, you'll get tired.' (B14)

See also (30) and (9-144).

Verbs in *-thikathika* are listed below according to whether the translation given is 'everywhere', 'here and there' (there is probably no real difference between these two) or 'everybody/everything' (i.e. affecting many objects — this again may not be clearly distinguished from the earlier translations).

(a) Everywhere:

purrithikathika	'to hide all over the place' (probably more appropriate in (b))
wawathikathika	'to look around', 'to have a good look around'
yawathikathika	'to spread all around'
parrkukathikathika	'to spill all over the place'
parndrithikathika	'to be on a hunting trip'

(b) Here and there:

minithikathika	'to run about here and there'
nhinathikathika	'to sit here and there'

(c) Everybody/everything:

karrukathikathika	'to initiate all the eligible people' (*karru* 'man', *-ka* 'causative')
nganathikathika	'to tell everyone'
ngunyithikathika	'to give around'
dringathikathika	'to scrape everybody' (?!)
thumbalkathikathika	'to show around'
windrithikathika	'to go around rubbing everybody'
yakathikathika	'to go around asking everybody'
mandrithikathika	'to go around and pick it all up'
mapathikathika	'to muster', 'to gather', 'to pick up'

Function not clear, perhaps (b)
> *thangguthikathika*   'to be somewhere for a while (used of a dog)'
> (*thanggu* 'to stand').

12.7 Action around a centre

The suffix *-waga* denotes motion located or directed around some object or place. It usually occurs reduplicated, in which case it probably refers to a more extensive area or other attenuation of the action than the simple form. When reduplicated it is, at least in many cases, interchangeable with *-thikathika* (§12.6). Note also that there seems to be a preference for *-wagawaga* on *thawa* 'to go' but *-thikathika* on *mini* 'to run', which seems to suggest that there is no difference in the functions. However, contrast *nhinathikathika* 'to sit here and there' with *nhinawagawaga* (see (31) below); when I asked about this pair on a later field trip, BK said: 'Well it's they scattered around, *nhinathikathikarla*. And *nhinawagawagarla* means they sitting in a round ring'. *Thangguthikathika* seems to mean 'to be around a place for a while' (another time translated as 'walking around and standing around') and was contrasted with *thangguwagawaga* 'to stand around'. Not too much weight should be attached to contrastive translations like this given by language speakers (in general); when asked for the difference between two forms people feel under pressure to find some difference even if none exists.

The difference between *-waga* and *-wagawaga* is illustrated by:

(28)   *Karrtjiwagarla.*
       turn-around-PRES
       '[He's] turning around'. (W8)

and

(29)   *Wathi   nhunuyi   karrtjiwagawagarla.*
       machine 3sg:NOM-HERE turn-around-around-PRES
       '[The tape recorder] is going round and round.' (W6)

Other examples include:

(30)   *Ngapala thawawagawaga-rnangardi   karru-ka-thikathikana —*
       well   go-around-around-CONT-EMPH man-CAUS-everywhere-?

       padlakurnu-padlakurnu.
       place-one-place-one
       'Well, they went around everywhere initiating all the young men.' (E1, =S6-17)

(31)   *Walya makayitji   nhinawagawaga, kudla-yindriyila   yini.*
       not   fire-LOC-EMPH sit-around-around burn-RR-POT-EMPH 2sg:NOM
       'Don't sit close around the fire or you'll get burnt.' (X19)

(32)   *Ngulu-ka-yindri-waganga, ya   winkathikapadakaldri.*
       end-CAUS-RR-around-FUT and disappear-return-in-again
       'He peeped around and then ducked back in again.' (B11)

(33)   *Palha pawayi tharrawagawagarla.*
       bird hawk   fly-around-around-PRES
       'The hawks are going round in circles.' (B17)

158   Chapter 12

(34) *Ay ngarru nganyi   thawawagawagarla.*
    oh only 1sg:NOM go-around-around-PRES
    'Oh, I'm just walking around.' (W8)

See also (1) for both *-waga* and *-wagawaga*.

Other words in *-waga* and *-wagawaga* include:[2]

kulpinawaga	'to surround'
dringawaga	'to scrape all around'
thambanawaga,	
thambanawagawaga	'to play around'
mandriwagawaga	'to go around and pick [it] all up' (cf. *mandrithikathika*)
purriwagawaga	'to hide all over the place'
thumbalkawagawaga	'to show around'
wapawagawaga	'to turn around (TR)', 'to twist round and round'
wawawagawaga	'to look around' (cf. *wawathikathika*)
yawawagawaga	'to spread (something) all round'

12.8 Continued action

The formative *-nhina* has two functions:

(a) to denote a continuing action or state, such as 'being seated' as opposed to 'the act of sitting down', and

(b) to denote action in the daytime. The second function has been discussed earlier (§11.4). In one case the translation of a verb with this formative, at least as it was given, is specialised to the extent that it is not completely predictable: *wawawawanhina* 'to expect', 'to watch out for' (*wawa* 'to see', 'to look').

As a free form *nhina* is the verb 'to sit', 'to stay', 'to be (in a place)'.

Examples of *-nhina* with function (a) include:

(35) *Thudanhinarla nhutjadu.*
    lie-sit-PRES   3sg:NOM-THERE
    'He's lying down.' (T7)

Contrast:

(36) *Thudapandhirla nhutjadu.*
    lie-down-PRES 3sg:NOM-THERE
    'He's (in the act of) lying down.' (W1, 2, 4)

(37) *Pipinhinanga nganyi,   makamakayi yina.*
    rest-sit-FUT 1sg:NOM fire-fire-LOC EMPH
    'I'll have a rest while it's hot.' (R6)

See also (1) and (8–36).

In the following examples it is not clear whether *-nhina* has the function (a) or (b):

---

[2] Note that some words in the lists given in this chapter do not occur in elicited or text material but were made up by me and suggested to BK, who gave a translation for them. For example, some words which occurred with *-thikathika* were tried with *-wagawaga* instead, and vice versa. Such suggested words were usually accepted and the translations given were what was expected.

(38) *Pirritjampanarla nganyi, minimini-nhinini-nguda.*
 tired-INCH-PRES 1sg:NOM run-run-sit-GER-ABL
 "I'm tired of running about all day." (W7)

(39) *Walarriyi nganyi nhinanhina-nhukada.*
 shade-LOC 1sg:NOM sit-sit-RECP
 "I was sitting under the shade yesterday." (R3)

In fact, the two functions certainly overlap; e.g. BK translated *nhinanhina* as "sat all day".

12.9 Habitual action

The suffix *-padapada* is used to mark habitual action, and in particular the gerund of a verb in *-padapada* denotes past habitual, normally translated as 'used to'. *-padapada* does not often occur with tense inflections. It is assumed to be a reduplicated form of the formative *-pada* (see §12.12), although there is no clear synchronic connection between their functions.

(40) *Wawa-padapadarlatji nganha nhulu, ngarru nganha parndripadangangu.*
 see-HAB-PRES-EMPH 1sg:ACC 3sg:ERG only 1sg:ACC hit-in-FUT-THEN
 'Whenever he sees me he hits me.' (P8)

(41) *Nganggalhildra thana wani thamba-na-padipadini, walya*
 owner-BUT 3pl:NOM corroboree dance-INCH-HAB-GER not

 yiwali wawini-ngadi yirrbandji yina.
 woman-ERG see-GER-DAT permitted EMPH
 'They used to dance on their own; the women weren't supposed to watch.' (P11)

There are many examples of *-padipadini* in the ethnographic text in the dictionary volume, especially in the second half. See also (1) and (14-45) and, for another present tense example, (16-84).
One slightly problematical example is:

(42) *Malkanpa nganyi nhina-padipadini nyangi parrkulu.*
 Innamincka 1sg:NOM sit-HAB-GER moon two
 'I stayed at Innamincka for two months.' (X5)

Actually, the sentence asked for involved two years, not two months; this seems to be a more reasonable time to justify the use of a 'used to' construction.

12.10 Action at night

The suffix *-yukarra*, denoting action at night, has been discussed above (§11.4).

12.11 Action in the morning

The formative *-warrka*, only rarely used and doubtfully translated as 'action in the morning', has been discussed in §11.4. Another meaning is suggested by the translation of the suggested verb form *thambanathikawarrkana* as 'went over and danced' and the added comment: '*-warrka* means "over there, way over"'.

12.12 Action directed in or across

The suffix *-pada* has a variety of functions, some of them imperfectly or not at all understood. They include:

(a) to denote that the action is carried out in or directed into a confined space;

(b) to denote that the object of the action is initially in a confined space;

(c) to denote that the action is directed to the other side (from the agent) of some barrier (such as a river) (but compare §12.15);

(d) to denote action early in the morning (there is only one example in the corpus);

(e) possibly to denote physical contact between the actor and the object;

(f) unknown functions.

As a free morpheme *pada* is an adverb, 'inside'.

As noted above (§12.9), the 'habitual' suffix *-padapada* is presumed to be a reduplicated form of *-pada*, and in theory it might be expected that the two of them could be combined. When I suggested the word *nhinapadapadapadarla* 'stops inside all the time' BK readily accepted it. (However, when I made up a comparable word with three occurrences of *thika* — as a stem with the reduplicated suffix *-thikathika*, see §12.6 — he did not accept it, but replaced the suffix with the adverb *purru*.[3])

Examples include:

function (a):

(43) *Kathi windripadana mardrayi.*
 snake enter-in-IP stone-LOC
 'The snake went under the stone.' (T3)

(44) *Ngandjarri thawawarrarla, muduwa yada winkapadani*
 rain go-arrive-PRES child hither disappear-in-PLIMP

 ngandjarri-puru.
 rain-AVER
 "Rain coming, come inside so you won't get wet." (W4)

(45) *Nhinapada!*
 sit-in
 "Go and sit inside!" (W4, word suggested by GB, repeated and translated by BK)

Other verbs in this category include *thawapada* 'to go in', *kurrapada* 'to put in', *thudapada* 'to lie inside', *windrimapada* 'to bring inside' (*windri* 'to enter', *-ma* causative) and *winkathikapada* 'to duck back in'.

function (b)

(46) *Kathi mandritharrapada mirrkayi nhunggatjaduyi.*
 meat get-fly-in bag-LOC 3sg:GEN:THERE-LOC
 'Take the meat out of the bag.' (T7) (See §12.18 for *-tharra*)

---

[3] One word occurs in a text with three occurrences of the morpheme *windri*, but there is another suffix intervening at one point: *windriwindrimawindrimalka* 'enter-enter-CAUS-enter-OPT' 'can put [water in the waterbag] to go away [with]'.

Bound verb aspect markers 161

Other verbs include *mandripada* 'to get (them) out' (also *mandrithikapada* 'to go in and bring (them) out') and *dukapada* 'to pull out' (e.g. a witchetty grub from a tree).

function (c):

(47) *Kinipapayi   nganha   warrkawindringa, ngapa   yulpurru yina*
     Cooper's.Creek-LOC 1sg:ACC   throw-enter-FUT   water   flood   EMPH

   ngaka-rlayi, walyala   ngani   purrkapadayi   wilpadalitji.
   run-SIM   not-EMPH   1pl:ex:NOM   cross-across-POT   wagon-INST-EMPH
   'They left me at Cooper's Creek because it was flooded and we mightn't have got across with the wagon.' (R9, =S10-2-3)

   See also (S10-8, 10, 12 and 21).

Other verbs of this type include:

thingapada	'to pull in' (used of the action of pulling a net, which had been stretched across a river, into the bank) (See (11-78)).
kanpapada	'to be visible on the other side'
karrkapada	'to call out (to someone on the other side)'
mandripada	'to get [something] on the other side'
thanmapada	'to swim across'
thawapada	'to go across'
tharrapada	'to fly across'
warrkapada	'to throw to the other side'
wawapada	'to see [someone/something] on the other side'
wawatharrapada	'to see [someone] going across'
yakapada	'to ask [someone on the other side]' (See (S10-8, 10, 12))
yinbapada	'to send across'
kadipada	'to chase across' (e.g. drive cattle across a river)

function (d):

The only verb in this class is *kuthipada*, said to mean 'to leave early in the morning'.

function (e):

(48) *Warlkana nganyi   walya nganha   yundru   pardrapadanatji.*
     fall-IP   1sg:NOM   not   1sg:ACC   2sg:ERG   hold-in-IP-EMPH
     'I fell because you didn't hold me.' (T11)

(49) *Warlu   nganha   milkapadana?*
     who-ERG   1sg:ACC   pinch-in-IP
     'Who pinched me?' (P25)

Other verbs include *parndripada* 'to hit' (with the hand?), *wikapada* 'to wipe', perhaps *mandripada* and *mandriyindripada* 'to marry' (*mandri* 'to get', *-yindri* reciprocal).

Note, however:

(50) *Kayidi pardra ngathu   mandripadarla   ngan.gutji.*
     now   ?   1sg:ERG   get-in-PRES   word-EMPH
     'I'm just beginning to understand the language' ("just getting hold of it"). (P13)

162   Chapter 12

function (f)

Verbs in which the function of formative *-pada* is not clear include *karrapada* 'to tie on', 'to tie up', *ngunyipada* 'to give (something to someone when he is going) away', *pulkapada* 'to light (a fire)' (*pulka* 'to blow'), *thinbapada* 'to chisel (a piece out of) something standing up' (compare *thinbapandhi* when the object is lying down).

12.13 Action directed downwards

Two bound morphemes, *-pandhi* and *-ngari*, may be used to denote action directed downwards. Both of these occur also as free forms, being adverbs with the meaning 'down'. Both as a free form and as a bound morpheme *(-)pandhi* is by far the more common. No consistent difference in function has been noted. The two seem to be interchangeable at least in some cases, possibly always.[4]

(51)   *Nhinapandhi!*
       sit-down
       'Sit down!' (T7)

(52)   *Thawapandhirla   nganyi   karirri-ngadi   ngapa   marndra-yindringa.*
       go-down-PRES   1sg:NOM   river-DAT   water   dip.up-RR-FUT
       'I'm going down to the river for water.' (T11)

(53)   *Kinipapa   nhulu   mulhatji   wawangarirla.*
       Cooper's.Creek   3sg:ERG   face-EMPH   look-down-PRES
       'He's facing towards the river.' (P3)

       See also (1, 15, 21).

-pandhi is one of the most common of all verb stem formatives, and is used in some cases where it is hard for an English speaker to see any idea of downward movement; in some cases, of course, there may be a quite obvious connection in the mind of the speaker which is simply omitted from his translation. It is interesting that in several of these cases 'up' is often used (similarly enigmatically) in English — cook up, mix up, eat up etc. The following list gives examples of such words, for *-ngari* as well as *-pandhi*. In general, the translation is the same as that of the verb root.

kudlapandhi	'to cook'
karrtjipandhi, karrtjingari	'to turn back', 'to turn around' (*karrtji* 'to roll over')
marndrapandhi	'to paint oneself'
nhapipandhi, nhapingari	'to mix (TR)'
panmapandhi	'to put out (fire)'
parndripandhi	'to kill'
thayipandhi	'to eat'
dirrkapandhi	'to turn off (the track)'
karrapandhi	'to tie up', 'to tie together'
wantjapandhi, wantjangari	'to try'
wangapandhi, wangangari	'to light (a fire)'

---

[4]   BK said on one occasion that 'if you up a tree you *wawangariri*, and if you standing you *wawapandhiri* (i.e. look down)'. However, other evidence does not support this distinction.

thangkakapandhi   'to make (a fire)'
wapapandhi   'to twist around (TR)'
papanangari   'to start' (*papana* 'to start', -*na* is probably a formative but the root *papa* is not known elsewhere).

In those cases where both a -*pandhi* form and a -*ngari* form appear in the above list (and in some other cases where both are attested) one of the two has been suggested by me as an alternative to the other (which has been elicited or heard in sentences or text) and has been repeated or at least accepted by the informant.

12.14 Action directed upwards

The formative -*thalka* denotes action directed upwards, or alternatively action carried out (early?) in the morning. The latter function has been discussed in §11.4. As a free morpheme *thalka* is the adverb 'up'.

(54) *Thangguthalka!*
     stand-up
     'Stand up!' (T7)

(55) *Minha kara   nhunuyi   marrkathalkarla maltji ngakaniyi.*
      what   maybe   3sg:NOM-HERE   crawl-up-PRES   leg   1sg:GEN-LOC
      'There's something crawling on my leg.' (C5)

(56) *Mayathali nhulu   yadamani pangkiparndrithalkana mardrawita-ngadi.*
      boss-ERG   3sg:ERG   horse   rib-hit-up-IP   stone-hill-DAT
      'The boss galloped his horse up the hill.' (R6)

See also (1).

It seems that it should be possible to have -*thalka*, with its time-related meaning, and -*pandhi* or -*ngari* co-occurring in the same verb. When I asked BK whether you could say *thawapandhithalkana* 'went down this morning' he said '*Thawathalkana nhunu, and thawapandhina nhunu*', but then agreed that you could say it the way I had (but did not repeat it). However, he would not accept *thawathalkathalkana* 'went up this morning', using -*thalka* once with its spatial and once with its temporal meaning.

12.15 Action directed across

There is a single example of an adverb *walpirri* 'across', given as (16-33). This is also known as a verb modifier, 'action across something', more specifically, 'action directed across something that requires going up and across and down to cross'. Thus you go *walpirri* a sandhill or a mountain, but you go *pada* (see §12.12) a creek or a road. Comparing *kulkumapada* and *kulkumawalpirri* (*kulkuma* 'to jump') BK said: 'Well, he's jumping across, and the other one is he's jumping over'. Another way of expressing this kind of movement is by combining -*thalka* 'up' with -*pada* 'across', as in *walkithalkapadari* 'climbed over'. It has been heard both as -*walpirri* and -*ngalpirri* (or even -*alpirri*). However, there is only one unelicited example (from a story) and other information was gathered in a discussion of the meaning of the form.

(57) Karna   muthu   kurnu nhunu   kankunu   durru-nguda, kulkuma-walpirringa.
     person indeed one   3sg:NOM   windbreak back-ABL   jump-across-FUT
     'The other man [sneaked up] behind the windbreak, and jumped over it.' (B26)

12.16 Going a different way

The suffix *-rdaka*, heard only in the last few days of the fieldwork, seemed to refer to a traveller's observation of the tracks, and perhaps of the camp or even the actual person(s), travelling in a different direction to the observer. It was not possible to determine its function with any semblance of certainty. In some cases it was combined with *-pada*, which itself can mean 'across' (although in the sense of 'to the other side' not 'in a crossways direction'). Also there was a change in some of the details during the course of our discussions; these concerned whether or not the person(s) themselves might have been seen, and whether or not the two parties could have been travelling the same way.

The initial occurrence of *-rdaka* was in the elicited sentence given in (58).

(58) Palthuyi   ngathu(nga?)   thina wawana, thawardaka-padini-nguda nhunu.
     road-LOC   1sg:ERG(-?)   foot   see-IP   go-rdaka-in-GER-ABL   3sg:NOM
     'He was heading right across our path.' (X25)

BK at this stage said that *-rdaka* would not be used if you actually saw the person heading across your path, and when asked what *-rdaka* meant said 'He's gone'. It was clear too that it could not be used of someone lying crossways to the path; *kunawarrku* would be used for that. However, when I tried the word *wawardakapada* he accepted it as meaning seeing someone as you passed. However, he did not accept the use of *-rdaka* in saying that you passed someone. He did accept it for passing someone's camp, and at this stage *-rdaka* was looking similar to *-thawa* and *-mini* (and BK accepted this) (see §12.2).

The next day BK accepted the use of *yada* 'hither' and *yita* 'away' and also of the bound morpheme *-ngalpirri* 'across' with *thawardaka*. The following day, in the last reference to this morpheme, he accepted a verb *thudardaka* (*thuda* 'to lie, to camp'), but again here it seemed, and was accepted, to be the same as *-thawa*.

12.17 Action for oneself

The formative *-thayi* denotes action performed for the actor's own benefit, and so seems to have the same function as that described in §14.1 for *-yindri*. There may, however, be differences in the verbs which can combine with these formatives, or the meaning of the formative when combined with a particular verb. Thus *wanthiyindri* is the normal form of the verb 'to look for'; although *wanthi* is sometimes used without *-yindri*. *Wanthithayi* was translated as "looking for my own". *Kudlayindri* means 'to cook INTR)' or 'to be(come) cooked' as in (14-8), while *kudlathayi* means 'to cook (it) yourself.' Another likely difference is that *-yindri* combines only with transitive verbs while *-thayi* may combine with either transitive or intransitive verbs; however, there are no examples of *-thayi* in combination with an intransitive verb and the only evidence is that a proposed form (*thambanathayi* 'to dance for oneself, not for others to watch') was accepted. There are few examples of *-thayi* in the corpus. As a free form *thayi* is the verb 'to eat'.

The only examples of *-thayi* in a sentence are:

(59)   *Mardra-ngadi   mandrithayinga   pirna.*
       stone-DAT   get-eat-FUT   big
       '[They're] going to win a lot of money [at the races].'   (T11, =S1-2)

(60)   *Mandrithayi(ri?)   pilthirri   thana   warrkathalkangatji.*
       get-eat-(UNSP?)   broken.pieces   3pl:NOM   throw-up-FUT-EMPH
       'They pick up the broken pieces of rock and throw them out [of the well].'
       (D3, in A-101)

The only other forms known are *walthathayi* and *pakathayi*, both 'to carry your own'.

12.18 Following and completion

The formative *-tharra* (related to the free form *tharra* 'to fly' and glossed 'fly') has a number of functions which can be grouped into two sets. The first set includes:

(1a)   action involving following or being behind someone or something (*kapitharra* 'to follow, to track', *kudhitharra* 'to hide behind someone who is going on ahead');

(1b)   action involving an object who/which is going away (*wawatharra* 'to see (someone) going', *ngunyitharra* 'to give to someone who is leaving');

(1c)   action directed away (*thumbakatharra* 'to point away', *nhinatharrathika* 'to visit' — go away[5] (*tharra*) and stay (*nhina*) a while and come back (*thika*). This set thus involves, usually not very directly, action directed away from the actor. This contrasts with *-windri* (§12.3), which involves action directed away from and by the actor. There is probably some overlap, however, as noted below.

The second set includes:

(2a)   all doing something (*thudatharra* 'all to be lying down, all sleeping');

(2b)   doing something to all (*wawatharra* 'to see all', *papurlakatharra* 'to hobble all the horses');

(2c)   doing something all over or all round an area (*windritharra* 'to rub all over', *purrilkatharra* 'to cover up', *pakutharra* 'to dig all around');

(2d)   do completely or thoroughly, in which case it is sometimes translated 'right' (*kulkupathalkatharrana* 'jumped right up', *mandritharrapada* 'to take right out').[6]

These different functions are not mutually exclusive; thus *wawatharra* can mean 'see going away' as well as the meaning given above. In another explanation, BK said: 'When you're pointing at the bloke that's walking away, *thumbakatharrari* [= 'point-fly-UNSP']. Or you're pointing at the place that you want to go, direction. *Thumbakatharra*. Or you might tell him to go over to that place over there ...' Functions (1a) and (1b) seem to be combined in BK's translation of *yinbatharrari* 'send-fly-UNSP' as 'You send somebody else after him'. *Kudhitharra* is 'to get lost' as well as the meaning given above. Another explanation of BK's is relevant to function (1a); when I asked if there was a word

---

[5] BK's explanation here was: 'That *-tharra* mean that he been there and back, that's all. You've got to put the *-tharra* in to make it rhyme'.

[6] This second set was originally thought to be the major function of this morpheme, and this section was then labelled 'thorough action'.

walkithalkatharrari ('climb-up-fly-UNSP') BK said: 'Say he went up first, then I went *walkithalkatharrari* then. I follow you up'.

Note the difference between *tharrawindritharra* 'to fly (right) away' and *tharratharrawindri* 'to hurry away'. The latter does not contain the formative *-tharra*, but the root *tharra* is reduplicated to give *tharratharra* 'to hurry'.

The actual function in a particular case is not always clear and in a few cases it may be idiosyncratic. For example, *warlkatharra* 'to fall over' was translated once as 'he went — flat, fell **over**', and on another occasion *warlkatharra* 'to fall over (while running)' was contrasted with *warlkangari* 'to fall down (as from a tree)'. The function in this case may belong to (2d). *Warrkatharra* (*warrka* 'to throw, to leave (behind)') is translated both as 'let (someone, something) go' and as 'leave'. The former is consistent with the functions of *-tharra*, specifically (1b), since it is the object that goes away, but the latter is not. 'To leave' would be expected to be (and normally is) *warrkawindri*. *Dukatharra* (*duka* 'to pull') is explained as follows: 'And *dukatharrari*, well you might spoil a net or something, and take it to pieces. It means other way about, see; it means pull it to pieces. Or dragging it back. You're sitting down here and drag it back'. This might be function (2d).

An example of overlap with *-windri* may be the pair *yinbawindri* and *yinbatharra*, which seemed on one occasion to be accepted as the same, 'send away' (but note, above, the different translation given for the latter on another occasion). Note also *ngunyiwindri* in §12.3.

The verb *kuditharra* 'to forget' may contain *-tharra* but *kudi* is not otherwise known. The compound nominal *warntatharra* 'a short time' (*warnta* 'short') probably involves a different *tharra*.

Examples include:

(61) *Ay   kilkarla   ngathu,   nhinggiwa   yini   nhinatharrathikana.*
      Hey   know-PRES 1sg:ERG   location-THERE   2sg:NOM   sit-fly-return-IP
      'Hey, you've been over there, I know'. (T8)

(62) *kadli   paldritharra-nhana*
      already   die-fly-NP
      '(My relations) have all died.' (B17)

(63) *Muduwa   pulyali   ngathu   wawatharrana   kurrupu   karrukarrutji*
      child   small-ERG   1sg:ERG   see-fly-IP   old.woman   old.man-EMPH

      nhina-rlayi   ya   thayi-yindri-rlayi.
      sit-SIM   and   eat-RR-SIM
      'When I was a little boy I saw the old women and old men, how they lived and fed themselves.' (D5, =A-173)

See also (46, 16-66, A-63, A-186).

12.19 *-thanggu*

There are three examples in texts of a verb in which *-thanggu* appears to function as some sort of aspect marker. As a free form *thanggu* is the verb 'to stand'.

(64) *Nhina-padapadanga nganyi — nhinathanggu-rnanga.*
    sit-HAB-FUT   1sg:NOM   sit-stand-CONT(?)
    'I stayed there for a while' (BK's translation "stopping for a week or two").
    (R9, =S10-19)

(65) *Thayi-yindringa nhinathanggu-rnangalatji.*
    eat-RR-FUT   sit-stand-CONT-EMPH-EMPH
    'He lives on it while he's staying there.' (E2, =A-188)

(No translation of this was given at the time; the translation given here was obtained later, and *thanggu* was said to denote 'for some time' — in this case, up to two or three months. On another occasion, when the sentence was discussed in isolation from its context it was said to mean: 'sit having a feed every day'. The 'every day' seems to refer to the *-thanggu*.)

(66) *Nga walya yartukini-ngaditji,   ngala palhali   ngarndri-ngapiri*
    then not full-CAUS-GER-DAT-EMPH then   bird-ERG mother-father

   thana   yartu-ka-thangguthalkarla yada,   marru-ngudalitji.
   3pl:NOM   full-CAUS-stand-up-PRES   hither lake-ABL-ERG-EMPH
   They don't have to feed them; the parents of the birds, the ones from the lake, feed them '?every day/?while they were there.' (E4)

No further examples could be recorded, but from a later discussion it seems that *-thanggu* means 'every day' and perhaps also 'all day'. The 'for some time' translation fits (64) better, while both it and 'every day' seem all right for (65) and (66).

12.20 Order of aspect markers

In view of the large number of conceivable combinations of aspect markers and the fact that most occur in only a very limited number of compounds with other aspect markers (*-thayi*, for example, is attested only directly attached to a verb root with no other formative following) only a very tentative attempt can be made to list these formatives in any order of precedence. However, there is only one case where two aspect markers seem to be permuted, and this may not be correct; in no other cases are there contraindications of a consistent order. Aspect markers always follow other formatives (including *-yindri*, which has a wide range of functions including marking aspect [see §14.1], and which follows all other verb stem formatives). The proposed order is:

-yindri
-mini, -thawa
-windri
-tharra
-thika
markers not listed elsewhere
-warra
-thikathika, -wagawaga, -padapada
time specifiers

This order is based on the following stems (among others) (abbreviations used are: N noun stem, V verb stem, Vbr verbaliser, Redup reduplication,)

ngulukayindriwaga	N + Vbr + *-yindri* + *-waga*	'to peep around'
kaldrithayiyindri	N + V + *-yindri*	'to swear at one another' (Note that *-thayi* here is a verb stem forming a compound verb, not an aspect marker)
warliwarlimayindri	N + Redup + Vbr + *-yindri*	'to help each other'
wiriwinmayindri	V + V + *-yindri*	'to exchange'
walthayindrithika	V + *-yindri* + *-thika*	'to carry back for oneself'
thangguminiwindri	V + *-mini* + *-windri*	'to stand up and walk away'
tharrawindritharra	V + *-windri* + *-tharra*	'to fly away'
nhinatharrathika	V + *-tharra* + *-thika*	'to go and visit'
kadithikathalka	V + *-thika* + *-thalka*	'to chase back up'
nhinathikapandhi	V + *-thika* + *-pandhi*	'to sit back down'
winkathikapada	V + *-thika* + *-pada*	'to duck back in'
thangguthalkawarra	V + *-thalka* + *-warra*	'to stand up'
thambanathikawarrka	V + Vbr + *-thika* + *-warra*	'to go and dance in the morning(?)'

The order includes a fair amount of guesswork, e.g. the grouping of *thawa* with *-mini*, the ordering of *-yindri* before *-mini*, *-thawa* and *-windri*, the ordering of the last two groups and the separation of the time functions of *-thalka* and *-nhina* from their other functions.

The one anomaly is *walkithalkatharra* 'to climb up'; *walkitharrathalka* has also been heard.

There is at least one example of a word with three aspect markers being accepted and used: *marndrayindrithikapandhinga* 'will go down and get [some water] for myself and bring it back'. It is not hard to think of other plausible words, such as *walthayindrithalkapada* 'to carry across for oneself', or *thangguthikathalkawarra* 'to stand back right up' (the English here is awkward; the idea is a combination of 'stand back up (again)' and 'stand right up'). However, perhaps speakers would prefer to find other ways.

13 Verb-stem formation

Verb compounding is a productive process in Yandruwandha and a wide range of possibilities of combination of verb, noun and adverb roots, formatives and even inflected nouns exists. Reduplication, either of root or compound, may also be involved. The following chart showing types of verb stem is probably not exhaustive. In this chart V stands for verb root, N for noun root, A for adverb root, R for reduplication, F for verb-stem formative and I for inflectional suffix. The roman numerals are a key to the examples below. Some of the nodes do not represent verb stems, and these do not have a number. R can be ambiguous; it could represent reduplication of the immediately preceding morpheme or of the whole preceding sequence (of two roots). In one case both are represented; (xiii) is a reduplication of the whole sequence and (xiv) a reduplication of the immediately preceding morpheme. The other ambiguity is at (xviii), and in this case the whole sequence is reduplicated. Numbers (x) and (xxxi) possibly do not represent productive types. Examples are:

(i)   *thanma* 'to swim', *warrka* 'to throw';

(ii) *thawathawa* 'to walk about' (*thawa* 'to walk'), *yandhayandha* 'to talk' (*yandha* 'to talk');

(iii) *minimininhina* 'to keep on running about' (*mini* 'to run', *nhina* 'to sit'), *ngarangarathawa* 'to hear while passing' (*ngara* 'to hear', *thawa* 'to walk');

(iv) *wawawawana* 'to look after' (*wawa* 'to look', *-na* applicative ('purposeful action')), *thayithayiyindri* 'to have a feed' (*thayi* 'to eat', *-yindri* 'action for oneself');

(v)   *wawawawanathika* 'to look after for someone else' (*wawa* 'to look', *-na* applicative, *thika* 'to return');

(vi) *windrima* 'to put in' (*windri* 'to enter', *-ma* causative), *mulpayindri* 'to cut oneself or one another' (*mulpa* 'to cut', *-yindri* reflexive/reciprocal);

(vii) *pakanathika* 'to bring back' (*paka* 'to carry', *-na* applicative, *thika* 'to return'), *walthayindrithika* 'to bring back' (*waltha* 'to carry', *-yindri* 'action for yourself');

(viii) *thanggunatharrathalka* 'to stand up (TR)' (*thanggu* 'to stand', *-na* causative, *tharra* 'to fly', *thalka* 'up');

(ix) *kadlinayindri* 'to put on (clothes)' (*kadli* 'to wear', *-na* causative, *-yindri* reflexive);

170   Chapter 13

Verb-stem formation chart

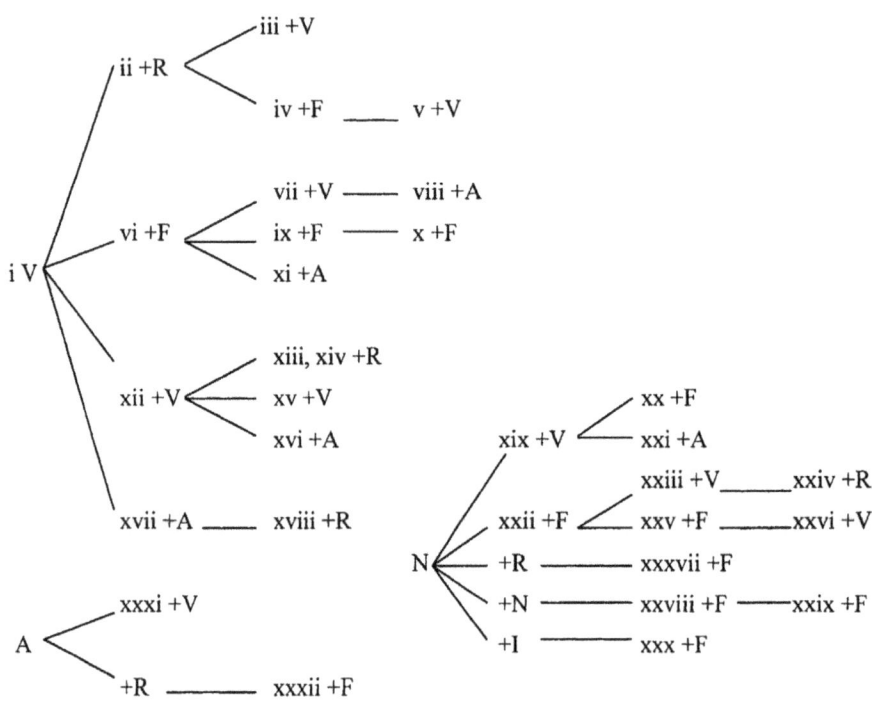

(x)   *nhambalkanayindri* 'to cover yourself' (*nhamba* 'to cover', *-lka* causative, *-na* causative, *-yindri* reflexive);

(xi) *wawayindripandhi* 'to look down at oneself' (*wawa* 'to look', *-yindri* reflexive, *pandhi* 'down'), *windrimapada* 'to put in' (*windri* 'to enter', *-ma* causative, *pada* 'in');

(xii) *paldritharra* 'to all die out' (*paldri* 'to die', *tharra* 'to fly'), *wawathika* 'to look back' (*wawa* 'to look', *thika* 'to return');

(xiii) *thudathawa-thudathawa* 'to travel for a few days, camping along the way' (*thuda* 'to lie', *thawa* 'to go'), *mandrithawa-mandrithawa* 'to pick up here and there' (*mandri* 'to pick up');

(xiv) *yingka ngunyingunyi* 'to make laugh' (*yingka* 'to laugh' — perhaps also a noun root, *ngunyi* 'to give'), *wawawagawaga* 'to look around everywhere' (*wawa* 'to look', *waga* 'to shift');

(xv) *thangguminiwindri* 'to stand up and go away' (*thanggu* 'to stand', *mini* 'to run', *windri* 'to enter'), *tharrawindritharra* 'to fly away' (*tharra* 'to fly');

(xvi)   *walkithikapandhi* 'to climb back down' (*walki* 'to climb', *thika* 'to return', *pandhi* 'down'), *mandritharrapada* 'to take out' (*mandri* 'to get', *tharra* 'to fly', *pada* 'in');

(xvii) *thikapandhi* 'to go back down' (*thika* 'to return', *pandhi* 'down'), *nhinapada* 'to sit inside' (*nhina* 'to sit', *pada* 'in');

(xviii) *warrkapandhi-warrkapandhi* 'to throw down (many things)' (*warrka* 'to throw', *pandhi* 'down');

(xix)   noun root plus verb root, e.g. *yambarrikurra* 'to flatten' (*yambarri* 'flat', *kurra* 'to put down'), *ngagapardra* 'to choke' (*ngaga* 'throat', *pardra* 'to hold');

(xx)   *marnaminina* 'to become brim full' (*marna* 'mouth', *mini* 'to run', *-na* inchoative(?));

(xxi)   *pangkiparndrithalka* 'to gallop (a horse) up' (*pangki* from *pangkithirri* 'rib', *parndri* 'to hit', *thalka* 'up');

(xxii) *pirnana* 'to grow' (*pirna* 'big', *-na* inchoative), *karruka* 'to initiate (into manhood)' (*karru* 'man', *-ka* causative);

(xxiii) *papurlakatharra* 'to hobble all (the horses)' (*papurla* 'hobble', *-ka* causative, *tharra* 'to fly'), *ditjipawindri* 'to put out in the sun to dry' (*ditji* combined form of *dritji* 'sun', *-pa* a formative of which there are no other examples, *windri* 'to enter');

(xxiv) *karrukathikathika* 'to initiate (young men) everywhere' (*karru* 'initiated man', *-ka* 'causative', *thikathika* from *thika* 'to return');

(xxv)   *pururrukayindri* 'to dry yourself' (*pururru* 'dry', *-ka* causative, *-yindri* reflexive); *marnipikana* 'to fatten' (*marni* 'fat', *-pika* 'characterised by', *-na* inchoative);

(xxvi) *ngulukayindriwaga* 'to peep around' (*ngulu* 'end', *-ka* causative, *-yindri* reflexive, *waga* 'to shift');

(xxvii) *kunakunana* 'to grumble' (*kuna* 'faeces', *-na* inchoative), *paltjapaltjaka* 'to strengthen' (*paltja* 'strong', *-ka* causative);

(xxviii) *kunapampuka* 'to make into a ball by rolling up (e.g. string)', (*kuna* 'faeces', *pampu* 'egg', *-ka* causative), *marnipirnana* 'to fatten' (*marni* 'fat', *pirna* 'big', *-na* inchoative);

(xxix) *warliwarlimayindri* 'to help one another' (*warli* 'help', *-ma* causative, *-yindri* reciprocal), *pilthipilthirrika* 'to shatter' (if *-rri* in *pilthirri* 'stone chips' is to be considered a formative, *-ka* causative);

(xxx)   *marnangadika* 'to put into the mouth' (*marna* 'mouth', *-ngadi* dative, *-ka* causative), *padlangadika* 'to throw (in wrestling)' (*padla* 'ground');

(xxxi) Rare, see §13.5 for the only examples;

(xxxii) *pudlupudluka* 'to be unable to (TR)' (*pudlu* 'can't', *-ka* causative), *walyawalyaka* 'to lose (*walya* 'not').

Probably all of the above categories can combine with the habitual formative *-padapada*, a reduplicated adverb (*pada* 'in'), as in *nhinapadapada* 'to stay habitually' (*nhina* 'to sit'), *yartunapadapada* 'to feed habitually' (*yartu* 'full', *-na* 'inchoative'), *thawathawapadapada* 'to walk about habitually' (*thawa* 'to walk'). Also many could be expanded by the use of

172 *Chapter 13*

such formatives as *-thikathika* 'to do everywhere' (from *thika* 'to return') and *-yindri* 'reflexive/reciprocal'.

Many aspects of verb-stem formation were discussed in Chapter 12, under the heading of 'Bound verb aspect markers', and some will be described in Chapter 14. The remainder are discussed below.

13.1 Verb roots

The vast majority of verb roots are disyllabic; the few ostensible verb roots that are not include some which probably include stem formatives (e.g. *-ka* in *pinaka* 'to rock (in a coolamon)', *-ma* in *panthama* 'to smell (TR)') although the supposed disyllabic root has not been noted in any other context) and others which are borrowed (*kartiwirri* 'to dive' is also found in Ngulupulu, in which it is composed of *karti* 'head' and *wirri* 'to enter'). The few roots which may be genuinely trisyllabic include *dadawa* 'to fan', *kayinta* 'to dry (TR)' and *yukarra* 'to lie', 'to spend the night'. Note also the possible defective verbs *kapada* 'come on' and *warrayi* 'leave it' (see §17.2.1).

13.2 Reduplication

Reduplication of verbal roots is normally quite straightforward; deviant forms which have been heard, such as *kilkalilka* and *kilkayilka* from *kilka* 'to know' and *mapaapa* from *mapa* 'to gather' have later been disowned by the informant and replaced by regular forms, *kilkakilka* and *mapamapa*, respectively.

The function of reduplication is superficially quite variable; it seems non-existent in some cases (e.g. *thikathika* 'to return', *thika* 'to return') while in at least one case the reduplicated form seems to bear no semantic relationship to the root (*thanggu* 'to stand', *thangguthanggu* 'to walk around'). In other cases it seems to denote intensification (*kilkakilka* 'to know all about', *kilka* 'to know'; *karrtjikarrtjima* 'to whirl (trans)', *karrtji* 'to roll over', *-ma* causative), repetition (*thudathawa-thudathawa* 'to spend nights on the road, while travelling', *thudathawa* 'to camp (one night) while travelling'; *panmapanmayindri* 'to go out all the time (of a fire)', *panma* 'to put out (a fire)', *-yindri* reflexive), or aimlessness (*thawathawa* 'to walk around', *thawa* 'to go', 'to walk'). It denotes the reverse of intensification in *pardrapardra* 'to feel (with the hand)' (from *pardra* 'to hold', 'to catch').

However, a closer look at the list of reduplicated verb roots shows that, in most cases, where any function can be assigned to the reduplication, it is that of denoting action at many points in a restricted area or limited time. Where no function can be assigned to the reduplication this is probably attributable to impreciseness of translation or lack of data, so that the function is simply not noticed. Thus *thangguthanggu* means 'to stand (briefly) in various places, in the same general area', which of course implies walking between these places. *Thawathawa* is similar, but with emphasis on the walking rather than the standing. *Pardrapardra* implies 'handling over an extended area', as compared to *pardra* 'holding (with a fixed grip)'.

Other examples where reduplication denotes action distributed over an area include *minimini* 'to run around' (*mini* 'to run', the area being, say, the vicinity of a campsite), *marrkamarrka* 'to crawl around' (from *marrka* ' to crawl', with possibly a more restricted area than *minimini* because of the nature of the action), *kapikapi* 'to follow round everywhere' (*kapi* 'to follow, to track'), *dramardrama* 'to cut up' (*drama* 'to cut', distributed over the whole area of the material, say a piece of meat, being cut), *kudrakudra* 'to break up', 'to shatter' (*kudra* 'to break'), *kurrakurra* 'to make camp' (*kurra* 'to put down'; one puts down one's goods, bedding, firewood and other requisites in the appropriate parts of the campsite), *ngarndangarndama* 'to block (i.e. to shut in on all sides)' (*ngarndama* 'to shut') and *thapathapa* 'to lick' (*thapa* 'to poke out (the tongue)').

Action repeated over a period of time is exemplified by *thudathawa-thudathawa* (the time being that of the journey), *panmapanmayindri* (presumably restricted to the time a fire might be expected to last) and *karrtjikarrtjima*, of the examples given above, as well as by *ngarnmangarnmayindri*, with various translations — 'to be halting of speech', 'to be hard to follow (of speech)', 'to be unable to walk freely (because of, say, a stiff leg)', 'to jib, or refuse to go (e.g. of a horse)' (from *ngarnma* 'to grip', 'to hold tight', 'to stick', -*yindri* reflexive; thus the basic meaning seems to be 'to keep on stopping'). Other examples are *warrkawarrka* 'to throw from one to the other' (also, probably idiomatically, 'to dislike') (*warrka* 'to throw'), *wawawawana* 'to look after', 'to care for', 'to watch' (*wawa* 'to look', 'to see', -*na* purposeful action), *thayithayiyindri* 'to have a feed' (*thayi* 'to eat', -*yindri* action for oneself).

This hypothesis as to the function of reduplication provides an explanation of the reduplication of verb stems when they are used with an aspect marker which implies motion, thus *ngurangurarduda* 'to hear while going along', *ngarangarathawa* 'to hear while passing', *ngarangaramini* 'to listen and go' (probably 'to go with occasional stops to listen') all from *ngara* 'to hear', 'to listen' and *yibayibarduda* 'to drink while going along' (from *yiba* 'to drink'; contrast *yibayiba* 'to suck' i.e. 'to make a drinking action over a surface'). It also explains the reduplication of roots in the formation of agent and instrument names, where the agent or instrument would be expected to carry out or be used for the appropriate action regularly over its working life. Examples are *kathi dramirdramini* 'butcher' (*kathi* 'meat', *drama* 'to cut'), *thinbithinbini* 'chisel' (*thinba* 'to chisel'), *wathi parndriparndrini* 'axe' (*wathi* 'tree', *parndri* 'to hit').

There is no difficulty in fitting an abstract verb like *kilkakilka* 'to know all about' into the above scheme. There are very few reduplicated verbs that do not fit easily; one example which does seem deviant enough to be idiomatic is *tharratharra* 'to hurry' (*tharra* 'to fly'), *warrkawarrka* 'to dislike' (see above) is another.

A reduplicated verb stem for which the simple form was not accepted as a stem is *katjakatja* 'to sting' (see the dictionary volume for its grammar).

13.3 Compounding of verbs

Those verb roots which function as productive stem-forming suffixes with aspectual functions are discussed in Chapter 12. No non-predictable verb + verb compounds are known, although there are, of course, a number of other four-syllable verbs which cannot at present be analysed. One second element which is known in two verbs (and, as recorded, with a slightly different form in each, is -*pantji* ~ -*pandji*, in *kaldripantji* and *ngarndapandji*, both meaning 'call out, sing out'. (*Kaldri* occurs in other compounds with related meanings — 'to argue', 'to swear', while *ngarnda* exists with other meanings which are not clearly related to this one.)

13.4 Compounding of nouns and verbs

This is a productive method of forming compound verb stems. A noun root and a verb root are juxtaposed, either as a two-word compound or, usually, as a single word. In certain cases it is not clear whether an expression is to be regarded as a compound verb or as a verb plus object or verb plus adverb; for example, *muka thuda* 'to sleep' (*muka* 'asleep', *thuda* 'to lie'), *yadhi kurra* 'to give birth' (*kurra* 'to put down', *yadhi* 'unborn baby' and other meanings related to birth), *marrka thawa* 'to go camping out' (*marrka* 'camping out', *thawa* 'to go'), *yulpu thawa* 'to travel' (*yulpu* 'travelling'), *minha ngana* 'to do what?' (*minha* 'what?', *ngana* 'to do'). All of these have a nominative subject except *yadhi kurra*, which also has an object, and *muka*, *marrka* and *minha* (at least) can be inflected as nouns (but not when they are part of the above expressions). See §14.2.

Compounds of noun root plus verb root can be classified according to the semantic relationship between the noun and the verb. The largest class is that in which the referent of the noun is the object of the action denoted by the verb. Examples are *pantjakurra* 'to kneel down' ('knee-put.down'), *makawarrka* 'to stack firewood' ('firewood-throw'), *marna yiba* 'to kiss' ('mouth drink') and perhaps *yaba ngunyi* 'to frighten' ('fear give')[1] and *yambarri kurra* 'to flatten' ('flat put down'). Note also *makawadhawarrka*, with a similar meaning to *makawarrka*; the meaning of *-wadha* is unknown. A number of nouns are formed by nominalisation of a compound verb of this type (and these compound verbs are not known to exist other than in this form). Examples include *purdathayini* 'plain turkey' (*purda* 'unripe', *thayi* 'to eat'), *padla pakuni* 'pick' (*padla* 'ground', *paku* 'to dig') and many others.

In a second class the referent of the noun functions as the instrument of the action denoted by the verb. Examples are *kupuwarrka* 'to wave' ('arm-throw'), *makumandri* 'to trip (INTR)' ('shin-catch') and — as a nominalised form — *marapardrini* 'handle' (*mara* 'hand', *pardra* 'to hold').

In a couple of cases the referent of the name seems to denote the location of the action, as in *marnaminina* 'to become brim full' (*marna* 'mouth', *mini* 'to run', *-na* 'inchoative'(?)[2]) and the nominalised form *mitjithulkini* 'glasses' (*mitji* 'eye', *thulka* 'to wear').

No compound verbs are known in which the noun is the subject of the verb root, but two nominalised forms, related semantically, are of this form. One of these is especially unusual in that the nominaliser is zero — *dritjirdunka* 'sunrise' (*dritji* 'sun', *dunka* 'to come out'). The other is *dritjiwindrini* 'sunset' (*windri* 'to enter').

In a few cases the relationship between the noun and the verb is not clear, e.g. *durruthanggu* 'to stoop' ('back-stand'), *warluparndri* 'to bark' ('bark-hit'; note that one can also "hit", i.e. sing, a song; cf. (16-85)), *marrikudhi* 'to get up early in the morning' (*marri* also occurs in *marripathi* 'tomorrow', *marriparrkulu* 'two days later' — *parrkulu* 'two', and *marrikudukudu* (also heard as *marrikurukuru*) 'early morning'; *kudhi* 'to hide'), *munapaka* 'to lie on one's front' (*muna* 'chest', *paka* 'to carry') and *thundruthuka* 'to lie on one's back' (*thundru* 'stomach', *thuka* 'to carry').

---

[1] An abstraction from the more concrete type of example, as suggested by a referee.
[2] One might perhaps expect *marnamimina*, derived from *marnamimi* 'lip' (*marna* 'mouth') and be tempted to think that that was what was meant.

13.4.1 Derivation of verb phrases from abstract nouns

A number of verb phrases with causative meaning are derived from abstract nouns denoting feelings or qualities with the verb *ngunyi* 'to give', usually reduplicated. Thus, with *yaba* 'fear' we have *yaba ngunyingunyi* 'to frighten' (also *yaba ngunyi*, which has been heard also as *yabangunyi*, see the previous section); compare the English 'give [someone] a fright'. The words which are known to take part in this construction include a number of the words which combine with *-li* to derive adjectives or adverbs (see §16.9); these include *mawa* 'hunger', *mura* 'thirst', *malthi* 'cold', *kinyi* 'stealth', *thidri* 'jealousy', *yunka* 'disgust', *ngidla* 'sorrow', *nhinda* 'shame' and *yingka* 'laugh' (which, as noted above, §10.5.9, seems to function as a noun as well as as a verb root). One word which does not combine with *-li* but does combine with *ngunyi(ngunyi)* is *mundja* 'sickness'. Some other words which combine with *-li* do not combine with *ngunyi(ngunyi)* but instead can be verbalised with the causative *-ka*; these include *kalga* 'loose; easy', *makamaka* 'hot' and *paltjapaltja* 'strong, hard'. Other words which can combine with *-li* are not known to be verbalised at all. The word *paka*, glossed 'quick' in the dictionary but perhaps better 'hurry' or 'immediate', is causativised with *-ka* (§13.7.3) but this follows the *-li*: *pakalika*, also *pakapakalika* 'to hurry someone up'. (BK contrasts with this the phrase *paka ngunyingunyi* 'to set the pace', i.e. 'to make someone go fast by setting a fast pace'.) Probably this ordering applies to *mura* 'thirst' too; *muralika* 'to make thirsty' (unconfirmed). It is not clear whether and/or how this is different from *mura ngunyingunyi*, although it was said that if it is something like salt meat that makes a person thirsty the latter construction is used. One word — *muka* 'sleep' — is known to combine with each of *-li*, *-ka* and *ngunyingunyi*: *mukali* 'sleepy', *mukaka* 'to put to sleep' (e.g. putting a baby to sleep) and *muka ngunyingunyi* 'to make sleepy'. In Yawarrawarrka *ngunyi* can be compounded with *kurrungkurru* 'cough' to make *kurrungkurru ngunyi* 'make cough' (compare *kurrungkurruka* 'to cough', which, with the causative formative, would be expected to be transitive). An adjectival word like *patji* 'good' or *marnipirna* 'fat' cannot take part in this construction.

On most occasions when this construction was discussed, BK used or accepted only the form with *ngunyi* reduplicated; however, it seems clear that the other form is acceptable at least with some words, and it may be that it is more likely when several syllables follow in the word. In other words, a citation form is more likely to have *ngunyi* reduplicated (and perhaps to have this insisted on) while the simple form is more likely to be found in text.

(1) *Ngapa kaldri nhanha(?) ngathu yiba-nhana, ngapa mura*
water salty 3sg:fem:ACC(?) 1sg:ERG drink-NP water thirst
ngunyingunyinga nganha.
give-give-FUT 1sg:ACC
'I drank salty water and it made me thirsty.' (X16)
(Note the use of the word *ngapa* 'water' with *mura*, as if to say 'water-thirsty'.)

(2) *Ngapala yingka-rnangala thili yabangunyi-yindrini-nguda ngala pula*
well laugh-CONT-EMPH DU fear-give-RR-GER-ABL then 3du
walypala-thili.
white man-DU
'Well, they both laughed then, the two white men, at the way they had frightened one another.' (R4, =S9-38)

176   *Chapter 13*

The Strzelecki dialect has *mana* 'to give', and *mawa manamana* 'to make (someone) hungry' and *mura manamana* 'to make (someone) thirsty' are attested.

13.5 Compounding of adverbs and verbs

Two verbs compounded of an adverb of place and a verb root are known: *ngardrawarrka* 'to leave behind' (*ngardra* 'behind', *warrka* 'to throw') and *kakayalba* 'to split the end (of a stick)' (*kaka* 'near', *yalba* 'to split').

13.6 Non-productive verb-stem formatives

A few verbs seem to involve no longer productive monosyllabic verb-stem formatives. These include *ditjipa* 'to spread in the sun to dry' (*dritji* 'sun') and *dakuma* and *dakunba*, both of which seem to mean 'to do well' as illustrated in the following examples. *Dakuka ~ dakurdakuka*, presumably with the causative suffix *-ka*, means 'to repair', 'to fix'. *Daku* has not been noted in any other context. The *-ma* of *dakuma* could be the causative suffix *-ma*. Note the absence of any inflection on *dakuma* in (3) (cf. *panina, panika*, §11.17).

(3)   Wawana   ngathu   yinha,   kanpa   dakuma.
      see-IP   1sg:ERG   3sg:ACC   right   do well
      'I saw him properly'. (B11)

In answer to the question "Is there a word *daku*?" BK said "No; only *dakunbari*, if he caught a ball, caught it good. Another fellow would say 'Oh *dakunbana nhuludu*'; or for hitting anything, you know, and he fired at it and he hit it."

Another interesting case is that of the verb *manhawakura* as in:

(4)   Parndripadipadini   ngani,   ngurra   thawarnanga,   manhawakurarla
      hit-HAB-GER   1pl:ex:NOM   always   go-CONT   become.infirm-PRES

      ngani.
      1pl:ex:NOM
      "We're getting too old, can't get out; we used to go [hunting often]." (T14)

This is derived from *manhawakuru*, defined by BK as "old fellow, can't move or walk about much". There seems here to be an inchoative formative *-a* which replaces the final vowel of the noun.

13.7 Productive verb-stem formatives

There are a number of productive formatives which either derive a verb stem from a non-verb stem, or derive a verb stem of one particular valency from a stem of a different valency. These will mainly be dealt with in the remainder of this chapter, but some more complicated or less understood aspects of transitivity will be described in the following chapter. The processes involved in the following subsections are verbalisation of nouns (including inflected nouns) and adverbs, transitivisation of intransitive verbs and intransitivisation of transitive verbs. The formatives involved cannot be dealt with conveniently under these headings because some of them have a function spread over two of these divisions, but they will be described in approximately the order implied.

13.7.1 Inchoative/transitiviser/applicative

The suffix *-na* may be added:

(a) to noun stems and to *kaka* 'near' and *kala* 'even', and perhaps some other adverbs, to form an intransitive verb,

(b) to an intransitive verb stem to form a transitive verb,

(c) to a transitive verb stem to form a ditransitive verb (see §14.3),

(d) to certain verb stems to denote purposeful action, and

(e) to a few verb stems with unknown function.

With function (a) it is glossed INCH for inchoative, with function (b) TVR for transitiviser and with functions (c) and (d) APP for applicative. These functions could be summarised as 'increasing the valency of the base by one'.

As an inchoative *-na* generally conveys the meaning 'to become the referent of the unverbalised stem'. The following examples illustrate this function:

(5) *Ngapala ngathu kathi parndriri, pirnanangatji nganyi*
well 1sg:ERG meat kill-UNSP big-INCH-FUT-EMPH 1sg:NOM

karru-ngaditji.
man-DAT-EMPH
'I'm going to be a butcher when I grow up.' (W4)

(6) *Nhadina-nhana, nhambana yinha kali.*
dead-INCH-NP bury-IP 3sg:ACC already
'He died and they've buried him.' (T8)

(7) *Ay darla nganyi withiwithinarla.*
oh skin 1sg:NOM sore-sore-INCH-PRES
'Ouch, my skin is chafed.' (T8)

(8) *Kakana yadaw, dranyingalatji yinha!*
near-INCH hither:DISTORT shoot-FUT-EMPH-EMPH 3sg:ACC
'Get closer, so you can shoot it!' (P11)

Other verb stems formed with this affix include:

yartuna	'to become full (of stomach)'
marnipikana, marnipirnana	'to get fat' (*marni* 'fat', *pika* 'characterised by', *pirna* 'big')
yimpana	'to be/become black/bruised' (*yimpa* 'black')
muduna	'to burn away to ashes' (*mudu* 'ashes')
makamakana	'to get hot'
thangkana	'to burn' (*thangka* not known as a free form; *thangkaka* 'to light (fire)')
kunapampuna	'to roll into a ball', 'to curl up' (*kunapampu* 'ball' presumably from *kuna* 'faeces', *pampu* 'egg')
kunakununa	'to grumble' (*kuna* 'faeces', literally *kunakunana* means 'to become shitty')

mundjana	'to become sick'
manyuna	'to get better' (*manyu* 'good')
patjina	'to get better' (*patji* 'good')
kaldrukaldruna	'to bark' 'to growl (of a dog)' (*kaldrukaldru* 'bark, growl (of a dog)')
marnkana	'to crack' (*marnka* 'crack')
yarrana	'to spread (as opening the arms, spreading the legs)' (*yarra* 'wide')
kanpana	'to appear' (*kanpa* 'visible')
panina	'to do completely' (*pani* 'none'; this verb is intransitive and has a transitive counterpart *panika*)
yabana	'to get frightened' (accepted).

Other verbs which may include this formative (presumably with function (a)) are *drulkurdrulkuna* 'to grunt', *papana* 'to start' and *pirritjampana* 'to be tired'.

When added to an intransitive verb stem (function (b)) *-na* is usually clearly causative. In some cases the verb stem is reduplicated. Examples include:

(9) *Muduwa   ngathu   yingkiyingkinana.*
     child   1sg:ERG   cry-cry-TVR-IP
     'I made the baby cry.' (W8)

(10) *Wathi   ngathu   yinha   thanggunana.*
     tree   1sg:ERG   3sg:ACC   stand-TVR-IP
     'I stood the post up.' (W8)

Other stems formed in this way are *yirrtjina* 'to wake up (TR)' from *yirrtji* 'to get up', *kirdrakirdrana* 'to make squeal' from *kirdra* 'to squeal' and *yarrana* 'to move [someone's] legs apart' from *yarra* 'to open one's legs' (also *yarra* 'wide'). Data in one case are contradictory: *kudhikudhina* 'to hide (intrans.)' (*kudhikudhi* 'hidden'), or *kudhikudhina* 'to hide (trans.)' (*kudhikudhi* 'to hide (intrans.)').

The function of the suffix is transitivisation but not causative in the following example; in fact it is exactly similar to the effect of the suffix with a transitive verb stem, applicative, as described in the next paragraph.

(11) *Mirrka   nganha   yundru   tjukurru   darla   nhinanarla.*
     rug   1sg:ACC   2sg:ERG   kangaroo skin   sit-TVR-PRES
     'That's my kangaroo skin you're sitting on.' (P15)

(Note *nganha* where *ngakani* 1sg:GEN would be expected.)

Addition of *-na* to a transitive verb in some cases (function (c)) makes it ditransitive, i.e. it takes two direct objects, one of which would otherwise have been expressed as an indirect object. Examples include:

(12) *Ngarru   ngamali   mulhudutji   walthanari   yinha.*
     only   mother's.brother-ERG tucker-EMPH   carry-APP-UNSP   3sg:ACC
     'Only his mother's brothers could take him food.' (W10)

This was soon afterwards repeated, without *-na*, as:

(13) *Ngarru   ngamali   walthapandhi-rnanga   mulhudutji*
     only   mother's.brother-ERG   carry-down-CONT   tucker-EMPH

nhungganingadi.
3sg:GEN-DAT

Note that the direct object *yinha* has been replaced by the dative indirect object *nhungganingadi.*

(14) *Ya   mulhudutji   yinha   thana   nguthu-ngamalitji*
and   tucker-EMPH   3sg:ACC   3pl:NOM   elder brother-mother's brother-ERG-EMPH

pakana-pandhi-malka.
carry-APP-down-OPT
'His relations could take food down to him.' (E2, in A-184)

(15) *Purtu   ngathu   yura-nhana   mandrinini-ngadi   nganha.*
goods   1sg:ERG   want-NP   get-APP-GER-DAT   1sg:ACC
"I wanted you to get me some things." (P8)

(16) *Yalkura   nhulu   nganha   wirninana.*
Dreaming.story   3sg:ERG   1sg:ACC   tell-APP-IP
'He told me a (Dreaming) story.' (X20)

An applicative form is intransitivised with *-yindri*, functioning as reciprocal, in *yalbanayindri* 'to share' (*yalba* 'to split'; BK pointed out that *yalbayindri* would mean 'split one another').

In some cases *-na* is added to a stem (sometimes reduplicated) to denote a purposeful action (function (d)). Verbs derived in this way include *wawana*, or more commonly *wawawawana* 'to watch', 'to care for' from *wawa* 'to look', 'to see', *wawawawa* 'to look about'; *kurrakurrana* 'to teach' from *kurra* 'to put down', *kurrakurra* 'to make camp'; *warrkawarrkanayindri* 'to throw from one to the other' (and also 'dislike one another') and possibly *warrkana* 'to spear', from *warrka* 'to throw'; *thirrithirrina* 'to be angry (about something)', 'to seek revenge' from *thirri* 'to fight'. Examples ((19) from Yw) include:

(17) *Nhuludu   windrali   warrkana-nhana,   nguthuyi   nhunu*
3sg:ERG-THERE   spear-INST   throw-APP-NP   elder.brother-LOC   3sg:NOM

thirrithirrina-nhana.
fight-fight-APP-NP
"He speared him when he was wild over his brother." (P4)

(18) *Muduwa   thanayi   patjikurnu   nhinarla,   wawawawana-rlayitji   thanha.*
child   3pl:NOM-HERE   good-one   sit-PRES   look-look-APP-SIM-EMPH   3pl:ACC
'The kids are good as long as I watch them.' (P4)

(19) *Ngathu   pulhayi   pardrapardranana,   pulayi   thirrirnanyi.*
1sg:ERG   3du:ACC-HERE   hold-hold-APP-IP   3du:NOM-HERE   fight-SIM
'I stopped them two from fighting.' (Y9)

See also (18-17). These examples all involve transitive verb roots. This function does not seem to apply with intransitive roots, unless the problematic example (9-25) could be construed as such. I prefer the explanation suggested there.

In a few cases no function of *-na* has been noted; in at least some of these cases the function might actually be that last described. Such words include *pipina ~ pipi* 'to have a spell' (both intransitive), *wathina ~ wathi* 'to build', *kimana ~ kima* 'to pour out', *nhambalkana ~ nhambalka* 'to cover' (all transitive). The last is interesting in that *-lka* is also a stem formative (although not productive); this is the only case in which *-na* follows another stem formative and the only case in which two monosyllabic stem formatives (i.e. excluding aspect markers) occur together. Note also that a couple of the verbs in *-na* in the above lists are (like the corresponding verbs without *-na*) intransitive.

Note also the verbs *thambana* 'to dance' and *thambathambana* 'to play', the latter intransitive and the former pseudo-transitive (see §14.2). *Thamba* never occurs in the Yandruwandha corpus without *-na* or *-ka*, the latter making it transitive ('play with'). However, there is one example (8-41) where it does in Yawarrawarrka.

There is an indication of flexibility in the ordering of *-na* and an aspect marker: *pakanawarrana* was accepted as an alternative to *pakawarranana* '[he] brought [them] to [me]'. The former corresponds to the order in (14) and other comparable forms as well as the order of the form *pakanawarranhana* (with near past tense instead of immediate past tense) which was used in the same discussion. Another unusual form appearing in the same discussion was *pakala warranana*, in which the compound was separated into two words and an emphatic suffix added to the first. There is not a free form **warra* 'to arrive' anywhere else in the corpus, although there is one occurrence of a homophone in Yw (see *dikilyarra warra* in the dictionary). However, it was used four times in this short discussion, and it may be that this was inspired by the context of discussion of language; two of the occurrences were in words *warranana* and *warranhana* which were apparently intended to contrast the pair of suffixes *-na-na* (applicative + immediate past) with the suffix *-nhana* (near past). A second example of *-na* following *-warra* was heard later the same day:

(20) *Warrkawarrana-nhanatji   ngathu   yinha ...*
      throw-arrive-APP-NP-EMPH   1sg:ERG   3sg:ACC
      'I left him ...' (X15)

The *-na* in the verb of the following sentence (a repeat of 9-25) is a problem. None of the uses of the suffix described above seem to fit it, unless *thika* here is to be understood as being an adverb (see §16.7).

(21) *Durruli   nganyi   thikathikanarla.*
      back-INST   1sg:NOM   return-return-INCH?-PRES
      'I'm walking backwards.' (P13)

13.7.2 Inchoative verb phrases

The verb *ngana*, normally a transitive verb meaning 'to tell', sometimes an intransitive verb 'to do', can act as an inchoative formative or a copula verb, 'to become'[3] in combination with nouns (abstract nouns with operative case inflection, or descriptive nouns in nominative case) to form two-word phrases which function as intransitive verbs. Examples include:

---

[3] In Diyari *ngana* functions as a copula verb, but with the meaning 'to be', not 'to become' (Austin 1981a:104) and so is equivalent to *nhina* in Yandruwandha.

(22) *Ngala malthilitji nganari, kali windripada-malka walpayi.*
then cold-INST-EMPH do-UNSP already enter-in-OPT humpy-LOC
'Then if you get cold you can go into the house.' (W4)

(23) *Kathikathi ngathu yinha wawa-nhana, nganyi yabali ngananga.*
snake 1sg:ERG 3sg:ACC see-NP 1sg:NOM fear-INST do-FUT
'When I saw the snake I got frightened.' (P10)

(24) *Ngapa nhutjadu purudu ngana-nhana pidri-ngadi.*
water 3sg:NOM-THERE dry do-NP anus-DAT
'The water dried up to the bottom.' (W9)

Note, *purudunganaarla* 'is drying up now' also is attested, with *-ngana* heard as a bound morpheme.

(25) *Ay, kilkarla ngathu; matja warlpara nganini-nguda.*
eh know-PRES 1sg:ERG long.time knowing do-GER-ABL
'I know all about it; I learnt a long while ago.' (B16)

Although nearly all of the evidence suggests that *ngana* is intransitive in this usage, there is one example that suggests that it may be transitive. The translation is not clear; the sentence asked for was 'Those two are jealous of one another' and the sentence was followed by a more faithful, although disjointed, translation using the phrase *thidriyi puladu* 'jealousy-LOC 3du:NOM-THERE'. Perhaps a different *ngana* is being used in (26) and the literal translation is something like 'Those two people are telling one another with aggression'.

(26) *Karna puladu thirrili ngana-yindrirla.*
person 3du:NOM-THERE aggression-INST do-RR-PRES (X42)

For some other uses of the very versatile verb *ngana* see §11.1, §11.3.1, §14.2 and §14.3.

13.7.3 Causative -ka

The suffix *-ka* may be added to any type of stem which can be verbalised, i.e. to those nouns and adverbs which can combine with *-na* (see §13.1) and to the negatives *walya* and *pudlu* and nouns in the dative and operative (cf. §9.1.3) cases. The stem so formed is a transitive verb, meaning generally 'to cause (someone/something) to be the referent of the unverbalised stem'.

In most cases the stem to be verbalised is a descriptive noun, describing some state or condition (i.e. it is translated into English by an adjective); however, other nouns too (often reduplicated) are commonly verbalised. (9-88) illustrates verbalisation of a kinship term. When a dative noun is verbalised, as in (29), the meaning of the verb is 'to cause (someone/ something) to go to the referent of the noun'. For additional examples of *-ka* see (9-15), (9-67) and (16-74).

(27) *Mardri mardra pudlupudlu kandrakarla ngathu.*
heavy stone can't-can't top-CAUS-PRES 1sg:ERG
'I can't lift the rock.' (T13)

(28) *Wawawawana yintjadu, thinkakayila yina nhuludu.*
 look-look-APP 3sg:ACC-THERE dead-CAUS-POT-EMPH 2sg:ACC 3sg:ERG-THERE
 "You want to watch him, otherwise he'll kill you." (W4)

(29) *Kathi thukali ngala thayi-rnangatji, marna-ngadikinitji,*
 animal mussel-INST then eat-CONT-EMPH mouth-DAT-CAUS-GER-EMPH

 mandrirnanga.
 get-CONT
 'They ate it by spooning it into their mouths with a mussel [shell].' (D4, =A-171)

Other verbs derived in this way and having approximately the expected meaning are listed below:

(a) derived from noun stems

dupurdupuka	'to bend' from *dupurdupu* 'round'
karruka	'to initiate (into manhood)' from *karru* 'initiated man'
mundjaka	'to hurt' from *mundja* 'sick'
paltjapaltjaka	'to strengthen', 'to tighten' from *paltjapaltja* 'strong'
patjipatjika	'to repair' from *patji* 'good'
pilthipilthirrika	'to shatter' from *pilthirri* 'stone splinters'
warlparaka	'to teach' from *warlpara* 'knowing', 'learned', 'used to'
wirlpaka	'to pierce' from *wirlpa* 'hole'
ngulukayindriwaga	'to peep around (from behind something)' from *ngulu* 'end', *yindri* reflexive, *waga* 'around'
yartuka	'to feed' from *yartu* 'full (in the stomach)'
yimpaka	'to blacken' (e.g. blacken someone's eye) from *yimpa* 'black'
kalgaka	'to loosen' from *kalga* 'loose', 'dim'
papurlaka	'to hobble (horses)' from *papurla* 'hobble' (borrowed from English)
puruduka	'to dry' from *purudu* 'dry'
thulathulaka	'to make (someone) out to be a stranger' from *thula* 'stranger' (see (S10-17, 26))[4]

(b) derived from dative noun

padlangadika	'to throw (in wrestling)' from *padla* 'ground'

(c) derived from negative adverbs

walyawalyaka	'to lose' from *walya* 'not'
pudlupudluka	'to be unable (TR)' from *pudlu* 'can't'

---

[4] No other examples of this usage — 'to make X out to be Y' — have been elicited or heard in text, but when I suggested one, using a fauna term, it was accepted.

(d) derived from other adverbs
manduka,
mandumanduka   'to join together' from *mandu* 'together'
panika   'to do completely (TR)' (cf. *panina* 'to do completely (INTR)')
kalaka   'to get even' from *kala* 'back', 'in return'
muthuka   'to get (e.g. to spear or shoot successfully)' from *muthu* 'well'

(e) derived from unknown stems
thangkaka   'to light (a fire)' (cf. *thangkana* 'to burn')
parrkuka   'to spill' (cf. *parrku-* 'two')

In one case the verb seems to have the meaning 'to use as an instrument the referent of the unverbalised stem'.

milarrika   'to hook (e.g. to hook down branches from trees)',
                 'to make a mesh (net)' from *milarri* 'hook'.

It is, of course, assumed that in many cases additional data would lead to a broadening of the known range of meanings of roots or derived forms.

In one case the suffix *-ka* is added to an intransitive verb root to form a transitive verb: *thangguka* 'to stand (something) up', 'to tail (cattle), i.e. to follow them and keep them moving in the right direction' from *thanggu* 'to stand' (note also *thangguna*, in (10)). A possible case of addition of *-ka* to a transitive verb root is exemplified by *pardaka* 'to get', possibly from *pardra* 'to hold' although BK did not accept any suggestion of relationship between these words.

The function of *-ka* is not clear in:

(30) *Kathi   durrukayi   warrkana-nhana   nhulu   tjukurrutji.*
      animal   back-CAUS?-LOC?   throw-APP-NP   3sg:ERG   kangaroo-EMPH
      "He speared him [kangaroo] from the back." (B14)

There is one example of a verb formative *-kV*, perhaps *-ka*, in the Nhirrpi corpus, but it forms an intransitive verb: *pundrakinga* 'will cool down' (with future *-inga*) from *pundra* 'cold'.

13.7.3.1 *-kanmana*

A morpheme *-kanmana* was heard on three occasions during the final few days of work with BK. BK said, in connection with the second example, that *-kanmana* meant 'they', but this does not seem to be right. It may be some sort of extension of *-ka* causative.

(31) *Wibu   nhuludu   karta-kanmana-rnanga.*
      whip   3sg:ERG-THERE   crack-KANMANA-CONT
      'He's cracking the whip.' (X8)

(Immediately before, he had given it as

      Wibu   nhuludu   parndrinhana   kartaka-rnanga,
      whip   3sg:ERG-THERE   hit-NP(?)   crack-CAUS-CONT

karta-kanmananma-rnanga.
crack-KANMANA-CONT

in which the *-ka* in the fourth word seems to be the causative suffix, and the *-kanma* in the fifth word seems to be partially reduplicated.)

(32) *Kinyili   nganha   mirrka   winka-ma-kanmana-nhana.*
     stealth-INST 1sg:ACC   blankets   disappear-CAUS-KANMANA-NP
     'Those fellows robbed me of my blankets.' (X43)

On the third occasion it did not occur in a sentence, but in the word:

(33) *waduwadu-kanmana-pandhiringa*   (repeated as)   *waduwadukanmanari*
      hang-hang-KANMANA-down-?-FUT   hang-hang-KANMANA-UNSP
      'hanging [the head] down [between the knees, when feeling sick]' (X50)

13.7.4 Causative -ma

The suffix *-ma* is added to some intransitive verb roots to form transitive verb stems. For example:

(34) *Windrima-pada   yintjadu   paltjayi.*
     enter-CAUS-in   3sg:ACC-THERE   bag-LOC
     'Put it into the bag.' (T7)

Other verbs in *-ma* include *winkama* 'to steal' (*winka* 'to run away', 'to disappear', 'to be lost') and *karrtjikarrtjima* 'to whirl' (*karrtji* 'to roll over'). Others which may involve this formative (but whose roots are not otherwise attested) include *panthama* 'to smell', *kandama* 'to count' (probably a borrowing from English), *nyandama* 'to block up' (*nyanma* has the same meaning) and *warlima ~ waliwarlima* 'to help' (but *warli* may be a noun; if so it is the only noun to combine with *-ma*).

A number of verbs with final *ma* may be historical compounds with *-ma*; these include *ngarnma* 'to grip, hold tight', *panma* 'to put out (fire)', *winma* 'to put in' (SY, YW, compare *windrima*), *yinma* 'to stick (something) in', *nyunma* 'to drown (trans.)', *wiriwinma* 'to swap' as well as *nyanma* (previous paragraph) and, less plausibly, intransitive verbs *manma* 'to tell (a lie), pretend', *thanma* 'to swim' and *tjarnma* 'to shine'. (The transitivity of *munma* 'to shut (mouth)' is not known.)[5]

13.7.5 Causative -lka

The suffix *-lka* combines with a few intransitive roots to form a transitive verb stem. This suffix, although rare in the Innamincka dialect, may be productive in the Strzelecki dialect. The function is causative in some cases, e.g. *purrilka* 'to turn over' from *purri* 'to be upside down', *wagalka* 'to shift' 'to move' (TR), from *waga* 'to shift', 'to move' (INTR), but not in *thumbalka* 'to show' from *thumba* 'to point'. In the last case it seems to have the same type of function as *-na* in (11).

---

[5] This paragraph follows a suggestion by a referee, who mentioned some of the verbs quoted and also *thinba* 'to chisel', *yinba* 'to send', *pirnpi* 'to scatter (TR)' and *darrpi* 'to turn back' as other possible historical compounds.

In one case *-lka* is added to a transitive verb; *nhamba*, *nhambalka* and *nhambalkana* are all translated 'to cover' and the formatives *-lka* and *-na* have no obvious function.

13.7.6 *Intransitivisation of transitive verbs*

The suffix *-yindri* has been briefly dealt with in §7.4 and will be further discussed in §14.1. See the latter section also on the verb *yura*.

14 *Variations on transitivity*

The simple situation described in Chapter 7, in which we have intransitive verbs which have a subject but no object, and transitive verbs which have a subject (or agent) and an object, does not exhaust the variety of combinations of basic valency of a verb and the number and nature of arguments that can occur with it. This is true for many languages, Australian and others, but in Yandruwandha the number and variety of combinations seems to be quite extraordinary, although it rarely uses dative for the object of verbs like 'look for', which have dative objects in many Australian languages, or for indirect objects of verbs like 'give'.

As a referee points out, the type of verbs that are involved in these alternations are often the type of verbs that, in other languages, might show alternations between ergative/absolutive, ergative/dative and absolutive/dative by reason of their in-between semantic transitivity status. (There are notable exceptions, though, as (54) shows.) Yandruwandha has more limited use of dative than many other languages, and uses the verbal suffix *-yindri* for some functions for which other languages use the nominal suffix, the dative. The fact that Yandruwandha was no longer in use at the time of this study and that there are no examples of its use in a real-world context may account for some of the alternations seeming to have no function — alternative ways of saying something are said to be 'the same'. This situation can be contrasted with that in more viable languages; see, for example, Hale (1982) for a clear exposition of case frames and their functions in Warlpiri, showing that every variant has its function.

14.1 Verbs with *-yindri*

The suffix *-yindri* is added to a transitive verb stem and has a number of functions, of which only the two most common are referred to in the interlinear gloss, RR. These are to mark:

(a) reflexivity; the object of the action is identical with or part of the agent. For example:

(1) *Maltji   nganyi   kudra-yindrina.*
     leg   1sg:NOM   break-RR-IP
     'I broke my leg.' (T8)

(b) reciprocity; the objects of the action are identical or partly identical with the subjects. For example:

(2)   *Mardramitjili   thanadu   dranyi-yindrirla.*
      stone-eye-INST 3pl:NOM-THERE hit (throwing)-RR-PRES
      'They're throwing stones at one another.' (W8)

These two functions have been described in §7.4.

(c) intransitivisation; a transitive verb stem is converted into an intransitive verb stem in that it has a nominative subject, but continues to take a direct object, and the formative *-yindri* in these cases denotes 'action on one's own behalf'. For example:

(3)   *Nhutjadu   parndri-yindrirla maka.*
      3sg:NOM-THERE hit-RR-PRES   fire
      'He's chopping some wood for himself.' (P7; contrast (14).)

(4)   *Karrundjatji   kathi   thana   thayi-yindrirla.*
      man-PL-EMPH   meat   3pl:NOM   eat-RR-PRES
      'The men were having a feed of meat.'[1] (X22)

(5)   *Karruwalili thanayi   pampu   pardakarla kudlini-ngadi*
      boy-ERG   3pl:NOM-HERE   egg   get-PRES   cook-GER-DAT

      thayi-yindringa   nganyi.
      eat-RR-FUT   1sg:NOM
      'The boys are bringing some eggs and I'm going to cook them and eat them.' (T14)

(6)   *Kali   ngaldra   murdana,   kurrathikapadaringu   purtutji*
      already 1du:in:NOM   finish-IP   put-return-in-UNSP-YET things-EMPH

      thanhadu.   Yinggani   waltha-yindri-thikangaldra   yini.
      3pl:ACC-THERE 2sg:GEN   carry-RR-return-FUT-BUT   2sg:NOM
      'Now we've finished, and we can put the things back. You can take yours back.'
      (Said when we finished a recording session and were ready to pack up.) (X14)

This construction was not always accepted; for example, *marndrayindrithikapandhi* 'to go down and get water and bring it back for yourself' was not accepted with a nominative subject.

A variant of this function is to denote something like 'action concerned with oneself', as in the verb *wirniyindri* 'to tell about yourself', from *wirni* 'to tell (a story)' (example from SY), or *mungkayindri* 'to hug something to yourself' from *mungka* 'to hug'. Another variant, found commonly in Australian languages, has the verb intransitivised but no object expressed, and in this case, perhaps, the function may be to focus on the action and not on the object (see footnote 1). The following example of this is from a text. This seems not to be a common construction in Yandruwandha; this sentence more or less repeated the preceding sentence, which had an overt object and this does not favour the idea that the

---

[1] A referee questioned whether the gloss 'action on one's own behalf' is appropriate for a verb like 'eat', since eating can hardly not be on one's own behalf. As the referee suggests, the function for verbs like this may (at least sometimes) be the typical antipassive function of focussing on the action and not on the object affected by the action.

A phrase *mundjungunkula thayiyindringa* 'will live on balls of flies — a lot of flies compressed into a ball' describing what people get to eat in Hell, had no subject expressed; it hardly seems likely to be expressing 'action on one's own behalf', but it most certainly is focussing on the object (which even has an emphatic suffix).

function of *-yindri* is not the same in the two. (The word written *ani* here may be the English 'only'.)

(7) Thayi-yindringa thana ani nhinanhinanga.
 eat-RR-FUT 3pl:NOM (only?) sit-sit-FUT
 'They just sit and eat.' (D1)

(d) passivisation; the subject of the verb is the affected object and is not the agent of the action. The verb is intransitivised. In most cases (of the few attested) it seems to be an agentless passive in that there seems to be no provision for inclusion of the agent; a sentence of the type of (8) with instrumental (= ergative) agent added was not accepted. Examples are:

(8) Kathi nhutjadu kudla-yindrirla.
 meat 3sg:NOM-THERE cook-RR-PRES
 'The meat is cooking.' (cannot locate original, but see B10, X33)

(9) Kudra-yindri-nhana nhunu, patjipatjikangala ngathu.
 break-RR-NP 3sg:NOM good-good-CAUS-FUT-EMPH 1sg:ERG
 'It broke and I'm mending it.' (P30)

and from SY:

(10) Ngakani nhunuyi mirrka purra-yindrirla.
 1sg:GEN 3sg:NOM.here clothes tear-RR-PRES
 'My dress is torn.' (M17)

However, there are a couple of examples of sentences which could perhaps be analysed as agentive passives (or, in (11), including an agentive passive clause):

(11) Thawarla nganyi Malkanpa-ngadi nhandulu thuka-yindri-rnanga.
 go-PRES 1sg:NOM Innamincka-DAT horse-INST carry-RR-CONT
 'I'm going to Innamincka on horseback.' (T11)[2]

(12) Ngapali yulpurruli nhunu nyunma-yindri-nhana.
 water-INST flood-INST 3sg:NOM drown-RR-NP
 'He was drowned in the flood.' (R8)

The alternative is to regard these as reflexive sentences, with the underlying agent treated as an instrument (like the sentence in (11)). Evidence that (11) is in fact to be regarded as reflexive is found in the existence of the nominalised form *thukayindrini* 'rider', and in the fact that locative marking on the word for 'horse' has (once, in Yw) been heard.[3] Note also the sentence

(13) Yadamani ngathu yintjadu thuka-yindringatji.
 horse 1sg:ERG 3sg:ACC-THERE carry-RR-FUT-EMPH
 'I'm going to ride that horse.' (R3)

---

[2] You can also 'go' (*thawa*) on a horse (instrument).

[3] A sentence in which MN used *thukanarla* 'carry-APP-PRES' with *nganyi* as subject seems like a mistake, as does the sentence in which BK used *nganyi* as subject of *thukayindri* but left the word for 'horse', *yadamani*, unmarked. The latter seems to imply that the root *thuka* means 'ride' rather than 'carry'. However, it seems that it is not safe to assume that any such sentence is wrong, as this chapter will show.

Variations on transitivity 189

in which *thukayindri* behaves as a transitive verb (both in having an ergative subject and in having an accusative object). Semantically, the reflexive analysis works well for (11): 'I'm going to carry (transport) myself with a horse'. It does not work well with (12), as this analysis would seem to imply that the person drowned himself of his own volition.

(e) action on one's own behalf; this is similar to (c) except that the verb is not intransitivised, i.e. the subject is ergative. For example:

(14) Nhuludu   parndri-yindrirla maka.
     3sg:ERG-THERE hit-RR-PRES   fire
     'He's chopping some wood for himself.' (B23; see also X22)

This sentence seems to have the same meaning as (3). (3) was given by BK as part of an elicited sentence. He was later (the following year) given the two versions — (3) and (14) — and asked which he would use. He replied "Both ways" and repeated both, in the order (14, 3) which was the order I had put them in, and added "just the same". The matter was discussed again in a later year and he did not at first use *-yindri* but used *nganggali* to express 'for myself'; he also suggested an alternative word for chopping and when the two alternatives (as in (3) and (14)) were put to him with this verb (*mulpa*) instead of *parndri*, he chose the version with the agent, *nhuludu*.

The strongest reason for not regarding (14) as a transitive sentence and not passive is (13) in which the object has accusative marking. Otherwise, the only indication that the examples of this type are actually transitive sentences and not passive is in the word order (e.g. *ngathu* in (16) appears to be a constituent of the sentence nucleus, not a peripheral constituent) and the apparent meaning (action for the actor's own benefit). Both are weak indications.

Discussing fishing on one occasion, BK said, 'You've got to put that *parndriyindrirla* in, you know, because if you say *karlukarlu parndrirla* it means you hit them, not caught them.' (In fact, though, he did use *parndri* for 'catching [fish]' on occasions.)

Another example of a pair of sentences with no clear difference in meaning, and differing only in that *-yindri* has rendered the verb intransitive in one case but not in the other, is:

(15) Ngarndri nganyi   wanthi-yindrirla.
     mother   1sg:NOM look.for-RR-PRES (T7)

and

(16) Ngarndri ngathu   wanthi-yindrirla.
     mother   1sg:ERG look.for-RR-PRES
     'I'm looking for my mother.' (T11)

Similarly, when I questioned the acceptance of the ergative subject in:

(17) Nhulu   wani   dranga-yindrina.
     3sg:ERG song   sing-RR-IP
     'He sang a song.' (X20, accepted)

I was told that you could say *nhunu* (3sg:NOM). The difference may be that in the type illustrated by (16) there is emphasis on 'for one's own benefit' (perhaps, in (17), 'for one's own amusement'). In Yw and SY sentences like (15) do not have an unmarked goal but use the locative. (18) is an example that was supposedly Yw but actually seems to be SY.

190   *Chapter 14*

Wanthi may be used also without the RR marking, but this is less common. There is even an example in the Yw corpus in which this was done but the subject was nominative and the goal locative. In a SY example, (19), there is a nominative subject and goal, but the last part of it, answering the question that the first part asks, seems to show that that goal should have been marked locative. The locative suffix is *-yi*, and it is easy to understand this being lost when the following word begins with /yi/. Similarly, it is easy to understand this suffix being lost, or at least not noticed, when the stem to which it should be affixed ends in /i/, as in (15). However, dative *-ngadi* (*-ma* in Yw) was used on the goal as an uncommon alternative to the unmarked goal as in (15) (one of the only two BK examples is in the *wanthi* entry in the dictionary; there is one, with no subject expressed, from MN). Furthermore, there is no question of any locative suffix being lost or not heard in (20).

(18) *Nganyi   pulganiyi   wanthi-yindri-nhana.*
      1sg:NOM   3du:GEN-LOC   look.for-RR-NP
      'I was looking for those two.' (Y15)

(19) *'Minha yini   wanthirla?'   'Muduwayi.'*
      what   2sg:NOM   look.for-PRES   child-LOC
      'What are you looking for?' 'For the child.' (M6)

(20) *Wanthi-yindrirla   yini   yinha.*
      look.for-RR-PRES   2sg:NOM   3sg:ACC
      'You're looking for him.' (X17)

Yet another verb for which a variety of case frames was accepted was *ku(d)la* 'to cook'; *kudlayindri* can be used with the thing cooking as subject, but BK also accepted it with the person as subject, either nominative or ergative, and the thing being cooked as object.

Another example where the verb is not intransitivised is:

(21) *Thawa-padapadarla   nganyi,   pandili   nhulu   kapi-yindri-rnanga   ngurra.*
      go-always-PRES   1sg:NOM   dog-ERG   3sg:ERG   follow-RR-CONT   always
      'Wherever I go the dog follows (me).' (R7)

In some cases, where the subject is omitted, the question of transitivity of the verb becomes irrelevant. For example:

(22) *Thawapandhirla   nganyi   karirri-ngadi   ngapa   marndra-yindringa.*
      go-down-PRES   1sg:NOM   river-DAT   water   dip.up-RR-FUT
      'I'm going down to the river for water.' (T11)

Another verb which behaves in some ways like *wanthi* is *windri* 'to paint, to rub', which is basically transitive but seems to be intransitivised, with or without affixation of *-yindri*, when it is used reflexively. Thus:

(23) *Windringa   ngathu   yinhayi   pirtipirti.*
      paint-FUT   1sg:ERG   3sg:ACC-HERE   red
      'I'm going to paint it red.' (P30)

(24) *Maltji withi   nganyi   windrirla*   (or, it seems,   *windri-yindrirla*).
      leg   sore   1sg:NOM   rub-PRES   rub-RR-PRES
      'I'm rubbing my sore leg.' (X24)

It was made clear, in a discussion about this verb, that using the nominative pronoun made the verb reflexive; replacing it with the ergative pronoun in (24) would mean that you were rubbing someone else's leg.

Other verbs in which -*yindri* is attested as denoting action on one's own behalf and not rendering the verb intransitive include *kulpinayindri* 'to surround', *walthayindri* and *pakayindri* 'to carry' and *parndriyindri* 'to kill'. Obviously at least some of these could also occur in reflexive and/or reciprocal clauses.

The constructions in which verbs which can combine with -*yindri* have been attested, then, are as follows (with A agent, S subject, O object, V verb, R reflexive/reciprocal marking, D nominal in dative case, L nominal in locative case, order of constituents, apart from R, variable):

A	O	V	(very common)
S	O	V	(uncommon)
S	L	V	(only SY, Yw; rare)
S		VR	(common; regular for reciprocal sentence)
A	O	VR	(uncommon)
S	D	VR	(uncommon)
S	O	VR	(common; regular if part–whole relationship between O and S)
S	L	VR	(only SY, Yw; seems to be common)

Words for 'look for' (*wanthi* in Yandruwandha, *nhingka* in Yawarrawarrka) are, between them, attested in all these constructions.

BK did not know a root *kaga*, which would be expected to underlie the verb *kagayindri* 'to burp' and/or 'to yawn'.

Yura 'to want, to like' will be considered here, as there is a single example of it with -*yindri* (in the *manu* entry in the dictionary). This is a verb that has been heard with up to twelve case frames (depending on how they are classified) and may well have more. It has been heard as:

(i) a straight transitive verb — ergative-accusative (25);
(ii) with a nominative subject and accusative object (26);
(iii) with a nominative subject and locative indirect object (from MN only, (27)).[4]

When the verb takes a verb-based complement (which is a much more common situation in the corpus), the possibilities are:

(a) subject is (i) ergative or (ii) nominative;
(b) *yura* (i) does or (ii) does not have a nominal object;
(c) complement is (i) a purposive verb (equivalent to a noun in the dative case) or is (ii) in the future tense form;
(d) complement verb is (i) transitive and has an object, or is (ii) intransitive.

This amounts to sixteen possibilities, of which nine are attested in the Innamincka corpus (all from BK). These are summarised in the following table, in which the case of

---

[4] MN would not use *yura* in a positive sentence, but only in a negative sentence with *wabya*. She used *ngandja* (a transitive verb) in a positive sentence. However, it may be that *yura* is Yandruwandha and *ngandja* Yawarrawarrka; the information on this is inconsistent.

192   *Chapter 14*

the subject (ERG or NOM) is given first, followed by 'like' representing the stem *yura* and its inflection, followed by O if there is a nominal object of *yura* (which would be coreferential with the deleted subject of the complement verb), followed by V representing the complement verb stem with *-iningadi* (indicating purposive) or *-nga* (future) and then O if this verb is transitive and takes an object. (There is one example where the verb is transitive but there is no explicit object, and a couple of other examples where an expected and implied object of *yura* does not appear. These are not included in the table.) The number following, if any, gives the number of examples in the corpus (of IY only), and the next number identifies the example given for this frame. There are other examples that cannot be assigned with certainty, such as a SY example of NOM like V-*nga* where the V is transitive but its O is understood, and others with a non-singular pronominal subject (which does not distinguish nominative from ergative). SY and Yw data on this verb are fragmentary.

Table 14-1: Case frames for *yura* with verbal complement

ERG like O V-*iningadi*	1	(28)	NOM like O V-*iningadi*		
ERG like O V-*iningadi* O	2	(29)	NOM like O V-*iningadi* O	2	(30)
ERG like V-*iningadi*			NOM like V-*iningadi*	3	(31)
ERG like V-*iningadi* O	3	(32, 33)	NOM like V-*iningadi* O	5	(34)
ERG like O V-*nga*			NOM like O V-*nga*		
ERG like O V-*nga* O			NOM like O V-*nga* O		
ERG like V-*nga*			NOM like V-*nga*	2	(35)
ERG like V-*nga* O	1	(36)	NOM like V-*nga* O	2	(37)

There are no obvious conditioning factors. With an ergative subject there are no examples where there is not a nominal object of either *yura* or the complement, but there are actually more examples where *yura* does not have a nominal object than where it does (and this would have seemed to be the most likely conditioning factor). It is not common for *yura* to have a nominal object when the subject is nominative, but it does happen. The fact that *yura* can combine with the reflexive-reciprocal suffix — a reflexive form is attested, which means something like 'to feel good about yourself' — suggests that it is basically transitive, but nevertheless the nominative subject is far more common in the corpus (and slightly more common where there is no verbal complement).

(25) *Karna   ngathu   yintjadu   walya yurarla,   ngurra yina*
      person   1sg:ERG 3sg:ACC-THERE   not   like-PRES   always EMPH

  nhutjadu   yandhayandha-yukarrarla   ngurra.
  3sg:NOM-THERE   talk-talk-at.night-PRES   always
  'I don't like that fellow; he talks all night.' (R7)

(26) *Ngathu   yina   mardra nguyiwindringa; wayini   yini*
      1sg:ERG   3sg:ACC stone   give-enter-FUT   how.much   2sg:NOM

  yurarlatji?
  like-PRES-EMPH
  "I give you money before I go and how much do you want?" (W4)

(27) *Walya nganyi yurarla yingganiyi. Yundru nganha yuparla.*
not 1sg:NOM like-PRES 2sg:GEN-LOC 2sg:ERG 1sg:ACC tease-PRES

Thawa yita!
go away
'I don't like you. You're teasing me. Go away!' (M6)

(28) *Walya nhuludu nganha karnali yura-nhana thawini-ngadi,*
not 3sg:ERG-THERE 1sg:ACC man-ERG like-NP go-GER-DAT

kathitji parndrini-ngadi.
animal-EMPH hit-GER-DAT
'That man didn't want me to go hunting.' (R10)

(29) *Ngathu yinha yurarla wawini-ngadi yina.*
1sg:ERG 3sg:ACC like-PRES see-GER-DAT 3sg:ACC
'I want him to see you.' (R3)

(30) *Walya nganyi yinha yurarla wawini-ngadi nganha.*
not 1sg:NOM 3sg:ACC like-PRES see-GER-DAT 1sg:ACC
'I don't want him to see me.' (R6)

(31) *Ngunda(?) thawini-ngadi nganyi yura-nhanatji, ngala wathi malkirrili*
? go-GER-DAT 1sg:NOM like-NP-EMPH then tree many-ERG

nganha ngarndangarndamaritji.
1sg:ACC block-block-CAUS-UNSP-EMPH
'I wanted to go through, but all the trees blocked me.' (P5)

(32) *Walya nhulu nganha dranyini-ngadi yura-nhanatji.*
not 3sg:ERG 1sg:ACC hit(throwing)-GER-DAT like-NP-EMPH
'He didn't mean to hit me.' (P5)

(33) *Walya ngathu yinha wawini-ngadi yurarla.*
not 1sg:ERG 3sg:ACC see-GER-DAT like-PRES
'I don't want to see him.' (R5)

(34) *Minhala yini yurarla ngarini-ngadi, nganyi yandha-rlayi?*
what-EMPH 2sg:NOM like-PRES hear-GER-DAT 1sg:NOM say-SIM
'What do you want to hear me say?' (W4)

(35) *Walarriyi kara yini yurarla nhinanga.*
shade-LOC maybe 2sg:NOM like-PRES sit-FUT
'You might like to sit in the shade.' (W4)

(36) *Ngathu yurarla karna yawarritji ngaranga.*
1sg:ERG like-PRES person language-EMPH hear-FUT
'I want to hear the Aboriginal language.' (P29)

(37) *Minhala yini yurarla yakayakanga nganha?*
what-EMPH 2sg:NOM like-PRES ask-ask-FUT 1sg:ACC
'What are you going to ask me next?' (W5)

There are a couple of examples of *yura* with 'contemporaneous action' suffix *-rnanga* used as a one-word clause with the meaning 'if you (or he, she, they) want to'.

Finally, *wada* 'to wait for' (*kalka* in SY, Yw) is a transitive verb which can take a nominal object or a purposive or simultaneous action verb complement; see its dictionary entry (including the *wadayindri* subentry) for examples, and note also that *nhandra* '3sg:fem:ERG' was accepted as an alternative to *nhani* in (38).

(38)   Nhipa   nhani   wadayindrirla.
       spouse   3sg:fem:NOM wait-RR-PRES
       'She's waiting for her husband.' (X31)

14.2 Pseudotransitive sentences

Certain intransitive verbs co-occur with nouns which function, in varying degrees, syntactically and semantically, as objects, and so have two nominative arguments. This includes verbs modified by the suffix *-yindri* (see §14.1). In a number of cases the noun and verb form a standard expression, perhaps best regarded as a compound verb; these include the inchoative verb phrases formed with *ngana* (see §13.7.2, and see §11.1, §11.3.1, and §14.3 for other uses of *ngana*, which is usually transitive). Others are *minha ngana* (or *minhangana*?) 'to do what?', not included in §13.7.2 because it differs from those inchoative verb phrases in the nature of the nominal constituent and in the nature of the derived verb phrase, and also such phrases (some, at least, involving cognate objects) as *muka thuda* 'to sleep' (*muka* 'sleep', *thuda* 'to lie'), *wani thambana* 'to dance a corroboree' (*wani* 'corroboree', *thambana* 'to dance'), *pukudu thuda* 'to dream'[5] (*pukudu* 'a dream'), and *marrka thawa* 'to go camping out' (*marrka* 'camping out').

(39)   Minha   nganarla   yiniyey?
       what   do-PRES   2sg:NOM-DISTORT
       'What are you doing?' (T10, see also M23, Y8)

(This example, with *ngana* intransitive, can be contrasted with the second example sentence in the dictionary entry for *ngana*.)

(40)   *Ay karrukarra, muka nganyi   thudapandhinga, yundru   nganha*
       eh   old.man-VOC sleep 1sg:NOM lie-down-FUT   2sg:ERG   1sg:ACC

       yirrtjinana.
       wake-CAUS-IP
       'Hey, old man, I was just going to sleep, and you woke me up.' (W1)

The following example shows that *muka* is a noun, not an adverb. (However, it is possible for certain nouns, if not all, to function as adverbs; see §14.). Similarly, *pukudu* and *marrka* are nouns.

(41)   Marna   kaga-yindrirla nganyi   mukali.
       mouth   yawn-RR-PRES   1sg:NOM sleep-INST
       'I'm yawning (with sleepiness).' (P17)

It seems in some cases that it would not be possible to regard the verb and 'object' as a compound verb. For example:

---

[5]   See (53) for a 'pseudo-ditransitive' sentence involving *pukudu*.

(42) *Yandruwandhatji   nganyi   yandhayandharla.*
      Yandruwandha-EMPH 1sg:NOM talk-talk-PRES
      'I talk Yandruwandha.' (T6)

and

(43) *Kuditharrana   nganyi   mardratji.*
      forget-IP   1sg:NOM   money-EMPH
      'I forgot the money.' (X35)

The ergative pronoun *ngathu* was not accepted as a subject of this sentence. Similar examples are found in the dictionary entry for *kuditharra*.

Sentences like (44) in which a part of the body has an effect on a person have a subject (the body part) which is unmarked and an object (the person) which is in the accusative case.

(44) *Thundru drakarla   nganha   mulhudu pirna thayini-nguda.*
      stomach stab-PRES   1sg:ACC   food   big   eat-GER-ABL
      'I've got a bellyache from eating too much.' (X16)

The verb *nhina* 'to sit' can function as a copula as in (10-2), (11-70) and (18-30); it may be that other stance verbs can too when they are more appropriate. These phrases — complement + *nhina* (+ inflection) — seem to be exactly similar to the phrase *muka thuda* (+ inflection) except that they do not normally occur in present tense.[6] Another example is:

(45) *Yada   nhutjadu   ngapiringi   nhina-padipadini, ngakanila*
      boomerang   3sg:NOM-THERE   father-1KIN   sit-HAB-GER   1sg:GEN-EMPH

      nhutjadu.
      3sg:NOM-THERE
      'That boomerang used to be my father's, but it's mine now.' (P12)

14.3 Ditransitive sentences

A few verb roots and a set of derived verb stems govern two object noun phrases, the nuclear sentence then being made up of subject noun phrase, two object noun phrases and a verb. The ditransitive verb roots include *ngunyi* 'to give', *ngana* 'to tell' (but note *ngana* with other meanings, see §13.7.2 and §14.2), *yaka* 'to ask', *ngarrka* 'to do' (in *minha ngarrka ~ minhaya ngarrka* 'to do what?', although *minhangarrka* — with stress as for a single word — has also been noted), *thumba* 'to show, to point' (IY), 'to call' (SY) and *drintha* 'to spit (at)'.

(46) *Minha ngarrkana yundru   marnitji.*
      what   do-IP   2sg:ERG   fat-EMPH
      'What did you do with the fat?' (R7)

(47) *Walypala   yintjadu   ngana kathi yina   ngunyini-ngadi.*
      white.man 3sg:ACC-THERE   tell   meat   2sg:ACC   give-GER-DAT
      'Tell the white fellow to give you some meat.' (R6)

---

[6] A possible example of *thanggu* 'to stand' as a copula, in present tense, occurs in the *thanggu* entry in the dictionary. (18-33) too has a present tense copula.

(48) Ngaltja drinthana nganhala muduwali.
spittle spit-IP 1sg:ACC-EMPH child-ERG
'That kid spat at me.' (X43)

Derived ditransitive verbs consist of a transitive verb stem plus the formative -na (see §13.7.1).

(49) Pukapaka ngathu ngunyi-nhana, kathila nhulu nganha
food-tobacco 1sg:ERG give-NP meat-EMPH 3sg:ERG 1sg:ACC

pakana-thikandji kidlatji.
carry-APP-return-then next-EMPH
'He gave me some meat in return for the tobacco.' (R6)

(50) Ngapiri nganha wirnina yinggani.
father 1sg:ACC tell-APP 2sg:GEN
'Tell me about your father.' (R2)

(51) Maya nganha drikana.
name 1sg:ACC name-APP
'Tell me his name.' (R2)

One verb derived with the causative suffix -ka also seems to be ditransitive.

(52) Nganhala warlparaka wanitji yintjadu.
1sg:ACC-EMPH knowing-CAUS corroboree-EMPH 3sg:ACC-THERE
'Teach me that song.' (R6)

The noun *pukudu*, which can form the 'object' of a pseudotransitive verb, is also involved in what may be describable as a 'pseudo-ditransitive' construction with a transitive verb. For example:

(53) Pukudu ngathuna pardra-nhana.
dream 1sg:ERG-2sg:ACC hold-NP
'I dreamt about you last night.' (T5)

In fact, this construction has been heard on two occasions with a nominative subject, despite the transitivity of the verb *pardra* in other contexts being very clear. Thus in the following sentence, from TG correcting an apparent mistake by BK (who had used *thudanhana* 'lie-NP' instead of *pardranhana*; he accepted TG's version and partly repeated it), there is a nominative subject and two nominative objects. *Pukudu* is a noun, as shown by two examples in the dictionary entry in which it has instrumental marking, and an occurrence of it with the ablative suffix.

(54) Pukudu nganyi yina pardra-nhana.
dream 1sg.NOM 2sg.ACC hold-NP
'I dreamt about you.' (C2)

The case of *windri* 'to paint, rub' which is a transitive verb that is intransitivised by the use of a nominative pronoun subject when the object is a body part of the subject, is mentioned in §14.1. In (23) the fact that *pirtipirti* 'red' is unmarked suggests that it is an object and since the thing being painted is also an object, this sentence too could be regarded as 'pseudo-ditransitive'.

15 *Coordination and subordination*

Sentences containing more than one clause are of three basic types. In compound sentences the constituent clauses are all of the same status — i.e. none is subordinated to any other — and they are linked by conjunctions or simply juxtaposed. In complex sentences there is one main clause and other clauses are subordinated to it, and are marked as subordinate in various ways, and depend on the main clause for some aspects of their meaning. In quotation sentences there is one main clause whose verb is an information verb, i.e. a verb denoting knowledge, or transfer or acquisition of information,[1] and a quotation clause, related to the information, which is not marked internally in any way as subordinate but is the object of the verb of the main clause.

Also described in this chapter are sentences which, although comprising only one clause, are incomplete in a similar way to subordinate clauses and depend on a preceding sentence to supply certain aspects of their meaning, and sentences which include a conjunction linking them to a preceding sentence. These are called subordinate sentences and coordinate sentences respectively.

In practice it is sometimes difficult to decide whether a boundary within an utterance is between clauses or sentences.

No exhaustive study has been made of the deletion of constituents from coordinate or subordinate clauses or sentences where they have been stated in an earlier clause or sentence. However, the rules appear on the whole to be straightforward and to allow deletion only when this does not lead to difficulty of interpretation. Thus if two successive clauses have the same subject it may be deleted from the second. Where they are not the same there is no subject deletion. Deletion may be obligatory when appropriate in certain types of clauses, such as those subordinate clauses involving nominalised verbs, but is not in other cases, e.g. in coordinate clauses (10, 6) and (18-30, 31). In some cases subject, verb and object may all be deleted, as where the function of the second clause is to suggest or negate a possible alternative to a peripheral constituent of the first clause ((2) and (8-30)) or where the second clause asks a question about the first ((3) and (8-15)). Note also those compound sentences where the second clause consists only of a negative particle and a nominalised verb (such as (4), and also — if this is correctly classed as a compound rather than a complex sentence — (8-32)).

---

[1] Note, however, that verbs of this type can also occur in the main clause of complex sentences, i.e. their object may be in the form of a subordinate clause rather than a quotation. See, for example, (10-45) or (18-11).

(1) *Thayi-padipadini ngani tjukurru, kathi ngalyila ngani*
 eat-HAB-GER 1pl:ex:NOM kangaroo animal other-EMPH 1pl:ex:NOM

 thayirlatji.
 eat-PRES-EMPH
 'We used to eat kangaroo, but now we eat other animals.' (T3)

(2) *Maltjili nhutjadu thanmarlatji, walya kupuli.*
 leg-INST 3sg:NOM-THERE swim-PRES-EMPH not arm-INST
 'He just swims with his legs; he doesn't use his arms.' (R9)

(3) *Walpa nhulu wathiri, wayini kara dritji.*
 humpy 3sg:ERG build-UNSP how.many maybe sun
 'He built a house; I wonder how long it took him.' (P5)

(4) *Patjikurnu nhuniyi, walya marrtjini.*
 good-one 3sg:NOM-HERE not bark-GER
 "He's a good dog, he never barks." (W7)

Where the subject of one clause is part of the subject of the other both subjects must be specified or at least the whole must be specified in one clause and the part (with the whole deleted) in the other. See (5) and (11-76), where the whole is specified in the first clause and the part only specified later, and (6), where both whole and part are specified in the first clause and the whole appears as subject of the second.

(5) *Man.gili nhunu mundja, patjarla, thawa-nhana nhunu*
 Ben.Kerwin 3sg:NOM sick be.sick-PRES go-NP 3sg:NOM

 kirri-ngadi; kintha yunggudu ngaka-rnanga.
 clever-DAT nose blood run-CONT
 "He's [Bennie] gone to see the doctor, he's sick, his nose is bleeding." (T14)

(6) *Martardaku nganyi dulyi-nhana, nganyi ngurrangu thawarla.*
 ankle 1sg:NOM twist-NP 1sg:NOM always-YET go-PRES
 'I hurt my ankle but I'm still going.' (R9)

Note (18-1) (which is also (S9-34)), where the participants who have been specified at an earlier stage are repeated in a sentence which sums up what has gone before.

Occasionally a subject or object is incompletely or not at all specified in an earlier clause but specified in a later one. Examples are (7), where the object is specified only by a pronoun in the main clause, but is more fully identified in the subordinate clause where it is subject, and (8-24), repeated here as (8), where the subject of the third and fourth clauses is the object of the first and second, and is deleted from the third but not from the fourth. In (11-85) the subject of the subordinate clause (which is an unknown person or thing) is omitted, but speculated on in the next clause. In (11-65) the subject of the subordinate clause is never actually specified, except as the owner of the object of the main clause.

(7) *Purrtjinana ngathu yinha, nga pandili nhulu nganha*
 fright-CAUS-IP 1sg:ERG 3sg:ACC then dog-ERG 3sg:ERG 1sg:ACC

 mathanga, kulkuma-thalkari mathanga.
 bite-FUT jump-up-UNSP bite-FUT
 'I frightened the dog and he bit me — jumped up and bit me.' (R9)

(8) *Ngathu   yinha   kapirla,   yakayakanga yinha,   mardra ngakani*
    1sg:ERG   3sg:ACC follow-PRES ask-ask-FUT   3sg:ACC stone 1sg:GEN

   winkama-nhana,   ngunyithikanga kara nganha nhulu, pani kara.
   disappear-CAUS-NP give-return-FUT maybe 1sg:ACC 3sg:ERG none maybe
   'I'm going to follow him "and ask that bloke whether he shook my money and whether he'll give it to me back or not."' (P7)

In some cases the subject of a second clause may be formally identical to the subject of the first, but is actually different and cannot be deleted. This happens in cases where the subjects involve *kurnu*, meaning 'one' in the first clause and 'another' or 'the other' in the second, *ngalyi*, meaning 'some' and 'others' or perhaps *thana* 'they'. See (13) and (18-44, 46); another example will be found in the entry for *karawarra* in the companion dictionary.

15.1 Compound sentences

Compound sentences can comprise a variety of combinations of the types of sentences described in Chapters 7, 8 and 14, i.e. verbless, intransitive, pseudotransitive, transitive, ditransitive, imperative, indefinite, interrogative and negative.

The basic types of compound sentences can be symbolised as 'a and b', 'a or b' and 'a not b'. Simple examples of these types are (respectively):

(9) *Parndrithikana nhulu   windra, thinbarla   nhulu.*
     hit-return-IP 3sg:ERG spear   chisel-PRES 3sg:ERG
     'He went and cut the spear, and now he's smoothing it.' (T8)

(10) *Karruwali ngala nhunudu   kayi man.garri?*
     boy   then 3sg:NOM-THERE   or   girl
     "Was it a boy or a girl?" (P8)

(11) *Walya ngathu   yinha   kandri-nhana, ngala nhunu   thawawarranangu.*
     not   1sg:ERG 3sg:ACC call-NP   then 3sg:NOM go-arrive-IP-YET
     'I didn't call him but he still came.' (P8)

Other examples are more complex; for example:

(12) *Warnu   kara   nhunu   thawawarrarla; karru kara,   nga yiwa*
     who:NOM maybe 3sg:NOM go-arrive-PRES man   maybe   then woman

     kara;   walyangu ngathu   kurrakurrarlatji.
     maybe   not-YET   1sg:ERG   put-put-PRES-EMPH
     'Someone's coming — "could be a man or could be a woman. I can't figure it out yet, who it is."' (P15)

Here there are four clauses; the second and third are related in an 'a or b' type relationship and this forms a unit which is related to the fourth clause (if this is not in fact a separate sentence) in an 'a not b' type, while these three form a unit related to the first clause in an 'a and b' type. Note that even if the fourth clause is a separate sentence (and so a coordinate sentence) this relationship still seems to hold.

The 'a not b' sentence type is a common means of making a comparison; a quality is not thought of as having an absolute value but as being relative, and so, for example, something

200 *Chapter 15*

that is normally thought of as big is called small when it is compared with something bigger. Compare also (9-53).

(13) *Palha pirnaldra nhutjadutji warruwitjitji, ya purdathayinitji*
bird big-BUT 3sg:NOM-THERE-EMPH emu-EMPH and turkey-EMPH

pulyaldra.
small-BUT
'Emus are bigger than turkeys.' (P14)

(14) *Karrukarruldra nganyi, ngala yinitji pulyaldra.*
old.man-BUT 1sg:NOM then 2sg:NOM-EMPH small-BUT
'I'm older than you.' (P14)

Conjunctions include *ya* 'and', *nga ~ ngala* 'then', *kara* which can sometimes be translated 'or', *kayi* 'or', perhaps *ngapala*, usually translated 'well' and the bound forms *-ngu* 'then', still', 'yet', *-ldra* 'on the other hand' and *-ldrangu* 'too'. The bound conjunctions are described below (§18.3), while the free conjunctions (except *kara*, §8.3) will be described in Chapter 17.

Combinations exemplified in examples given in other sections of this grammar or in dictionary entries include (positive statement clauses where not specified otherwise):

verbless + verbless (18-37)
intransitive + intransitive (6) and *karawarra* entry
transitive + transitive (1)
transitive + verbless (18-31)
transitive + intransitive (18-30)
verbless + verbless negative (4) and (10-51)
ditransitive + intransitive question *wayini* entry
intransitive + intransitive negative question (18-39)
transitive + imperative + negative verbless (8-32)
transitive negative + verbless negative (8-36)
transitive + transitive + transitive (also with a subordinate clause) (A-67)
ditransitive + intransitive + transitive (18-29)
intransitive + verbless + verbless (18-36).

The more complex sentence (12) above is intransitive indefinite + verbless indefinite + verbless indefinite + transitive.

15.2 Coordinate sentences

It is common in texts for a sentence to begin with, and be linked to what has gone before by, *nga ~ ngala* 'then' or *ngapala* 'well' (although it is not certain that the latter really has a coordinate function). Other free conjunctions are less common sentence-initially but do occur. Bound conjunctions may also relate the sentence to a previous one; see the subsections of §18.3. Many examples of conjunctions occurring sentence-initially can be found in the two text chapters in the dictionary volume, especially texts 8 and 9.

15.3 Complex sentences

Complex sentences are divisible into two classes according to the degree of subordination of the subordinate clause. Sentences in which the subordinate clause is of the type which can occur as the main clause of a subordinate sentence involve verbs with the suffixes *-nga*, called 'future' but with a much wider range of functions, *-ri* 'unspecified tense', *-kaldri* 'repeated action', *-rnanga* 'contemporaneous action' and *-ndji* 'immediate sequence' and are often linked to the main clause by conjunctions. They thus have something of the nature of coordinate clauses; in fact it is difficult to make a definite separation of compound and complex sentences, because a coordinate clause may be dependent on the clause it is coordinated with in that, for example, it may rely on this clause to supply the identification of a subject which has been deleted.

The second class of complex sentence involves subordinate clauses which do not normally occur without modification as main clauses. Some types involve nominalised verbs and in the other cases the verbs do resemble nominalised verbs in some ways: potential verbs resemble aversive nouns (see §11.7) and verbs denoting simultaneous action may involve the locative suffix *-yi* (see §11.12).

Sentences using those verb forms — *-ri*, *-rnanga*, *-kaldri* and *-ndji* — which appear in subordinate clauses and subordinate sentences but not, or not typically, in independent sentences, are illustrated in §11.8 to §11.11. The suffix *-nga*, which can also occur in the main verb of an independent sentence, is described in §11.3. Further examples of its use in subordinate clauses are given below. Its function is to indicate that the action concerned followed that denoted by the main clause (without necessarily being a consequence of it).

(15) *Mardrayi nganyi thina yilkana, warlkanga.*
stone-LOC 1sg:NOM foot slip-IP fall-FUT
'I slipped on a rock and fell down.' (W3)

(16) *Yundra ngathu yina wawana, walya yina kilkanga.*
far 1sg:ERG 2sg:ACC see-IP not 2sg:ACC know-FUT
"I seen you a long way and I didn't recognise you." (W5)

(17) *Walyawalyaka-nhana ngathu windratji ngakani; ngarrula nganyi*
not-not-CAUS-NP 1sg:ERG spear-EMPH 1sg:GEN only-EMPH 1sg:NOM

nhinanhinanga walyala thawini kathi parndringa.
sit-sit-FUT not-EMPH go-GER animal kill-FUT
'I lost my spear so I can't go hunting now.' (R10)

(18) *Thika-lapurra nganyi wawawawanga yinha.*
return-REMP 1sg:NOM see-see-FUT 3sg:ACC
'I went back and saw him.' (C5)

(19) *Walyala yina kara nhunuyi puthakurnu thikanga*
not-EMPH EMPH maybe 3sg:NOM-HERE occasion-other return-FUT

yakayakangatji, ngathunha panipanikala ngananga.
ask-ask-FUT-EMPH 1sg:ERG-3sg:ACC none-none-CAUS-EMPH tell-FUT
'He mightn't come back again and ask me to tell him everything.' (D6)

Of those verb forms occurring exclusively, or almost exclusively, in subordinate clauses, *-yi* is described in §11.7 and *-rlayi* in §11.12. Subordinate clauses involving the gerund form of the verb are illustrated below. There are two types, both very common — those in which the dative suffix *-ngadi* is affixed to the gerund, and those in which the ablative suffix *-nguda* is used. (These are, of course, not strictly clauses in that they do not have a verb, but rather an inflected nominalised verb.) The former type expresses purpose or goal, and seems in many cases to be interchangeable with the future tense form of the verb, with suffix *-nga*; compare (23) and (24). It occurs frequently after verbs such as want, ask, tell, send in a context such as 'V someone to do something'. As noted above (§11.3), Austin (1981b:319) says that *-nga* and *-iningadi* (see §11.3) form a same subject/different subject pair in implicated (i.e. purposive) clauses. This requires qualification: *-iningadi* is indeed used in sentences that speak of someone doing something so that someone else does something (like 'I told him to go') but it is used also with verbs such as 'want' even when no object is expressed ('I want to go'). See (23) and (25) below; also (28) and (29) which are similar. Furthermore, it is used to express the purpose of something which is better thought of as an instrument than an agent (as 'They made nets for catching fish' — it is 'they' who catch the fish). There are many examples in the ethnographic text; see (A-2, 3, 10, 19, 25, 40, 92, 96, 107, 134) and probably others. Other examples below where the two subjects are the same are (22) and (26).

In these two types of complex sentence a participant which is common to both clauses is not normally made explicit in the second; one where this is done is (27). When I made up sentences, along the lines of some of the following examples (for example, by adding *ngathu* '1sg:ERG' after *kathikathi* in (20)) BK usually (but not always) accepted them. I suspect that when he was younger and more alert he would not have been so likely to. A participant seems to be more likely to be expressed in both clauses when the subordinate clause uses *-nga*, as in (16), (17) and (19).

(20) *Wathi nganha yada ngunyi, kathikathi parndrini-ngadi.*
stick 1sg:ACC hither give snake hit-GER-DAT
'Give me a stick to hit the snake.' (T2)

(21) *Mirni ngaldra wadarla man.garri nhani thikawarrini-ngadi.*
wait 1du:in:NOM wait-PRES girl 3sg:fem:NOM return-arrive-GER-DAT
"We'll have to wait till that girl comes home." (W3)

Contrast (9-45) in which *man.garri* is part of the main clause.

(22) *Minha-ngadi pandi nhuliyi ngurukarla parndrini-ngaditji.*
what-DAT dog 3sg:ERG-HERE own-PRES hit-GER-DAT-EMPH
"Why does he own a dog if he's going to belt it?" (W7; see also X44 where *ngurukarla* is corrected to *nganggalikarla*.)

(23) *Nhunu thangguthangguni-ngadi yurarla.*
3sg:NOM stand-stand-GER-DAT want-PRES
'He'd like to stand up' (of a baby who can't yet). (P8)

(24) *Walarriyi kara yini yurarla nhinanga.*
shade-LOC maybe 2sg:NOM want-PRES sit-FUT
"You like to go and sit out in the shade." (W4)

Note that in (23) the subordinate clause is embedded in the main clause. Another example of this type is (25).

(25) *Karru nhutjadu thawarla yada ngakani-ngadi. Walya ngathu*
man 3sg:NOM-THERE go-PRES hither 1sg:GEN-DAT not 1sg:ERG

yinha wawini-ngadi yurarla. Dirrkapandhirla nganyi
3sg:ACC see-GER-DAT want-PRES turn-down-PRES 1sg:NOM

paladila, warrakurnula thawanga.
individual-EMPH side-other-EMPH go-FUT
'That man's coming here. I don't want to see him; I'll go the other way and dodge him.' (R5)

The subordinate clause precedes the main clause in:

(26) *Wani thambanini-ngadi, marndrapandhirla nganyi.*
corroboree dance-INCH-GER-DAT paint-down-PRES 1sg:NOM
'I'm going to paint myself for the corroboree.' (T12)

The subject and object of the subordinate clause are inflected as they would be in the corresponding independent clause; see (20), (21), (25) and (27). However, when I made up sentences in which they were inflected with the dative (for example, *kathikathingadi* instead of *kathikathi* in (20)) BK accepted them. There could have been some confusion involved, as *kathikathingadi* would be correct if the verb (*parndriningadi*) were omitted.

(27) *Kapada, thumbalkarla ngathuna kardratji pakuni-ngadi,*
come.on show-CAUS-PRES 1sg:ERG-2sg:ACC yam-EMPH dig-GER-DAT

padla yundru kilkini-ngadilatji.
place 2sg:ERG know-GER-DAT-EMPH-EMPH
'I'll show you where the yams are so you can dig them up. "So you'll know where it is."' (P11)

In (28) the subordinate clause contains a noun in dative case, but this has an allative function:

(28) *Kuditharra-nhana nganyi thuwa-ngaditji thawini-ngadi.*
forget-NP 1sg:NOM store-DAT-EMPH go-GER-DAT
'I forgot to go to the store.' (R3)

A subordinate clause may be governed by a verbless main clause, as in:

(29) *Patjikurnu nhutjadu mayikurru parndrini-ngadi.*
good-one 3sg:NOM-THERE rat kill-GER-DAT
'He's good at catching rats.' (of a dog) (R6, X33)

In (30) a purposive clause acts as a main clause, answering a question asked in the preceding sentence, and is itself qualified by a clause which has the form of an independent clause but functions here as a relative clause qualifying the object of the purposive clause.

(30) '*Minha-ngadi yundru windra pakarleyéy?*' '*Pandi yinha*
what-DAT 2sg:ERG spear carry-PRES-DISTORT dog 3sg:ACC

warrkanini-ngadi matha-nhana yina nganha nhulu.'
throw-APP-GER-DAT bite-NP EMPH 1sg:ACC 3sg:ERG
'What are you doing with that spear?' 'I'm going to spear that dog that bit me.' (R2)

(The second sentence of this example was repeated with the future form of the verb, *warrkananga*, instead of *warrkaniningadi*. This entails a focus on the person who is to do the spearing rather than the instrument with which it is to be done.)

In (31) a subordinate clause has another clause of the same type subordinated to it.

(31) *Walya nhuludu nganha karnali yura-nhana thawini-ngadi,*
not 3sg:ERG-THERE 1sg:ACC person-ERG want-NP go-GER-DAT

kathitji parndrini-ngadi.
animal-EMPH kill-GER-DAT
'That fellow didn't want me to go hunting.' (R10)

In (32) the subject of one of the clauses forms part of the subject of the other (the other part of the latter subject being the object of the first clause).

(32) *Karrkarla ngathu nguthingi; ngali kandrakini-ngadi.*
call-PRES 1sg:ERG elder.brother-1kin 1du:ex:NOM top-CAUS-GER-DAT
'I'll call my brother and the two of us will be able to lift it.' (T13)

The use of the gerund with the ablative inflectional suffix in a subordinate clause denotes that the action referred to preceded the action referred to in the main clause. The subjects of the two verbs may or may not be the same. In many cases the action referred to in the subordinate clause caused or contributed to that referred to in the main clause, but this is not always so. It is not clear whether, where the subordinate clause is transitive, the word denoting the object can also carry the ablative suffix; it certainly can if the verb is deleted and there are no semantic problems (for example, in (33), in which *kathi kuthawirringuda* could be substituted for the last three words, or (16-26)). Compare the remarks above about an object being marked dative in a purposive clause.

(33) *Patjarla nganyi kathi kuthawirri thayini-nguda.*
be.sick-PRES 1sg:NOM meat rotten eat-GER-ABL
'I'm sick because I ate rotten meat.' (T11, X25)

(34) *Pirritjampanarla nganyi minimininhinini-nguda.*
be.tired-PRES 1sg:NOM run-run-sit-GER-ABL
"I'm tired of running about all day." (W7)

(35) *Panmana ngani, walya panipanika manggini-nguda.*
put.water.on-IP 1pl:ex:NOM not all-all-CAUS burn-GER-ABL
'We put [the fire] out before it did much damage.' (R7)

(36) *Walya nganha ngunyi kudrini-ngudatji.*
not 1sg:ACC give break-GER-ABL-EMPH
'Don't give me the broken one.' (X16)

This was the second translation given for this English sentence. The first was:

(37) *Walya nganha kudrikudrinitji yinha(?) ngunyi.*
not 1sg:ACC break-break-GER-EMPH 3sg:ACC(?) give (X16)

There is one probable case of operative suffix *-li* following *-nguda* on a nominalised verb (compare §9.1.6, especially (9-62) and also (9-176)).

(38) ...(inaudible)... *pangkithirri-ngarnmini-ngadi nganha yingkani-ngudali.*
               rib-grip-GER-DAT   1sg:ACC   laugh-GER-ABL-INST
      "He got a stitch in the belly from laughing." (B24)

Sentences including clauses in which the verb is nominalised but not inflected, or sentences with the form of a single clause which includes a nominalised verb, are not regarded as involving a subordinate clause, even though, as in (39), they may involve a subordinate clause (here a relative clause) in the English translation. (For examples of the former type see §8.4.1, and for the latter type see (10-41) and (10-44).)

(39) *Kurrakurrari nhutjadu,   muduwa kadikadini,   parndri-nhana*
      mad-mad   3sg:NOM-THERE   child   chase-chase-GER   hit-NP

      nhuludu   nhipatji   ngakani.
      3sg:ERG-THERE   wife-EMPH   1sg:GEN
      'That fellow that's always chasing the kids, he belted my wife yesterday.' (R6)

15.4 Subordinate sentences

Clauses of the type which occur as subordinate in the first class of complex sentences described in §15.3 frequently occur as the main clause of a sentence. Such a sentence then relies on a preceding sentence or the context to specify the tense of the verb. Some examples will be found in §11.7 to §11.10. Two others, including one in which the main clause of the subordinate sentence governs a subordinate clause, are given below. Subordinate sentences are common in texts; (40) is taken from a text and it is only the context that shows that it is subordinate.

(40) *Ngapala pula   thingapadanga yada.*
      well   3du:NOM   pull-in-FUT   hither
      'Then [after the men throw the net down] they pull [it] in [to the bank].'
      (D2, = A-52))

(41) *Ngarru nhunu   kulkupa-thalka-warrandji,   purrtjinanga   nganha.*
      only   3sg:NOM   jump-up-arrive-SEQ   nervous-CAUS-FUT   1sg:ACC
      "He jumped around from behind my back and frightened me." (P5)

15.5 Quotation

A quotation sentence consists of a main clause containing a transitive verb and its subject but no object or a ditransitive verb with subject and one object phrase, followed by a clause which is formally identical to an independent clause; this clause functions as the object of the verb of the main clause but there is no morphological marking to denote this fact. The verb of the main clause is an information verb (defined in the first paragraph of this chapter), i.e. a verb related to the possession, acquisition or transfer of information or awareness. This is to be contrasted with the case where the verb of the main clause is a verb of sensing; in that case the verb of the dependent clause is marked by the simultaneous action suffix *-rlayi*. Note, however, that an information verb is not necessarily followed by a quotation clause (see (19), (28), (9-165), (10-45), (18-11)).

(42) *Ay kilkarla ngathu, nhingguwa yina nhinatharrathikana.*
 eh know-PRES 1sg:ERG location-THERE EMPH sit-fly-return-IP
 'I know you've been over there.' (T8)

Contrast this example (in which the subject of the quoted clause is omitted, being clear from the context) with the next one, in which the object is marked with the dative, presumably because *kilkarla* here means 'know how' rather than 'know that'.

(43) *Ay kilkarla ngathu pukatji kudlini-ngadi.*
 eh know-PRES 1sg:ERG tucker-EMPH cook-GER-DAT
 'I know all about cooking.' (T8)

(44) *Nhuludu nganha ngana-nhana, yundru kathi kantu*
 3sg:ERG-THERE 1sg:ACC tell-NP 2sg:ERG animal wallaby

 windrali warrkana-nhana.
 spear-with throw-APP-NP
 'That man told me about you spearing the wallaby.' (R3)

(45) *Ngana-yindringa nganyi, 'Walya yabalitji ngana mayi.'*
 tell-RR-FUT 1sg:NOM not fear-INST-EMPH do EMPH
 "Telling myself not to be frightened." (R8)

(46) *Pukudu ngathu pardra-yukarrana, tjukurru ngathu warrkana-nhana*
 dream 1sg:ERG hold-at.night-NP kangaroo 1sg:ERG throw-APP-NP

 windrali; manipirna, kathi marnipirna.
 spear-INST fat-big, animal fat-big
 'I dreamt I speared a fat kangaroo.' (P11)

(47) *Ngathu yina walya wirnina-nhana, thantjiyipa-ngadi nganyi*
 1sg:ERG 2sg:ACC not tell-APP-NP town-DAT 1sg:NOM

 thawa-nhana, yaba ngunyinga nganha thana.
 go-NP fear give-FUT 1sg:ACC 3pl:NOM
 "I never tell you, about me taking a fright in the town; or [correction] they frightened me in the town." (P11)

(48) *Yakalarla ngathuna, minha nganarla nhunuyi walya*
 ask-NOW-PRES 1sg:ERG-2sg:ACC what do-PRES 3sg:NOM-HERE not

 yandhiyandhini ngakaniyi.
 talk-talk-GER 1sg:GEN-LOC
 "I'm asking you why he don't talk to me." (P15)

Note that the quoted clause is verbless in (8-14). In (49) the quoted clause is not formally identical to an independent clause, but its verb is nominalised and ablative, referring to a (supposed) event in the past.

(49) *Ngara-nhana ngathu paldrini-nguda yina yini.*
 hear-NP 1sg:ERG die-GER-ABL EMPH 2sg:NOM
 'I heard you had died.' (P8-9)

16 *Adverbs*

Adverbs are uninflecting words which form adverbial phrases (see Chapter 5) or part of adverbial phrases, and thus can modify a verb phrase or a noun phrase. Adverbs are — to use Lyons' (1968:326) words — a very heterogeneous class, and can be divided into many subclasses according to their semantic properties and syntactic functions. Subclassification is difficult in some cases, especially where the function of the adverb is not clear, and it has been found necessary to group a few unclassified items together. Membership of some subclasses is obvious; other subclasses include modal adverbs, the negatives and the potential *kara*, aspectual adverbs — *kali* 'already', *ngada* 'still' and *ngurra* 'always', and reciprocal adverbs — *kala* 'back', 'in return', 'in revenge' and *kidla* 'in turn'. The adverbs of manner include *ngarru* 'only', 'just', *muthu* 'very' and *marndu* 'together'. A set of derived adverbs is considered in §16.9.

Some adverbs are often cliticised, i.e. pronounced with no main stress as if part of the preceding word. These include *ngada, nguka* 'too', the demonstrative adverbs and occasionally others such as *kara*.

Some adverbs can be verbalised by means of the inchoative suffix *-na* and/or the causative suffix *-ka*. These include *kaka* 'close', 'near', *kala* 'in return', *pudlu* 'can't', *walya* 'not', *marndu* 'together' and *muthu* 'very'. Reduplication may be involved in some cases. *Nguka* forms a transitive verb stem when reduplicated, no verbalising affix being used.

A few descriptive nouns (corresponding to English adjectives) may function as adverbs (and compare the use of nouns such as *muka* in pseudotransitive sentences, §14.2).

(1) *Kundangali paltjapaltja   pulkarla.*
     wind   strong-strong blow-PRES
     'The wind is blowing hard.' (P14; see also X25, X33)
     (This is a doubtful case; the word order suggests that *paltjapaltja* is
     functioning as an adjective.)

(2) *Ngarru nganyi   warnta thudapandhinatji; walya yina nganyi ngurra*
     only   1sg:NOM short   lie-down-IP-EMPH not   EMPH 1sg:NOM always

     thudathudanhina-nhana.
     lie-lie-sit-NP
     'I only lay down for a little while; "I haven't been sleeping all day."' (P15)

Patji 'good' has been heard with an adverbial function in its normal form, *patjikurnu*, the uncommonly heard short form *patji*, and as a reduplicated stem *patjipatji*.

(3) *Maka nhutjadu walya thangkanarla patjikurnu;*
fire 3sg:NOM-THERE not burn-INCH-PRES good-one

panmapanma-yindri-rnanga ngurra.
put.out-put.out-RR-CONT always
'The fire's not burning properly; it's going out all the time.' (P14)

(4) *Walya nhandradu muduwa wawawawanarla patji.*
not 3sg:fem:ERG-THERE child look-look-APP-PRES good
'She's not looking after the baby properly.' (P14)

(5) *Patjipatji nhulu thinbarla.*
good-good 3sg:ERG chisel-PRES
'He's doing it [i.e. making a boomerang] very carefully.' (P14)

The noun *kurnu* 'one' seems to function as an adverb in:

(6) *Yini thangguthikanga thannganiyi, karna thulayitji?*
2sg:NOM stand-return-FUT 3pl:GEN-LOC person stranger-LOC-EMPH

Parndriyila yina, kurnutji thawa-rlayi.
hit-POT-EMPH 2sg:ACC one-EMPH go-SIM
'Are you going to visit those strangers? You shouldn't go alone, they might kill you.' (R1)

16.1 Modal adverbs

The modal adverbs are the negatives *walya*, *pani* and *pudlu* and the potential adverb *kara*. These have been described in §8.3 and §8.4.

16.2 Aspectual adverbs

16.2.1 kali

Kali 'already' denotes completion, either in the sense that an action has been completed or that an action has been commenced and (in either case) that the previous state of affairs no longer exists. In some cases — possibly always — it implies that the speaker believes that the hearer thinks that the previous state of affairs still applies. It is usually associated with a verb in the immediate past tense or present tense. See the dictionary entry for additional examples. The combination of *kali* with the negative adverb *walya* means 'nearly' (see the last part of §8.4.1).

(7) *Nhadina-nhana nhunu, nga nhambana yinha kali.*
dead-INCH-NP 3sg:NOM then cover-IP 3sg:ACC already
'He died, and they've buried him.' (T8)

(8) *Kali nhunu manyunalarla; kali walya nhunu paldri-nhana.*
already 3sg:NOM good-INCH-NOW-PRES already not 3sg:NOM die-NP
'He's getting better now; he nearly died.' (P10)

(9) *Kali ngathu yawarri panikala kilkarla.*
already 1sg:ERG language all-CAUS-EMPH know-PRES
'I know the language completely now.' (P13)

(10) *Kali nhunuyi manggalarla.*
 already 3sg:NOM-HERE burn-NOW-PRES
 'It's burning now' (i.e. I have succeeded in getting it to burn). (P12)

Kali is associated with a verbless sentence and with an optative verb in the two following examples. Its function in the second of them is not clear; BK translated it there as 'well'.

(11) *Kali nhutjadu ngan.gutji yinggani patjikurnu.*
 already 3sg:NOM-THERE word-EMPH 2sg:GEN good-one
 'That's right.' [more literally, 'Your words are good.'] (C2)

(12) *Ngala malthilitji nganari, kali windripada-malka walpayi.*
 then cold-INST-EMPH do-UNSP already enter-in-OPT humpy-LOC
 "If ... he's cold, he go in the humpy and sit down inside." (W4)

16.2.2 ngada

Ngada 'while' occurs only a few times in the corpus and is used to state that something is in progress while something else is done. It may be a clitic. It follows a locative noun phrase which refers to the continuing situation; it was not accepted as a suffix to a verb. The action denoted by the verb in the clause takes up only a small part of the time during which the situation is continuing; as BK put it, referring to the word (or phrase?) *mukayingada* 'sleep-LOC-while', 'That's if you want to do anything quick while he's asleep'. Thus it was acceptable for 'Let's sneak off while he's asleep' but not for 'I kept on watching him while he was asleep.'

(13) *Malthiyi-ngadatji, kathi kudlapandhiri.*
 cold-LOC-while-EMPH meat cook-down-UNSP
 'Let's cook our meat now, while it's still cool.' (R6)

(14) *Thawarla ngandra kayidi, malthiyi ngada.*
 go-PRES 1pl:in:NOM now cold-LOC while
 'We'll go now while it's still cool.' (R6)

(15) *Thayinhana walya ngathu, kanpayi ngada.*
 eat-NP not 1sg:ERG visible-LOC while
 'I should have eaten it "while it was there."' (R8)

See also (S7-4).

16.2.3 ngurra

Ngurra denotes that an action or state is frequent, habitual or continuing for a long period. In (2) it is contrasted with *warnta* '[for a] short [time]'. Other examples of its use are (3) and (72). It is very common.

(16) *May! Ngurra nganyi yandharla.*
 well always 1sg:NOM talk-PRES
 'Well! I've been talking all the time!' (D6)

210   *Chapter 16*

(17) *Pandi nhutjadu   karna   mathini   ngurra, ngurra mathini.*
     dog   3sg:NOM-THERE person bite-GER always always bite-GER
     'That dog's a terror to bite.' (R6)

(18) *Parndri-padipadini   ngani,   ngurra thawa-rnanga.*
     kill-HAB-GER   1pl:ex:NOM   always go-CONT
     'We used to go hunting a lot.' (T14)

The combination of *ngurra* with *-ngu* 'yet' means 'still'.

(19) *Thawa-nhana nganyi,   kalkayila   dritjitji,   ngala nganyi*
     go-NP   1sg:NOM   afternoon-LOC-EMPH   sun-EMPH   then   1sg:NOM

     ngurrangu   thawa-rlayi.
     always-YET   go-SIM
     'It got late while I was still going along.' (R8)

The reduplicated form *ngurrangurra* is translated 'for good':

(20) *Ngurrangurra   kara,   ya   thikanga   kara   nhunu   walpi kara.*
     always-always   maybe   and   return-FUT maybe 3sg:NOM   when   maybe
     'He might go for good, or he might come back some time.' (D6)

16.3 Reciprocal adverbs

The two reciprocal adverbs *kala* (sometimes *kadla*) and *kidla* are both uncommon; only two examples of the latter are known. The difference between the two may lie in the desirability of being the recipient of the action; *kala* refers to an action in revenge, or to get even, or to an action taken in turn or as someone's part in a sequence and *kidla* to a return of a favour. BK translated *kala* 'back' and *kidla* 'next' or 'take a turn'. There seems to be overlap, however.

(21) *Kalala   ngathu   yinha   nganathikandji,   yarnduldrangu.*
     back-EMPH   1sg:ERG 3sg:ACC tell-return-SEQ   how-BUT-YET
     'I told him back [the same way].' (B15)

(22) *Parndripada-nhana   nhulu   yina,   yundru   kalala   walya*
     hit-in-NP   3sg:ERG 2sg:ACC   2sg:ERG   back-EMPH   not

     parndrithikari,   or parndripadari.
     hit-return-UNSP   or hit-in-UNSP
     'You should have hit him back when he hit you.' (R1-2)

(23) *Ngapa   yundru   kidlala   marndrathikanga.*
     water   2sg:ERG   next-EMPH   dip up-return-FUT
     'It's your turn to go and get the water.' (R6)

(24) *Pukapaka   ngathu   ngunyi-nhana, kathila   nhulu   nganha*
     tucker-tobacco 1sg:ERG give-NP   meat-EMPH   3sg:ERG   1sg:ACC

     pakana-thikandji   kidlatji.
     carry-APP-return-SEQ   next-EMPH
     'He gave me some meat in return for the tobacco.' (R6)

Kala can be verbalised. For example:

(25) *Nganha   yundru   parndripadana;   mirni   wada,*
     1sg:ACC 2sg:ERG hit-in-IP   how.about   wait

   kadlakini-ngadilatji   ngathu.
   back-CAUS-GER-DAT-EMPH-EMPH   1sg:ERG
   'You hit me; you wait; I'll get even with you.' (P31)

16.4 Adverbs of time

Much of the time specification in Yandruwandha is expressed in the verb, which can do this more precisely than most other languages (see Chapter 11). Time is frequently specified also by adverbial phrases based on common nouns such as *nyangi* 'month', 'moon', *malthi* 'cold weather', 'year', *nguni* 'day', *dritji* 'sun', 'day' and *kalka* 'afternoon' or by location nouns (see §9.6) such as *marripathi* 'tomorrow' and *matja* 'a long time away' (i.e. long ago, or a long time in the future, according to the tense of the verb). Note also the specification by such phrases as *muduwayi* 'when a child' or clauses like *man.garri nhani thikawarriningadi* 'until that girl cames home', and special inflected verb forms like *ngananhinanhukada* 'yesterday'.

The other method of specifying time is by means of adverbs of time such as *kayidi* 'now', 'soon', 'today', *ngakamarra* 'a while ago', *thakurru* 'in a while', *ngardra* 'later', 'after' and *kambarri* 'before'. The last two can refer to place as well as to time. See the various dictionary entries.

(26) *Kayidi   nhunu   thikawarrana   nguthu   wawathikini-nguda.*
     now   3sg:NOM   return-arrive-IP   elder brother   see-return-GER-ABL
     'He's just came home from visiting his brother.' (P12)

(27) *Thawa-nhana   ngani   wani-ngadi   ngala thana   kadli*
     go-NP   1pl:ex:NOM   corroboree-DAT   then 3pl:NOM   already

   thambanari,   ngardratjila   ngani   thawawarra-nhana.
   dance-INCH-UNSP   later-EMPH-EMPH   1pl:ex:NOM   go-arrive-NP
   'We went for the corroboree but we got there too late.' (R2)

The morphology of the word based on *ngardra* in the following example is not clear.

(28) *Thawarla nganyi,   ngala nhunu   kuthiwarra-rlayitji   ngadratji-kala*
     go-PRES 1sg:NOM   then 3sg:NOM come-arrive-SIM-EMPH   later-EMPH-?

   kadli   nganyi   thawari.   Yakayakarlayitji   nhulu,   nganandji yinha,
   already   1sg:NOM go-UNSP   ask-ask-SIM-EMPH   3sg:ERG   tell-SEQ   3sg:ACC

   'Ay   marrikudhi-nhana   nhunu.'
   eh   go early-NP   3sg:NOM
   'I'm going, and he'll be coming later, when I've already gone. If he asks you, tell him, "Oh, he went early".' (P8)

A reduplicated form of *kayidi* is translated 'now and then'.

(29) *Kundrukundrurla   nhutjadu   kayidi-kayidi.*
     cough-cough-PRES   3sg:NOM-THERE   now-now
     'He's coughing now and then.' (P15)

212 *Chapter 16*

An adverb of time that occurs only once in the corpus (from TG) is *yuri*, translated (by her) "a good while". It was not used by BK and may have been a loan from English, 'hour'.

(30) *Yuriyi   puladu   yandhayandharla.*
     hour(?)-LOC 3du:NOM-THERE   talk-talk-PRES
     'They're talking for a long time.' (T12)

See also *ngala*, §17.1.

16.5 Adverbs of place

Location is expressed by means of nouns in the locative case, location nouns (e.g. place names) in the nominative case and adverbs of place (which may form a phrase with one or more of the others). Adverbs of place include *thanu ~ thanuthanu* 'between', *kaka* 'near', 'close', *walpirri* 'on the other side', 'across' (possibly a directional adverb; see §12.15), *pada* 'inside', *parrari* 'underneath', *pandhi* 'down', *thalka* 'up' and others. *Kambarri* 'in front' and *ngardra* 'behind' (as noted in §16.4), and possibly others, can refer to location in time as well as place. See the dictionary entries.

(31) *Kurrapandhi nhinggudu,   thanuthanu. Mandrithawarla ngathu   yita.*
     put-down   location-THERE   between   get-go-PRES   1sg:ERG   away
     "Put it down in the middle. I'll pick it up as I'm going home." (P4)

(32) *Wayi kaka kara.*
     how near maybe
     'I don't know how far.' (P5)

(33) *Kathi   puluka walpirri miriyi   thanggukarlatji.*
     animal bullock across   sandhill-LOC stand-CAUS-PRES-EMPH
     "Tailing cattle over the hill." (P4) (tailing = herding)

(34) *Thilthirri nhutjadu   pada, darlamurruyi.*
     centipede   3sg:NOM-THERE   in   bark-LOC
     'There's a centipede under the bark.' (B14)

Ngardra forms the initial component of a compound verb *ngardrawarrka* 'to leave behind':

(35) *Pirnalatji   nhunu   payirrila, ngardrawarrkangala   kara*
     big-EMPH-EMPH   3sg:NOM long-EMPH   behind-throw-FUT-EMPH maybe

     yina.
     2sg:ACC
     "He might pass you in height." [lit. 'He's tall, might leave you behind.'] (P8)

While most adverb stems are monomorphemic, two formatives, *-palapala* 'on both sides' and *-thanuthanu* 'between' can be used to derive an adverb of place from a noun. Since these derived forms are adverbs and not noun + adverb phrases, locative marking, as on the nouns in (33) and (34), is not used. *Thanuthanu* (and possibly *palapala*) can function as an adverb in its own right, with the meaning 'in the middle'.

An example of the use of an adverb formative in a sentence is:

(36) *Pandi-thanuthanu nhinarla nhunu.*
     dog-between   sit-PRES   3sg:NOM
     'He's sitting in amongst the dogs'. (X35)

Other adverbs derived in this way are *mardrathanuthanu* 'between the hills', *yiwathanuthanu* 'between the women' (note, heard as two words), *pirithanuthanu* 'in the space between the legs', *thadripalapala* 'on both banks' (*thadri* 'bank (of river)') and *palthupalapala* 'on both sides of the road'. See also (18-20).

Some adverbs of place — *pandhi, thalka, ngari, pada* and *walpirri* — form verb aspect markers as described in Chapter 12. See §16.6 for the combination of *pandhi* with *yita*.

Some compounds with *kurnu* 'one' may function as adverbs of place, e.g. *marndakurnu* 'half way', *padlakurnu-padlakurnu* 'everywhere'.

16.6 Directional adverbs

Direction (not only of motion, but also, for example, of gaze or of giving) may be expressed by adverbial phrases involving nouns (with dative or ablative case marking) and/or compass points and/or the adverbs *yada* 'hither', *yita* 'away' 'over there' and perhaps *walpirri* 'across' and *kunawarrku* 'crossways'. Additional examples will be found in the dictionary. See also (11-67).

(37) *Ngarru nganha yada wawari   walya yandhini.*
     only   1sg:ACC hither look-UNSP not speak-GER
     "He looked at me and never said a word." (W1)

(38) *Kathi yita pandi ngunyikow!*
     meat away dog   give-away:DISTORT
     'Give the dog some meat!' (T7)

(39) *Mardra thanayi   thitathita yitatji.*
     stone 3pl:NOM-HERE rough   away-EMPH
     '[The rocks were smooth up there but] they're rough from there on.' (C4)
     (Note that this sentence is verbless.)

(40) *Ngapala, kurrupu   karrukarru, pundrayi kara, makamakayi kara,*
     well   old.woman old.man   cold-LOC maybe fire-fire-LOC maybe

     ngapala ngarru kankunu   kurraringa   makawarrkanga,
     well   only   windbreak put-UNSP-EMPH   fire-throw-FUT

     kunawarrkutji   thuda-yukarrangatji.
     crossways-EMPH   lie-at night-FUT-EMPH
     'Well, the old women and the old men, in winter and in summer, only put up a windbreak, threw some firewood down and slept crossways.' (D4, = A141)

The two directional adverbs *yita* and *yada* may be combined to express a reciprocal action as in:

(41) *Yitayada   ngali   parndri-yindrina.*
     away-hither 1du:ex:NOM hit-RR-IP
     'We hit each other.' (T3)

Contrast

(42) *yitala   yadala   minimini-rnanga*
     away-EMPH   hither-EMPH   run-run-CONT
     'running here and there' (E5)

Yita also combines with the adverb *pandhi* 'down' to form the adverb *yitapandhi* 'down there, further down a slope or bank'.

16.7 Demonstrative adverbs

Demonstrative adverbs may be divided into one group which is more often cliticised than stressed as free morphemes, and another group which behaves as free morphemes. The first group includes *waka*, *widi*, *walha* and *nhayi*, all of which seem mainly to reinforce other demonstratives without carrying much meaning in themselves. They may have some function of more precise specification but the data are not sufficient to reveal this. *Walha* and *nhayi* seem to be interchangeable and were used only by TG. They are all glossed DEM.

Waka may follow or be affixed to a demonstrative pronoun (most commonly), a noun (especially a location noun), another demonstrative adverb or a directional adverb. BK has translated it 'over there'. On another occasion he said: '*Waka* means anybody coming this way', which does not fit some of the following examples. Other examples are in the dictionary entry.

(43) *Waranu   nhutjadu   wakayey.*
     who-NOM   3sg:NOM-THERE   DEM-DISTORT
     'Who is he?' (T5)

(44) *Wathi ngathu   mamathikana   yintjadu-waka.*
     stick 1sg:ERG   steal-return-IP   3sg:ACC-THERE-DEM
     "I took the spear off that fellow over there." (?) (W8)

(45) *Thutjutju-wakana nhadi?*
     dog-DEM-?   dead
     'Is your dog dead?' (T5)

(46) *... padla yundra-waka,   ngapa-paniyi*
         place far-DEM   water-without-LOC
     '... in a far country, without water' (D2, in A-96)

(47) *Hey, warnu   kara   yita-wakaya   thawawarrarlaya.*
     hey who:NOM maybe   away-DEM-?   go-arrive-PRES(?)-DISTORT
     'Hey, someone's coming.' (?) (T6)

(48) *Warnu   puladu   yundratji   waka.*
     who:NOM   3du:NOM-THERE   far-EMPH   DEM
     "What them two fellows way over?" (W5)

(49) *Karna thana   nhina-thikathikarla,   nhinggiyi   ya   nhingguwa   waka.*
     person 3pl:NOM sit-everywhere-PRES   location-HERE   and   location-THERE DEM
     'People sitting round, here and there.' (P13)

See also (A-127).

Widi seems to have a similar distribution to waka and no difference in meaning has been noted.

(50) *Karrkarla   nganha   nhulu-widay.*
      call out-PRES 1sg:ACC   3sg:ERG-DEM:DISTORT
      'He's calling out to me.' (T6)

(51) *Nganyi   thawarla nhinanga nhungganiyi-wida.*
      1sg:NOM   go-PRES   sit-FUT   3sg:GEN-LOC-DEM:DISTORT
      'I'm going over to sit with that fellow.' (W6)

(52) *Thalkatji widi, Yinimingka.*
      up-EMPH   DEM   Innamincka
      'Up there, at Innamincka Waterhole.' (P3-4)

(53) *Nguda nhinggiwa   ngali   thudarla, kurrakurrana, miriyi   widi.*
      camp location-THERE 1du:ex:NOM lie-PRES   put-put-IP   sandhill-LOC DEM
      'Our camp is over there in the sandhills.' (T5)

The only examples of *walha* and *nhayi* are as follows:

(54) *thalkatjiwalha*
      up-EMPH-DEM
      'up there' (T8)

(55) *Thawana   nganyi   kathi mandrithikanga, nhungganiyi-walha.*
      go-IP   1sg:NOM   meat   get-return-FUT   3sg:GEN-LOC-DEM

      ['*thawana nganyi*' repeated by GB] *kathi   mandrithikanga, nhunggani-nhayi.*
                                          meat   get-return-FUT   3sg:GEN-DEM
      'I went and got some meat from him.' (?) (T10)

The second group of demonstrative adverbs consists of *kanta* 'over there' and the doubtful cases *kala* and *thika*. These seem (from the little evidence available) not to be cliticised, but there are very few examples.

(56) *Thawa-nhana nhunu   ngakani-ngadi yandhayandhanga-nyadi nhinggiyi,*
      go-NP   3sg:NOM 1sg:GEN-DAT   talk-talk-FUT-like   location-HERE

      walyangu nhunu   thawawarrana, nga   yini   thawa   mayi
      not-YET   3sg:NOM go-arrive-IP   then   2sg:NOM go   EMPH

      yandhayandhanga nhungganiyi   nhingguwa   kantanga.
      talk-talk-FUT   3sg:GEN-LOC   location-THERE   over.there-?
      'I thought he was going to come here and talk, but he hasn't come yet, so you go over there to his place.' (X25)

(The meaning or function of the final *-nga* is not known.)

Yundra kanta (*yundra* 'far') is acceptable but *nhinggiyi kanta* (*-yi* 'here') is not. Note that *thalka*, which has been regarded as an adverb of place, occurs in the phrase illustrated in (57), which is exactly similar to that in (56) (apart from the unexplained ending on *kantanga*).

216   *Chapter 16*

(57) *Minha ngana-lapurra yini   nhinggiwa   thalka.*
 what   do-REMP   3sg:NOM location-THERE up
 "What you doing up there?" (W7)

Kala may simply be the suffix *-kala* (see §9.10) or at least related to it.

(58) *Nhunu   kala   yada   kanpanalarla.*
 3sg:NOM DEM? hither   visible-INCH-NOW-PRES
 "There he is, showing up now." (B24)

(59) *Ngathu   yina   yurarlala   wawini-ngaditji   karna   yina*
 1sg:ERG 2sg:ACC want-PRES-EMPH see-GER-DAT-EMPH person   EMPH

 (or *yinha* ?) *kala   ngakani-ngadi.*
  3sg:ACC DEM ? 1sg:GEN-DAT
 'I want you to see him for me.' (R3)

There is one example in which *thika*, normally a verb stem 'to return', functions as a demonstrative adverb (or directional adverb, or adverb of place?) 'back here'.

(60) *Kathi   tjukurru   ngathu   wawana,   thawa-rnanga   nhinggiyi-ngadi,*
 animal   kangaroo 1sg:ERG   see-IP   go-CONT   location-HERE-DAT

 parrkulu pulayi   thika.
 two   3du:NOM-HERE back.here
 "That means two kangaroos back here; I seen them when I was walking home, I seen two kangaroos back here." (W1)
 See also (9-25).

16.8 Adverbs of manner

Adverbs of manner resemble directional adverbs in that they can be used in response to *yarndu* 'how?', 'which way?'. In general, manner is specified by means of nouns used as adverbs (as in (1)–(6) above) or by means of nouns in the operative case (see §9.1.3, especially the second half). Words which are basically adverbs of manner are rare; those exemplified below are *ngarru* 'just', 'only', *purru* 'completely' and *muthu* 'very', 'well'. Another is *marndu* 'together' (used only of feet in this corpus) which can be verbalised to form the stem *marnduka ~ marndumarnduka* 'to join (TR)'.

Ngarru is used to specify that an action involves nothing more than what is specified in the utterance (i.e. that something additional which might be expected is not), or that something does not come up to expectations, or that an action has no reason or justification. See also (A-152) and the dictionary entry.

(61) *Ngarru   puladu   ngan.guli   yandri-yindri-nhana.*
 only   3du:NOM-THERE   word-INST   scold-RR-NP
 "They only roused on each other." (They didn't fight.) (B13)

(62) *Ngarru   marrkamarrkarlangu   nhunu.*
 only   crawl-crawl-PRES-YET   3sg:NOM
 "He's only crawling yet." (He hasn't learnt to walk yet.) (P8)

(63) *Parndripada-nhana nganha ngarru, minhayi kara.*
    hit-in-NP   1sg:ACC only what-LOC maybe
    'He just hit me, for no reason.' (P6)

(64) *Dritji parrkulu nganyi thawa-nhana, walya karna wawini. Ngarru*
    sun two 1sg:NOM go-NP not person see-GER only

   ngathu makaparu wawa-nhana ngapakurnayitji, walya thawapandhini.
    1sg:ERG fire-light see-NP waterhole-LOC-EMPH not go-down-GER
   'I was travelling for two days and didn't see anyone. I just saw the light of a fire by a waterhole, but I didn't go down.' (R7)

Purru denotes completeness; there are only three examples in the corpus.

(65) *Purru   ngathu yinha   kuriyirrikana.*
    completely 1sg:ERG 3sg:ACC clean-IP
    'I cleaned it all over.' (B23)

(66) *Ngapa yulpudu wambatharrarla nhulu padlatji, purru.*
    water flood   cover-fly-PRES 3sg:ERG place-EMPH completely
    'The floodwater's covering everything.' (B11)

Muthu seems to denote a high degree or high intensity, but there are few examples. The verbalised form *muthuka* means 'to do successfully' and is used of spearing or shooting something; it may have a much wider range of uses. (It is not clear whether there is also an intransitive equivalent, *muthuna*; a short sentence using it was accepted, but it has not actually been heard from a speaker.) The function of *muthu* in (S8-10) is not known. See also the dictionary entry.

(67) *Parndringa muthu ngathu yinha.*
    hit-FUT   very 1sg:ERG 3sg:ACC
    'I'm going to really belt him.' (X37)

A similar sentence to (67), but in past tense and with third person subject, was first given as *Parndrinhana nhulu muthu*, but then corrected to *Parndri muthu nhulu*, with no inflection on the verb. This can be compared to the similar omission of tense inflection before *-ldrangu*, as noted in §18.3.3. In the case exemplified here a later discussion led to the conclusion that the verb should have been *parndriri*, with the 'unspecified' inflection. Perhaps (as a referee suggests) *muthu* must immediately follow what it modifies and that is why the first form given was not acceptable.

The combination of *muthu* with *kanpa* will be referred to in the next section.

16.9 Adjectives/adverbs derived with the operative suffix

As noted above (§9.1.3), the operative suffix can be added to certain nouns, mostly abstract, to form words which function as adjectives or adverbs. The meaning generally seems to be 'affected by the emotion or having the quality named by the root'. The same process is known to occur in Diyari (Austin 1981a:121–122, with suffix *-li*) and Ngamini (with *-nu*), in Arabana/Wangkangurru (Hercus 1994:213–216) in which the suffix involved is *-li* but the inflectional suffix has undergone a sound change and is *-ri ~ -ru* (equivalent to *-di ~ -du* in my spelling for Yandruwandha), and in Arrernte (Wilkins 1989:339) where *-l* has the same functions (and is used also for locative). Operative forms used in this way include *mawali* 'hungry' from *mawa* 'hunger' (cf. *mawapika* 'person with a big appetite'), *murali* 'thirsty' from *mura* 'thirst', *mukali* 'sleepy' from *muka* 'sleep', *yabali* 'frightened' from *yaba* 'fear' (cf. *yabapika* or *yabakanpa* 'frightened person', *yaba ngunyi* 'to frighten' — lit. 'fear give', *yabayabana* 'to become a little frightened'), *kinyili* 'dishonestly' from *kinyi* 'dishonesty, stealth' (cf. *kinyipurra* 'thief'), *nhindali* 'shy' from *nhinda* 'shame' (note also *nhinda* 'shape, appearance'), *ngidlali* 'sorry' from *ngidla*, probably 'sorrow', *yunkali* 'disgusted' from *yunka* 'disgust', *kalgali* 'dimly; easily' from *kalga* 'dim, loose, weak; easy', *pakali* 'quickly' from *paka* 'quick' and perhaps *marrkali* from *marrka*, both translated 'camping out'. *Thidrili* 'jealous' and *marnkamarnkali* 'slowly' are attested only for the Strzelecki dialect although *thidri* 'jealousy' and *marnka(marnka)* 'slow(ly)' are known also for the Innamincka dialect. *Yingkali* (from *yingka* 'laugh') was accepted but its meaning is not clear — perhaps 'amused'. Another probable example is *kidlali* 'in turn'. See also the dictionary. Sentence examples are:

(68) *Yabali   yini   kathikathi-puru?*
     fear-INST 2sg:NOM meat-meat-AVER
     'Are you frightened of the snake?' (T2)

(69) *Ngurrangu   nganyi   mawali   nganarla.*
     always-YET 1sg:NOM hunger-INST do-PRES
     'I'm still hungry.' (R5, M22)

(70) *Marrkali   ngani   thudathika-nhana.*
     camping.out-INST 1pl:ex:NOM lie-return-NP
     'We went out camping.' (R2)

(71) *Kalgali   nhutjadu   tjarnmarla.*
     dim-INST 3sg:NOM-THERE shine-PRES
     'It's shining dimly.' (B11)

In the case of *pidipidi(li)* 'hard, vigorously' and *paltjapaltja(li)* 'hard, strongly' it seems that the suffix may be optional, although speaker error may be involved. We have *pidipidili ngindrarnanga* 'breathing hard', *kururruparla pidipidili* 'rubbing hard (as in grinding something)', *pidipidili warrka* 'throw it hard!', *mathana pidipidili* 'bit hard', *thingari pidipidili* 'pulling hard'. However, *minirla pidipidi* 'running hard' was heard, *wakanarla pidipidi* 'working hard' was accepted, and BK said *Kukathanggunhana nganyi pidipidi* for 'I've been thinking hard' but in the ensuing discussion said 'I've been thinking, *kukathangguri pidipidilitji'*. On balance I would suggest that the occurrences with adverbial function without *-li* are not correct. *Paltjapaltja* (but not *paltja*) is used as an adjective while both *paltjali* and *paltjapaltjali* can function as adverbs, as in *paltja(paltja)li warrka* 'throw it hard'. However, it may be that you can also say *paltjapaltja thadra* 'push hard' and *paltjapaltja thingarla* 'pulling hard'. Another word with a similar meaning is *mampali*.

A concrete noun which forms an adjective with the operative is *thiltja* 'sinew'; *thiltjali* means 'cramped'.

(72) *Thiltjali   nganyi   ngurra   nhinini-nguda.*
     sinew-INST 1sg:NOM always sit-GER-ABL
     'I've got a cramp from sitting a long time.' (R10)

An alternative to this sentence is:

(73) *Thiltja ngarnma-yindrirla nganyi, ngurra nhinininguda.*
     grip-RR-PRES

In the case of *makamakali* 'hot', the derivation is from *makamaka* 'heat, summer' which in turn is derived from the concrete noun *maka* 'fire'.

It is not clear whether *malthi* 'cold' belongs to this group of words. Although there is no reason to doubt (12), BK did not accept *malthili nganyi* for 'I'm cold' but corrected it to *pundrali nganyi*. This suggests a contrast between *pundra* referring to the feeling and *malthi* referring to the state. Other data do not all support this, however; both can refer to the weather, your hands can be *malthi*, and *malthi ngunyingunyirla* was given as the translation of 'making [us] cold' (but perhaps it is really 'making it cold'). Perhaps also (12) would be more correctly translated with 'if it gets cold ...'.

An example of verbalisation of a noun of this type with *-li* affixed is shown in

(74) *Pakapakalikana   ngathu   yintjadu.*
     quick-quick-INST-CAUS-IP 1sg:ERG 3sg:ACC-THERE
     'I hurried him up.' (P30)

Compare

(75) *Pakali   nganaw!*
     quick-INST   do:DISTORT
     'Hurry up!' (B8)

See §13.4.1 on combination of some of these adverbs with *ngunyi* 'to give' or its reduplication.

16.10 Other adverbs

The existence of the intransitive/transitive verb pair *panina/panika* 'to do completely' (see §11.17) seems to imply a form *pani-* 'all' or 'completely'. In fact, however, these verbs are clearly derived from the noun root *pani* 'none', 'nothing'; after all, 'all done' implies 'nothing left to do'. This etymology is supported by the example

(76) *Kali   nhunu   paninalarla.*
     already   3sg:NOM   none-INCH-NOW-PRES
     'It's easing up now' (of the wind, which had been blowing hard), (P14)

and further consideration of other examples makes it seem more plausible.

The root (or pair of homophonous roots) *kanpa* occurs as a noun (adjective) meaning 'visible' and as an adverb, meaning not clear, possibly best translated as 'right' or 'properly', perhaps also 'very'. A phrase using it is *kanpa kudrini* 'easily broken'. The compound *kanpapardra* has been translated as "first shot" and *kanpangu* seems to have a similar meaning. The force of the adverb seems to be strengthened in the compound *kanpamuthu*. There are only a few examples in which *kanpa* occurs as an adverb; they include three in the dictionary entry, taken from a text. They appeared in quick succession in the same section of the text.

(77) *Wawana ngathu   yinha   kanpa   dakuma.*
     see-IP   1sg:ERG 3sg:ACC   right   succeed
     'I saw him properly.' (B11) (For *dakuma* see §13.6)

(78) *Karna wirrpa kanpamuthu nhutjadu minirla yabayi, nhandunyadi.*
person fast right-very 3sg:NOM-THERE run-PRES fear-LOC horse-like
'That fellow can run fast, like a horse.' (T11)
(The translation takes no account of *yabayi* and its function is not clear. The sentence was repeated with *muthu* omitted.)

(79) *Muduwa thanayi ngakanili kilkarla mardramitjili*
child 3pl:NOM-HERE 1sg:GER-ERG know-PRES stone-eye-INST

dranyiri kanpapardra.
hit(throwing)-UNSP 'first shot'
'My kids think I can hit that bird first go.' (P12)

Pardra occurs as the verb root 'to hold'; the only examples of a possible adverb *pardra* are in *kayidi pardra,* which seems to have the same meaning as *kanpapardra*; (80) and (81) are two of the only three examples (and see the dictionary entry for the third).

(80) *Nhapina ngathu kayidi pardra.*
mix-IP 1sg:ERG now ?
'I made it first go.' (made a cake, successfully, at the first try) (X27)

(81) *Kayidi pardra ngathu mandripadarla ngan.gutji.*
now ? 1sg:ERG get-in-PRES word-EMPH
"I've just got the words."
(What was asked was 'I'm just beginning to understand the language'; the meaning may be 'I'm catching the words for the first time'.) (P13)

Nguka (~ *yuka*) appears to mean 'too' or sometimes 'other' (i.e. another of the same, not something different); however, little is known about its function. Another meaning, illustrated in (84) and confirmed in later examples and discussions, is 'in case'. It could be related to *-ngu* 'yet, still'. It is often cliticised and the first consonant is sometimes deleted; in fact, in most cases where *yuka* is written a vowel /i/ precedes it and these could be cases of deletion of /ng/ from *nguka*. *Ngaliyuka*, repeated by GB (some time after it had been recorded) was corrected by BK to *ngalinguka* and translated "me and him too" (*ngali* '1du:ex:NOM'). Asked for 'me and you too' he gave *ngaldranguka* (*ngaldra* '1du:in:NOM'). Other examples include:

(82) *Walya ngathu ngananhina-nhana, minha kurnu ngukatji.*
not 1sg:ERG do-sit-NP what one too-EMPH
"I never did anything at all." (P15)
(Note that *ngana* here is transitive; normally with the meaning 'to do', it is intransitive.)

(83) *Kurnungukala yada ngunyi.*
one-too-EMPH hither give
'Give me another one.' (X28)

(84) *Ngapakurna-ngadi nganyi thawarla, makita ngala ngathu pakarla,*
waterhole-DAT 1sg:NOM go-PRES gun then 1sg:ERG carry-PRES

palha kara, palhanguka ngathu wawayi.
bird maybe bird-too 1sg:ERG see-POT
'I'll take my gun to the waterhole just in case I see any ducks.'
(*palhanguka* was given as a replacement for or correction of *palha kara*.) (R8)

(85) *Minha-ngadi yintjadu   wani   kurnu yundru parndri-padapadarla,*
     what-DAT   3sg:ACC-THERE corroboree one   2sg:ERG hit-HAB-PRES

   walya wani   kurnunguka drangini? Ngarru kurnungu yundru
   not   corroboree one-too   sing-GER only   one-YET   2sg:ERG

   kilkarla?
   know-PRES
   'Why do you always sing that same song, and never any other? Is that the only one you know?' (P12)

There are several other sentences in texts, of the form 'they used to eat/catch/visit … too', using *nguka* or *yuka*; see, for example, (A-174).

If the speculation that the verb *ngukanguka* 'to mix' is derived from this adverb is correct,[1] this is the only example of derivation of a verb stem by simple reduplication of an adverb. (The *ngukanguka* appearing in (A-179) is, however, interpreted as a reduplicated adverb.)

(86) *Yambarriyi kurranga, padla paltjapaltja yina wipingini-ngudaatjinha,*
     flat-LOC   put-FUT   ground hard-hard   EMPH sweep-GER-ABL-?-?

   mitji thaka ngukanguka-yindriyi.
   seed clay mix-RR-POT
   'They put them on the hard ground, after sweeping it so that the seeds wouldn't get mixed up with the dirt.' (E4, = A-164)

Yala 'same' is tentatively classified as an adverb. It was heard only in (87), although on another occasion a similar sentence was accepted.

(87) *Pandi puladu   nguya   yala.*
     dog   3du:NOM-THERE appearance same
     'Our two dogs both look the same.' (P14)

The converse is expressed by means of *paladi-paladi* 'different', a reduplicated form of the noun *paladi* 'individual', 'separate'.[2]

---

[1] BK did not think it was.
[2] BK accepted *palapaladi* as an alternative to *paladi-paladi*.

17 *Conjunctions, interjections and emphatic particles*

17.1 Conjunctions

Conjunctions have the following functions in Yandruwandha:

(a) to link phrases within a compound phrase,
(b) to link clauses within a compound sentence,
(c) to link clauses within a complex sentence,
(d) to link a sentence to a preceding sentence.

However, they are obligatory in none of these cases. Even in noun phrases where there is no verb morphology to show that there is coordination or subordination, juxtaposition may be used:

(1) *pandi thanayi nhiwa karrukarru thawathawarla*
dog   3pl:NOM-HERE female old.man   go-go-PRES
'dogs and bitches walking around here' (X45)

The only conjunction which can be said with certainty to fulfil function (a) is *ya* 'and', although *kayi* 'or' may possibly do so. *Kayi* does not fulfil functions (c) or (d), unless its function as illustrated in (S10-9, 11) (where it could perhaps be translated as 'how about?') comes under (d). *Ngala* and *nga* are confined mainly to functions (c) and (d), although they may also fulfil function (b). Thus they are frequently associated with subordinate clauses and subordinate sentences.

The adverb *kara* 'maybe', described in §8.3, functions as a conjunction in some cases, especially in the clause *pani kara* 'or not': note also (8-17). It seems to be interchangeable with *kayi* in some circumstances, and they are thought to be the same word, although because of the rarity of *kayi* it is impossible to be sure. Note the occasional pronunciation of /y/ as [ɹ], e.g. in *kurrayi* 'mad', *warrayi* 'it's all right'. Note also the following examples:

(2) *Man.garri kayi karruwali.*
girl   or   boy
"Was it a boy or a girl?" (BK's translation, with stress on 'or'), repeated as:

(3) *Man.garri kara, karruwali kara.* (B18)

When asked if 'Is it a man or a woman?' would be *karru kayi yiwa* BK replied 'That's right; same if we say "or it's a woman"; *yiwa kayi*; "or a woman"'. This material was recorded in a discussion of a sentence recorded some time earlier. In another discussion, of the use of *kayi* in the text sentences referred to above, BK said that *kayi* there was not the same as *kara*.

Other examples of *kayi* (sometimes heard and written as *kay*) include:

(4) Karruwali ngala nhunudu,   kayi man.garri.
    boy   then 3sg:NOM-THERE or   girl
    "Was it a boy or a girl?" (P8)

(5) Kilkarla   ngathunow   muduwa paninyadi,   kayi
    know-PRES 1sg:ERG-2sg:ACC.DISTORT child   without-like but

    muduwa-mindji ngala yina. (or yini '2sg:NOM'?)
    child-PROP   then EMPH
    "I thought you never had a kid" (but you have). (P8)

In the latter, *kayi* is equivalent to English 'but' rather than 'or'. There is also a doubtful example from a text, with *kayi* again perhaps translatable as 'but':

(6) Karnalitji   thana   pulka-padipadini kathi mardramitjiyi walya
    person-ERG-EMPH 3pl:NOM   grill-HAB-GER   meat stone-eye-LOC not

    maka-mukuruyi. Mardramitjiyi kay.
    fire-coal-LOC   stone-eye-LOC but(?)
    'The Aborigines used to grill their meat on the (hot) stones, not on the coals.' (D3)

Examples of *ya* include (7) and (8), linking noun phrases, (9) linking demonstratives, (10) which could perhaps be thought of as creating a complex word, and (11) linking clauses. See also (A-41), where it introduces a new topic in a narrative.

(7) karruwali malkirri ya man.garri kurnu
    boy   many   and girl   one
    'a mob of boys and one girl' (W2)

(8) Wathi windra ya yada   nhulu   waltharla.
    tree spear and boomerang 3sg:ERG carry-PRES
    'He's bringing his spear and his boomerang.' (P7)

(9) Karna thana   nhina-thikathikarla, nhinggiyi   ya nhingguwa   waka.
    person 3pl:NOM sit-everywhere-PRES location-HERE and location-THERE DEM
    'People sitting round, here and there.' (P13)

(10) Mara parrkulu ya thinamitji parrkulu.
     hand two   and foot-eye   two
     'Twelve' (two hands and two toes). (P13)

(11) Kali   thana   thukaringu   ngapa-ngudatji, ya pirditjirranga
     already 3pl.NOM take.out-UNSP-THEN water-ABL-EMPH and strip-FUT

     thana.
     3pl.NOM
     'Then they took it out of the water and peeled it.' (D1, = A-6)

There are rare examples of *ya* (or *-ya*) as some sort of emphatic marker; compare the usage of *kayi* as described above. BK said the *ya* in (12) meant 'eh' and translated the sentence as 'Who's laughing, eh?'

(12) *Warnu   nhunu   yingkarla   ya?*
     who   3sg:NOM   laugh-PRES   eh

   (*ya* here was heard first as a clitic, then on repetition as a separate word) (X50)

There are one or two examples of a possible conjunction *yi*:

(13) *Kirri   yinhayi   wantja, patji   kara,   yi   thungga   kara.*
     please   3sg:ACC-HERE   try   good   maybe   or(?)   rotten   maybe
     'Will you taste this and see if it's all right.' (P22)

Ngala and *nga* share the same functions and may share the same morpheme; the /la/ of *ngala* could possibly be the emphatic suffix *-la*. They can often be translated 'and then', 'then' 'this time' or 'now', but often they need not be translated at all and seem to have little meaning (like English 'well' introducing a sentence). As the translations suggest, they (or at least *ngala*) sometimes have a subsidiary function of time specification, and in some cases this function is predominant and the linking function, implied by the first translations given for it above, may be non-existent. On other occasions an emphasising function may be predominant. As noted in §5.3, *ngala* very commonly begins a clause in text, and in this position it normally has the linking function. The new clause may or may not have the same arguments as the previous one. *Ngala* is more common than *nga*, the latter occurring mostly (but still less frequently than *ngala*) in texts and possibly being basically a rapid speech variety. Either may begin a sentence; note that a realisation [a] is interpreted as *nga* with /ng/ realised as zero rather than *ya* with /y/ realised as zero. Text examples include, among others, (A-41, 50, 62, 73 and 121) and other examples include (5-19), (9-12), (11-34) and the following:

(14) *Kathi   tjukurru   ngathu   parndri-lapurra   muduwalitji,   ngala*
     animal   kangaroo   1sg:ERG   kill-REMP   child-ERG-EMPH   then

   karrukarrula   ngala   nganyi.
   old man-EMPH   then   1sg:NOM
   'I used to kill a lot of kangaroos when I was a young fellow but "I'm getting old now."' (W2)
   (In this example the first *ngala* acts as a conjunction and the second as a time specifier, 'now'.)

(15) *Walya   yarndudutji   ngaldra   yita   thawarla,   ngala   yarnduyi*
     not   how-THERE-EMPH   1du:in:NOM   away   go-PRES   then   how-HERE

   ngala   ngaldra   yita   thawarla.
   then   1du:in:NOM   away   go-PRES
   'Let's go this way, not that way.' (P4)
   (This resembles (14) except that the second *ngala* probably provides emphasis rather than time specification. The first clause was first given with *thawa* instead of *thawarla*.)

(16) *Pandi   nhuniyi   ngurra   mirrtjarla,   karna   ngalyi   ngala*
     dog   3sg:NOM-HERE   always   be.noisy-PRES   person   some   then

   nhulu   walya   matharla.
   3sg:ERG   not   bite-PRES
   "He's always barking but he never bites anybody." (W7)

(17) *Mawalila   nganyi; kathi-pani ngala ngandra.*
      hunger-INST-EMPH 1sg:NOM meat-PRIV   then   1pl:in:NOM
      "I'm hungry and we got no meat." (P5)

(18) *Minha kamiri   ngala yini?*
      what division then   2sg:NOM
      'What "meat" are you?' (W5)

Ngala is sometimes used in association with *-ldra* 'contrast', glossed '-BUT', as in (19). For further examples see §18.3.2.

(19) *Muduwa nhunggani putha-pika ngala muduwa ngakani puthapirnaldra.*
      child 3sg:GEN   fast-CHAR   then child 1sg:GEN fast-big-BUT
      "Your [*sic*] kids can run but my kids can run faster." (P12)

There are two examples in text of a morpheme *ka* which seems to have a similar function to *nga*, as far as can be seen. It may simply be a mispronunciation. See (A-44 and 73).

17.2 Interjections

Interjections are subdivided into sentence introducers, sentence substitutes and exclamations. The first, as their name implies, introduce a sentence and serve to give some idea of the type of sentence to follow, gain the hearer's attention and sometimes possibly to link the sentence loosely to a preceding one. Sentence introducers include *kapada* 'come on', *warrayi* 'all right', *mirni* and *kirri*, both translated (among other ways) as 'how about', *ngapala* 'well' and *mayi* 'well!' (which also sometimes functions as an emphatic particle — see §17.3 — and also has some of the features of an exclamation). In addition such extraphonemic forms as *ay* and *ey* could be regarded as sentence introducers and/or as exclamations.

Sentence substitutes stand alone to function as sentences, usually as the answer to a question. They include *kawu* and *ngaandi* 'yes', *pani* 'no' and *ngalaaku* 'I don't know'.

Exclamations also can stand alone, but convey emotion rather than meaning. They include *ngandra ~ ngaldra* and some extraphonemic forms.

17.2.1 Sentence introducers

Kapada and *warrayi* seem to have some of the properties of imperative verbs and to paraphrase the sentence which they introduce. *Kapada* is translated 'come on' and is usually followed by a clause containing a verb of going (this may however be implied); *warrayi* can be translated by expressions such as 'it's all right', 'leave it alone' or 'never mind' and is followed by a clause expressing a permission or desire, not necessarily involving the optative form of the verb. See the dictionary entries for more examples, also (9-124), (11-64) and (15-27).

(20) *Kapada, thawarlala   ngaldra.*
      come.on go-PRES-EMPH   1du:in:NOM
      "Come on, me and you are going." (W2)

(21) *Mirni   warrayi   nhutjadu   yandharlangu may.*
      how.about all.right 3sg:NOM:THERE   talk-PRES-YET well
      'Let him talk.' (B19)

(22) *Warrayila   waw!*
or   *Warrayila   wawa!*
      all.right-EMPH look
      "Never mind!" (X28)

Mirni and *kirri* — the former much more common — have both been translated by BK as "will you" or "can you". These translations are quite acceptable for many cases but are not suitable sometimes, for example where the clause that follows has a first person subject (where 'let's' or 'let me' would be more appropriate). The translation 'how about' has been adopted as most nearly suitable for all occurrences; it is a weak imperative with little or no interrogative connotation. Another translation that has been given for *mirni* is "wait!"; *mirniwa*, which probably includes an emphatic suffix, was also translated this way. It does not seem appropriate in most cases, but see *mirnimirningu* in the dictionary. Another translation given for *kirri* was "if".

Both *mirni* and *kirri* almost invariably occur clause-initially. Where *mirni* does not appear initially it may sometimes be better glossed as 'before', as in two of the dictionary examples. In one case it appears that *mirni* may function as a verb, as it seems to govern a subordinate clause (25). It may be that *mirni*, *kirri*, *kapada* and *warrayi* can all be regarded as defective verbs occurring only in the imperative.[1]

Kirri also occurs as the noun 'clever', 'clever person', extended to 'doctor'. The reduplicated form *kirrikirri* is translated 'lively'.

(23) *Mirni   nganha   ngana-malk-ardi   yilanggi nhunu   ngapatji   pararla.*
      how.about 1sg:ACC   tell-OPT-EMPH   where   3sg:NOM   water-EMPH lie-PRES
      'Tell me where the waterhole is.' (P3)

(24) *Walya thawatji pipatji   drakanga   mundja yina yini;   nhinanhina*
      not   go-EMPH paper-EMPH   pierce-FUT   sick   EMPH 2sg:NOM sit-sit

      patjinini-ngadi   mirni.
      good-INCH-GER-DAT   how.about
      'You'd better not go [to work, writing] while you're sick. Stay home until you're better.' (P13)

(25) *Mirniwa   ngapuna-rlayi.*
      how.about-?   quiet-INCH-SIM
      'Wait till they shut up.' (B16, X28)

(26) *Kirri   nganyi   marripathi thawarla   thangguthikanga.*
      how.about   1sg:NOM   tomorrow   go-PRES   stand-return-FUT
      'I'll go tomorrow and visit [them].' (E7)

(27) *Kirrita —   wirni   dan.gaka,   pandi   karrini-ngadi.*
      how.about-? string   find-AWAY   dog   tie-GER-for
      'See if you can find something to tie the dog up with.' (R8)

---

[1] At an early stage in the analysis *warrayi* was thought to be the imperative form of a verb 'to let, to allow'. It governs a subordinate clause in (11-64). *Kapada* seems to govern a subordinate clause in *Kapada mandrithikanga* 'Come and get it'.

See also (13), (21), (32), (34) and the dictionary entries (including that for *mirnimirningu*, which includes the only example in a sentence of *mirni* reduplicated).

The use of *mirni* in the following rather elliptical Yw sentence is obscure; perhaps too much has been left out.

(28) *Ngathu   mirni,   mayi   nhulula   nganha.*
     1sg:ERG   how.about   EMPH   3sg:ERG-EMPH   1sg:ACC
     (approx.) 'I've [painted him], he's got to [paint] me now.' (Y10)

Ngapala is very common, especially in texts, where it occurs usually as the first word of a sentence or clause. It never introduces an isolated utterance or a text. It may function to some extent as a link between sentences or clauses. There are over eighty examples in the two text chapters.

(29) *Ngapala   karna   ngalyitji   nhulu   purnunukari.*
     well   person   some-EMPH   3sg:ERG   itchy-CAUS-UNSP
     "He teased the other jokers." (W4)

(30) *Ngathu   yina   wawana   yundratji,   ngapala   yina   walya   kilkanga.*
     1sg:ERG   2sg:ACC   see-IP   far-EMPH   well   2sg:ACC   not   know-FUT
     "I seen you a long way and I didn't recognise you." (W5)

(31) *Kudru   ngathu   pakuna,   ngapala   wuthi   yinhu   thanggunari.*
     hole   1sg:ERG   dig-IP   well   stick   3sg:ACC   stand-CAUS-UNSP
     "I dug a hole and stuck the post up." (W8)

Mayi (often pronounced as a monosyllable and spelt *may*) is less common than *ngapala* and differs in that it has more force and no suggestion of the function of a conjunction. It may introduce an isolated sentence and serves to gain the hearer's attention. In these ways it resembles such extraphonemic interjections as *ay* or *ey* (see (35)). *Mayi* occurred once in isolation as a sentence and was translated "What? What's next?" Note (9-43), in which *mayi* seems to function as a verb governing a subordinate clause (as did *mirni* in (25)). Another function of *mayi* will be dealt with in §17.3.

(32) *Mayi   yada   patji;   yundru   mirni   nganha   ngunyi.*
     well   boomerang   good   2sg:ERG   how.about   1sg:ACC   give
     'That's a good boomerang, I'd like to have it.' (C4)

(33) *A'ay   ngari-widi   mayi   Kilyalpa.*
     eh   down-DEM   well   Gidgealpa
     'He's down there at Gidgealpa.' (B17)

(34) *Mirni   mayi   mandrithikanga   ngakani   yurarla   nganyi   yinhayi*
     how.about   eh?   get-return-FUT   1sg:GEN   want-PRES   1sg:NOM   3sg:ACC-LOC

     (or *mini   mayi?*)
         run   eh?
     "Will you run over and get what I want?" (W6)

(35) *Ey   yalbangari   yintjadu!*
     eh   split-down   3sg:ACC:THERE
     'Split that [log]!' (T8)

228 *Chapter 17*

17.2.2 Sentence substitutes

- *Kawu* and *ngaandi*, 'yes', are used as sentence substitutes to give an affirmative answer to a question, or may be tagged on the end of a sentence or interpolated in text as a sentence or clause with the meaning, 'Yes, that (what I have just said) is right'; see (S6-11) and (S10-13). They may also occur initially in a sentence, followed by the sentence for which they substitute, as in (S9-35).

- *Pani* is used as a negative adverb (see §8.4.2) or, as a bound form, as a privative suffix on noun or verb stems (§10.5.5 and §10.6), or may occur alone as a negative answer to a question: 'no', 'none' or 'nothing'. An extraphonemic particle *aʔey ~ aʔay* used to signify refusal of a request is used in (S10-9, 10, 11 and 13).

- *Ngalaaku* 'I don't know' (also *ngalaku*) is used alone as a sentence substitute, see (S10–7), or may be tagged on to the beginning or end of a sentence.

(36) Yilanggitji   kara   thana   pitjidi   mandri-padipadini, ngalaaku.
      where-EMPH maybe   3pl:NOM   pitchery get-HAB-GER   I.don't.know
      'I don't know where they used to get the pitchery.' (D3, =A-114)

(37) Ngalaaku,   wagalkanga   kara   ngathu   yintjadu.
      I.don't.know move-CAUS-FUT   maybe   1sg:ERG 3sg:ACC:THERE
      "I don't know whether I can shift it." (P2)

Note that *ngalaaku* is redundant in such sentences, just as *kawu* and *ngaandi* are when tagged on to the beginning or end of a sentence. *Kara* is sufficient to supply the concept 'I don't know'.

17.2.3 Exclamations

Since the corpus lacks natural conversation, little is known about exclamations. The only phonemic word classified as an exclamation is *ngandra ~ ngaldra*, translated "Oh!" by BK. Perhaps this may be better described as a sentence introducer; alternatively perhaps some occurrences of *mayi* should be called exclamations. For examples see (S6-6, 10) and (S9-13, 20 and 36).

17.3 Emphatic particles

Mayi often follows an imperative verb and serves to strengthen the command. It is often heard and spelt *may*. See (34, 8-2, 11-57).

(38) Nhina mayi!
      sit   EMPH
      'Sit down!' (Y16)

Yina is a fairly common emphatic particle. It appears to occur usually following the first phrase of a clause and to follow any type of word, even if a bound emphatic marker also follows it. See also the last page of §18.4.

The identification of a word or clitic as emphasising the word or phrase or sentence to which it is attached is problematical; if the linguist cannot find a meaning for something the temptation is to call it an emphatic marker. Old and illiterate language speakers cannot easily explain their function, but may try to do so by simply translating the stretch of speech to which it refers, in an emphatic way. Part of the justification for regarding *yina* as emphatic particle is given in the following exchange between GB and BK, in which emphasis is marked by underlining.

GB: 'How do you say, "I'm not strong enough?"' BK: '*Walya yina nganyi paltjapaltja.*' GB: 'What's the *yina* mean there?' BK: 'You say I'm not strong.' GB: 'What if you just say, "*Walya nganyi paltjapaltja*"?' BK: '*Ngaan* [= 'yes'], that's short. "*Walya yina nganyi paltjapaltja.*" "*Walya nganyi paltjapaltja*", you can say that. (*Yina*) means I ain't.'

(39) *Paltjapaltja   yina   nhunu.*
 strong-strong   EMPH   3sg:NOM
 'He's very strong.' (P2)

(40) *Kayidi   yina   nhutjadu   thudapandhina.*
 now   EMPH   3sg:NOM:THERE   lie-down-NP
 "He just went to sleep." (W2)

(41) *Muduwa   pirnali   yina   parndri-nhana, pulya   yina   yini;   nganha*
 child   big-ERG   2sg:ACC   hit-NP   small   EMPH   2sg:NOM   1sg:ACC

 yundru   ngana-nhana   walya.
 2sg:ERG   tell-NP   not
 'That big kid hit you, and you only little. You should have told me.' (R2)

(42) *Walya   ngathu   nhipakari   nhanadutji,*
 not   1sg:ERG   spouse-CAUS-UNSP   3sg:fem:ACC-THERE-EMPH

 pirni nguru   yina   ngakani   nhatjadu.
 not.a.potential.spouse   EMPH   1sg:GEN   3sg:fem:NOM:THERE
 'I couldn't marry that woman, "she's sort of related to me."' (P11)

See also the *yina* entry in the dictionary volume.

18 Clitics and emphatic suffixes

In Yandruwandha bound morphemes combining with more than one part of speech include dual and plural markers (which can function as stem formatives with nouns, as seen in §10.5.1 and §10.5.2, but are also combinable as clitics with pronouns and inflected verbs), a marker of similarity, some conjunctions and some emphatic suffixes.

18.1 Dual and plural

The suffix *-thili*, used occasionally as a stem formative on nouns to mark dual number, has also been noted in text affixed to an inflected verb:

(1) *Ngapala yingka-rnanga-thili yabangunyi-yindrini-nguda ngala pula,*
well laugh-CONT-DU fear-give-RR-GER-ABL then 3du:NOM

walypala-thili.
white.man-DU
'Well, they both laughed then, the two white men, at the way they had frightened one another.' (R4, = S9-38)

When further enquiries were made BK repeated the sentence as:

(2) *Yingka-nhana ngali-thili.*
laugh-NP 1du:ex:NOM-DU
'We both laughed.' (B18)

The phrase '*thili ngali*' was not accepted.

Similar sentences using the plural suffix *-ndja* were then suggested.

(3) *Thana yandhayandharlandja.*
3pl:NOM talk-talk-PRES-PL
'They're all talking.' (B19)

was accepted and repeated, and the form *nganindja* 1pl:ex:NOM-PL, 'we (plural, exclusive)' was also accepted. However, no occurrences of *-ndja* other than as a plural noun stem-formative have been elicited or have occurred in text. The word *ngaldrathili* 1pl:in:NOM-DU 'we (dual inclusive)' appears in the Yw corpus.

18.2 Similarity

The suffix *-nyadi* (occasionally pronounced as a separate word) may be added to almost any word, including inflected words, to mark a resemblance or a mistaken belief. It is most commonly translated 'like' or 'as if'. *-nyadi* has been noted in seven types of constructions,[1] which can be divided into two groups according as the denotation is resemblance (a, c, e) or mistaken belief (b, d, f, g). Constructions (a) and (b), (c) and (d), (e) and (f) form pairs; it is not known whether there is a partner for (g). In the following description the abbreviations used are N1 and N2 noun phrases, NO a noun phrase denoting an observer, Vk a verb of knowing or believing, Adv1 and Adv2 adverbial phrases, Neg a negative adverb and S a sentence nucleus or clause (positive in type (g)). Alternatively, where appropriate, a symbol represents not the linguistic form but its referent. Present tense will be used in the explanations, as representative of whatever may be the appropriate verb form in an actual instance.

The seven construction types are:

(a) N1 N2-*nyadi*, which denotes that N1 shares some characteristic with or acts in a way characteristic of N2, or, briefly, N1 is like N2, as in:

(4)   ... *mulpini-nguda warnta payipayirru yina mara witjunyadi.*
        cut-GER-ABL   short   long-long   EMPH hand finger-like
   "... after they cut them into short lengths, about the length of a finger."
   (D1, in A-16)

(5)   *Thudarla yini   kunapampu-na-rnanga pandinyadi.*
       lie-PRES 2sg:NOM ball-INCH-CONT   dog-like
   'You're lying curled up like a dog.' (P14)

(6)   *Minha-ngadila yundru   parndri-nhana yintjadu,   nganggali-nyadi?*
       what-DAT-EMPH 2sg:ERG hit-NP   3sg:ACC:THERE owner-like
   'What right did you have to hit him as if you owned him?' (R8)

See also (7-18) and (S8-5).

(b) NO Vk N1 N2-*nyadi*, which is (a) as the object of Vk, denotes that NO believes or is led to believe, wrongly, that N1 is N2.

(7)   *Kilkarla   ngathu   muduwa-paninyadi.*
       know-PRES 1sg:ERG child-PRIV-like
   "I thought you never had a kid." (P8)

(8)   *Ngaran.ga ngathu   pirnanyadi ngala yini.*
       hear-FARP 1sg:ERG big-like   then 2sg:NOM
   'You were supposed to be a big fellow.' (P9)

(9)   *Nganyi yukarra-pandhirla, mukanyadi nganha nhulu   kilkini-ngadi.*
       1sg:NOM lie-down-PRES   sleep-like 1sg:ACC 3sg:ERG know-GER-DAT
   'I'll lie down so he'll think I'm asleep.' (R6)

---

[1] See also Breen (1984).

(c) N1 (N2) V-*nyadi*, where N2 is present or absent according to whether V is transitive or intransitive, denotes that N1 seems to be performing the action denoted by V or is performing an action that resembles V in some way.

(10) *Ngaga nganha nhulu parndripada-nhana, ngaga-pardrari-nyadi.*
 throat 1sg:ACC 3sg:ERG hit-in-NP throat-hold-UNSP-like
 'He hit me on the throat; I felt as if I was choking.' (B17)

(d) NO Vk N1 (N2) V-*nyadi*, which is (c) as the object of Vk and denotes that NO believes or is led to believe, wrongly, that N1 is performing the action denoted by V.

(11) *Ngathu kilka-nhukada patjina-rlayinyadi nhunu, mundjanaldrangu.*
 1sg:ERG know-RECP good-INCH-SIM-like 3sg:NOM sick-INCH-BUT-YET
 'I thought he was getting better but he got sick again.' (P10)

(12) *Kilka-nhana ngathu warlkini-ngadinyadi.*
 know-NP 1sg:ERG fall-GER-DAT-like
 'I thought you were going to fall.' (P8)

(13) *Ngaran.ga ngathu paldrini-ngudanyadi yina yini.*
 hear-FARP 1sg:ERG die-GER-ABL-like EMPH 2sg:NOM
 'I heard you had died.' (P8-9)

 N1 is NO in the following example.

(14) *Thawini-ngadinyadi nganyi ngana-nhana, ngala nganyi*
 go-GER-DAT-like 1sg:NOM do-NP but 1sg:NOM

 patjapatjanarla walyala nganyi kara thawanga.
 sick-sick-INCH-PRES not-EMPH 1sg:NOM maybe go-FUT
 'I was ready to go, but I'm getting sick and I mightn't go now.' (X38)

 (See 11.3.1 for this usage of *ngana*)

(e) S Adv1 Adv2-*nyadi* denotes that Adv1 modifies S in a way which resembles the way in which Adv2 would modify it.

(15) *Kathi thanayi pulkapulkaringu maka-mukuruli-nyadi, ngala*
 meat 3pl:NOM-HERE grill-grill-UNSP-THEN fire-coal-INST-like then

 mardramitjili.
 stone-eye-INST
 'They grilled their meat on the [hot] stones, and you would think it had been grilled on the coals.' (D3, = A-139)

(f) NO Vk S Adv2-*nyadi* denotes that NO believes or is led to believe, wrongly, that S is modified by Adv2. In this construction an (e) type construction is the object of Vk.

(16) ... *ngapala thana kathi nalybali-nyadi dramirdramini-nguda kilkari.*
 well 3pl:NOM meat knife-INST-like cut-cut-GER-ABL know-UNSP
 '.... and you would think it had been cut with a steel knife' (referring to meat cut with a stone knife). (D3, in A-111)

(17) *Matja ngathu yina wawawawa-na-nhina-nhanatji padlakanpayi*
 long.time 1sg:ERG 2sg:ACC look-look-APP-sit-NP-EMPH dawn-LOC

nyadi, yini   thawawarrini-ngadi.
like   2sg:NOM go-arrive-GER-DAT
'I was expecting you to come earlier.' (P12)

(g) NO Vk Neg-*nyadi* S denotes that NO thinks or is led to believe, wrongly, that S is not true. Note how -*nyadi* attaches to the first constituent of the clause and has scope over the whole clause.[2]

(18) *Kilkarla   nhulu   walyanyadi kara   ngathu   wawa-rlayi.*
      know-PRES 3sg:ERG not-like   maybe 1sg:ERG see-SIM
      'He thinks I can't see him.' (R6)
      See also (34).

In the following example, *nyadi* follows *kara* and seems to be a separate word, which raises the question of whether it should always be regarded as such.

(19) *Ngathu   kilka-nhana   thikawarrini-nguda   kara   nyadi nhunu.*
      1sg:ERG know-PRES return-arrive-GER-ABL maybe like   3sg:NOM
      I thought he'd come back.' (or perhaps better 'I thought he might have come back.') (X27)

18.3 Bound conjunctions

The three suffixes described in this section are -*ngu* 'yet', 'still' or 'then', -*ldra* 'on the other hand' and the combined form -*ldrangu* 'too'.

18.3.1 -ngu

The suffix -*ngu* 'still, yet, then' may be added to nouns (possibly only those denoting qualities, i.e. those translated by adjectives in English, and others referring to non-permanent situations, such as *muduwa* 'child', *ngandjarri* 'rain'), inflected verbs (including inflected gerunds), pronouns (third person, at least), demonstratives, the negatives *walya* 'not' and *pani* 'none', a reduplicated form of *mirni* (see §17.2.1), *yarndu* 'how' (with a suffix -*ru* intervening), *ngurra* 'always', *ngarru* 'only, just' and possibly to some other words.

-*ngu* is used frequently in texts affixed to the unspecified tense form of the verb (-*ri*) and in these cases it is translated as 'then' and denotes that this action follows (in time) the one(s) described in the preceding sentence(s). A similar translation seems to be appropriate when -*ngu* is added to *ngarru*; *ngarrungu* seems to be best translated as 'and then ... just ...'.

(20) *Ngapala thana   tharrapandhiri yada, ngala   karna   nhunu(?)*
      well   3pl:NOM fly-down-UNSP hither then   person 3sg:NOM(?)
      wada-yindrirla   thadri-palapala,   yadatji   warrkanga,
      wait-SELF-PRES bank-both sides boomerang-EMPH throw-FUT

---

[2] As pointed out by a referee.

234 *Chapter 18*

      ngapala palhatji thana kartiwirriringu.
      well   bird-EMPH 3pl:NOM dive-UNSP-THEN
      'Well they come flying down, while the men are waiting on both banks and they throw the boomerang. Well the birds dive down then.' (D2, = A-46)

(21) *Thawa-nhana ngani marrka, ngapala kuthiwarraringu,*
      go-NP   1pl:ex:NOM camping.out well   come-arrive-UNSP-THEN

     thudini-ngadilatji ngani; nga puka-pani ngala ngani
     lie-GER-DAT-EMPH-EMPH 1pl:ex:NOM then tucker-PRIV then 1pl:ex:NOM

     thawa-nhana.
     go-NP
     'We went out [into the bush] to camp overnight. Well we got there and were going to camp, but we had come without any food.' (R2)

(22) *Yiwali nhandradu muduwa yinha wawawawana-nhana*
     woman-ERG 3sg:fem:ERG-THERE child 3sg:ACC look-look-APP-NP

     ngarrungu yinha ngapala warrkawindri-rlayi yina.
     just-THEN 3sg:ACC well throw-enter-PRES EMPH
     'That woman was looking after the kid but now she's just leaving him.' (R3)

In its other occurrences *-ngu* denotes that a state or action or situation which applied earlier and which is denoted or partly denoted or referred to by the word to which the suffix is added still applies, and sometimes also that it may continue to apply for some time.

(23) *'Yigatji wayi patji?' 'Ay kaldringu; thana walpi kara*
     orange-EMPH how good oh bitter-YET 3pl:NOM when maybe

     pirtipirtinangatji.'
     ripe-INCH-FUT-EMPH
     'What are the wild oranges like?' "Oh, bitter yet. Don't know when they're going to get ripe." (P14)

(24) *Nguni pirnangu ngaldra.*
     day big-YET 1du:in:NOM
     'We've got a big day yet." (i.e. plenty of time) (R10)

(25) *Nga nhinggiyingu nhunu, yilanggi kara.*
     then location-HERE-YET 3sg:NOM where maybe
     'It's still here, somewhere.' (X17)

(26) *Mirniwa yandhayandha-malk-árdi, ngararlangu yina ngathu*
     wait-EMPH talk-talk-OPT-EMPH listen-PRES-YET EMPH 1sg:ERG

     yina.
     2sg:ACC
     "You can keep on talking, I'm still listening to you." (B15)

     See also (11-1, 16-62) and the *mirnimirningu* and *yarndudungu* entries in the dictionary.

Another function is to denote that someone or something involved in a situation is the same one that was involved in an earlier situation.

(27) *Karna   nhulungutji   nganha   parndri-nhana.*
      person 3sg:ERG-YET-EMPH 1sg:ACC hit-NP
      'The same man hit me.' (X16)

(28) *Yarru nhantjadu   yundru   wawarla,   nhinggudungu   nganha*
      yard   3sg:fem:ACC:THERE 2sg:ERG see-PRES location-THERE-YET 1sg:ACC

      yadamanalitji   warrka-nhukada.
      horse-ERG-EMPH throw-RECP
      'That yard is the place where the horse threw me before.' (R3)
      (See also (11-1). Note also *nhantjadu*, a feminine form, where *yintjadu* would
      be expected.)

Ngurra 'always', 'all the time' is frequently in combination with *-ngu*, and *walyangu*
'not yet' is also common. *Paningu* also can mean 'not yet' (*pani* 'none').

(29) *Pudlu ngunyingunyina, walya nhunu   yurana,   ngathu   ngurrangu*
      can't give-give-IP   not   3sg:NOM want-IP 1sg:ERG always-YET

      thanhayi   pardrarla.
      3pl:ACC-HERE hold-PRES
      'I tried to give them to him but he didn't want them, so I've still got them.' (P7)

(30) *Mulhudu pulya nhuludu   thayirla,   ngurrangu   ngala nhutjadu*
      tucker   small 3sg:ERG-THERE eat-PRES always-YET then   3sg:NOM:THERE

      marnipirna nhinarla.
      fat-big   sit-PRES
      'He doesn't eat much, but he's still fat.' (R9)

(31) *Mulhudu nganyi   thayiyindrina, ngala walyangu nganyi   yartu.*
      tucker   1sg:NOM eat-RR-IP   then   not-YET   1sg:NOM full
      'I had a feed but I'm not full yet.' (R5)

(32) *Ay   paningu,   walyangu nganyi   papana-nhana.*
      oh   none-YET not-YET   1sg:NOM start-NP
      'I haven't started yet [cooking the dampers].' (P12)

See also (15-12).

(33) *Wadarla   ngali   yinha.   Thangguthalkana nganyi   palthu wawanga,*
      wait-PRES 1du:ex:NOM 3sg:ACC stand-up-IP   1sg:NOM road   look-FUT

      paningu   nhunu.
      none-YET 3sg:NOM
      'We're waiting for him. I stood up to look at the road, but he's not coming yet.'
      (R7)

Kayidingu may mean something like 'only just now (after all this time)':

(34) *Wadana ngathu   yina,   matja,   ka   kayidingula   yini.*
      wait-IP   1sg:ERG 2sg:ACC long.ago maybe(?) now-YET-EMPH 2sg:NOM

      thawawarrarla. Kilkana   ngathu   walyanyadi kara   yini   thawa-rlayi
      go-arrive-PRES know-IP 1sg:ERG not-like   maybe 2sg:NOM go-SIM

yada.
hither
'I waited for you for a long time and you've only just arrived. I thought you weren't coming.' (X21)

18.3.2 *-ldra*

The suffix *-ldra* is used to denote a contrast between the referent of the word to which it is affixed and something referred to earlier (not necessarily in the same sentence), or it may be affixed to two or more words in a sentence (or perhaps in successive sentences) to denote contrast between the referents. Where it occurs only once, as in (35, 38, 39, 40), it can be translated 'on the other hand' or 'as for', or, as in (41), 'contrary to expectation'. Where it occurs more than once, as in (36, 37) the first occurrence is translated 'on the one hand' and later ones 'on the other hand'. See (A-57) for a sentence with three occurrences. In interlinear translations it is glossed as 'BUT'. In (42) the function is not clear at all.

-ldra is affixed frequently to nouns (inflected or not) and adverbs (including *walya* 'not'), but only rarely to verbs, two examples being (14-6) and (S6-7). Text examples include (A-25, 42, 79, 94, 147, 151, 152, 159, 162) and (8-9, 9-5, 9-22, 9-25, 10-5, 10-36). A variant *-ndra* has been heard (S9-21).

(35) *Nhatjadu   kudla-rnanga manyumanyu, ngala thana*
     3sg:fem:NOM:THERE cook-CONT   good-good   then   3pl:NOM

   ngalyitji   madlamadlandjildra kudlari.
   others-EMPH   bad-bad-BUT   cook-UNSP
   'She's the best cook in the camp.' (lit. 'She cooks well, all the others cook not so well.') (P14)

(36) *Ngapala ngali   parrkulu ngana warlkari,   nhunutji*
     well   1du:ex:NOM two   ?   fall-UNSP   3sg:NOM-EMPH

   parrarildrala   nganyi   kandraldra.
   bottom-BUT-EMPH 1sg:NOM   top-BUT
   'We both fell down; I was on top and he was underneath.' (R3)

(37) *Ngalyitji   mardramardraldra ngala ngarru padlaldra ngalyitji.*
     some-EMPH   stone-stone-BUT   then   only   sand-BUT   some-EMPH
   'Some places are stony and some are sandy.' (P30)

(38) *Wayipalatji,   walyaldra   thanayi   yarndukalatji   nhina-lapurra.*
     white.man-EMPH not-EMPH   3pl:NOM-HERE how-about-EMPH sit-REMP
   '[On the other hand] the whitefellows never used to live that way.' (W10)

(39) *Karna   thana   panipanina   thawa-nhana, ngala yinitji,*
     person 3pl:NOM all-all-INCH go-NP   then   2sg:NOM-EMPH

   minhayildra   walya thawa-nhana?
   what-LOC-BUT   not   go-NP
   'All the [other] men went away, why didn't you go?' (P15)

(40) *Ay, pandi nhutjadutji   ngakani-nyadildra.*
     eh   dog   3sg:NOM:THERE-EMPH   1sg:GEN-like-BUT
   'Eh, that dog's like mine!' (T11)

(41)   ... walyaldra   ngalunha   wawapadana.
           not-BUT   1du:ex-ACC   see-in-IP
       '[We waved to him on the opposite bank] but he didn't see us.' (X21)

(42)   Manyuldra   nganha   yundru   nganana.
       good-BUT   1sg:ACC   2sg:ERG   tell-IP
       'It's a good job you told me.' (P8)

18.3.3 -ldrangu

This suffix is presumably a compound of the two discussed previously although it is difficult to see how its function could be predicted from a knowledge of their functions. It can usually be translated 'too'; the translation is 'again' in (47) and (48). It seems, though, that a subtlety has been missed; when I asked BK on one occasion whether it meant 'again', he replied: 'Yes; go again; though, **though** I went again, -ldrangu means'. The 'though' clearly relates to the -ldra part of the suffix; see the previous section. BK was not able to specify any difference between this and -kaldri; see §11.10. -ldrangu has been noted in combination with both inflected and uninflected nouns and verbs, and also with the interrogative yarndu 'how' (also 'thus'; the form yarnduldrangu is translated 'in the same way') and with paladi 'separate', 'individual' to form paladildrangu 'different'. With parrkulu 'two', and presumably other words denoting numbers, -ldrangu means 'more'. It seems that when the tense is past (perhaps only one or a selection of the past tenses) the tense inflection is omitted and -ldrangu is suffixed directly to a verb stem ((11) and (48)). Text examples of -ldrangu are (A-25, 40-42, 83, 150-1, 156-7) and (S8-1, 9-3, 5, 37, 10-27).

The order of the constituents of this suffix is reversed in one occurrence of -nguldra ((A-152) in the dictionary volume) and there is also one possible (but unclear) example of -nguldrangu, and one example of -nguldra which seems to have the same meaning. The last does not occur in a sentence but in a mainly English explanation (see E3) of a sentence of text (A-57); thananguldra 'they [took a few each] too'. There is also an unclear example of -ldranguldra. These may be errors, although BK did accept them (apart from the last, which was heard only in the last couple of days of fieldwork) when asked about them on a later occasion. There are other examples of this type of error in the corpus.

(43)   ... kaku-ngurru   pula   thirri-nhanaldrangu.
           elder.sister-COM 3du:NOM   fight-NP-BUT-YET
       (The two brothers were fighting and) 'the two sisters were fighting too.' (P3)

(44)   Yiwa   nhatjadu   mundjaldrangu.
       woman   3sg:fem:NOM:THERE   sick-BUT-YET
       'That woman's sick too.' (P8)

(45)   Pulayi   parrkululdrangu   thawawarrarla.
       3du-HERE   two-BUT-YET   go-arrive-PRES
       'There's two more coming.' (X16)

(46)   Parndripada-nhana   nganha   nhulu,   ngathu   yinha
       hit-LOC-NP   1sg:ACC   3sg:ERG   1sg:ERG   3sg:ACC

238   Chapter 18

> *parndrithika-nhanaldrangu.*
> hit-return-NP-BUT-YET
> 'He hit me and I hit him back.' (B14-15)

(47) *Parndringaldrangu ngathu yinha.*
hit-FUT-BUT-YET 1sg:ERG 3sg:ACC
'I'm going to hit him again.' (X34)

(48) *Parndrildrangu ngathu yinha.*
hit-BUT-YET 1sg:ERG 3sg:ACC
'I hit him again.' (X34)

18.4 Emphatic suffixes

A number of suffixes, combinable with almost any word in a sentence, inflected or not, and having no apparent pragmatic, semantic or grammatical function, are here grouped together under the heading of 'emphatic suffixes'. These include *-la*, *-tji* and *-ardi*. A few rare suffixes — *-ni*, *-nga*, *-wa*, *-ka*, *-ma* — may also belong to this category; however, some of these have been noted only once or twice and may not be genuine.

-tji is probably the most commonly occurring morpheme in the language; in a text of about two hundred sentences and about 1550 words it occurred about 180 times. Some investigation into the occurrence of *-tji* in this text has been made, in order to determine whether any function other than emphasis, either phonological (for example, to generate a more acceptable stress pattern) or syntactic or pragmatic, could be discerned. Very little of any significance was found; *-tji* does not often occur on the first word of a sentence (7% of occurrences) and shows some preference for sentence final (27%) or before a significant pause (20%); it occurs indiscriminately on inflected and uninflected words; it shows a preference for nouns (about 60%, excluding nominalised verbs which account for another 10%) rather than verbs (22%, excluding nominalised verbs) and combines only rarely with pronouns and adverbs; it probably shows no significant preference for following any particular vowel (although this is not certain as the frequencies of the vowels in word-final position have not been calculated); it shows no particular preference for words with an odd or even number of syllables, or for short words as against long words (there are a number of occurrences of *-tji* as the eighth or ninth syllable of a word). It is tentatively assumed therefore that the function is to denote emphasis, although in view of its frequency of occurrence (it occurs up to at least four times, separately, in a sentence; see (11-32)) it cannot be strong emphasis. It may even have degenerated to a meaningless habit, although this also seems unlikely.

(49) *Walya nganyitji thawanga putha-ngaditji.*
not 1sg:NOM-EMPH go-FUT races-DAT-EMPH
'I'm not going to the races.' (T11, = S1-3)

(50) *Kathi-ngadi ngaldra thawarlatji parndrithikanga.*
meat-DAT 1du:in:NOM go-PRES-EMPH kill-return-FUT
"We're going out kangaroo hunting today." (C2)

(51) *Ngathutji yinha windrali warrkana-nhana.*
1sg:ERG-EMPH 3sg:ACC spear-INST throw-APP-NP
'I was the one who speared that [wallaby]' (someone else having claimed to have). (The second word was unclear, and could have been *yina* 'emphatic'.) (R3)

-la is another very common morpheme; there are about fifty occurrences in the text referred to above. In addition, *ngala*, a conjunction normally translated 'then', which may contain the suffix *-la*, occurs 33 times. (*Nga* also occurs with the same function as *ngala*.) Of the 50 occurrences of *-la*, 20 are in a combined suffix in which *-tji* follows. There are some differences in the distribution of *-tji*, *-la* and *-latji* (references to *-la* and *-tji* in this paragraph exclude *-latji*):

(a) *-la* shows a greater tendency than *-tji* to occur on the first word of a sentence (20% — but see (e)) and a lesser tendency to occur sentence-final (6%) and before a pause (3%). *-latji* shows a tendency, which may not be significant, to occur sentence-medially, but on a word which follows a pause.

(b) *-la* shows a strong preference for uninflected words (80% or more) while *-latji* occurs mostly (about three quarters of occurrences) on inflected words, and where it does combine with uninflected words they are compound or reduplicated forms.

(c) It follows from (b) that *-la* shows a strong preference for combining with disyllabic words (70% of occurrences) although it can also be the sixth, seventh, eighth or ninth syllable of a word (one example of each in the text). *-latji* prefers longer words, usually of three to five syllables (not including the *-latji*), never of two.

(d) *-latji* frequently (40%) follows the dative suffix *-ngadi* and, mainly because of this, prefers /i/ in the last preceding syllable (about two thirds of occurrences). *-la* shows some preference for following /a/ (two thirds).

(e) *-la* shows a preference (about 50%) for combining with noun stems, but also combines with verbs, pronouns, adverbs and some other words. There are five examples in the text, all sentence-initial, of *walya* 'not' combined with *-la*. *Walya* does not seem to combine with *-tji* or *-latji*, although it does combine with *-ardi* (see below). *-latji* most frequently combines with inflected nouns and nominalised verbs (there are no examples in the text of addition of *-la* to the latter). There are three apparent examples (not in this text) of *-la* being suffixed to a verb stem and being followed by other bound morphemes (the first of them being stressed as a separate word); these are discussed in §11.1 and the introduction to Chapter 12.

-la and *-latji* thus show some noticeable tendencies to occur in certain situations in strong contrast to *-tji*. However, there seems to be no indication of any function other than emphasis.

Note that *ngapangadilatji* and *ngapangaditji* occur in successive sentences, as do *puthakurnulatji* and *puthakurnutji*. Note also that the combination *-tjila* has been noted, although not in this text.

(52) ... *ngala yini   thawawarrana, kathi-paniyila   ngakani.*
          then   2sg:NOM go-arrive-IP   meat-PRIV-LOC-EMPH 1sg:GEN
      "... but you came when I got no meat." (W2)

(53) *Marripathi yini   thawawarranga, kaku   ngakani wawanga,*
       tomorrow   2sg:NOM go-arrive-FUT   elder.sister 1sg:GEN see-FUT

      nhani   thikawarra-rlayilatji.
      3sg:fem:NOM return-arrive-SIM-EMPH-EMPH
      "You come tomorrow and you'll see my sister; she's coming home tomorrow."
      (W2)

An example with both -*tji* and -*la* (separately) is (11-100).

-*ardi* is probably the strongest marker of emphasis — it carries a strong stress on its initial vowel which replaces the final vowel of the word to which it is added. It occurs only three times in the text referred to above, but occurs five times in a much shorter text of a type in which strong emphases would be more likely (S9-13, 16, 20, 21). -*ardi* has been noted in compound emphasis markers -*tjardi*, -*lardi* and -*latjardi*.

(54) *Thawa-malkakan-árdi!*
go-OPT-AWAY-PLIMP-EMPH
'Go away you lot!' (P3)

(55) *Ngandra maka ngala nhunuy-árdi   thangkanarla   ngurrangu!*
oh   fire then 3sg:NOM-HERE-EMPH burn-INCH-PRES always-YET
'Well, so the fire is still burning here!' (R3, in S9-13)

-*kala*, as noted above (§6.3), seems to be used as an emphatic marker on third person pronouns, but there are no convincing examples.

-*ni* is rare but seems to belong with the emphasis markers as it can combine with them; thus -*nitji* (A-110) and -*latjini* (A-140) occur in the long text. A few other unexplained syllables have been noted once or twice attached to the tail end of a word; these include -*ma*, -*wa*, -*ka* and -*nga*.

Note that emphasis may also be marked by strong stress, by distortion of word-final vowels (see §3.2.1) or by means of emphatic particles such as *yina* and *mayi*. *Yina* may combine with -*la* or -*tji* as in:

(56) ... *makala   yina   thangkaka-thalkanga.*
fire-EMPH EMPH burn-CAUS-up-FUT
'... and lit up the fire.' (R4, in S9-26)

Apart from -*ardi* and sometimes *mayi*, emphatic suffixes and particles are unstressed, and may emphasise the word to which they are added or which they follow by prolonging the time during which it is in focus before the next word is spoken.

18.5 -*yukala* (clitic with unknown meaning)

There are two occurrences in the corpus of an ending -*yukala*, once on a noun and once on a verb. On the noun it could perhaps be translated 'along'. In the other example it could be based on the potential suffix -*yi* with an addition.

(57) *Kilkalikarla   thawanga ngapa-ngaditji,   ngarru   pulyala*
know-know-PRES go-FUT   water-DAT-EMPH   only   small-EMPH

pakari   tjukurru   darla   yibini-ngadi   palthu-yukala
carry-UNSP kangaroo   skin   drink-GER-DAT   road-?

yitalayi   thawa-rnanga.
away-EMPH-DISTORT go-CONT
'They know it is there and they need carry only a small kangaroo skin [waterbag] for drinking from while they are going along.' (D3, = A-107)

(58) *Thawa-nhana, yini   thangguthikanga   thannganiyi,   karna*
go-NP   2sg:NOM stand-return-FUT 3pl:GEN-LOC   person

thulayitji.	*Parndri-yukala yina*		*walya*	*kurnulitji*
stranger-LOC-EMPH	hit-?	2sg:ACC	not	one-INST-EMPH

thawa-rnanga.	*Parndriyila*	*kara* —	*parndriyila*	*yina,*
go-CONT	hit-POT	maybe	hit-POT-EMPH	2sg:ACC

kurnutji	*thawa-rlayi.*	*Walya*	*kurnutji*	*thawala.*
one-EMPH	go-SIM	not	one-EMPH	go-EMPH

'You went to visit those strangers. They might have killed you, going without someone else, on your own. Don't go on your own.' (R1)

References

Austin, Peter, 1981a, *A grammar of Diyari, South Australia*. (Cambridge Studies in Linguistics, 32.) Cambridge: Cambridge University Press.

—— 1981b, Switch-reference in Australia. *Language* 57(2):309–334.

—— 1988a, Phonological voicing contrasts in Australian Aboriginal languages. *La Trobe Working Papers in Linguistics* 1:17–42.

—— 1988b, Trill-released stops and language change in Central Australian languages. *Australian Journal of Linguistics* 8:219–245.

—— 1990, Classification of Lake Eyre languages. *La Trobe University Working Papers in Linguistics* 3:171–201.

Blake, Barry J., 1988, Redefining Pama-Nyungan: towards the prehistory of Australian languages. *Aboriginal Linguistics* 1:1–90.

Bowern, Claire Louise, 1998, *The case of Proto-Karnic: morphological change and reconstruction in the nominal and pronominal system of Proto-Karnic (Lake Eyre Basin)*. BA Honours sub-thesis. Canberra: The Australian National University.

—— 2000, Nhirrpi sketch grammar. Unpublished draft.

Breen, Gavan, 1971, Aboriginal languages of western Queensland. *Linguistic Communications* 5:1–88.

—— 1974, On bivalent suffixes. In B. Blake, ed. *Papers in Australian Aboriginal languages*, 22–58. Linguistic Communications 14. Melbourne: Monash University.

—— 1975, Innamincka Talk (The Innamincka dialect of Yandruwandha. Preliminary version). Unpublished manuscript.

—— 1976a, Proprietive markers and kinship terms. In Topic A: The derivational affix 'having'. In Dixon, ed. 1976:290–297.

—— 1976b, Yandruwandha. In Topic D: Are Australian languages syntactically nominative-ergative or nominative-accusative? In Dixon, ed. 1976:594–597.

—— 1976c, Yandruwandha. In Topic E: Simple and compound verbs: conjugation by auxiliaries in Australian verbal systems. In Dixon, ed. 1976:750–756.

—— 1984, Similarity and mistake in two Australian languages. *Language in Central Australia* 2:1–9.

—— 1990b, Stories from Bennie Kerwin. In Peter Austin, R.M.W. Dixon, Tom Dutton and Isobel White, eds *Language and history: essays in honour of Luise A. Hercus*, 67–87. Canberra: Pacific Linguistics.

—— 1993, East is south and west is north. *Australian Aboriginal Studies*, No 2:20–33.

—— 1994, entry on Benny Kerwin in the *Encyclopaedia of Aboriginal Australia*. Canberra: Australian Institute of Aboriginal and Torres Strait Islander Studies.

—— 1997, Taps, stops and trills. In D. Tryon and M. Walsh, eds *Boundary rider: essays in honour of Geoffrey O'Grady*, 71–93. Canberra: Pacific Linguistics.

Capell, A., 1963, *Linguistic survey of Australia*. Sydney: Australian Institute of Aboriginal Studies.

—— n.d., *Linguistic materials for fieldworkers in Australia*. Canberra: Australian Institute of Aboriginal Studies.

Cornish, W.H., 1886, Cooper's Creek, to the eastward of its northern branch. In Curr (1886–87) 2:28–29.

Curr, E.M., 1886–87, The Australian race: its origin, languages, customs, place of landing in Australia, and the roots by which it spread itself over that continent. 4 volumes. Melbourne: John Ferres.

Craig, Beryl F., 1970, *North-West-Central Queensland: an annotated bibliography*. Australian Aboriginal Studies No. 41. Canberra: Australian Institute of Aboriginal Studies.

Dixon, R.M.W., 1972, *The Dyirbal language of north Queensland*. London: Cambridge University Press.

Dixon, R.M.W., ed., 1976, *Grammatical categories in Australian languages*. Linguistic Series No. 22. Canberra: Australian Institute of Aboriginal Studies.

Dixon, R.M.W., W.S. Ransom and Mandy Thomas, 1990, *Australian Aboriginal words in English: their origin and meaning*. Melbourne: Oxford University Press.

Hale, Kenneth, 1982, Some essential features of Warlpiri verbal clauses. In Stephen M. Swartz, ed. *Papers in Warlpiri grammar: in memory of Lothar Jagst*, 217–315. Work Papers of SIL-AAB Series A Volume 6. Darwin: Summer Institute of Linguistics, Australian Aborigines Branch.

Henderson, John and Veronica Dobson, 1994, *Eastern and Central Arrernte to English dictionary*. Alice Springs: Institute for Aboriginal Development.

Hercus, Luise, 1990, Aboriginal people. In M.J. Tyler, C.R. Twidale, M. Davies and C. Wells, eds *Natural history of the northeast deserts*, 149–159. Adelaide: Royal Society of South Australia,

—— 1994, *A grammar of the Arabana-Wangkangurru language, Lake Eyre Basin, South Australia*. Canberra: Pacific Linguistics.

—— 2001, Language and groupings of Wangkumara and Punthamara people. Unpublished draft.

Hercus, Luise and Peter Sutton, eds, 1986, *This is what happened*. Canberra: Australian Institute of Aboriginal Studies.

Horton, David R., general ed., 1994, *Encyclopaedia of Aboriginal Australia: Aboriginal and Torres Strait Islander history, society and culture.* Canberra: Aboriginal Studies Press.

Howitt, Alfred W., 1878, Notes on the Aborigines of Cooper's Creek. In R.B. Smyth *The Aborigines of Victoria*, vol. 2, 300–309. Melbourne.

—— 1886, Cooper's Creek, in the neighbourhood where Burke and Wills died. In E.M. Curr *The Australian race*, vol. 2, 30–31. Melbourne.

—— 1891, The Dieri and kindred tribes of central Australia. *Journal of the Royal Anthropological Institute* 20:30–104.

—— 1904, *Native tribes of south-east Australia.* London: Macmillan (republished 1996 by Aboriginal Studies Press).

Howitt, Alfred W. and O. Siebert, 1904, Legends of the Dieri and other kindred tribes of central Australia. *Journal of the Royal Anthropological Institute* 34:102–128.

Kerwin, Ben, 1986, The way it was. Transcribed and translated by J.G. Breen with the help of the narrator. In Hercus and Sutton, eds 1986:17–40.

Kerwin, Ben and Gavan Breen, 1981, The land of stone chips. *Oceania* 62:286–311.

Lyons, John, 1968, *Introduction to theoretical linguistics.* Cambridge: Cambridge University Press.

Mathews, R.H., 1899, Divisions of some Aboriginal tribes, Queensland. *Journal of the Royal Society of New South Wales* 33:108–114.

—— 1900, Divisions of the South Australian Aborigines. *Proceedings of the American Philosophical Society* 39:83, 84, 91.

Menning, Kathy and David Nash, 1981, *A sourcebook of Central Australian languages (pilot edition).* Alice Springs: Institute for Aboriginal Development.

O'Grady, G.N., C.F. Voegelin and F.M. Voegelin, 1966, Languages of the world: Indo-Pacific fascicle six. *Anthropological Linguistics* 8(2).

Paterson, Aaron, n.d., Yandruwandha research project [Pundulmurra College].

Reuther, J.G., 1981, *Three Central Australian grammars: Diari, Jandruwanta, Wonkaŋuru.* (Translated by T. Schwarzschild and L.A. Hercus, edited by L.A. Hercus and J.G. Breen) being vol. 5 of *The Diari*.

Salmon, H.G., 1886, Cooper's Creek. In Curr (1886–87) 2:24–27.

Sharpe, E, 1901, Yandra Wandra tribe. *Science of Man* 3 (12):208–209.

Smyth, R.B., 1878, *The Aborigines of Victoria: with notes relating to the habits of the natives of other parts of Australia and Tasmania.* 2 volumes. Melbourne: Government Printer.

Tchekoff, Claude, 1985, Aspect, transitivity, 'antipassives' and some Australian languages. In Frans Plank, ed. *Relational typology*, 359–390. (*Trends in linguistics: studies and monographs*, 28). Berlin: Mouton.

—— 1987, 'Antipassif', aspect imperfectif et autonomie du sujet. *Bulletin de la Societé de Linguistique de Paris* 82:43–67.

Tindale, Norman B., 1974, *Aboriginal tribes of Australia: their terrain, environmental controls, distribution, limits, and proper names*. Berkeley: University of California Press/Canberra: The Australian National University.

Tolcher, H.M., 2003, Seed of the coolibah: a history of the Yandruwandha and Yawarrawarrka people. Adelaide: the author.

Trefry, David, 1970, The phonological word in Dieri. In D.C. Laycock, ed. *Linguistic trends in Australia*, 65–73. Canberra: AIAS.

Wilkins, David P., 1989, Mparntwe Arrernte (Aranda): studies in the structure and semantics of grammar. PhD dissertation, The Australian National University.

Wimberley, Colin C., 1899, Yarrawurka tribe vocabulary. *Science of Man* 2(4):69–70.

Wurm, S.A., 1967, *Linguistic fieldwork methods in Australia*. Canberra: Australian Institute of Aboriginal Studies

www.ingramcontent.com/pod-product-compliance
Lightning Source LLC
Chambersburg PA
CBHW060930180426